Political Parties and American Political Development
from the Age of Jackson to the Age of Lincoln

Political Parties and American Political Development
from the Age of Jackson to the Age of Lincoln

Michael F. Holt

LOUISIANA STATE UNIVERSITY PRESS
Baton Rouge and London

Manufactured in the United States of America
First printing
01 00 99 98 97 96 95 94 93 92   5 4 3 2 1

Designer: Glynnis Phoebe
Typeface: Caslon O.F. #2
Typesetter: G & S Typesetters, Inc.
Printer and binder: Thomson-Shore, Inc.

Library of Congress Cataloging-in-Publication Data
Holt, Michael F. (Michael Fitzgibbon)
    Political parties and American political development from the age
of Jackson to the age of Lincoln / Michael F. Holt
        p.   cm.
    Includes index.
    ISBN 0-8071-1728-5 (cloth)
    1. United States—Politics and government—1815–1861.
    2. Political parties—United States—History—19th century.
    I. Title.
    E415.7.H75   1991
    320.973—dc20   91-31506
                                                                CIP

The author is grateful to the following publishers and journals for permission to reprint the essays
noted: "The Democratic Party, 1828–1860" and "The Antimasonic and Know Nothing Parties,"
in *History of U.S. Political Parties*, ed. Arthur M. Schlesinger, Jr. (4 vols.; New York, 1973), I,
497–536, 575–620, Chelsea House Publishers; "Winding Roads to Recovery: The Whig Party
from 1844 to 1848," in *Essays on American Antebellum Politics, 1840–1860*, ed. Stephen E. Maizlish and John J. Kushma (College Station, Tex.: Texas A & M University Press, 1982), 122–65,
used by permission of the Walter Prescott Webb Memorial Lectures Committee, University of Texas
at Arlington; "The Politics of Impatience: The Origins of Know Nothingism," *Journal of American
History*, LX (1973), 309–31; "The New Political History and the Civil War Era," *Reviews in
American History*, XIII (1985), 60–69; "Two Roads to Sumter," *Reviews in American History*, III
(1975), 221–28; "The Problem of Civil War Causation," *Virginia Quarterly Review*, LIII (1977),
166–76. "Abraham Lincoln and the Politics of Union" first appeared in *Abraham Lincoln and the
American Political Tradition*, ed. John L. Thomas (Amherst: University of Massachusetts Press,
1986), copyright © 1986 by the University of Massachusetts Press. "The Election of 1840, Voter
Mobilization, and the Emergence of the Second American Party System: A Reappraisal of Jacksonian
Voting Behavior" is reprinted by permission of Louisiana State University Press from *A Master's
Due: Essays in Honor of David Herbert Donald*, edited by William J. Cooper, Jr., Michael F. Holt,
and John McCardell, copyright © 1985 by Louisiana State University Press.

The paper in this book meets the guidelines for permanence and durability of the Committee on
Production Guidelines for Book Longevity of the Council on Library Resources. ∞

For Adam, Erin, and Annie

Contents

Acknowledgments

I want to take this opportunity to thank numerous colleagues, friends, and other scholars who gave me good advice while these essays were originally drafted and revised: Gary D. Allinson, John Ashcroft, Edward L. Ayers, John M. Blum, Robert Bruce, William J. Cooper, Jr., David Herbert Donald and the members of his American Studies colloquium at Harvard University, Nicholas Edsall, John Ferejohn, Paul M. Gaston, William E. Gienapp, William H. Harbaugh, Martin J. Havran, Joseph F. Kett, Richard L. McCormick, Richard P. McCormick, Charles W. McCurdy, Angus Macintyre, members of the Commonwealth Fund Memorial Lecture symposium, University College London, February, 1990, Joel H. Silbey, John L. Thomas, and Mark Thomas. I am especially grateful to Ed Ayers and Bill Gienapp for their helpful comments on the introduction to this volume. None of these individuals, of course, is responsible for any errors of fact or interpretation that remain.

Finally, I owe a heavy debt of gratitude to the secretarial staff of the Corcoran Department of History at the University of Virginia who, over the years, typed and retyped what must have seemed like innumerable drafts of these pieces: Lottie M. McCauley, Kathleen Miller, Elizabeth Stovall, and Ella Wood.

Political Parties and American Political Development
from the Age of Jackson to the Age of Lincoln

Introduction

The invitation from the Louisiana State University Press to publish this collection of essays is welcome for at least two reasons. It provides an opportunity to bring together in one place articles that have previously appeared in scattered publications, some of which may have escaped the eye of all but the most assiduous students of nineteenth-century political history. It also offers me an occasion to reflect upon certain themes that have guided my research for twenty-five years and to articulate as well why some of my approaches and concerns have changed over that time.

The essays gathered here were written between 1970 and 1990, and all but one have previously been published. Some were commissioned for collections edited by others on topics about which, at the time, I had no special expertise. Others originated as public lectures. Still others shared a more normal birth, emerging as efforts to make sense of my then-current research. Despite their disparate origins, all of these essays deal with the mass political parties that began to be formed in the third decade of the nineteenth century and with their relationship to broader American political developments from the 1820s, when Andrew Jackson first emerged as a national political figure, to the presidency of Abraham Lincoln. In particular, they address the integral connection between politics and the causes and course of the American Civil War.

Rereading what one wrote as long as twenty years ago can be a chilling experience, and I have occasionally winced as I did so. Because a few of the essays, especially those on the Know Nothings, were written at the same time for different audiences, moreover, there is some repetition. Nonetheless, aside from correcting typographical, stylistic, and a few egregious factual errors, I have not attempted to revise the essays. They are presented here essentially as they originally appeared. One reason for this decision is that so much scholarship relevant to the earlier essays has subsequently been published that any attempt to incorporate or address it would divert too much of my time from another project—a full-scale history of the Whig party—on which I have already labored far too long and am eager to push to completion. In addition, some of the subsequent scholarship by others was undertaken to pursue leads or refute interpretations advanced in the original essays, and it seems only fair to present the essays in the form that helped launch those later investigations. Most important, leaving the essays unrevised best allows the reader to see how my thinking about what is important in political history has changed over the years. Indeed, a major purpose of this introduction is to address those changes in approach and focus, and the reasons for them.

Before undertaking that explanation, let me say something about the order and provenance of the essays, how I might change them if I were to rewrite them today, and the common themes that link them to each other. Although this book does not purport to present a comprehensive history of political events from the Age of Jackson to the Age of Lincoln, the essays are arranged here in chronological order of the parties and topics they analyze, not in the order I wrote them. The two essays following this introduction reproduce two long articles prepared for a four-volume reference work edited by Arthur M. Schlesinger, Jr., on the history of American political parties from the debate over ratification of the Constitution to the present.[1] Aimed at a general audience, these essays were to be unfootnoted, and the various authors of that compendium were instructed to provide as comprehensive a narrative history of the party or parties assigned to them as was possible in the space allotted.

The first of these essays traces the history of the Democratic party from the early 1820s until 1860, when its rupture during the presidential campaign foreshadowed the secession of the Deep South states in response

---

1. "The Democratic Party, 1828–1860" and "The Antimasonic and Know Nothing Parties," in *History of U.S. Political Parties*, ed. Arthur M. Schlesinger, Jr. (4 vols.; New York, 1973), I, 497–536, 575–620.

to Lincoln's election. When I was asked to prepare this essay, my own primary research had focused exclusively on the period between 1848 and 1860, and had concentrated on opponents of the Democrats rather than that party itself. As a result, it differs from all of the other essays collected here, except the review essays, in that it is based almost entirely on a synthesis of secondary literature, not primary sources. Careful readers will note that it differs from the others in another important regard as well. I now believe—and have for some time—that the essay form is most successful when an author begins either by asking, implicitly or explicitly, a fresh question that he or she then attempts to answer or, alternatively, by laying out an argument at odds with the conventional wisdom on some subject, that he or she then attempts to prove. Although the essay on the Democrats met the narrative requirements prescribed by Professor Schlesinger, it lacks that kind of explicit revisionist thrust. Thus, were I to rewrite it today, I would attempt to impose such a fresh interpretative framework on it as well as alter certain emphases to respond to the vast literature that has appeared since it was written.

Although the essay on the Democratic party is less revisionist than other pieces presented here, I have still chosen to begin with it. The remainder of the book focuses on political foes of the Democrats—Antimasons, Whigs, Know Nothings, and Republicans—and a sense of balance (or justice) alone requires giving the Democrats their just due. Moreover, this essay comes closer than any of the others to providing a comprehensive sketch of political events and developments between 1820 and 1860. Hence it supplies the necessary context or background against which to read those other, more specialized, studies.

The second essay from the Schlesinger compendium, an article on the Antimasonic and Know Nothing parties, was commissioned after the piece on the Democrats had been accepted. Obviously, the material on the Know Nothings deals with the 1850s, but I have placed the article next because of the segment on the Antimasons, who mushroomed into political prominence in the 1820s and 1830s. Actually, when I was asked to prepare this essay, I knew as little about the Antimasonic party as I did about the Democrats in the Jacksonian period. But I had done substantial research on the Know Nothing movement, and my article on the origins of Know Nothingism, which appears later in this collection, had already been accepted for publication. Because I wanted to use that primary research on the Know Nothings, I decided that I must immerse myself in as much primary source material about the Antimasons as possible in a limited time before drafting an essay that dealt with both parties.

Happily, the very phenomenon of third parties like the Antimasons and Know Nothings, who protested so stridently against the existing major parties, raised the kind of explicit questions in which I was then most interested. Because most Americans for most periods of American history have operated politically through a system of two major parties, what explains the origins and appeal of third parties? Why do some voters take that route, whereas others remain within the confines of major parties? What impact do third parties have on the formation or dissolution of two-party systems? Given the intensity of dissatisfaction with major parties that contributed to the creation of dissident third parties in the first place, how can we account for their rapid collapse and absorption by major parties, whether new or old? Finally, is it possible to weigh the relative importance of ideological, economic, and social factors and grievances, on the one hand, versus political context and structure, on the other, in addressing these questions? For example, did the presence or absence of partisan competition or alternative channels for political action, rules of the political game, the policy output of government, and the division of jurisdictional authority over different policy areas within the American federal system influence the formation and dissolution of third parties? In short, to what extent is politics itself an independent variable in explaining the phenomenon of dissident minor parties?

By and large, my answers to those questions seem to have withstood the test of time. Subsequent research on the Antimasons does suggest that I may have exaggerated the economic deprivation or impoverishment of Antimasonic voters who, at least in some places, apparently represented middling rather than propertyless classes. But that research echoes my emphasis on egalitarian resentment of privileged groups, religious evangelicalism, and the party's populistic message of political empowerment as keys to Antimasonic strength.[2]

---

2. Kathleen Smith Kutolowski, "Antimasonry Reexamined: Social Bases of the Grassroots Party," *Journal of American History*, LXXI (1984), 269–93; Ronald P. Formisano, *The Transformation of Political Culture: Massachusetts Parties, 1790s–1840s* (New York, 1983), 197–98; Paul

Were I to rewrite the study of the Antimasonic party, I would focus much more specifically on the relative weights of social and ideological versus political factors in explaining the strength of the Antimasonic party as distinct from the Antimasonic movement. Social, economic, and ideological grievances can generate a grass-roots protest movement, but they do not necessarily explain why popular protest assumes the form of a separate political party that succeeds, if only briefly, in some places but not in others. Specifically, I would now stress even more than I did that it was a political vacuum caused by the weakness or absence of two-party competition that best explains why the Antimasonic party flourished in some states but not in others. One of the greatest mysteries concerning the Antimasonic party, for example, is why it was virtually nonexistent in New Hampshire whereas it achieved its greatest strength in neighboring Vermont—a state whose geography, climate, and socioeconomic structure were virtually identical to New Hampshire's—and also gained substantial political clout in other New England states comparable to New Hampshire, such as Massachusetts and Connecticut. The same question is raised by a comparison of Pennsylvania, where the Antimasonic party thrived for almost ten years, with its neighbors New Jersey and Maryland, where the party, if not the movement, was negligible. Table 1, which simply lists the proportion of the popular vote won by Andrew Jackson and John Quincy Adams in the 1828 presidential election, goes far toward answering that question.

Where competition between Jacksonians and Adams men was close, as is in New Hampshire, Maryland, and New Jersey, the latter possibly having had the most fully elaborated two-party system in the country by 1828, the emergence of a strong third party was aborted.[3] Opponents of the dominant party saw no need for a new organization because victory was already within their reach. In contrast, where the "out" party—be it Jacksonians or their opponents—languished in a hopelessly uncompeti-

---

Goodman, *Towards a Christian Republic: Antimasonry and the Great Transition in New England, 1826–1836* (New York, 1988), 39–53, 156–57, and *passim*. Goodman's splendidly imaginative study explores aspects of Antimasonry that never occurred to me in the early 1970s.

3. On New Jersey politics in the 1820s, see Michael Birkner, *Samuel L.Southard: Jeffersonian Whig* (Rutherford, N.J., 1984).

Table 1 Proportion of the Popular Vote Won
by Jackson and Adams in 1828

State	Adams	Jackson
Vermont	75%	25%
New Hampshire	53%	47%
Massachusetts	83%	17%
Connecticut	75%	25%
Pennsylvania	33%	67%
New Jersey	52%	48%
Maryland	51%	49%

tive minority, as in Vermont, Massachusetts, Connecticut, and Pennsylvania, the Antimasonic party prospered because it displaced the impotent opposition party to become, if only temporarily, the primary opposition party in the state. New York, as explained in the original essay, provides a variation on this same theme. There Jackson and Adams were relatively evenly matched in 1828 if only because many Antimasons supported Adams in the presidential election. Once New York's Adams men were deprived of the stimulus of a presidential election and of the support of the national administration, however, their organization collapsed, and for four years most opponents of the dominant Democrats rallied behind the Antimasonic party.

This kind of revision is relevant to a more general point I will make below. In the early 1970s, my primary method for explaining the popularity of the Antimasonic party was to try to infer the motives of Antimasonic voters by examining Antimasonic rhetoric and the social and economic conditions in which those voters lived. Now, had I to write the essay over again, I would probably give less weight to the motives of voters than to the nature of the political structure in which the Antimasonic party attempted to operate, a structure that was necessarily grounded in, but can nonetheless be conceptualized and analyzed independently of, the social and economic environment in which voters lived.

Following the two essays on the Democratic and Antimasonic parties come three that grow out of my current research on the Whig party and that together outline the major developments in its history between 1836 and 1856. The first, which originally appeared in a *festschrift* for my graduate school mentor David Herbert Donald, attempts to revise traditional interpretations of popular voting behavior between 1836 and 1844 and of the reasons for the Whig victory in the presidential election of 1840.[4] Consciously extrapolating from the research of political scientists on modern voting behavior and adopting a rational choice model, I seek to refute arguments that hoopla, interparty competition, and ethnocultural tensions explain either the extraordinary jump in voter turnout or the Whigs' dramatic surge to power and equally dramatic decline from it during those years. Instead, I contend that changing economic conditions and, even more important, the contrasting programmatic responses of the Whig and Democratic parties to those conditions generated political developments in that period.

The next essay, originally delivered as one of the Walter Prescott Webb Memorial Lectures at the University of Texas at Arlington in the spring of 1981, explores the fluctuating electoral fortunes of the Whigs between 1844 and 1848 as the party tried to recover from the traumatic defeat of Henry Clay in the presidential election of 1844.[5] It also disputes the usual reasons historians have offered for the Whigs' decision to nominate Zachary Taylor as their presidential candidate in 1848 and offers an alternative explanation based on the variation across both space and time in Whig electoral fortunes and the course of events over which Whigs had little control.

The third essay on the Whigs, published here for the first time, was prepared for delivery as the Commonwealth Fund Memorial Lecture at University College London in February, 1990, and revised in accordance with the stimulating (and telling) criticism I received in London during a daylong symposium on that lecture. It addresses the puzzling question

4. "The Election of 1840, Voter Mobilization, and the Emergence of the Second American Party System: A Reappraisal of Jacksonian Voting Behavior," in *A Master's Due: Essays in Honor of David Herbert Donald,* ed. William J. Cooper, Jr., Michael F. Holt, and John McCardell (Baton Rouge, 1985), 16–58.

5. "Winding Roads to Recovery: The Whig Party from 1844 to 1848," in *Essays on American Antebellum Politics, 1840–1860,* ed. Stephen E. Maizlish and John J. Kushma (College Station, Tex., 1982), 122–65. Used by permission of the Walter Prescott Webb Memorial Lectures Committee, University of Texas at Arlington.

that first aroused my interest in writing a history of the Whig party, namely, why did the Whig party die? By comparing the fate of the Whigs in the 1850s with that of our own Republican party in the twentieth century and of the British Conservative party in the 1840s and 1850s, this essay seeks to demonstrate how exceptionally rare and mysterious the utter disappearance of a major political party is. It also uses those comparisons to highlight certain unique structural and ideological aspects of American politics in the 1850s that help explain why the Whigs succumbed in that decade, whereas the modern Republicans and contemporaneous British Conservatives, who faced similar, and in some cases even graver, challenges did not.

The collapse of the Whig party in the mid-1850s both helped cause and resulted from the voter realignment and party reorganization of that decade. Those transformations then paved the way for the rise and triumph of the Republican party, which in turn provoked southern secession and Civil War. The next group of essays addresses those interconnected developments. First comes an analysis of the origins of the Know Nothing movement, an analysis that appeared in the *Journal of American History* in 1973 and was inspired by my first book on the formation of the Republican party in Pittsburgh.[6]

My research on Pittsburgh, which has since been confirmed for other areas of the North by a number of studies, had convinced me that the Know Nothing party's meteoric rise and fall between 1853 and 1857 played a vital transitional role between the collapse of the second party system of Whigs and Jacksonian Democrats and the emergence of the third, or Civil War, party system.[7] Equally if not more important, Know Nothing voters and the nativist and especially the anti-Catholic animosities vented by the Know Nothings contributed significantly to the electoral

6. "The Politics of Impatience: The Origins of Know Nothingism," *Journal of American History*, LX (1973), 309–31; *Forging a Majority: The Formation of the Republican Party in Pittsburgh, 1848–1860* (New Haven, 1969).

7. See, for example, William E. Gienapp, "Nativism and the Creation of a Republican Majority in the North Before the Civil War," *Journal of American History*, LXXII (1985), 529–59; Gienapp, *Origins of the Republican Party, 1852–1856* (New York, 1987); Joel H. Silbey, *The Partisan Imperative: The Dynamics of American Politics Before the Civil War* (New York, 1985), 127–65; and Paul Kleppner, *The Third Electoral System, 1853–1892: Parties, Voters, and Political Cultures* (Chapel Hill, 1979).

success of the Republican party. When I completed my book on Pittsburgh, therefore, I turned to a more general study of the Know Nothings.

The essay begins with a question that links it to the three previous essays on the Whigs. Because the northern voter realignment clearly worked against the Democrats and reduced their share of the northern electorate from 49.8 percent in the presidential election of 1852 to 41.4 percent in the presidential election of 1856, why didn't the traditional opponents of the Democrats, the Whigs, profit from the issues that propelled the realignment? In every other realignment in American history, the existing "out" party benefited from the movement of voters against the incumbent majority party, yet in the 1850s the "out" Whigs suffered as much from the realignment as did the incumbent Democrats. Why did voters who hated the Democrats also turn against the Whigs and instead channel their wrath against the Democrats through new parties? Rejecting as illogical and unpersuasive the traditional argument that antislavery and antisouthern outrage provoked by the Kansas-Nebraska Act drove northern voters from the Whig party, I argue instead that the surging Know Nothing movement gutted Whig voting support. Furthermore, the Know Nothing explosion was fueled not just by powerful nativistic and anti-Catholic prejudices but also by a ferocious hostility toward both old major parties and the selfish and unresponsive politicians who led them. Finally, I attribute the mushrooming of both antipartyism and anti-Catholicism in the early 1850s to fears and grievances generated by sudden economic and social dislocations in those years.

Although I would not recant anything in this essay, I no longer find this early effort to identify the social origins of Know Nothingism completely sufficient. As I have tried to demonstrate in a second book on the politics of the 1850s, the hostility to both the Whig and Democratic parties derived in large part from the prior disappearance of issue-differences between them that made both organizations seem hollow, meaningless, and spoils-oriented machines that now seemed to threaten, rather than protect, the cherished American ideal of republican self-government.[8] Know Nothingism, in other words, had political as well as social sources, and its appeal can and must be understood in terms of fundamental ideological values that suffused American politics since the Revolution. I

8. See Michael F. Holt, *The Political Crisis of the 1850s* (New York, 1978).

would also amend my analysis of the economic pressures that turned resident Americans against immigrants by incorporating a brilliant insight recently made by Professor Robert W. Fogel. I argue that the massive railroad construction between 1849 and 1854 helped cause the Know Nothing outburst by bringing immigrant construction crews into areas that had never seen a foreigner and by destroying the jobs of workers in communities hitherto dependent on water transportation or opened for the first time to competition from eastern and European products. He compellingly makes the additional point that when railroad construction slammed to a halt during the recession of 1854–1855, immigrant construction crews were dumped into the labor pools of numerous communities to compete with resident blue-collar workers for a dwindling number of jobs.[9] Even more economic contingencies than I had thought had decisive political impact.

Following the essay on Know Nothings come three brief review essays. They are included here because they allowed me to address certain critical issues concerning politics in the Civil War era more directly than I have done in the other essays. These issues include: the historiographical controversy over the validity of the ethnocultural interpretation of northern politics during the 1850s and the utility of the realignment/party system model characteristic of the so-called "new political history" written during the 1960s and 1970s; the problem of why slave states from the Upper and Lower South reacted so differently from each other during the secession crisis; and the general issue of Civil War causation.[10]

These essays, like virtually everything else I have written on the 1840s and 1850s, are shaped by certain convictions about the relationship between politics and the coming of the Civil War. It may help the reader if those convictions are spelled out here so that he or she can understand why I side where I do in the historiographical wars over these subjects and can better judge the persuasiveness of my case. Although political developments in the 1840s and 1850s can be, and in some cases must be, understood without reference to the subsequent Civil War, the obverse is

9. Robert William Fogel, *Without Consent or Contract: The Rise and Fall of American Slavery* (New York, 1989), 358.

10. "The New Political History and the Civil War Era," *Reviews in American History*, XIII (1985), 60–69; "Two Roads to Sumter," *ibid.*, III (1975), 221–28; and "The Problem of Civil War Causation," *Virginia Quarterly Review*, LIII (1977), 166–76.

not true. The outbreak of a shooting war between North and South in April, 1861, can be explained only by accounting for the chain of specific political events that precipitated it. Time is the subject of historians, and any creditable explanation of a historical event like the Civil War must be grounded in a specific chronology that demonstrates why the event occured at one point in time rather than another. Invoking the notion of inevitability simply will not do, nor will explanations of the war that cite broad ideological, cultural, social, and economic differences and disagreements between North and South prior to its outbreak, unless it can be proved that those differences and conflicts caused the specific sequence of chronological developments that led to war in 1861.

Most, though hardly all, of those developments were political. The firing on Fort Sumter would not have occurred without the previous secession of seven Deep South states, which was itself a political decision. Their secession was a direct response to Abraham Lincoln's election as president in 1860. Although it can be argued that neither Lincoln's election nor secession made war inevitable, the incontrovertible fact is that the outbreak of war in 1861 is inconceivable without secession and Lincoln's election. Lincoln's triumph, in turn, could never have occurred without the formation of the exclusively northern Republican party in 1854 and its rise to power in the North between that date and 1860. That development was absolutely dependent upon and could never have occurred without still earlier political transformations, the voter realignment of the mid-1850s and the collapse of the Whig party. I firmly believe, therefore, that any persuasive interpretation of what caused the Civil War must, at a minimum, account for *all* of those chronological developments, and one could with justice push the chain of indispensable, contingent political events as far back as 1840.

The corollary of this line of reasoning is that I reject as incomplete and therefore inadequate the contention of most historians that sectional conflict over slavery and slavery expansion caused the Civil War. Conflicting sectional attitudes and animosities played some role in all of the specific chronological developments that led to war and a primary role in certain of them. By itself, however, sectional conflict cannot explain all of the critical turning points on the road to war. Sectional conflict over slavery cannot account for the differences among the slave states themselves during the secession crisis, let alone for the northern voter realignment of mid-decade or the disintegration of the Whig party, which had to be displaced before the Republicans could rise to power. In much of the North, for example, it was the Know Nothings, not the Republicans, who ruined Whiggery and decimated the Democracy. The very existence of a powerful Know Nothing movement whose focus was on Catholics, immigrants, and unresponsive politicians, not the slavery issue, therefore, undermines the argument that slavery alone caused the Civil War.

At the same time, proponents of the slavery causation thesis who fault the ethnocultural interpretation of northern politics in the 1850s for its inability to explain the Civil War have a valid point.[11] Zealous proponents of the ethnocultural interpretation who insist that ethnic and religious antagonisms almost always shaped voting behavior in the nineteenth century *do* engage in reductionism, and they *do* incorrectly ignore the impact of contingent events, such as the caning of Charles Sumner, in changing the course of development. Nor do evangelical Protestant religious values fully, or even primarily, account for the northern outrage that fed the growth of the Republican party. Moreover, despite the imaginative efforts of some historians, the ethnocultural model explains next to nothing about southern politics in the prewar years and secession crisis.[12] Nonetheless, the ethnocultural interpretation of northern voting behavior is more relevant to the causes of the Civil War than its dismissive critics admit.

A single example illustrates why the sectional conflict and ethnocultural theories must be combined to account for the war. The pivotal proximate cause of the Civil War, because of the responses it provoked, was Abraham Lincoln's election in 1860. There are at least two ways to address the question of why Lincoln won. One is to ask why it was the

11. See, for example, Willie Lee Rose, "Comment on Robert Kelley's 'Ideology and Political Culture from Jefferson to Lincoln,'" *American Historical Review*, LXXXII (1977), 577–82; and Don E. Fehrenbacher, "The New Political History and the Coming of the Civil War," in his *Lincoln in Text and Context: Collected Essays* (Stanford, 1987), 72–92.

12. Silbey, *The Partisan Imperative*, 166–89. Much, however, can be learned about southern politics by employing the quantitative techniques associated with the "new political history," which should not be identified exclusively with the ethnocultural interpretation. See, for example, Peyton McCrary, Clark Miller, and Dale Baum, "Class and Party in the Secession Crisis: Voting Behavior in the Deep South, 1856–1861," *Journal of Interdisciplinary History*, VIII (1978), 429–57; and Daniel Crofts, *Reluctant Confederates: Upper South Unionists in the Secession Crisis* (Chapel Hill, 1989).

Republicans, rather than the rival Know Nothings, who aggregated the polyglot northern opponents of the Democracy between the end of 1855 and 1860. Events that intensified sectional animosity in the North provide a far better explanation of the Republican success in that regard than do ethnic and religious tensions, even if a considerable portion of Republican voters were former Know Nothings who continued to be motivated, in part, by anti-Catholic sentiment. Yet the question of why voters supported the Republican rather than some other anti-Democratic party is analytically separate from the question of why they opposed the Democrats in the first place.

Thus another way to address the question of why Lincoln won in 1860 is to ask why the Democrats lost. Proponents of the sectional-conflict interpretation might point to the sectional rupture of the party that year as the reason, but the fact is that even if the votes for Stephen Douglas and John C. Breckinridge had been combined behind single tickets, Lincoln would still have carried enough northern electoral votes to win. Alternatively, one might plausibly argue, as many Democrats did in 1860, that the record of the Buchanan administration was such a disaster that the Democrats were doomed to defeat that year no matter who their opponent was. Surely, however, the most fundamental reason the Democrats lost is that by 1856 they had already been reduced to less than 42 percent of the vote in the northern states that put Lincoln in the White House. The northern voter realignment of the mid-1850s, in short, played an absolutely critical role in causing the Civil War, and the evidence is simply indisputable that ethnocultural issues and tensions had a decisive impact in permanently converting a substantial majority of northern voters against the Democracy.

At the very least, in sum, any persuasive interpretation of the political origins of the Civil War must incorporate both a sectionalist and an ethnocultural perspective. None of the essays in this volume purports to advance such a comprehensive interpretation, although I have attempted to do so elsewhere.[13] But the line of argument laid out here should help the reader understand the stance I have taken in many of the essays contained herein.

The book's final essay departs wholly from the antebellum era to

13. Holt, *The Political Crisis of the 1850s.*

which I have devoted almost all of my research and deals with the politics of the Civil War itself. Based on admittedly limited forays into the primary sources for the war years, it attempts to marshal evidence for an intuitive argument I had been making for some years in my undergraduate lecture course. The resulting paper was first presented at a symposium entitled "Abraham Lincoln and the American Political Tradition" at Brown University in June, 1984.[14]

This essay is perhaps the most speculative in the entire book, and it evoked considerable skepticism from other participants at the Brown symposium who were disconcerted that such a novice in the study of Lincoln as I should advance such a brash thesis. Surely, far, far more research in the incoming correspondence of Lincoln and other northern politicians than I attempted is needed either to prove or disprove that thesis. I confess, however, that the interpretation continues to make eminently good sense to me.

The essay begins by challenging the insightful argument of Eric McKitrick that the presence of a two-party system in the North during the Civil War and the absence of such a system in the Confederacy helped the North to win the war.[15] Because Republicans of all persuasions rallied behind the Lincoln administration in order to defeat the common Democratic enemy, McKitrick contends, the North remained more united than the strife-torn Confederacy. I assert, instead, that the contrasting political responses of Lincoln and congressional Republicans to that Democratic threat were the source of the conflict between them over wartime policies. I also advance the heretical notion that Abraham Lincoln, the patron saint of the Republican party, set out to displace it with a new and differently constituted organization almost from the day he was elected.

If a major theme linking these essays has been my continuing fascination with the relationship between party politics and the outbreak and outcome of the Civil War, other concerns also permeate many of them. One grows out of my current project on the Whig party. It is to rebut, if

---

14. "Abraham Lincoln and the Politics of Union," in *Abraham Lincoln and the American Political Tradition*, ed. John L. Thomas (Amherst, Mass., 1986), 111–41, copyright © 1986 by the University of Massachusetts Press.

15. Eric McKitrick, "Party Politics and the Union and Confederate War Efforts," in *The American Party Systems: Stages of Political Development*, ed. William N. Chambers and Walter Dean Burnham (New York, 1967), 117–51.

further rebuttal is any longer necessary, the old-fashioned, unduly hostile, and wrong-headed caricature of the Whigs as an unprincipled, heterogeneous coalition held together by nothing other than common antipathy toward Democrats. The congenital weakness of this crippled invalid was supposedly demonstrated by its inability to win the presidency unless it opportunistically shunned platforms, concealed programs, and ran popular military heroes in hurrah campaigns, and by its entirely predictable disintegration in the 1850s. The Whig *were* an opposition party whose history can only be understood in terms of its changing relationship with the Democratic party during the life of the second party system. Its existence and success *did* depend upon it ability to provide a viable and genuine alternative to the Democrats. Otherwise, this biased lampoon is nonsense.

For one thing, it gives far too much weight to presidential races and drastically discounts the record of Whigs in state legislative, gubernatorial, and congressional elections, to say nothing of the cohesive and frequently successful legislative performance of Whigs at the state and national levels. Those who mock the supposed feebleness and unpopularity of the Whigs, who label the Whig party "still-born" during its early years and "moribund" during the last decade of its existence, would do well to take a look at the woeful electoral fortunes of the Republican party in the 1930s and mid-1970s. Compared to that pathetic record, the Whig party, throughout its existence, epitomized health and vigor.

As these essays try to demonstrate, moreover, Whigs won elections because and only when they advocated programs and policies different from those offered by the Democrats. They also seek to show—and my book on the Whigs will demonstrate in more detail—that the Whigs nominated William Henry Harrison in 1840 and Zachary Taylor in 1848, not because of intellectual bankruptcy or a conviction that the American electorate disagreed with their stand on issues, but because of temporary, contingent circumstances prevailing at the time of their national nominating conventions that convinced delegates they could not run the issue-oriented campaigns most preferred.

In both instances, ironically, those circumstances changed almost immediately after the conventions adjourned, and it is simply not true that either Harrison or Taylor won election, as opposed to nomination, primarily because of his allure as a military hero. Harrison was nominated in December, 1839, and in the early months of 1840 the economy went into a tailspin. That depression virtually guaranteed sweeping Whig victories in the state legislative, gubernatorial, congressional, and presidential elections that year. Similarly, Taylor was nominated in June, 1848, in large part because Whigs believed that the prosperity fueled by European grain sales and the Polk administration's financing of the Mexican War precluded the use of the economic issues on which they had won the congressional elections of 1846 and early 1847. Starting in July, 1848, however, the economy began the downward slide that Whigs had been predicting since 1846, and exultant Whigs trotted out the economic appeals that only one month earlier they had considered futile. It is true that the disruption of the northern Democratic party, reflected in and exacerbated by the formation of the Free Soil party, probably played the biggest role in electing Taylor. But it is also true that Whig attacks on the Walker Tariff and Independent Treasury Act helped limit northern Whig defections to that party and brought to the polls to vote for Taylor tens of thousands of other northern Whigs who considered his nomination an abomination precisely because they viewed it as an abandonment of Whig principles and programs.

Implicitly, these essays on the Whigs also suggest a point that merits explicit emphasis here. Close examination of the contingencies that shaped Whig presidential politics in the 1840s starkly underlines how extraordinary ill-starred the career of Henry Clay actually was. It is well known how close he came to victory in the election of 1844, even if the reasons for his defeat are more complex than many have thought. Less well known is how close he came to capturing the Whig nomination in 1840 and 1848. Had the Whig convention been held in the spring of 1840, rather than in December, 1839, I am absolutely certain that Clay would have been nominated and elected. Even in December, 1839, he almost grasped the prize. Clay was denied the nomination at that convention primarily because his northern opponents successfully adopted a unit rule that deprived Clay of his substantial support among northern delegations. Clay's friends lost that vote, in turn, not only because South Carolina, Tennessee, and Georgia, for reasons I still cannot fathom, sent no delegates to the convention, but also because the Arkansas delegation failed to reach Harrisburg in time for the convention. Had those states been represented, their delegates most likely would have voted as did every other southerner at the convention—for Clay. If so, under the unit rule, Clay would have come within five votes of the nomination on the first ballot. Even the wiles of Thurlow Weed and Thaddeus Stevens probably could not have stopped his nomination in that event. But if all southern states had been represented, there would have been no unit rule, for southern Whigs along with Clay's northern supporters would have defeated it. In sum, with full southern attendance, Clay would have won the nomination on the first ballot even in December. And given the plummeting economy of 1840, any Whig candidate would have won the election.

Similarly, between December, 1847, and early March, 1848, Clay emerged as the clear front-runner for the Whig nomination. He did so primarily because of Whigs' disgust with the "No Party" antics of Taylor and a dramatic speech in November, 1847, in which he condemned the Mexican War, vowed opposition to any territorial acquisition from Mexico, and pledged that slavery would never expand westward. Had Nicholas Trist not violated his instructions and negotiated a peace treaty with Mexico and had the Senate not ratified that treaty on March 10, Clay most likely would have won the nomination because so many Whigs believed they could win the election on that platform. Certainly, Taylor would not have been nominated in those circumstances. Whether Clay could have won election in 1848 is more difficult to say, for no Whig could mobilize Democrats in opposition as readily as he. Yet the creation of the Free Soil party would probably have secured his election just as it did Taylor's.

Skeptics might well ask what the point of these might-have-beens is. The point is the same one that drives some of the later essays in this volume. It is to show how untenable the notion that the Civil War was inevitable is, or at least the Civil War that actually started in 1861. The election of Clay at any point in the 1840s would have decisively altered the chain of events that explains why war did break out in that year. Had Clay been nominated in 1840, neither John Tyler nor any other southerner would have been his running mate. Had Clay been elected, Texas would not have been annexed during the next four years or perhaps for the remainder of the decade. Had Clay been elected in 1844, as he most likely would have been had the delegates to the Whig convention that year not thoughtlessly saddled him with Theodore Frelinghuysen as a running mate, there would have been no Mexican War, no Wilmot Proviso, and no territorial issue to fight over. Had Clay been elected in 1848, even after the Mexican Cession, it is likely that the attempt of Congress to find a solution for the territorial problem would not have been as long and rancorous as it was. It is certain that the Whig party would not have been as badly divided as it became during the administration of Taylor and Millard Fillmore. And a more unified and cohesive Whig party might have survived the turmoil of the 1850s, thus preventing the formation of a strong sectional party like the Republicans, whose victory in 1860 drove Deep South states to secede. Thus did contingencies, unthinking decisions, and unforeseen events have very large consequences.

This emphasis on the importance of contingent events in shaping the course of political development in part reflects a fundamental change in my thinking about the study of political history in general. Readers should note that the three essays on the Whig party and the analysis of Lincoln's political strategy, all of which were written after 1980, differ sharply in approach and focus from the three essays written in the early 1970s on the origins of Know Nothingism, the Antimasonic and Know Nothings parties, and the Democratic party. These changes reflect not simply a shift in my interests from grass-roots politics to national parties and national political elites. They also stem from a growing dissatisfaction with the limitations of my early approach.

The early essays, like my first book on the formation of the Republican party in Pittsburgh, embraced in whole or in part certain central tenets and assumptions of the so-called "new political history" and the related ethnocultural analysis of voting behavior with which I was then, quite properly, identified.[16] According to these models, which came to prominence in the 1960s and 1970s, analysis of the underlying patterns in, and transformations of, grass-roots voting behavior provided the best way to understand American political development. American political history could be periodized in terms of successive two-party systems that were defined primarily by distinctive cleavages in the electorate, not by the issues they contested, the programs they enacted, or the events that transpired during their existence. Those system-defining voter cleavages,

16. See, for example, Richard L. McCormick, "Ethnocultural Interpretations of Nineteenth-Century American Voting Behavior," in his *The Party Period and Public Policy: American Politics from the Age of Jackson to the Progressive Era* (New York, 1986), 29–63.

in turn, were first forged during relatively brief periods of voter realignment that originated in concerns of the electorate. Once voters formed attachments to one party or another in a realignment, their partisan loyalties remained remarkably stable—"fixed and fierce," I once called them—for long periods of time until the next voter realignment. Issues might change voters' preferences during realigning elections, in other words, but during the longer stable phases of party systems voters' partisan affiliations remained virtually unshakable no matter what happened. Concomitantly, most voters aligned with one party or another, not in response to national issues or the actions of presidents, Congress, governors, and state legislatures, but because of their local social and economic experience, their membership in social reference groups that shaped and reinforced partisan predispositions, and their rivalries with other, negative reference groups. Finally, according to some, though certainly not all, proponents of the "new political history," ethnic and religious attitudes and rivalries were the chief determinants of voting behavior during most of the nineteenth century, at least in the numerically dominant North. Therefore, voters, their social identities and attitudes, and their movements during periodic realignments, not governmental policies or leadership decisions, were the engines that drove political development.[17]

Although my early work focused heavily on grass-roots voting behavior and periods of voter realignment, I have never posited an exclusively ethnocultural interpretation of voting behavior. Moreover, I have always paid close attention to chronology and the impact of events, not just underlying structure and voters' attitudes. Nonetheless, like many of the "new political historians," I placed voters at the center of the political universe. Over the years, however, I have become increasingly doubtful about the adequacy and validity of both the party system and ethnocultural models as frameworks for structuring the history of political development. As a result, in different ways each of the essays gathered here that was written after 1980 reflects that disenchantment.

For one thing, both the portrait and explanation of popular voting behavior that I once embraced no longer seem accurate. Studies of voting

---

17. For a thorough description, if skeptical appraisal, of the methods and tenets of the "new political history," see Fehrenbacher, "The New Political History." A much more positive assessment by one of the genre's leading practitioners can be found in Silbey, *The Partisan Imperative*.

behavior conducted during the late 1970s and 1980s that employed more sophisticated statistical techniques than I and other scholars had previously used revealed that a small fraction of the electorate almost always switched from one party to another in successive elections.[18] Those findings challenged the notion that party systems had prolonged stable phases during which voter preferences remained rigidly fixed. Far more important, those later analyses of voting were more inclusive than earlier efforts in that they incorporated eligible voters who abstained from, as well as those who participated in, elections; and they demonstrated that there was usually considerable movement into and out of the active or participating electorate from election to election, a volatility that undermined assertions of voter stability.

These findings also exposed fundamental weaknesses in any explanation of voting behavior based on social experiences or reference group behavior. What usually determined the outcome of elections—who won and who lost—was not which social groups voted for which party but differentials in the turnout rates of different parties' supporters. Reference group membership and local social experience seemed unable to account for changes in turnout rates, whether they were the quantum leap in voter participation between 1836 and 1840, the short-term fluctuations during the remainder of the century in subpresidential as well as presidential elections, or the long-term secular decline during the twentieth century. An individual's social identity, which supposedly determined his partisan affiliation, remained fixed. Certainly, his ethnic and religious identity remained fixed. Manifestly, however, his decision whether or not to vote in any particular election was not fixed. On certain occasions, for example, when prohibition was a salient issue, ethnic identity and religious affiliation might influence turnout rates, but on others they did not.

---

18. The method employed was usually ecological regression estimation of voter movement between elections. Among other studies that reveal voter volatility are the following: Gienapp, *Origins of the Republican Party*, 482–85; McCrary, Miller, and Baum, "Class and Party in the Secession Crisis"; Jerome M. Clubb, William H. Flanigan, and Nancy Zingale, *Partisan Realignment: Voters, Parties, and Government in American History* (Beverly Hills, 1980); Kevin Sweeney, "Rum, Romanism, Representation, and Reform: Politics in Massachusetts, 1847–1853," *Civil War History*, XXII (1976), 116–37. Sweeney's superb study focuses on gubernatorial rather than presidential elections, and a number of unpublished papers by my graduate students also show that party switching between elections was especially prevalent in subpresidential elections.

Obviously, therefore, one has to look beyond the realm of social experience to explain changes in turnout rates.

At the same time that more recent studies of nineteenth-century voting behavior shook my faith in my earlier interpretations, I became aware of compelling analyses of contemporary voting behavior by political scientists that suggested that nineteenth-century voters may have been far more issue oriented and responsive to governmental actions than I had once believed.[19] The idea that voters reacted in a rational way to what national and state governments did comported far better than did my earlier grass-roots explanations of voting behavior with the evidence I was finding about the campaign tactics of political leaders who operated out of state capitals and Washington. Between 1830 and 1900, those politicians went to quite extraordinary lengths to inform the electorate of their party's record in Congress, statehouses, and state legislatures. Simultaneously, legislators in Washington and state capitals behaved in ways that clearly indicate that they expected party roll-call voting records to be used as platforms in subsequent elections. If popular voting behavior was determined only by grass-roots social experience, why did legislators behave that way, and why did party leaders circulate hundreds of thousands of copies of detailed, fact-laden, and often exceeding boring congressional speeches or print addresses at the end of state legislative sessions that detailed the voting records of their own and opposing parties? Did it make sense to believe that national and state politicians were so completely out of touch with the concerns of the grass-roots electorate?

In sum, as my research interests shifted from grass-roots politics and periods of realignment to national political parties as competitive institutions, I became convinced that it was a fundamental mistake to focus so exclusively on determining the social identity and values of voters, to heed the clarion call of the 1960s that political historians should devote their energies to a "social analysis" of politics.[20] Political parties were not

19. These studies are cited in my essay on the election of 1840. To reject their findings about twentieth-century voters as inapplicable to the nineteenth-century electorate is to insist that voters in the nineteenth century were utterly different political animals than their twentieth-century counterparts. I cannot accept such an assumption.

20. The chief proponent of this approach was Samuel P. Hays. See his "The Social Analysis of American Political History, 1880–1920," *Political Science Quarterly*, LXXX (1965), 373–94; and *American Political History as Social Analysis* (Knoxville, 1980). For an exceedingly shrewd and

simply voter coalitions, and the political system as a whole consisted of far more than the electorate. Just as the party system/realignment model seemed incapable of explaining voters' movements between periods of realignment, so voters' attitudes seemed incapable of explaining political developments between elections and outside of the electoral arena like, for example, the annexation of Texas, the initiation of war with Mexico, and the introduction of the Wilmot Proviso, all of which occurred during the supposedly stable phase of the second party system.

Indeed, from the perspective of developments such as these and of political parties that operated at all levels of the federal system both during and between elections, it seemed far more interesting and important to figure out how popular elections related to other aspects of the political system than merely to identify who voted for whom. In attempting to link popular voting to other political actions like policy making, patronage distribution, or the nomination of certain candidates, moreover, one conclusion became inescapable. What mattered most about elections to political leaders who acted in other arenas of the political system was not who voted for whom but which party's candidates won. For proponents of a "social analysis" of politics and the ethnocultural voting model, however, the results of elections were largely irrelevant. Frequently insisting that historians must focus on underlying structures and durable patterns of group behavior, they dismissed elite decisions as idiosyncratic, events like election outcomes as ephemeral, and traditional chronological narratives that sought to illuminate the causal sequence of events as episodic and impressionistic. In terms of understanding American political development over time, this emphasis on structure at the expense of events and chronology has always struck me as the most grievous flaw of the "new political history," and my shift in focus from local politics to national parties and political elites measurably increased that conviction.

In part, the rethinking outlined above was compelled by the sheer force of a critique of the ethnocultural voting model raised by a few of the most astute political historians in the profession. What, they asked, was the connection between popular voting behavior and governance, the

insightful appraisal of studies that embrace this approach, see McCormick, *The Party Period and Public Policy*, 89–140.

formulation and implementation of public policy?[21] Specifically, if conflicting ethnic and religious attitudes caused people to vote for one party or another, how can we explain why most public policies enacted by national, state, and local governments in the nineteenth century had little or no explicit ethnocultural content and were instead concerned with other things—economic development, sectional and racial relations, public health, or whatever? To be sure, some state and local legislation—statutes concerning prohibition, Bible reading in public schools, tax support for Catholic schools, and Sunday blue laws, for example—did have explicit ethnocultural content, but the vast bulk of governance did not. Unless we are to believe that voters and policy makers, be they executives, legislators, or judges, dwelled in entirely separate political universes, the question must be faced. What linked grass-roots voters to actions of the state? In particular, what linked local voters to more remote arenas of governance than their own local governments, such as state legislatures or Congress?

I would place this problem at or near the top of any agenda that political historians should address over the next decade, for answering it opens up all kinds of possibilities for integrating our comprehension of the political system as a whole. Although my own efforts at unraveling that puzzle are preliminary, the essays included here suggest at least three separate but related solutions, all of which posit that political parties constituted the institutional linkage between voting and policy output. First, in terms of the causal connection between voters' decisions and *subsequent policy making*, voters' motives mattered far less than did election results. During most of the nineteenth century political parties developed considerable internal cohesion on roll-call votes in Congress and state legislatures, and usually voted on opposite sides of public policy questions from their opponents. Therefore, which party won control of government in a particular election largely determined the shape of subsequent governance and policy making.

Second, in terms of a causal connection between governance and *subsequent voters' decisions*, both whether and how to vote, the retrospective and negative voting models developed by political scientists possess sub-

---

21. In one form or another, this question and imaginative answers to it constitute the theme of McCormick, *The Party Period and Public Policy*.

stantial explanatory power. According to these models, elections do not represent choices about the future but are referenda on the past actions of government and on the records of the rival parties, especially the incumbent majority party. Moreover, disapproval of an incumbent party's record provides a much more powerful incentive for voting than does approval of that record. Voters use the ballot more frequently to punish than to applaud. By this model, for example, voters' choices in the presidential election of 1860 could be understood not so much as preferences about the future, whether it was to attack slavery, secede, start or avert a Civil War, but as judgments on the Buchanan administration. In sum, assessments of the past action of government, not simply reference group membership, influenced which party one voted for and helped determine whether or not one bothered to vote at all.

Third, the legitimacy of any particular two-party system with the electorate depended heavily on the partisan dimensions of governance. The ability of any single party first to mobilize and then to maintain popular voting support was a function of the clarity or sharpness of its programmatic conflict with rival parties and of its success in enacting policies it had promised when it had the chance. Both large and small fluctuations in turnout rates as well as the ability or inability of minor parties to make incursions into the major parties' voting support and to mobilize previously inert voters against both of them were largely, though not exclusively, determined by the major parties' success in demonstrating to voters that they did indeed adhere to alternative positions on public policy. Failure to demonstrate policy differences eroded voters' faith in the responsiveness of the political system as a whole, drove down turnout rates, and encouraged the formation of third parties. Those consequences were as apparent in the 1870s as in the 1850s, in the South as in the North.[22]

The need to try to bridge the gap between voting and policy making that had been opened by the ethnocultural voting model, however, was only one of the impetuses for the shift in focus from the earlier to the later essays. More broadly, it stemmed from my growing alarm about the

22. On the electoral volatility and mushrooming of third parties in the 1870s, which so closely resembled the experience of the 1850s, see Kleppner, *The Third Electoral System, 1853–1892;* Dale Baum, *The Civil War Party System: The Case of Massachusetts, 1848–1876* (Chapel Hill, 1984); and Michael Perman, *The Road to Redemption: Southern Politics, 1869–1879* (Chapel Hill, 1984).

increasing incoherence or fragmentation of political history as a field of scholarly investigation during the 1960s and 1970s. Just as the flowering of the "new social history" and its immediate fragmentation into specialized subfields during those years produced lamentation about the disintegration of history as a discipline and calls for new syntheses that could integrate the findings of social historians with traditional narratives, so, it seemed to me, the study of political history itself had become dangerously balkanized. Just as some social historians had criticized their colleagues for mistakenly ignoring the importance of events, chronology, and the exercise of political power by groups that controlled government, so, it seemed to me, much of the political history written in those decades was dangerously ahistorical and apolitical.[23]

By 1980, for example, we had some superb studies of political ideology, especially republicanism, and of "political culture" that only indirectly, if at all, examined the motives of officeholders, the actions of government, and popular elections. We had, as noted above, analyses of popular voting that ignored election results and what winners did in office. We had as well excellent quantitative analyses of roll-call voting patterns in Congress and state legislatures, but their methodology often obscured important changes over time within a particular legislative session. In addition, they usually said nothing about who won and who lost particular roll calls, whether bills passed into law, how laws were implemented if they did pass, or what impact they had on the electorate.

As I confronted the task of writing the history of a political party as a whole, moreover, I wondered how any of these new findings could be integrated with the concerns of traditional political history that was now disparaged as old-fashioned and elitist. What, for example, did ideology, legislative voting, and popular voting behavior have to do with the decisions of presidents and other party leaders, with the distribution of patronage, with intraparty factionalism among the leadership, and with the flow of events over time? For that matter, how could one bring together the many traditional studies that focused on a single individual, a single

---

23. For examples of social historians who have faulted their colleagues for ignoring politics, see Elizabeth Fox-Genovese and Eugene D. Genovese, "The Political Crisis of Social History: Class Struggle as Subject and Object," in their *Fruits of Merchant Capital: Slavery and Bourgeois Property in the Rise and Expansion of Capitalism* (New York, 1983), 179–212; and Sean Wilentz, "On Class and Politics in Jacksonian America," *Reviews in American History*, X (1982), 45–63.

state, or a single event into a coherent whole with each other and with the more recent findings? Before a successful synthesis of the "new social history" and political history could be written, it seemed clear to me, political history itself had to be reintegrated.

My diagnosis of the maladies afflicting political history, especially its fragmentation and incoherence, is hardly original, and at least one historian has recently suggested that employment of rational-choice theory in all subfields of the discipline might produce the necessary integration.[24] My own prescription for attempting to reintegrate political history is less ambitious and theoretically oriented than that remedy. Its outlines appear in the three essays on the Whig party and the analysis of Lincoln's conflict with Republican congressmen. At the risk of redundancy and belaboring what may be obvious in those essays, it seems fitting to conclude this introduction by listing some of the ingredients of that prescription.

An integrated and comprehensive history of American political development, I am now convinced, must be written as a chronological narrative that pays close attention to short-term changes over time and the causal sequence of events. Rather than simply stressing the stability or predictability of underlying, structural patterns of group behavior that defined two-party systems, it must allow room for the impact of individual decisions, contingencies, and unforseen events both inside and outside of the political arena that altered the course of political development. Emphasis on chronological change is necessary not only to present a more accurate portrait of what happened but also to comprehend the motives and actions of the historical actors themselves. What most struck both voters and politicians in the nineteenth century was not the permanency of any party or two-party system or the predictability of political outcomes. Rather, they experienced a political system that seemed volatile, fluid, and constantly open to the possibility of change. It was, indeed, precisely this perception of a plastic, rather than an immutable, political universe that shaped many of the key decisions that altered the course of American political development from the Age of Jackson to the Age of Lincoln.

Historians who characterize the nineteenth century as "the party period" and who speak of "the partisan imperative" during those years

24. J. Morgan Kousser, "Toward 'Total Political History': A Rational-Choice Research Program," *Journal of Interdisciplinary History*, XX (1990), 521–60.

make a valid point. Political parties in that century were far stronger than they now are, and they played a more important role in people's lives than they do today. They had considerable power to shape the behavior of voters and officeholders alike. They elicited unparalleled loyalty. They could mobilize astonishingly high proportions of the potential electorate. In competition with each other, they did mold relatively stable patterns of electoral and legislative behavior. Therefore, from the vantage point of today's attenuated partisan culture, powerful and popular political parties do appear to have been the dominant influence on political life in the previous century.

At the same time, however, compared to the stagnant and discouragingly predictable partisan politics in the twentieth century, when the same two major parties have exercised an apparently unshakable monopoly over access to political office, when one party has controlled the House of Representatives for forty years, and when incumbents in Congress seem unbeatable, nineteenth-century politics seems open and malleable, not closed and rigid. Similarly, "strong" nineteenth-century parties appear considerably more vulnerable than do their "weak" modern counterparts. Only in the nineteenth century, after all, did new major parties appear and then disappear. Only in the nineteenth century did third parties constantly emerge to challenge the major parties in local, state, and national elections; and whether those minor parties became powerful, as did the Antimasons and Know Nothings, or remained inconsequential, the ease with which they were formed and the sheer frequency with which they appeared constantly reminded voters and politicians alike that change might be possible. Only in the nineteenth century did politicians as diverse as Daniel Webster, John Tyler, Zachary Taylor, John Clayton, Howell Cobb, Abraham Lincoln, and Andrew Johnson—to confine myself to the period covered in this book—believe that they had a realistic chance, through actions at the top of the political system, to displace existing major parties with differently constituted organizations. And only in the nineteenth century did politicians committed to the existing major parties regard those threats as entirely credible and react accordingly. Voters and politicians who lived through the 1820s, 1830s, 1840s, 1850s, 1860s, and 1870s, unlike their twentieth-century descendants, personally experienced rapid changes in party politics. Consequently, they saw change and uncertainty, not stability, as the political norm. Only by recognizing this sense of openness and possibility in the system can historians understand many of the things they did.

If surprise, contingency, and a perception of political fluidity were central ingredients of nineteenth-century politics, it is nonetheless true that far more than in the twentieth century most people who sought to influence what government did or did not do channeled political activity through political parties and partisan competition for control of government. Put differently, an administrative, bureaucratic state that operated independently of electoral politics and that might be susceptible to interest-group lobbying rather than partisan control had only rudimentary beginnings in the nineteenth century.[25] Therefore, the most inclusive focus for a chronological narrative history of political development in that century is political parties and their competitive relationship with other parties.

That story, in turn, can most profitably be told from the perspective of political leaders, rather than voters, for it seems clear that at most times the motives, decisions, and actions of officeholders and other politicians had greater impact in causing political change than did the values of voters. Political leaders, of course, never completely disregarded the electorate, and voters and popular elections would be integrated into the story in terms of the reciprocal relationships outlined above. By putting one party rather than another in power at a certain level of government, the results of elections helped determine its subsequent policy output. Those governmental actions, in turn, helped shape subsequent decisions among the electorate about whether and how to vote.

Voters and election results, in fact, have even broader ramifications for the study of parties and political development than just their important relationship to governance. For one thing, the most fruitful way to incorporate analysis of political ideology—particularly the much-studied republican ideology—into the story of political development is not simply to explicate the particular principles, worldview, or "political culture" of specific parties but also to relate it to a more fundamental question: What expectations did the electorate have about political parties and the political system as a whole? Ideology, that is, might not explain what leaders did,

---

25. Stephen Skowronek, *Building a New American State: The Expansion of National Administrative Capacities, 1877–1920* (New York, 1982), 3–46; but see also Richard Bensel, *Yankee Leviathan: The Origins of Central State Authority in America, 1859–1877* (New York, 1990).

what kinds of public policies were enacted at specific times, or why certain events transpired, but it can help us understand voters' responses to those developments in terms of changing attitudes toward the legitimacy of particular parties, the responsiveness of the system as a whole, and the political efficacy of the vote itself.

Equally important, the relationship between voters and politicians has even richer analytical potential than the causal linkages between elections and governance suggested above. Election results affected other kinds of leadership decisions than policy making. And they influenced the formulation and enactment of public policy in other ways than determining which parties controlled the executive, legislative, and judicial branches of government. To exploit that potential and thus write more integrated and comprehensive political histories, two further points must be emphasized.

First, a comprehensive history of political development in the nineteenth century must take into account the impact of the American federal system on politics and the interrelationship among politicians and events at the local, state, and national levels. Voters formed judgments of parties based on their record at all levels of the federal system, not just on what national leaders in Washington did. A positive reaction to the record of a party in a state legislature might offset a negative reaction against its officeholders in Washington. In addition, during most sessions of Congress, state legislatures were simultaneously meeting, state nominating conventions were being held, and, occasionally, state constitutional conventions were at work. What happened in those state political institutions influenced what the congressional delegations from those states did, just as what was transpiring in Congress often influenced state assemblages.

More basically, politicians in the nineteenth century seemed to have cared far more about the institutional success of their party at all levels of the federal system than do their modern counterparts. It was not simply the power of state legislatures to draw congressional districts and elect United States senators that explains the solicitude of national officeholders for the welfare of state parties, although that authority surely contributed to it. Political leaders, like voters, conceived of politics in terms of parties as organizations, not the individuals who composed them. Put somewhat differently, the tenure of individual officeholders was usually so short, their loyalty to party principles and programs when in office so firm, and the rotation of party nominations so extensive that politicians were viewed by the public, and they frequently viewed themselves, as interchangeable parts. What mattered to those who wanted to use government for some end and to those who judged what government did was the performance of the party as a whole, not the individuals who temporarily represented it. Most people, that is, voted for or against parties, not particular candidates. In addition, partisan politics in the nineteenth century generated a highly competitive ethos akin to athletics. Members of a particular party wanted their team to win no matter what arena it was playing in: elections for state legislatures, roll-call votes in Congress, debates on the hustings, or the allocation of government jobs.

The critical impact of federalism on political development between the Age of Jackson and the Age of Lincoln is, in fact, a theme that pervades the essays in this book. Thus I argue that many of Lincoln's actions can be explained by the calendar of conventions and elections in the states. Thus I contend that a string of defeats in state elections in the fall of 1839 turned Whig delegates toward a military hero at the national convention in December of that year. Thus I try to demonstrate that the division of jurisdictional authority over different policy areas between state and national governments largely accounts for the appearance of third parties like the Antimasons and Know Nothings. And the list of reciprocal impacts hardly stops there. For example, tables in the essay on the election of 1840 indicate that the Whig party suffered one of the most stunning reversals in American history in the congressional elections of 1842–1843. Having won 61 percent of the seats in the House of Representatives in the elections of 1840–1841, they captured only 29 percent in the elections of 1842–1843. As I argue in that essay, the major reason for this dramatic setback was the failure of Whigs in Congress to enact a program for economic recovery the party had promised in 1840–1841. But that failure was not the only reason. Tables in that essay also show that beginning in the fall of 1841 and extending into 1842 and 1843 Democrats made massive gains in state legislative elections, winning control of legislatures Whigs had dominated when Harrison was inaugurated. Those Democratic legislatures flagrantly gerrymandered congressional districts during the reapportionment following the census of 1840, and that gerrymander measurably contributed to the Whigs' debacle. The lesson is clear. Those who would understand nineteenth-century political development cannot focus on any single level of government. All of the parts must be incorporated to comprehend the whole.

Second, historians of nineteenth-century politics must pay far more systematic attention than they have to longitudinal trends in congressional and state elections. If historians bother to study those elections at all, it is usually for a single year or in a single state rather than all such elections in all states over extended periods of time. Indeed, one of the most striking differences between historians who study nineteenth-century elections and political scientists who study twentieth-century elections is that the latter, but not the former, frequently employ statistically elaborate time-series analyses of congressional elections that cover fifty or sixty years and that place great interpretive weight on biennial fluctuations in behavior. The failure of historians to make such longitudinal analyses leads to the embarrassing conclusion that historians are more ahistorical than are political scientists; that is, they are less sensitive to the importance of short-term change over time.

No time-series analysis of congressional elections that I have seen extends backward in time farther than 1876. Prior to that date, different states held congressional and state elections in different months of both odd- and even-numbered years, not on the same day in November of even-numbered years. That peculiar election calendar may have inhibited both historians and political scientists from extending time-series analyses to earlier elections, for no single month or even year would have a sufficient number of cases to be statistically significant. As my essay on the election of 1840 attempts to illustrate, however, those earlier congressional and state elections are susceptible to a cruder form of time-series analysis.

More important, it was precisely the chronological spread of elections prior to 1876 that explains their impact on policy makers and other political leaders. In every year, a congressional, gubernatorial, or state legislative election was held somewhere in every month between March and November except June, and local elections were often held in other months of the year. Whatever motivated voters in particular elections, political leaders in Washington and state capitals regarded them as the nineteenth-century equivalent of public opinion polls, as running tabulations of public attitudes toward their parties and their own performance in office. Thus, while presidents were allotting federal jobs, while congressmen were debating and voting on legislation, and while presidential campaigns were being conducted, elections were taking place that influenced, and sometimes decisively changed, the decisions and tactics of political leaders.

In sum, once one realizes that both voters and politicians cared deeply about the electoral and legislative performances of rival political parties at all levels of the federal system, not just at any single one, that state legislative and congressional sessions had a reciprocal influence on each other, and that the month-to-month fluctuation of election results influenced decisions made in other sectors of the political system, the potential for reintegrating political history becomes readily apparent. One can address traditional questions like elite actions and intraparty factionalism without discounting the importance of voters' concerns and behavior. Simply put, incumbent officeholders responded to the results of elections, state conventions, and other political developments in their own and opposing parties. Those developments, especially election results, thus influenced the decisions of presidential nominating conventions, tactical shifts during presidential campaigns, the allocation of patronage and formulation of political strategies by presidents and governors, the balance and competitive tactics of warring factions within a particular party, and changes of course by congressmen and state legislators during the course of particular legislative sessions. By remaining alert to the impact of events, by considering parties as federal organizations whose activities at different levels of the federal system were interconnected, and by seeking to understand the reciprocal relationship between voters and leaders, it is as possible as it is imperative to bring together into a comprehensive whole the many diverse sectors of the political system that have hitherto too often been treated in isolation from each other.

The Democratic Party, 1828–1860

$\mathbf{T}$ he Democratic party between 1828 and 1860 was a changing coalition of men with different interests joined by a common desire for its success at the polls. Ambition, prejudice, economic concerns, sectional loyalties, and personal animosities as well as principle influenced Democratic voters and leaders, and motives varied from time to time and man to man. Formed behind the presidential candidacy of Andrew Jackson in 1828, the party was a heterogeneous alliance that cut across the regional, economic, ethnic, and religious lines fragmenting American society. As the party's policies were more clearly defined and as new issues arose, the composition of this initial coalition changed. These realignments were the products of both internal leadership decisions and transitions in the rapidly growing and diversifying society. Developments external to the party not only provided the issues it addressed and shaped the electorate to which it appealed, but also defined the rules of the political game in which it was a contestant.

The party's origins lay in the political situation of the 1820s. By 1820, the first American party system of Jeffersonian Republicans and Federalists had collapsed. Aside from isolated pockets of strength, the Federalists had disappeared, and almost all active politicians considered themselves Republicans. One party rule gave apparent validity to the title applied to the period—"The Era of Good Feelings"—but beneath this facade raged bitter antagonisms. The inclusiveness of the party diluted its ideology. To the dismay of purists known as Old Republicans, or Radicals, the state rights, strict construction, small government principles of the original Jeffersonians no longer prevailed, and the party had acquiesced in nationalistic programs pushed by younger men. In addition, state organizations were rent by factional struggles. At both the national and state levels, however, political battles reflected in part the reaction to two profoundly disturbing events—the depression following the Panic of 1819 and the angry division between North and South that emerged in the Missouri debates between 1819 and 1821.

The result of a complex combination of events, the Panic of 1819 had enormous political impact. Many southerners and westerners who faced the foreclosure of mortgages held by banks blamed the Bank of the United States and the eastern elite at its Philadelphia headquarters for causing the panic. This inflamed sectional animosity toward the East influenced congressional debates over issues like the tariff, internal improvements, and land policy for years, and made the juggling of sectional interests part of the task of constructing a national party. More important, the panic resulted in part from an overextension of bank credit and rampant speculation in land. It ignited working-class and agrarian hostility to paper money and the private banking system that seemed to favor a few at the expense of the many and to cause economic fluctuations that were catastrophic to the little man. Farmers clamored for relief from debts and became more active politically in order to get it. In frontier states like Mississippi, they wanted more paper money, but in more settled regions like Tennessee and Ohio, farmers, along with Jeffersonian ideologues and urban workers, increasingly opposed any kind of paper money, especially that issued by privately controlled banks.

To fathom the intensity of this attack on banks, one must understand that it represented in part a protest against the entire course of the American economy. Between 1815 and 1860, a rapidly growing capitalistic and commercial economy replaced the simpler agrarian society cherished by so many Americans. The dislocation and psychological malaise caused by this transition were basic forces behind the Democratic party. A closer look at this development, then, is imperative for an understanding of the nature of the Democracy throughout the period.

The days of the self-sufficient yeoman farmer were gone before Andrew Jackson's victory at New Orleans in 1815, but the following years witnessed extraordinary growth in speculative activity, in the number of commercial and manufacturing enterprises, and in market-oriented agriculture. Government policies and the opening of the West encouraged land speculation. Transportation improvements—turnpikes, canals, and, in the 1840s and 1850s, railroads—facilitated and made cheaper the transfer of goods from one region to another and thus created a national market. To take advantage of this market and the faster transportation, merchant capitalists established relatively large-scale manufacturing operations in shops and mills and, in the 1840s and 1850s, increasingly in machine-powered factories. All of these developments tended to reduce skilled and semiskilled workers to dependent wage-earner status.

This commercial economy required new institutions to fuel its mechanisms with capital and currency. To supply capital for speculative investments and credit to finance the transfer of goods, banks were chartered as corporations with the privilege of issuing paper bank notes. Along with other advantages, the stockholders in banking corporations had limited individual liability. Because corporations enjoyed this and other privileges denied to individuals, the corporate form spread to insurance companies, turnpikes, canals, and railroads as well. It became a central political issue in the 1830s and 1840s.

If many people profited from the burgeoning economy, others suffered from it and began to demand a change in government policies. The transportation revolution that opened eastern markets to the booming agricultural production of western areas injured farmers in New England and the older areas of the Middle States and Old South, who lost their competitive advantage in those markets. Conversely, businesses in the West faced increased competition from the East. Advantages of location were destroyed. Merchants, farmers, and manufacturers who lacked access to adequate transportation or financial facilities could not match competitors who had them, and they often demanded for themselves the opportunities extended to others—more roads and canals, more chartered corporations, and more bank notes.

On the other hand, many farmers and workers despaired at the trend of the economy and turned against the institutions that epitomized speculative capitalism. Artisans who were reduced to wage-earner status, who could not compete with large-scale enterprises, or who were paid in undervalued paper scrip began to blame banks for their problems. Accustomed to a simple, stable economy, farmers felt threatened in the rapidly changing society after 1815. They resented the privileges given an elite few by the mechanisms of capitalism. Deploring the subversion of an earlier and, to them, more moral society where honest toil and thrift were valued, perplexed by the vacillations of an economy they did not understand, they turned on the bankers and speculators who seemed to grow wealthy through arcane manipulations of an artificial currency. Whether caused by specific economic grievances or qualms about the perversion of the proper moral order, antibanking sentiment was a major political force until the 1840s.

The Panic of 1819 and subsequent depression crystallized this nascent antibanking sentiment for the first time, and it along with antieastern prejudices helped shape the Jackson movement that became the Democratic party. The Bank of the United States was a target of popular wrath in Ohio. Hatred of it, the East, and the American System, which seemed to favor the East, was universal in Missouri in the 1820s. In Kentucky, politics revolved around the issue of granting relief to debtors, and those who voted for the Relief party, which denounced bankers, would later vote for Andrew Jackson. Antibank sentiment was so strong in Tennessee that it threatened to overthrow those politicians who owned the state's banks. To save their political lives, the leaders of the dominant bank clique—John Overton, William Lewis, and John Eaton—began to boom General Andrew Jackson, their ally, but a renowned foe of banks, for president. Expecting only to use Jackson's immense popularity to protect themselves in Tennessee, these managers did not anticipate the nationwide enthusiasm for Jackson that exploded in 1823 and 1824. Thus the prejudices against banking formed in the 1820s account not only for later votes for Jackson but also, in part, for his ever being a candidate.

Equally important in the creation of the Democratic party were the bitter attacks on slavery that emerged in Congress between 1819 and 1821. The unity of northern hostility to the admission of Missouri as a slave state revealed to perceptive observers the possibility that politics might be reorganized along sectional lines and that the northern majority could be used against slavery. As John Quincy Adams wrote, the potential northern party was "terrible to the whole Union, but portentiously terrible to the South—threatening in its progress the emancipation of all their slaves, threatening in its immediate effect that Southern domination which has swayed the Union for the last twenty years." Because southerners considered slavery their exclusive problem, they would not tolerate northern discussion of it, let alone attacks on it. Those of Old Republican persuasion blamed the potential sectional realignment on the fact that there was only one party, whose discipline and adherence to principle had collapsed because of the lack of competition. They thought, moreover, that new men like Henry Clay and John C. Calhoun had corrupted the Republican party with nationalism and jettisoned the pure principles of strict construction, laissez faire, and state rights.

To smother the slave issue and prevent a permanent realignment of free states versus slave states, Old Republicans like Thomas Ritchie of Richmond wanted, in effect, to reconstruct the old national party lines on economic and constitutional questions, to restore the Republican party to first principles, and to impose such strict discipline on its members that no sectional debate would ever be allowed and that nationalistic backers of the American System of high tariffs, federal internal improvements, and a national bank would be driven from the party. Throughout the South, in the early 1820s, Old Republicans dedicated to these tenets competed for state and national offices with the followers of Calhoun and others who favored a vigorous national government. If westerners opposed the American System because it seemed to favor the privileged eastern establishment, Old Republicans in the South opposed it because its call for a strong national government seemed to threaten slavery. As early as the 1820s, southerners were consciously espousing state rights and laissez faire as bulwarks in the defense of the slave system.

Thomas Ritchie and the Richmond Junto led most Old Republicans in the South, but Martin Van Buren, head of the Albany Regency and Bucktail faction of the Republican party in New York, quickly assumed national leadership. Van Buren was inclined philosophically toward Jeffersonianism, and the fact that New York was building the Erie Canal at its own expense strengthened his opposition to federal internal improvements. Moreover, he was a shrewd and ambitious politician who saw the advantages of the state rights, laissez faire position. By stressing the value of the old national Republican party and its principles, he could quash the slavery issue that his opponents in New York, the Clintonians, were using against him, and by aligning with southern Old Republicans, he could increase his own influence within the national party. Elected to the United States Senate in 1821, he worked in Washington with the Virginians and other Old Republicans from the South.

The American System and nationalistic direction of the Republican party became important, if not open, issues in the election of 1824, which reopened the contest for the presidency and forever fragmented the Jeffersonian party. Five men, all of whom claimed the Republican mantle, sought the office. Henry Clay, John C. Calhoun, and John Quincy Adams were known supporters of the American System. Old Republicans led by Van Buren and Ritchie called a congressional caucus, which nominated William Henry Crawford of Georgia, Monroe's secretary of the treasury and an advocate of the state rights principles they cherished. Although this caucus became a major issue in the campaign as a vestige of corruption and elitism, its real function was to revive the New York–Virginia axis in the party and to regain power for the state rights wing. Old Republicans, frightened by the acerbic debate over slavery in 1820, revered tight party discipline, and they regarded the caucus as a way to impose it. The final candidate was Andrew Jackson, whose views were unknown but who was untainted by the caucus system.

The election of 1824 set the stage for the creation of the Democratic party. Although Jackson won a plurality of the popular and electoral vote, no candidate had a majority, and the election went to the House of Representatives. There, Henry Clay threw his formidable support to Adams, who won. When Adams then espoused ardent nationalistic policies, he united in opposition those who wanted to protect slavery as well as those who resented the American System for economic reasons. The appointment of Clay as secretary of state provided evidence for charges of a "corrupt bargain" that Jackson hurled soon after the election, and this cry rallied everywhere those who disliked established politicians.

One can follow the formation of the Jackson party in rough chronological order. First were the original Jackson men, those who pushed and supported him in 1824. An amorphous lot, this group included opportunistic state politicians like the Tennesseans who used Jackson to protect themselves, men who jumped on the Jackson bandwagon for reasons of local advantage. It also included voters throughout the country, except New England, but especially in the West, Pennsylvania, and New Jersey. Jackson's popularity with the voters had many sources, but among his supporters were men who feared that speculation, elitism, and corruption were perverting Old Republican values of simplicity, democracy, and equal opportunity. Whether they located the privileged elite in a certain class or region, some original Jacksonians were motivated by hostility to the establishment. What is most important about the original Jackson men, however, is that they alone could not command an electoral majority. Other groups were needed before the Democrats could forge a majority.

First to join the original Jackson men were the followers of Calhoun. In 1824, the South Carolinian was just beginning his conversion from ardent nationalist to foremost defender of southern rights, and men throughout the country were dedicated to his presidential aspirations. His supporters were especially numerous in North and South Carolina. Detesting the Crawford Old Republicans, most of them supported Jackson in 1824 after the Calhoun boom had collapsed. Then they expected Calhoun, who was elected vice-president in 1824, to follow Adams as president. The bargain between Clay and Adams seemed to doom this hope. Clearly, Clay was Adams' choice as a successor, and Calhoun's path to the presidency might be blocked for as long as sixteen years. Calhoun himself, a lifelong opponent of spoilsmen and the use of patronage for political manipulations, was deeply offended by the "corrupt bargain." Moreover, South Carolina and other southern states were vigorously protesting the Tariff of 1824. To maintain his political base in the South, Calhoun found it expedient to oppose the nationalism of the Adams administration. His early support of a high tariff had, in any case, derived from a belief in its military necessity, and by 1825 he thought that necessity was gone. Principle and political needs, then, turned him against protective tariffs. In 1827, he cast the deciding vote against the Woolens Bill, and in 1828 he secretly wrote the *South Carolina Exposition and Protest*, affirming the right of a state to nullify a tariff it considered unconstitutional. Principle and political needs also threw Calhoun into the arms of Jackson. In 1826, Calhoun's supporters in Congress joined the antiadministration coalition emerging there. Calhoun's lieutenant, Duff Green, edited an opposition sheet in Washington, and other Calhoun men there and in South Carolina entered into regular correspondence with Jackson's managers in Nashville. By serving as Jackson's vice-presidential running mate in 1828, Calhoun hoped to speed up his presidential timetable and to influence the new party to lower the tariff.

Calhoun's conversion made possible the most significant addition to the coalition. Between 1826 and 1828, Van Buren brought the Old Republicans, who initially distrusted Calhoun and hated his southern followers, into the party. In December, 1826, the Little Magician promised Calhoun the support of New York for Jackson in 1828. In January, 1827, he wrote Ritchie to urge him to back Jackson as a way to reconstruct the old party lines and prevent the formation of an antislavery sectional party in the North. A party formed on old principles would be a "complete antidote for sectional prejudices by producing counteracting feelings." Ritchie went along, and the Richmond Junto was soon in constant communication with the Nashville Junto in preparing strategy and propaganda. Van Buren traveled through the South in the spring of 1827 persuading the Old Republicans in North Carolina and Georgia to support Jackson, although the North Carolinians wanted Calhoun dropped from the ticket. From the time of its formation, then, an important wing of the Democratic party was determined to protect slavery with state rights doctrines and to prevent its emergence as an issue in the political arena by focusing attention on other issues. Unlike other elements of the 1828 Jackson coalition, almost all of this strict construction wing would remain in the party, and its principles would dominate Democratic ideology.

Once the essential elements were in the coalition, the Jacksonians in Congress tried to enhance the hero's chances in 1828. To lure the votes of men in Kentucky, Missouri, Ohio, Pennsylvania, and New York who wanted higher tariff rates on certain raw materials and other goods, the Jacksonians in the House wrote a bill raising the rates on hemp, molasses, raw wool, and iron products but lowering those on woolen goods that were manufactured in New England, Adams' impenetrable stronghold. When the New Englanders in the Senate threatened to kill the measure unless the rates on woolens were raised as well, Jacksonians like Martin Van Buren and Levi Woodbury supported them in order to keep the high rates the West and Middle Atlantic states wanted. With the aid of key Jacksonians, the so-called Tariff of Abominations passed in 1828. While claiming credit for raising rates where it would do them the most good, the Jacksonians tried to mollify the outraged southerners. They knew the South would never desert Jackson to vote for Adams, but Van Buren wrote soothing letters to southern friends, and Calhoun intended the *South Carolina Exposition* in part to reassure southerners that a Jackson administration with him as vice-president would move for a lower tariff.

While Jacksonian politicians maneuvered in Congress, they also began to construct the machinery necessary to elect their champion. By 1828, the suffrage had been extended so that in most states almost all adult white males could vote. More important, by that year presidential electors were chosen by the people rather than the legislature in all but two states. Because most states adopted the system of statewide slates of presidential electors that gave the winner all the state's votes, there was a need for state party machinery that could mobilize voters throughout a state. Increasingly, therefore, professional politicians adept at manipulating the machine replaced influential local gentry as the key men in building political parties. Such was the case with the Jackson party, which was constructed by men who made direct appeals to the voters rather than assembling an alliance of local elite groups.

Riding and channeling the wave of resentment against Adams and enthusiasm for the hero of New Orleans, the supremely talented Jacksonian managers organized the Democratic party from the top down. Central committees were established in Nashville by Jackson's friends and in Washington by Van Buren, Calhoun, and other Jackson cronies. These committees, and Jackson himself, corresponded voluminously with state politicians, urging them to build state organizations that in turn established Jackson clubs or committees in each county and most localities. Once completed, the Democratic organization consisted of a multitude of conventions and committees built in pyramid fashion from the locality to the county to the state to the central national committees. The national committees and Jacksonian congressmen disseminated propaganda to the local committees to keep Old Hickory in the public eye. A politician of superb instincts, Jackson himself directed much of this propaganda, making sure that the public remembered he was the victim of a cynical and corrupt bargain. The politicians in Washington also raised money to support an extensive chain of newspapers they had established across the country, and these sheets brought the Jacksonian gospel to the people.

State and local politicians aided in this last endeavor as they did in constructing state machines. Recognizing the possibilities of the broader electorate—rather than causing the reforms that democratized politics— these Jackson men developed techniques to catch the imagination of the voters. Local clubs organized conventions and rallies, barbecues and hickory pole raisings to arouse the public. Local politicians flocked to the Jackson banner, often in the hope that a Jackson victory would mean an office for them. Isaac Hill, an editor, organized the New Hampshire Jackson machine. In Massachusetts, David Henshaw of Boston, unhappy with his lack of influence among the state's Republicans, organized the Jackson party in part to increase that influence. Van Buren swung the formidable Regency machine behind the General in New York. Rival factions in Pennsylvania, the Family and Amalgamation parties, fought for the leadership of the Jackson cause to gain control of the state. In New Jersey, out-of-office politicians, especially erstwhile Federalists, organized the party. Ambitious politicians led the way in Mississippi and North Carolina as well, and the Maryland Jackson party's leadership was a coalition of unhappy politicians—former Federalists, friends of Calhoun, Old Republican Crawfordites, and younger men on the make.

If sheer opportunism caused many state politicians to follow Jackson, it cannot explain why voters supported the organizations they created. The enthusiasm for Jackson had, after all, often antedated the formation of organizations. The reasons why people vote for parties often differ from the reasons why politicians organize them. Certainly, the thirst for office hardly influenced the bulk of voters.

One must look elsewhere to explain their behavior. To some extent, the mass techniques of the Jacksonians, the barbecues, pole raisings, and parades, drew new voters to the Jackson cause. The General's popularity as a military hero unstained by corrupt politics undoubtedly helped him. In the South and West, voters regarded Jackson as one of their own, a firmer friend of slavery and foe of the Indian than the New Englander Adams. In some cases, previous alignments of voters existed in a state, and antagonistic forces fell into line behind opposing candidates. Thus, in New York, Van Buren's Bucktails backed Jackson, whereas the Clintonians favored Adams. In Delaware and Maryland, where regional differences had helped preserve the Federalist party, Federalist voters supported Adams and Republicans, Jackson, although their leaders followed more complex courses. In Kentucky, areas that had supported the Relief party of the early 1820s, a party that favored debtors and was hostile to the Bank of the United States, voted for Jackson; areas that had opposed relief supported Adams. Jacksonians hurled charges in some areas that Adams hated Catholics and in others that he violated the Sabbath, and religious convictions and prejudices probably influenced some to vote for Old Hickory. It seems clear that in cities like Philadelphia and New York

Jackson was popular with the Irish and Germans. Finally, the outbreak of Antimasonry in New York and Pennsylvania drove into the Democratic party many Masons who probably would not otherwise have supported Jackson, for they comprised part of the elite other Jacksonians opposed.

The attitudes molded in the 1820s, the loyalties formed in this campaign, and the magnetism of Jackson would keep many of these voters in the Democratic party for the rest of their lives. They would be concerned with Democratic victory in future elections, not necessarily for reasons of policy or interest in issues, but because of a rabid enthusiasm for their party and a competitiveness akin to the present-day fans' passionate loyalty to the local football team. Despite bitter ideological and personal divisions among the leaders of the party at the national and state level, much grass-roots support remained constant, at least until the 1850s.

If some voters remained Democratic no matter what Jackson and other leaders did, other voters left the coalition as leadership policy was clarified. The coalition that elected the hero in 1828 was too broad and heterogeneous to be stable. For example, Jackson's overwhelming popularity in the South and West camouflaged deep differences among his followers, some of which would appear during his presidency and others of which would cause defections once the northerner Martin Van Buren became his successor. In 1829, there was a Jackson coalition; by 1837 there would be a smaller but more homogeneous and unified Democratic party.

Andrew Jackson's actions in his first term streamlined the Democratic party. As long as Jackson was president, he was master of his administration. He determined its policies, not Van Buren, the Kitchen Cabinet, or anyone else. Jackson's tendency to personalize issues, to make them death struggles with a hated foe, explains his vehement determination in pursuing some policies, but he made his decisions in part to strengthen and refine the Democratic party. To simplify again, that party was a coalition of original Jackson men from Pennsylvania and the West, Old Republicans, and Calhoun supporters. By the end of the first term, the main result of Jackson's policies was the ascendancy of the Old Republicans and their leader Van Buren, and the exile of Calhoun from the party.

In responding to western aspirations, Jackson alienated other groups. His vigorous support for the removal of the Indians still east of the Mississippi River to the west of that stream was vastly popular in the West, but it apparently drove from the party some of the Quakers and Methodists who had supported him in 1828. The western desire for internal improvements proved a thornier issue to handle. In 1830, Jackson vetoed the Maysville Road bill, which would have provided federal funds for the construction of a twenty-mile road in Kentucky. This veto angered westerners and may have cost votes, especially in Kentucky, but Jackson's arch foe, Henry Clay, was so popular in his home state that the impact of the veto in adding to anti-Jackson sentiment is difficult to assess. On the other hand, Jackson approved other internal improvement projects, and federal expenditures for those amounted to about one million dollars a year. As long as Jackson himself ran, he remained the favorite in the West.

One reason for the Maysville veto was to reassure the Old Republicans in the party, especially the southerners, that Jackson favored limitations on the powers of the national government. The veto message took a strict constructionist line, denying that the national government could undertake such a project. Jackson seemed to reassert his state rights convictions when he refused to enforce a Supreme Court ruling against the right of Georgia to extend its authority over Cherokee Indians in the state. Because the Court's decision reduced the power of the state, Jackson's refusal to enforce it seemed to uphold that power. Jackson brilliantly cemented the support of the Old Republicans in 1832 with his veto of the bill to recharter the Second Bank of the United States. Parts of his veto message denounced the subversion of state rights by actions of Congress.

By ensuring the allegiance of the state rights wing with pronouncements against a strong national government, Jackson was in a position to lop off Calhoun and his followers when the proud South Carolinian tried to dominate his administration. It is true that Calhoun did much to bring on his own demise by initiating hostilities with Jackson, but in the process of driving Calhoun out of his coalition Jackson displayed considerable political skill. Jackson had long known that Calhoun, while Monroe's secretary of war, had wanted to censure the general for his activities during the Seminole War of 1818–1819. Furious about that attack, Jackson never mentioned it until his administration was well launched. He needed Calhoun's aid in the election of 1828 and in Congress in his first few years in office. When, however, Jackson was confident of the Old Republicans, those longtime foes of Calhoun who controlled every southeastern state except South Carolina in 1830, Calhoun became expendable.

The South Carolinian had thrown his support to Jackson in return for the vice-presidency, which he expected would lead to the presidency. As head of the party, Calhoun hoped to lead it in lowering the tariff that was so offensive to his constituents. The vice-president was quickly dismayed by Jackson's use of the patronage and rotation in office to build the Democratic machine and by his reluctance to move against the tariff. Even before Jackson's inauguration, Calhoun had begun to regard Van Buren as a potent rival, especially when Jackson appointed the New Yorker secretary of state. Van Buren's leadership of Calhoun's southern foes and his willingness to support the Tariff of Abominations only added to Calhoun's jealousy and fear. To establish his own domination of the administration, Calhoun had hoped to control the other cabinet appointments and especially to make a South Carolinian secretary of war. To his chagrin, Jackson had appointed one of his Tennessee friends, John Eaton, to that post, and Eaton, not Calhoun, picked the other southerners in the cabinet—John Branch for the Navy and John M. Berrien as attorney general. Although one of his Pennsylvania allies was secretary of the treasury, Calhoun was humiliated. To show his power, he determined to drive Eaton from the cabinet.

It was this determination that precipitated the cabinet crisis of 1831. Eaton had recently married the widow Peggy O'Neal Timberlake, whose husband had reportedly committed suicide because of disgrace at being cuckolded by Eaton. The scandalized wives of Calhoun and the cabinet members refused to receive Peggy socially, but it is probable that Calhoun encouraged his wife in an effort to make Eaton resign through social pressure. Only the widower Van Buren was polite to Peggy, and his behavior gratified Jackson, who was furious at the snubbing.

Jackson regarded the whole Eaton affair as a Calhoun plot to "weaken me . . . and open the way to his preferment on my ruin." It was at this time as well that he asked Calhoun about his criticism of Jackson during the Seminole War. Although he and Calhoun exchanged letters on the matter, Jackson carefully avoided a split in 1830. Gradually, however, he began to deprive the Calhoun faction of patronage. In December, 1830, he replaced Duff Green's *United States Telegraph*, a Calhoun sheet, with Francis P. Blair's Washington *Globe* as the official administration paper. Then in February, 1831, Calhoun published a pamphlet detailing his correspondence with Jackson on the Seminole matter and revealing the personal feuds in the cabinet. Because it brought the rift among party leaders into the open, this publication made Calhoun's break with Jackson final.

In April, 1831, the cabinet was reorganized to expunge the Calhoun influence. Van Buren and Eaton resigned, and Jackson asked for the resignation of the others. When Jackson appointed Van Buren minister to England, Calhoun completed his estrangement from Jackson by casting the deciding vote against his confirmation in January, 1832. But that was a gesture. Van Buren would be Jackson's running mate in 1832, and Calhoun would be in opposition. Indeed, in July, 1831, Calhoun had openly endorsed the nullification doctrine, and he prepared to oppose the administration on the tariff issue.

The breakup of the cabinet had other political results. Branch of North Carolina and Berrien of Georgia furiously blamed Van Buren for their dismissals. Both were popular at home, and their firings were the most significant factors in the creation of opposition parties in both states.

The replacement of Calhoun by Van Buren as the probable successor to Jackson had significant impact on the sectional alignments within the Democratic party. Both Van Buren and Calhoun opposed the nationalistic program of internal improvements, high tariffs, and a national bank, but for different reasons and in different ways. Van Buren looked to a North-South alliance, with a stress on Old Republican principles and on economic matters explicitly as a way of avoiding sectional antagonism over slavery and the tariff. Instead, he would emphasize opposition to the Bank of the United States and internal improvements about which strict constructionists in both sections could agree. Calhoun, on the other hand, increasingly the champion of southern rights, wanted to confront the North with southern demands, not align with it in order to avoid divisive issues. Southern rights would only be safe, he thought, if the North accepted southern domination of the party. In Congress, he and his lieutenants worked to effect a South-West alliance, working for cheaper lands for the West and a low tariff for the South. Because others favored this alliance, it appeared to be working the first two years of Jackson's term. The isolation of Calhoun from the party, however, discredited his leadership in this strategy and kept intact the North-South alliance by preventing a concerted attack on the tariff.

By the spring of 1832, then, Calhoun was cut off from the party, and the followers of Branch and Berrien were alienated. South Carolina refused to support Jackson in the election of 1832, but dissidents in Alabama, Virginia, Mississippi, Georgia, and North Carolina dared not back another man for president. Instead, they cooperated with Jackson's enemies in an effort to block Van Buren's election by running P. P. Barbour of Virginia for vice-president on Jackson–Barbour tickets against the regular Jackson–Van Buren tickets. Though unsuccessful, their revolt portended one of the defections from the Democratic party in the South during Jackson's second term. By 1836, the number of southerners who would not accept the northerner Van Buren had grown considerably, and the New Yorker that year commanded only a fraction of the vote in the South and West that Jackson had won.

What drove some of these southerners out of the party was the Nullification Crisis in the winter of 1832–1833. Many southerners had complained about the high Tariff of 1828, and Jackson's approval of the Tariff of 1832, which restored rates to 1824 levels, did not appease them. In November, 1832, after Jackson's reelection, South Carolina nullified the Tariffs of 1828 and 1832 and threatened secession if the federal government attempted to collect tariff duties. This action changed the issue from the justice of the tariff to the power of the state to defy the national government. Responding with a carrot and a stick, Jackson worked for a lower tariff while denouncing in a proclamation to South Carolinians both nullification and secession and requesting from Congress additional powers to collect revenues. Congress passed both a Force Bill giving Jackson more military power and a compromise tariff gradually lowering rates, and Jackson signed both on March 2, 1833. South Carolina nullified the first but accepted the tariff, and the crisis passed.

But Jackson's firm action against South Carolina angered extreme state rights men throughout the South, and they openly broke with the Democratic party. Although not all Branch men were Nullifiers, his followers withdrew from the party in North Carolina. Virginia's Barbour supporters made an open alliance with National Republicans in that state against Jackson. In Georgia and Mississippi in 1833 and 1834, independent State Rights parties were created. John Berrien led the bolters in Georgia, and the faction later became the Whig party there. Though not forming a formal organization, state righters in Alabama also bolted under the lead of Dixon H. Lewis.

What is most significant about these southern Nullifiers, however, is that they were a small minority of Jackson's original supporters in the South. No other state joined South Carolina in its defiance of the national government, and the vast majority of southerners applauded Jackson's strong defense of the Union. Indeed, the name State Rights parties is misleading, for the Nullification Crisis did not drive most state rights southerners from the party. Nullifiers actually demanded state sovereignty. On the other hand, Old Republicans wanted to protect state rights by limiting the powers of the national government, but they scorned secession and extremism. One of the reasons Calhoun and South Carolina were so isolated was that the Old Republicans in Virginia, North Carolina, Georgia, and Tennessee remained in the Democratic party. The bitter feuds between Calhoun men and Old Republicans in the 1820s, Van Buren's success in convincing southern Old Republicans that slavery would be safe if the Jeffersonian party were reconstructed behind Jackson, and Jackson's masterful politics bore fruit in 1833 when so few southerners joined the Nullifiers. Most state rights southerners would still trust the Democratic party to protect southern rights. Looked at another way, there were still many southerners in the Democratic party to make sure it did nothing to offend the South.

If sectional antagonisms and political jealousies provoked the first split in the Democratic ranks and contributed to southern suspicion of Van Buren, disagreements on economic issues caused even more dissension. Jackson's war on the Bank of the United States and his other financial policies drove large numbers of leaders and wealthy voters from the party everywhere, split those who remained into conservative and radical wings, and led to the creation of the Whig party, an opponent with larger national support than the National Republicans had ever mustered.

Precisely what motivated Jackson's war on the bank is still a subject of dispute among historians. It seems clear he did not act in response to popular demand or on behalf of Wall Street. Jackson decided to kill the bank on his own. In part, his animosity sprang from his agrarian suspicion of all banks and paper money. In part, his attack derived from jealousy of the uncontrolled political power of the bank. First, he learned that some of its branches had used funds against him in 1828. Then, when the bank asked for recharter in 1832, Jackson regarded it as an attempt to embarrass him by reducing his majority in the election that year. Thus he determined to strip the institution of its malign political power. Once engaged in the contest, he personalized the dispute into a death struggle between himself and the bank, and he set out to destroy it.

One can isolate three major phases of Jackson's assault that together had profound political results. First was the veto of the bill to recharter the bank on July 10, 1832. A masterpiece of political propaganda that appealed to popular fears of foreign influence, state rights fears of strong central government, lower-class fears of a privileged aristocracy, and democratic fears of uncontrolled power, this veto undoubtedly irritated some Democratic leaders. Over a third of the Democrats in Congress had voted for recharter. The Bank had support everywhere, except the South, and solid support in New England and the Middle States. It seems, however, that most Democratic politicians grinned and bore their anguish even in such probank states as Pennsylvania; Jackson's word was party law. Nor did it cause mass defections of voters. Although Jackson's proportion of the popular vote declined between 1828 and 1832, his actual vote was larger in the latter election. If some left the Jackson party in 1832 because of the veto, their numbers were small.

Much more important in driving conservative Democrats from the party were the other two phases of Jackson's program. In September, 1833, the president announced that federal revenues would no longer be deposited in the Bank of the United States and would be placed instead in carefully selected state banks, later to be called pets. It soon became clear that Amos Kendall selected these pets less on the basis of banking practices than for their Democratic pedigree. The reallocation of the deposits was thus used to build up the Democratic machine and reward the faithful. Finally, between 1834 and 1836, Jackson in a series of steps made a definite move in the direction of hard money—that is, using what powers he had to drive paper bank notes from circulation. In 1834, he asked Congress for a law to prevent deposit banks from issuing bills valued at under five dollars, and the limitation was gradually to rise to bills under ten dollars and then twenty dollars. Jackson repeated this request in December, 1835, and Congress finally passed such a law in 1836. Before that, Jackson had had his secretary of the treasury issue circulars in April, 1835, and February, 1836, directing the deposit banks not to issue or receive notes worth less than five dollars and then ten dollars. In April, 1835, land offices were ordered not to accept paper worth less than five dollars, and in July, 1836, the Specie Circular prohibited the purchase of public lands in anything but coin.

Removal of the deposits and the drive for hard money terrified certain segments of the Democracy. An ardent Jacksonian wondered "what temporary illness and imbecility persuaded [the President] to lay violent hands on the public treasure and transfer it." Many who had resentfully acquiesced in the bank veto because it was Jackson's command bolted the party when he removed the deposits. Others left when he attacked bank notes. Recognizing the need for currency and credit to foster economic growth, friends of the bank and state banks in Pennsylvania, New York, and other states joined the opposition now organizing as the Whig party in response to Jackson's alleged executive tyranny. Twenty-eight of the forty-one Democrats who voted for recharter in 1832 were in the Whig ranks by 1836. Probank Democrats who broke with Jackson over removal of the deposits were especially important in Whig leadership in the South. In Jackson's own Tennessee, his early managers such as John Overton, John Eaton, and Hugh Lawson White split with him on this issue. Willie P. Magnum bolted to the Whigs in North Carolina. In 1828, a respectable number of wealthy businessmen supported the initial Jackson coalition; but Jackson's policies, along with the antibusiness rhetoric of state Democratic parties, tended to drive the vast majority of the rich, especially the urban rich, into the Whig party. For example, one-third of the men worth $100,000 or more in New York City who had been Democrats in 1828 were Whig by 1845. At that date, 85 percent of the 642 men worth that amount whose political affiliations could be identified were Whigs. If Jackson's stance toward South Carolina drove off some southern dissidents, his economic policies alienated the wealthy throughout the country.

Although Jackson's financial program caused some to defect, it also split those who remained in the Democratic party into probanking and antibanking factions, or conservatives and radicals. Some conservatives like Benjamin Butler and Thomas Olcutt of the Albany Regency and David Henshaw in Boston hoped to create a new national bank under

Democratic control. Other Democratic conservatives were content with the state deposit bank system because it pumped more paper money into circulation than the Bank of the United States had allowed. Both groups were appalled by Jackson's hard money tendencies. By prohibiting land offices and pet banks from accepting small notes of certain denominations, Jackson undermined popular faith in such notes and thus reduced the profits of note-issuing banks. Taking the lead for the conservatives at the national level, Senators Nathaniel P. Tallmadge of New York and William C. Rives of Virginia cooperated with the Whigs to pass a law that, in effect, repealed the Specie Circular, only to have Jackson pocket-veto it.

The rift, however, went deeper than a division in Congress. In many states, bitter battles developed between probank and antibank wings of the party. Despite Jackson's hard money policies, conservative Democratic officeholders in states like New York, Pennsylvania, New Jersey, and Ohio gave special charters to banks and other corporations from which they often profited directly. Protesting the dominance of conservatives in the party and the unequal privileges of corporations and monopolies, the minority hard money wings in these and other states, like the Locofocos of New York City, demanded a cessation of such policies and fought for control of the party.

The Panic of 1837 and the resulting depression that lasted into the 1840s exacerbated the divisions in the party and reversed the balance of power. When banks suspended specie payments and foreclosed mortgages, and when the depression dragged on and on, the agrarian hatred of banking and of the commercialization of the economy that had flared in the early 1820s was rekindled. Antibank men demanded that banks resume specie payments or forfeit their charters and that paper money be destroyed. Probank Democrats, on the other hand, blamed the depression on hard money policies and were more convinced than ever of the need for paper money and credit to bring about economic recovery. Because many states had plunged into debt before the panic by financing internal improvements and citizens were faced with increased taxes to pay off that debt, friends and foes of speculative capitalism within the party also debated the broad issue of the use of the state to foster economic growth through direct expenditures and the creation of institutions such as banks and corporations.

In the fall of 1837, President Martin Van Buren provided national leadership for the hard money wing. According to law, the pet banks that suspended should have surrendered their federal deposits to the government; and throughout the summer of 1837, Democrats debated whether the national government should continue the system of deposit banks— thereby making public funds available for private commercial enterprise—or divorce itself from the economy by removing the funds from the banks. Calling Congress into special session in September, Van Buren chose the latter course. Absolving Jackson's hard money policies of any responsibility for the panic, he blamed instead overbanking, excessive credit, and overspeculation, and called on Congress to create independent subtreasuries where government monies could be deposited and thus be inaccessible for private use. He also urged that Congress put the government on a hard money basis by refusing to accept or pay out state bank notes. Van Buren specifically denied that the government should manage domestic trade or provide special aid to individuals ruined by the panic, and he even called on the states to reform their banking systems after the federal government withdrew its funds. After this message, the hard money, antimonopoly, anticorporation principles of the antibank Democrats became official Democratic dogma both in the states and at the national level.

Paradoxically, although Van Buren's Independent Treasury plan delighted the egalitarian wing of the party, it also lured back to the Democracy John C. Calhoun and the southern Nullifiers, who had bolted the party in 1833 and 1834. Calhoun liked the strong attack on national governmental interference in the economy and Van Buren's argument that the subtreasury system would reduce executive patronage. Moreover, he hoped again to gain control of the Democratic party to use it to protect southern rights. As will be shown below, Democratic leadership had already made concessions to southern pressure on the slavery question, and Calhoun's conversion hastened the process by which the Democracy became an open defender of southern interests.

If Van Buren's message brought back Calhoun and the Nullifiers, it further alienated Democratic conservatives, who deplored the proposed removal of public funds from private banks and the attack on paper money. In Congress, Tallmadge and Rives led the most outraged conservatives out of the party, and they cooperated with the Whigs in preventing the passage of the Independent Treasury Act until July, 1840. Rives's defection badly split the Virginia Democracy; his die-hard followers, already miffed at Van Buren because Rives failed to get the vice-presidential nomination in 1836, bolted the party with him. By 1840, these secessionists, although claiming independence, were in effect Whigs.

When action stalled on the Independent Treasury bill in Congress in the late 1830s, the intraparty battle over banking shifted to the states where the effects of the depression were most severe. Now in the majority in most states, hard money Democrats fought against Whigs and conservative Democrats to restrict banking privileges. The intensity of this intraparty strife varied from state to state, as did the goals of the hard money wing. In the Northeast, the impetus behind antibanking sentiment was egalitarian antimonopolism. Radicals there would grudgingly accept banks if the system of special charters were replaced by free banking or general incorporation laws and if the state imposed reforms on the banks such as increased stockholder liability, the requirement of adequate specie reserves, and the prohibition of small notes. In both the North and Southeast, hard money Democrats thought that the public should have more control over corporations and the currency supply. In the West, on the other hand, where the effects of bank suspensions were most severe and agrarian resentment of banks was strongest, hard money Democrats wanted to abolish banks and paper money altogether. In this section, divisions over the banking issue lasted well into the 1840s, whereas they were settled much sooner in the East. The rift was particularly serious in Ohio, where a conservative minority led by Governor Wilson Shannon cooperated with the Whigs to frustrate the desires of the hard money majority of Democrats. By the mid-1840s, southwestern Democrats led the antibanking forces in the party. Louisiana, Texas, and Arkansas Democrats succeeded in prohibiting the renewal or further chartering of banks, and in 1843 Mississippi Democrats overwhelmingly repudiated the state's obligation, made in 1838, to redeem the bonds of the state-chartered Union Bank.

The bitter division over banking was confined primarily to the western states by the early 1840s, but the personal antagonisms engendered since 1837 remained a source of division within the party. Conservatives blamed Van Buren for delaying recovery and stifling economic growth. Many supported him only halfheartedly, if at all, when he ran for reelection in 1840, and his defeat that year made them more determined than ever to oppose his leadership in the future. The hard money followers of Van Buren who controlled the party, on the other hand, were its ideological wing. Viewing the currency issue as a moral one, they furiously blamed the conservatives for the long delay in passing the Independent Treasury Act and for Van Buren's defeat, and they resolved to purge the Democracy of all traitors and restore Van Buren to the presidency.

Although the rancorous division over banking continued to infect the leadership of the party, and although some Democratic organizations like that in New Jersey continued to ally with corporations, by the early 1840s Democrats in most places had adopted a remarkably coherent view of the proper role of the government in the economy. Championing the individual and the common man, Democrats denounced tariffs and corporations for benefiting the wealthy few at the expense of the poor. Because Democrats argued that most legislation by the government acted unequally on the public, they opposed it as class legislation and called for strict economy and minimal governmental action. They were especially united in opposition to a vigorous economic role for the national government, and Democrats in Congress formed a solid bloc against a national bank, a protective tariff, and most internal improvements. This belief in the virtues of the negative state reflected not only the biases of the hard money wing, who were now Van Buren's staunchest supporters, but also the militant state rights sentiments of Calhoun and other southerners who were becoming increasingly concerned in the late 1830s about protecting slavery and southern rights from governmental interference.

If the Democrats had adopted a consistent economic program by 1840, their voting support had solidified by that date as well. Despite persistent bickering and personal antagonisms among leaders, despite the apparent hypocrisy of some Democratic machines in chartering and cooperating with corporations, and despite the emergence of new sectional issues in the 1840s that would strain and eventually disrupt the bonds of party cohesion in Congress, many voters supported the Democracy by 1840 and would continue to do so because of habit or a passionate loyalty that seemed impervious to issues or changes.

Identifying the precise composition of the Democratic coalition is a problem that has baffled historians, but to a certain extent the Democracy's claims of representing the common man were accurate. True, Democrats rarely drew their leaders from the poor, and often they were as wealthy as the supposedly aristocratic Whigs. Indeed, the higher the level of office-holder—congressmen, state executive officials, state legislators, and so forth—the more Democrats probably approximated Whigs in wealth and occupational status. But at the local level, although the situation varied and although it was sometimes religion or ethnic background rather than wealth that differentiated Democrats from Whigs, Democratic leaders frequently did have less social status than the Whigs. In many areas, Whigs drew their local leadership from the community's social elite, whereas the Democrats built their machines around professional politi-cians who had little prestige other than what their party or patronage positions gave them. As James Buchanan wrote of his most trusted lieu-tenant in Pittsburgh, "He does not move in the first circle of fashionable society, but exercises more influence than any other Democrat in that region."

Generalizing about the voting support of the Democrats is equally hazardous. For many, as noted earlier, initial support of Jackson made them Democrats forever, and this group included both rich and poor. Although the Democrats enlisted some of the wealthy in their coalition, however, their antibank, antibusiness, and often prolabor rhetoric drove the vast majority of the rich, especially in cities, into opposition. More-over, if the popular vote was too closely divided between the parties for the Democrats to have drawn a disproportionate share of the votes of poor farmers and workers, most Democratic voters came from less privi-leged groups. In states as diverse as New Hampshire, Tennessee, Ohio, Virginia, and Mississippi, the farmers from the least prosperous areas or those whose fortunes were declining because transportation developments helped competing regions formed the backbone of Democratic strength.

What prevented the Democrats from securing more unified support from the poor and middle classes were usually noneconomic considera-tions. In the South, regional animosities within states often determined voting alignments. In some cases, these reflected class lines, but in others they cut across class lines. In cities and other areas with large concentra-tions of immigrants and Catholics, the heavy support those groups gave the Democrats drove many native-born American workers who despised them and yearned for middle-class respectability to support the Whigs, thus dividing the middle and lower classes along ethnic and religious lines. In 1840, this division was still none too sharp because many native-born workers voted Democratic and some immigrants, especially those of British origin, voted Whig, but it would become more clear-cut in the next two decades. In other areas, longtime feuds between more and less established Protestant denominations apparently determined voting behavior. In Massachusetts and New Hampshire, for example, Congregationalists from all social classes supported the Whigs, whereas the less established denominations like Baptists and Methodists backed the Democrats. To an extent, the same was true in Connecticut, where a bitter fight between Congregationalists on the one hand and Baptists and Episcopalians on the other had culminated in the disestablishment of the Congregational Church in 1818. The antagonisms and group loyalties engendered in that struggle continued to influence voting alignments in the Nutmeg State into the 1840s and 1850s. Throughout the country, but especially in northern states, Democratic opposition to active governmental interference in the society attracted those who resented the aggressive do-goodism of the evangelical Protestants who joined the Whigs to press for prohibition and legislation outlawing activities on Sunday. Beneath the Democratic standard, hard-drinking natives could join Germans and Irishmen in opposing the temperance crusade they identified with Whiggery. In short, many affiliated with the Democracy for reasons other than class interest, often because they disliked the people they perceived as Whigs or because of loyalties formed many years earlier. But if one accepts nationality and religion as well as wealth as indices of social status, it seems safe to conclude that substantially more Democratic voters than Whig voters came from the less privileged groups in the society, and these groups formed the majority of Democratic voters.

The peculiar blending of elements in the Democratic coalition augured future trouble for the party. Ethnocultural, religious, and economic resentments could be complementary pressures in forging an alliance of the underprivileged, but they could also be conflicting and divisive forces. Protestant resentment of Catholic influence within the party and of Catholic demands for separate, tax-supported schools constantly threatened to disrupt working-class support. For example, in New York City in the mid-1830s and again in 1843, dissident anti-Catholic Democrats, largely from the lower classes, broke from the party to help form the Native American Democratic Association and the American Republican party, both of which protested the number of Democratic Catholic officeholders.

Equally dangerous was the fragile alliance between North and South that Martin Van Buren and other Democrats had worked so hard to preserve. Since the 1820s, Van Buren had tried to suppress or avoid divisive sectional issues and to reassure southerners by stressing state rights, laissez faire principles on economic issues. When Calhoun and the South Carolina Nullifiers had tried to force the North and Jackson to accept their demands on the tariff and the idea of state sovereignty in 1832, most southerners had remained in the Democratic party, confident of its ability to stop northern attacks on slavery. During Jackson's second term and Van Buren's administration, however, holding the allegiance of skittish southerners proved more difficult. In 1834 and 1835, abolitionists began to bombard Congress with petitions to abolish slavery in the District of Columbia and to inundate the South with antislavery material, and Jackson and Van Buren could no longer suppress the slave issue. Particularly threatening to the Democrats was the effort of Calhoun to unite southerners of all political persuasions behind himself. He would confront the North with nonnegotiable demands that slavery could not be touched in the District because abolition there endangered it in southern states, that southern postmasters could purge the mails of material they found incendiary, and, in 1837 and 1838, that the North must accept the annexation of Texas as a slave territory in order to strengthen slavery in the South.

Steering a middle course between the extremes of antislavery men and Calhoun, Jackson and especially Van Buren sought compromise positions to keep their southern support. In doing so, however, they risked the anger of northern Democrats as they swung the party more and more toward a prosouthern position on the slavery issue. Jackson's Postmaster General Amos Kendall unofficially ordered southern postmasters to seize abolitionist literature in 1835, Jackson himself asked Congress to ban its circulation through the mails, and eventually Vice President Van Buren cast the deciding vote in the Senate for a measure, pushed by Calhoun, ordering southern postmasters to seize any mail banned by state law. Van Buren also engineered a compromise on the petition question. Resisting Calhoun's demand that the North disavow the right to abolish slavery in the District, he arranged the introduction of the famous "gag rule" that automatically tabled antislavery petitions in the House of Representatives but called emancipation only inexpedient, not unconstitutional. From 1836 until 1844, Democrats in the House, with a very few northern exceptions, voted in a bloc to sustain the gag. Democratic leaders again managed to suppress the divisive issue. Their wish to do this caused both Jackson and Van Buren to balk at southern demands to annex Texas, the proslavery republic that had won its independence in 1836. Northern resistance to the move made it too hot to handle. Party unity had been maintained, but at the price of markedly increasing southern influence in the formulation of national policy.

Both ethnocultural and sectional tensions would be important in weakening the Democrats in the 1840s and shattering their majority in the 1850s, but until 1843 the Democrats maintained their voting support and their cohesion in Congress by stressing the traditional economic positions on which there was substantial party agreement. These issues took a natural saliency because of the depression wracking the country until 1843, and uneasy northern Democrats could content themselves with southern support for their economic program of negativism. Defending the rights of the individual against corporate privilege, castigating the immoralities of paper money while moderating their actual bank reform programs in crucial eastern states, and denouncing vigorous national government as a threat to state rights and individual freedom, they held together native-born Protestants and Catholic immigrants, northerners and southerners, entrepreneurs and antibank agrarians. Though defeated in 1840, their popular vote was half again larger than in 1836, and in the congressional elections of 1842–1843 they captured almost a two-to-one majority in the House.

As long as traditional economic issues occupied the attention of Democrats, especially in Congress, the party could stand united. Between 1842 and 1844, however, during the presidency of the former Democratic Whig John Tyler, the slave question flared again. Both major parties were forced to address the demand for the annexation of Texas, even though the leadership of both hoped to suppress this question and concentrate on other issues.

How the slavery and Texas questions were allowed to reemerge against the will of so many leaders, especially the Van Buren men in the Democracy, is a fascinating problem. Abolitionists in Congress were too few and too isolated from the reins of power to impose their demands on the major parties. And although there was popular enthusiasm for the idea of territorial expansion once politicians agitated it in 1844, the doctrine of Manifest Destiny—the idea that the United States was preordained to spread across the continent—was more a Democratic rationalization after the fact of expansion than a cause of it. In short, an upswelling of public opinion, either against slavery or for expansion, cannot explain the emergence of the slavery issue in national politics after 1842. Not popular pressure, but the decisions of a few leaders in both parties account for the reappearance of the slavery issue. Those decisions were made because of preexisting factionalism in the parties that had little or nothing to do with slavery.

By the end of 1842, John Tyler, the state rights Whig from Virginia who had succeeded to the presidency upon the death of William Henry Harrison, had irreparably split with the Whig leaders in Congress on economic issues. Having frustrated Whig plans for a new national bank and the distribution of the revenue from land sales to the states, he was left with meager support in Congress. Some like Caleb Cushing of Massachusetts and Henry Wise and Thomas Gilmer of Virginia soon joined the Democratic party. Others like Robert J. Walker of Mississippi were already Democrats. Speculators in Texas lands and ardent advocates of its annexation, Walker, Wise, Gilmer, and other Virginian friends of Tyler persuaded him to annex Texas. Tyler then replaced Daniel Webster as secretary of state with another Virginian, Abel P. Upshur, and in the summer of 1843 Upshur began secret negotiations with Texas. At the same time, Walker and Gilmer stealthily prepared a propaganda campaign to convince the country it needed Texas. As early as February, 1843, they secured a letter from former President Jackson demanding Texas annexation to protect Americans from British aggression.

If the Texas promoters were using Tyler to forward their land schemes, Tyler was using Texas to rehabilitate his political fortunes. Cut off from the Whigs, he hoped to have a treaty with Texas in hand before the 1844 campaign and to use it either to build a third party based on the expansion issue or preferably to secure the Democratic presidential nomination that year. To this end, in 1843 and 1844 he frantically appointed Democrats to his cabinet and to local offices everywhere. In 1844 he planned to hold a separate convention in Baltimore at the same time as the Democratic convention in hope that the Democrats would embrace him.

For it was only through the Democratic party that pro-Texas men could gain success. Bitter at Tyler anyway, the Whigs were deeply opposed to territorial expansion on principle. Tyler needed Democratic support in the Senate to ratify any treaty he concluded. It was because Democratic sponsorship of Texas was so vital that Gilmer and Walker had sought Jackson's letter in 1843, a letter they kept secret until 1844. Walker, who still favored Van Buren for the Democratic nomination, was using Tyler to force the Democrats to endorse expansion in their 1844 campaign.

By the early 1840s, it will be recalled, Democratic leadership was already fragmented over banking and other issues. Dominant in most states, the moralistic hard money wing was determined to renominate Van Buren in 1844 and to drive the conservatives from the party. The Van Burenites seemed to control a sufficient number of states in the spring of 1843 to lock up the national convention. Equally determined to stop Van Buren, the soft money, probank wing of the party rallied around various candidates. Their favorite was Lewis Cass of Michigan, whose prominence won him the hatred of the Van Buren men. Also opposed to Van Buren's nomination were the followers of John C. Calhoun who hoped to capture the nomination for the South Carolinian. Calhoun never trusted a party he could not control to protect southern interests, and he considered Van Buren too pronorthern. He was particularly angry that in the House session of 1843–1844, some New York Democrats had voted against the gag rule while Democrats from New York, Pennsylvania, and New Jersey had prevented southern legislation lowering the high Whig Tariff of 1842. What Calhoun was looking for was an issue that would destroy Van Buren's support in the South and unite the section behind himself so that he, or at least the South, could control the Democratic party.

Walker and the Texas men skillfully exploited these divisions in the Democracy. In Washington, they secured the aid of Calhoun's lieutenants, who knew that Calhoun would have no chance for the nomination unless Texas were made an issue and that only President Tyler could make it one. The prospect of Texas annexation might stir up enough antislavery sentiment in the North to disillusion Van Buren's southern followers and send them scurrying to Calhoun for protection of southern rights. As Calhoun's loyal Virginia friend R. M. T. Hunter wrote him in December, 1843, upon learning of Tyler's plans, "It will be something if we could really make an issue with the antislavery feeling and arouse the public to its importance."

While the Texas men were winning the support of Calhoun, which they needed in the Senate, they also delayed the Democratic national convention until Texas sentiment could be whipped up in the party. The convention was scheduled for November, 1843, before Congress met, but in late February, 1843, Walker persuaded Silas Wright, Van Buren's chief lieutenant in Washington, to postpone the convention until May, 1844. Van Buren was sure to win anyway, Walker argued, and postponement would conciliate the soft money men and Calhoun, who wanted a later convention. What Walker did not tell Wright was that Tyler was secretly moving to get Texas, that he already had Jackson's letter demanding Texas, and that he wanted the delay so negotiations could be completed and Democratic annexation sentiment could be aroused with Jackson's letter before that convention met.

Van Buren and his followers desperately sought to quell the Texas issue. He had backed away from it as too divisive during his administration, and in 1842 he had apparently arranged with Henry Clay, the certain Whig candidate, to keep it out of the 1844 campaign. Van Buren had always thought that the Democratic party should be broad enough to allow diverse opinions on slavery but that no official position, either for or against, ought to be forced on the party as a whole. As early as 1842, he wrote about the liability of appearing too prosouthern in New York: "The truth is that the Democrats of this State have suffered so often, and so severely in their advocacy of Southern men and Southern measures, as to make them more sensitive in respect of their conduct from that quarter, than I could wish." Even when Walker opened his propaganda campaign for Texas in early 1844, Van Buren remained silent on the issue. In state after state, his followers captured control of the delegations to the Baltimore convention, and angry probank and Calhoun men searched for a device to stop the Van Buren steamroller.

Texas provided it. On February 29, 1844, Secretary of State Upshur was killed in an explosion on the warship *Princeton*. After maneuvers by Henry Wise, Tyler appointed Calhoun as his successor to complete the Texas negotiations. In March, Walker released the Jackson letter as part of a bold propaganda campaign in the press and in Congress. On

April 12 the treaty was signed. On April 15 the Washington *Globe*, Van Buren's sheet in Washington, editorially endorsed annexation. Assuming that editor Francis P. Blair spoke for Van Buren, Tyler and Calhoun feared that the Little Magician was trying to rob them of the credit for pushing annexation. Tyler therefore delayed submission of the treaty to the Senate, and Calhoun, specifically attempting to make annexation a proslavery measure so obnoxious that Van Buren would have to oppose it, hastily wrote a letter to British Minister Richard Pakenham, which he sent on April 18. Defending slavery as a beneficial institution "essential to the peace, safety, and prosperity of those states of the Union in which it exists," he argued, in effect, that the United States was annexing Texas in order to protect slavery. The treaty, along with the Pakenham letter, was submitted to the Senate on April 22, and on April 27, Van Buren, who had been warned that Texas could "prostrate, at the North, every man connected with it," released a public letter opposing immediate annexation. In late April, as well, Robert Walker, that brilliant engineer of the Texas scheme, organized the anti–Van Buren Democrats in Congress and told them to agitate the Texas issue constantly so that it could not be avoided at the Van Buren–controlled convention. Thus Calhoun men and interested speculators in Texas land were joined by the conservative backers of Cass, who took up the Texas cry solely from a bitter desire to stop Van Buren.

At the Baltimore convention in May, the polyglot foes of Van Buren prevented his nomination. Walker and the Texas men persuaded the convention to adopt the two-thirds rule. Relieved delegates, long pledged to the former president but now disillusioned with him, could vote for him on the first ballot and then desert him. Unable to attain a two-thirds majority, the Van Burenites still prevented the nomination of Cass. To break the deadlock, the convention, with the blessings of the Van Burenites, then nominated James K. Polk of Tennessee, who had come out for Texas and had carefully ordered his managers to back Van Buren so that he might get Van Buren's support if the New Yorker were stopped. After the nomination, Robert J. Walker wrote the Democratic platform, which called for "the reoccupation of Oregon and the reannexation of Texas at the earliest practicable period." To balance the expansionist aims of the party, solicit western support, and mitigate the prosouthern appearance of the platform, the Oregon plank was tacked to it at the last moment.

There had been no great popular demand for it before the convention.

Texas was the crucial issue. Its incorporation into the platform and, above all, the brutal shelving of Van Buren had momentous consequences for the leadership of the party. Although the expansionist alliance of South and West that deposed Van Buren and now controlled the party was led by Polk, not Calhoun, Van Burenites, long imbued with a belief that Calhoun was conspiring to usurp control of the party, viewed the convention as his triumph. As a result, they developed a hatred of southern political power that continued until the Civil War, and they blamed southern Democrats, the Slave Power, for forcing the slavery issue on the party when Van Buren had tried to suppress it throughout his career. Although they campaigned hard for Polk in 1844, the Van Burenites refused to accept Texas, and they cooperated with the Whigs to defeat Tyler's treaty in the Senate that summer.

If the Texas issue divided Democratic leadership, its contributions to Polk's victory in 1844 are less clear. By that year, voting alignments were remarkably fixed in most areas of the country, and the campaign merely brought out traditional Democratic strength. The vast majority of Democratic voters were probably unaffected by the issue. The election was close, however, and Texas may have brought crucial swing voters to the Democrats. In all probability, though, Texas helped the Democrats carry only Georgia and Indiana of the states they would not have won anyway, and it may have cost them Ohio because of the defection of antislavery Democrats.

Much more important in retaining strength for the Democrats and in gaining new voters were economic and ethnocultural issues. By giving a qualified endorsement to a protective tariff, Polk held the votes of pro-tariff Pennsylvania Democrats. Moreover, when the Whigs formed open alliances with the nativist American Republican party in Philadelphia and New York City in 1844, it solidified immigrant support for the Democrats and brought more of them to the polls. Throughout the 1840s and 1850s, the growing size of the immigrant vote would help maintain Democratic strength in crucial northern states.

Polk's actions in office did much to fragment the national Democratic party. Determined to command his own administration, free from the control of Van Buren, Cass, or Calhoun, he alienated all factions. The Van Buren men, concentrated mainly in New York, Ohio, Pennsylvania, and parts of New England, were estranged before the end of 1845. If they accepted Polk's nomination, they could not tolerate his cabinet selections or his handling of Texas. Van Buren's followers in New York, the hard money, anti-Texas Barnburners, expected that one of their number would head the State or Treasury department, but Polk appointed James Buchanan to the former and, to the outrage of Van Burenites, Robert J. Walker, the Texas agitator who had done so much to depose Van Buren in 1844, to the latter. Compounding his sins in Barnburner eyes, Polk then appointed as secretary of war William L. Marcy, who had broken with Van Buren and joined the Hunkers, their soft money, pro-Texas foes in New York. The Hunkers received many local appointments as well. Polk's replacement of Blair's Washington *Globe* with Thomas Ritchie's Washington *Union* as the official administration newspaper also infuriated the Van Burenites.

The Texas issue further estranged them. Between the election in November and Polk's inauguration in March, 1845, President Tyler and Calhoun pushed for the annexation of all of Texas as a slave state by a joint resolution of Congress. Because most people believed that Texas would be divided into four additional slave states, annexation on such terms was intolerable to northern Van Buren men, who feared that growing antislavery sentiment at home would defeat any Democrat who voted for it. As Senator John M. Niles of Connecticut wrote to Gideon Welles, the South "will consent to no compromise to reconcile the measure to the opinions or prejudices of the north, and make it more safe for northern democrats to vote for it." These Van Burenites bitterly disliked southern Democrats' forcing this plan upon them, and they were adamant about preventing the growth of the Slave Power's influence within the party that the Texas plan entailed.

The Van Burenites hoped for some compromise—such as the proposal to have part of the unsettled area of Texas admitted as free territory—that would make Texas more palatable to their constituents. But southern Democrats and Tyler refused to make any compromise. The House, over the opposition of twenty-eight northern Democrats and the Whigs, passed Tyler's plan virtually intact. In the Senate, however, the Van Burenites combined with the Whigs to stop it, and in February, 1845, a compromise plan was adopted that would give the president the option of accepting the House bill or negotiating a new treaty with Texas that, as the Van Buren men hoped, would mollify northern sentiment. The Van Burenite senators supported this plan only because they expected Polk, not Tyler, to act on it, and Polk had promised John A. Dix, Thomas Hart Benton, and others that he would renegotiate the treaty. To their dismay, Tyler asked Texas to consent to annexation under the House plan, and it did. Polk could have reversed this decision, but he did not. His agents even assured the Texans that the Polk administration would uphold their claim to the Rio Grande River as Texas' southern border. Fearing that this claim would bring on war with Mexico, the Van Burenites were convinced by Polk's treachery that the hated Slave Power controlled his administration.

The outbreak of war with Mexico in the spring of 1846 confirmed this conviction and persuaded the Van Burenites to repudiate their president. As early as February, 1845, Van Buren had warned that northern Democrats must avoid a war "in respect to which the opposition shall be able to charge with plausibility, if not truth, that it is waged for the extension of slavery." When Polk asked for a two million dollar appropriation, they feared he meant to buy territory for slavery. To guarantee their northern constituents that such was not the case, in August, 1846, they eagerly introduced an amendment to the appropriation bill. Named for its author, David Wilmot of Pennsylvania, the Wilmot Proviso would prohibit by law the introduction of slavery into any territory won or purchased from Mexico.

The proviso attracted support from other northern Democrats whose anger at other policies of Polk provoked them to rebel against the apparent southern domination of the party. The low Walker Tariff of 1846, which had been pushed by the administration, outraged Pennsylvania Democrats, all of whom except Wilmot voted against it. More damaging, Polk seemed to desert the Northwest. Hoping to intimidate the British into compromising the conflicting American and British claims to the Oregon Territory, which had been jointly occupied by both since 1818, Polk pressed claims to the entire territory and called on Congress to abrogate the treaty with England. Taking their lead from Polk, northwestern Democrats like Cass of Michigan, William Allen of Ohio, and Edward Hannegan of Indiana raised the cry in Congress of "Fifty-Four Forty or Fight." They were quickly opposed by a peace bloc of Whigs and southern Democrats led by Calhoun, who feared war with

England. Although few southern Democrats joined Calhoun in this effort, northwestern Democrats, who had solidly voted for the annexation of Texas, angrily charged that once slave territory had been expanded, southerners deserted them. When, in 1846, Polk negotiated a treaty with England dividing Oregon at the forty-ninth parallel, the northwesterners were furious at his duplicity. They were even angrier when the president stopped promoting a bill for the graduation of land prices, which they desired, and when he vetoed a rivers and harbors bill in early August.

By that month, then, westerners who did not share the Van Burenites' anger over Texas were ready to join them in opposing southern influence in the administration. Congressional Democrats split completely on the appropriation bill to which the rebellious northerners attached the proviso. Fifty-two northerners voted for it, whereas fifty southerners and four northern men opposed it.

Because the proviso was introduced at the end of that session of Congress and because party leaders wanted to maintain harmony in the state and congressional elections of 1846, the slavery issue did not rupture the Democracy that year. Throughout the country, most Democrats did not want to hamper the war effort or prevent any territorial expansion by dividing the party over slavery, and they would argue that the proviso was unnecessary because no territory had as yet been acquired. Even in New York the Barnburners did not agitate the proviso because they wanted Hunker help in reelecting Silas Wright governor. When Hunker officeholders successfully engineered Wright's defeat in that election, however, restraints were removed from younger Barnburners like Preston King who were morally opposed to slave extension.

The Barnburners reintroduced the proviso into Congress in 1847, and when northern state legislatures began to endorse it, the Democracy divided seriously along North-South lines. Arguments over the proviso became more heated in early 1848 when the United States acquired the Mexican Cession, which included present-day California, New Mexico, Arizona, and Utah. The disposition of slavery in the territories won from Mexico was no longer a hypothetical question. Pressed by extremists from both the North and the South, frantic party leaders tried to develop a compromise formula on which the party could be united for the election of 1848.

In both the second session of the Twenty-ninth Congress (1846–

1847) and the Thirtieth Congress (1847–1849), agitation of the issue split the party along sectional lines. Whereas Barnburners demanded the proviso, Calhoun insisted that Congress had no power to deny the South equal rights by prohibiting slavery from the territories. Southern Democrats joined with southern Whigs to vote against the proviso, which the majority of northern Democrats continued to support. Already, however, moderate northern Democrats like Lewis Cass, who wanted to preserve party unity to achieve expansion and to woo southern support for the 1848 election, were voting against the proviso. Indeed, if most northern Democrats did not vote with the proslavery southern Democrats, close analyses of roll-call voting reveal that most did not vote with northern Whigs either. If there was southern sectional unity on the issue, there was as yet no northern unity. Moreover, Democratic cohesion on traditional issues like land, finance, and the war itself remained high. In sum, the slave extension issue in Congress could divide Democrats internally, but longtime loyalties and antagonisms prevented northern Democrats from joining northern Whigs in a purely sectional phalanx. Though weakening party lines, the slavery issue could not yet replace them with sectional ones.

Nor between 1846 and 1848 did the extension issue permanently divide voting support. In both the North and the South, party regulars managed to fend off extremists. True, in New Hampshire, antislavery Democrats had bolted the party in 1846. In addition, the Barnburners and the Hunkers were irreparably split in New York. The Hunkers seized control of the party in 1847, and the Barnburners, who probably represented the majority of New York Democrats, held a separate convention and ensured Hunker defeat in the general election. In 1848, the two factions again held separate conventions and sent separate delegations to the Baltimore national convention. There were problems in the North, then, but in most states party leaders sat on the issue and prevented it from seriously dividing the voters.

They were aided in this endeavor by a compromise solution advocated most ardently by Cass in a public letter to A. O. P. Nicholson in December, 1847, and by Stephen A. Douglas of Illinois. Known variously as squatter sovereignty or popular sovereignty, this doctrine said that Congress should not establish or prohibit slavery in a territory by law. It should not interfere with the problem. Rather, the settlers in the territory themselves should decide if slavery would be allowed there. Although northerners sometimes argued at home that the decision on slavery would be made in the territorial stage by the territorial legislature, the doctrine was sufficiently ambiguous to allow southerners to argue that it would be made in the constitution when the territory applied for statehood. Because it renounced the obnoxious Wilmot Proviso and endorsed congressional noninterference, many southerners could accept popular sovereignty as a viable solution.

Even before the emergence of popular sovereignty, Democratic regulars in the South had been fairly successful in resisting the demands of proslavery extremists. Calhoun, who was jealous of Polk's leadership of the South-West alliance in the party, had broken with the president by opposing the Mexican War and moving to have Thomas Ritchie, the administration editor of the *Union*, barred from the Senate. Unable to control the Democratic party, he made one of his periodic efforts in the summer of 1847 to persuade southerners to drop party allegiances and unite behind him in an independent Southern Rights movement to force the major parties to protect southern interests. Led by Ritchie, Democratic regulars responded as they had since 1826 that, in spite of the Barnburners, northern Democrats were firm allies of the South and that only through a national party, not an independent sectional movement, could southerners protect their rights. In southwestern states, the regulars were successful as Democrats there omitted reference to slavery in 1847 and accepted Cass's popular sovereignty doctrine in 1848. In the southeastern states, however, the Democratic friends of Calhoun, known as the Chivalry, were stronger. Unable to lead a bolt from the party, they were powerful enough in Alabama, Georgia, and Virginia to pledge the state parties to support no man for president in 1848 who endorsed the Wilmot Proviso. Nor did they find popular sovereignty acceptable, and in 1848 the Alabama, Virginia, and Florida Democratic parties adopted the so-called Alabama Platform, which denounced territorial prohibition of slavery as well as congressional prohibition as pernicious to the South and pledged the delegations from those states to the national convention to oppose any man who did not renounce both doctrines.

The Baltimore convention, seating both Barnburner and Hunker delegations from New York, then proceeded to ignore both and nominate Cass, a prominent foe of the Wilmot Proviso and advocate of popular sovereignty. Denouncing abolitionists and denying the power of Congress to interfere with slavery in the states, their platform omitted any direct reference to the problem of slavery in the territories, much to the chagrin of both Barnburners and southern rights extremists.

Extremists from neither section were satisfied with the result. William Lowndes Yancey, author of the Alabama Platform, tried to persuade southerners to nominate an independent on that platform, but he failed everywhere as southern Democratic parties ratified the Cass nomination. Yancey's attack on popular sovereignty as free-soilism in disguise, however, may have influenced some southern Democrats to support the Whig candidate, Zachary Taylor, a Louisiana slaveholder, in the election. Equally unhappy, the Barnburners were more successful in forming an independent party. Combining with Liberty party men and Conscience Whigs, they formed the Free Soil party and nominated Martin Van Buren for president.

The motives of the Democrats who joined the Free Soil party varied. Some were loyal followers of Van Buren, who had hated Cass and his followers since the early 1840s before slavery was even an issue. Ensuring Cass's defeat was reason enough for many of these men to defect. Some undoubtedly found slavery morally intolerable and were determined to prevent its spread. Others were racists who wanted to preserve the territories for white northerners instead of Negro slaves. Most shared a resentment of the political power of the South and its domination of the Democratic party. Bruised and battered by their unsuccessful attempts to defeat the Slave Power within the Democratic party, they sought independent action to prevent its growth. As David Wilmot wrote Franklin Pierce when he grudgingly returned to the party in 1852:

> I am jealous of the *power* of the South. . . . [T]he South holds no prerogative under the Constitution, which entitles her to wield forever the Scepter of Power in this Republic, to fix by her own arbitrary edict, the principles & policy of this government, and to build up and tear down at pleasure. . . . Yet so dangerous do I believe to be the spirit and demands of the *Slave Power,* so insufferable its arrogance, if I saw the way open to strike an effectual & decisive blow against its domination at this time, I would do so, even at the temporary loss of other principles.

This same bitter jealousy that caused many northern Democrats to bolt to the Free Soil party in 1848 would later spur most of them to leave the Democracy in the 1850s and join the incipient Republican party. At that time they would be joined by many others.

The formation of the Free Soil party foiled the Democratic effort to avoid the Wilmot Proviso as an issue in 1848. In response, Democrats ran two very different campaigns. In the South, they emphasized Cass's pledge to veto the proviso should Congress ever pass it. In the North, they stressed other issues but argued, when forced, that a territorial decision on slavery would result in free soil as surely as congressional prohibition and without threatening the bonds of the Union. As in Congress, the Democratic party was split on North-South lines over the slavery question in 1848.

Despite this split, that issue was not yet strong enough to cause massive defections from the party in most states. The Democratic vote did drop by 117,000 (10 percent) since 1844, declining 123,000 in New York alone. Losses were probably even larger than this figure, because some of the Democratic total came from new states that had not voted in 1844, and new immigrant votes in all northern states partially camouflaged defections. Clearly, the Democrats lost votes to the Free Soilers in New York, Ohio, Vermont, Maine, and Massachusetts, and some Democrats may have defected to the Whig Taylor in Alabama, Virginia, and Georgia. Except in these states, however, habitual party loyalty and antagonism to the Whigs continued to keep the vast majority of the party's voters faithful, both North and South. In 1848 as in 1844, the slavery issue apparently had less impact on popular voting than on party leadership.

The defeat of Cass and the increasing need in 1849 to establish civil governments in the territory won from Mexico strengthened the hands of extremists in both sections. Blaming Cass's loss on the defection of southerners, northern Democrats in state after state came out openly against slavery extension. In some states like Vermont and Ohio, the Democrats formed open alliances with the Free Soilers in 1849. Southerners, on the other hand, became firmer in their hostility to the proviso and their demand for equal treatment in the territories. When California applied for admission as a free state, southern Democrats stoutly opposed it. Mississippi Democrats, encouraged by South Carolina, called for a southern convention in Nashville, Tennessee, in June, 1850, to determine a common southern strategy in resistance to northern pressure. By the end of 1849, there was a serious danger of southern secession if the Wilmot Proviso were applied to the Mexican Cession, as northerners demanded.

Although the Compromise of 1850 alleviated this danger of secession, it failed to unite the Democratic party. By that compromise, the South acquiesced in the admission of California, and the North dropped its demand for the proviso and accepted popular sovereignty in Utah and New Mexico Territories. The slave trade in the District of Columbia was stopped and a harsher Fugitive Slave Law passed. More Democrats than Whigs supported the compromise measures in Congress, and the Democrat Stephen Douglas engineered their passage. But southern Democrats were far less enthusiastic about the compromise than were their northern comrades. Party cohesion in Congress was sundered, and on key bills like the Fugitive Slave Act and California bill the Democracy was almost polarized on North-South lines.

Moderate Democrats endorsed the compromise and hoped it would settle forever the sectional issue, whereas dissidents in both sections refused to accept it as a finality. For example, in Massachusetts, the Democrats, against the wishes of a conservative minority led by Caleb Cushing, formed an alliance with the Free Soilers and sent Charles Sumner to the Senate in 1851. In New Hampshire, the Democratic nominee for governor denounced the Fugitive Slave Act, so the conservative Democrats led by Franklin Pierce nominated another candidate, who eventually won the election. Despite grumbling from antislavery men about the Fugitive Slave Act, the procompromise Democrats dominated the party organizations in most northern states. Even in New York, where factionalism was more confused than ever, the party endorsed the compromise.

Similarly, moderate Democrats in the southern states accepted the compromise so long as the North abided by it, but the Democratic organizations in Missouri, Mississippi, Alabama, and Georgia split wide open between friends and foes of it. In the last three states, party lines were temporarily erased. Procompromise Union parties composed of a minority of Democrats and majority of Whigs successfully ran candidates against Southern Rights parties, which the bulk of Democrats normally joined.

During the presidential campaign of 1852, most southern Democrats returned to the regular party fold despite the efforts of Alabama's Yancey to maintain an independent Southern Rights organization. When the more established candidates, Cass, James Buchanan, and Douglas, blocked each other at the national convention, Franklin Pierce of New Hampshire, a procompromise conservative and Mexican War veteran, obtained the Democracy's nomination. Avoiding division by refusing to call the Compromise of 1850 a finality, the Democratic platform endorsed and pledged to enforce all the compromise measures and vowed to "resist all attempts at renewing in Congress, or out of it, the agitation of the slavery question, under whatever shape or color the attempt may be made." Moreover, it explicitly lauded the state rights principles of the Kentucky and Virginia Resolutions. To remold their North-South alliance in 1852, the Democrats openly stated in their platform the premise underlying that alliance since 1826—the Democrats would protect southern rights by quashing the slavery issue whenever it raised its head and by following a state rights course.

Almost all elements of the party rallied behind Pierce's candidacy, and the Democratic vote rose by 380,000 over 1848. Because the Barnburners had returned to the New York Democracy in 1849 and because the Free Soil vote dropped by 135,000 since 1848, much of this gain represented Van Burenites returning to the party. In the South, on the other hand, some of the increase may have come from the accession of slave-owning Whigs who could not stomach the Whig nominee Winfield Scott. The Democrats themselves, however, lost votes in Alabama and Georgia and gained nothing in Mississippi, the states that saw the greatest Whig losses, so the number of Whig conversions should not be exaggerated. It was the Democratic success in attracting new, non-Whig voters in the free states that accounts for most of the increase. The procompromise stand may have contributed to this, but probably more important was the additional support from German and Irish immigrants. Observers everywhere noted that more immigrants voted in 1852 than ever before, and because of Scott's reputed nativism and the Whigs' association with the temperance movement they went for Pierce in a phalanx.

By 1852, then, the Democracy had regained its majority position. Solidifying most of its leadership behind an inoffensive dark horse, reuniting its northern and southern wings behind the longtime pledge to crush slavery agitation, and attracting the bulk of the country's new voters, the party seemed stronger than ever. By 1856, however, it lost its majority status, and by 1860 it lost the White House. In the next eight years, the Democracy suffered division and defection. Both Democratic decisions at Washington and local tensions that sapped grass-roots support caused the political realignment of the mid-1850s which forever destroyed the Jacksonian Democratic coalition.

When Franklin Pierce prepared to dispense patronage, he found bitterly divided parties in almost every state. In Mississippi, Alabama, and Georgia, both Union and Southern Rights Democrats claimed to be the true party that exclusively deserved appointments. In Ohio, Indiana, Iowa, Pennsylvania, Massachusetts, and other northern states, longtime rivals competed for office and angrily blamed Pierce when the other side got the plum. As usual, New York presented the most perplexing problem. The party there was rent into three factions: the Barnburners, who had returned to the party, now led by John A. Dix; the Softshell Hunkers, who were willing to welcome the Barnburners back into the Democratic fold, headed by William L. Marcy; and the intransigent Hardshell Hunkers, led by Daniel S. Dickinson, who believed that the Barnburners should be punished for their apostasy and denied any patronage. Vindictive foes of the antislavery wing and the Softs, the conservative Hards were in turn the particular favorites of southern Democrats.

Hoping to reunite the party by an even distribution of the patronage among all factions, Pierce rewarded both free-soil Democrats and Southern Rights Democrats. To the anger of Union Democrats in the South, he appointed Southern Righters Jefferson Davis of Mississippi secretary of war, John Campbell of Alabama to the Supreme Court, and Louisiana's Pierre Soulé minister to Spain. To the dismay of regular Democrats in New England, he made Massachusetts' Caleb Cushing, an erstwhile Tyler Whig, attorney general. Marcy's appointment as secretary of state infuriated Dickinson and the Hards, as did the selection of Dix as subtreasurer in New York City. When the Hards and the Softs, aided by the Barnburners, nominated separate Democratic tickets in 1853, Pierce's administration blamed the Hards and removed that faction's appointee as head of the New York Customs House.

Hunkers and southern Democrats, furious at Pierce's appointments of free-soilers, threatened not to confirm these appointments when Congress convened in December, 1853. At this stage, two different groups of senators decided to provide the leadership for the party that Pierce had failed to supply. Ambitious for the nomination in 1856, Stephen A. Douglas hoped to divert the party's attention from patronage squabbles and sectional division, and rally Democrats behind a program of western development. More ominously, a powerful clique of southern senators who roomed together on F Street—R. M. T. Hunter and James M. Mason of Virginia, A. P. Butler of South Carolina, and David R. Atchison of Missouri—were determined, in the tradition of Calhoun, to assert southern control of the party. They would define a prosouthern program in the Senate and force all Democrats, especially Pierce's antislavery appointees who still needed Senate confirmation, to hew to this line of party orthodoxy or face mortal southern opposition.

When Douglas' committee on territories began in December, 1853, to consider a bill to organize the Nebraska Territory in the remainder of the Louisiana Purchase from which slavery had been banned since 1820, the "F-Street Mess" made it clear that they would prevent passage of the bill unless a concession were made to the South allowing slavery in the territory. After a series of complex maneuvers in which Douglas surrendered to southern pressure, the result was the Kansas-Nebraska bill, which explicitly repealed the Missouri Compromise prohibition of slavery north of 36°30' and applied popular sovereignty to Kansas and Nebraska territories. Needing Senate votes to confirm his appointments and ratify a foreign policy of aggressive expansionism, which he hoped to pursue, Pierce threw his support behind the measure and tried to force reluctant northern Democrats to vote for it. As was the case with Texas and the Wilmot Proviso, internal Democratic factionalism had brought the slavery issue back into the political arena.

Passed in May, the Kansas-Nebraska Act precipitated a widespread revolt in the North. Democrats along with other northerners protested the reintroduction of the slavery question and especially the repeal of the Missouri Compromise that made slavery expansion a vital possibility. Unlike the Mexican Cession, these territories were contiguous to settled parts of the Midwest, and many free white farmers expected to move there. The act seemed concrete evidence of a Slave Power plot to use the federal government to spread slavery against the will of the North, a plot abolitionists had warned about since the 1830s. Anti-Nebraska, antiadministration coalitions, some already called Republicans, sprang up throughout the North, and in the fall elections of 1854 these fusion parties swept the Democrats out of office. The number of Democratic congressmen from the free states fell from ninety-three to twenty-seven.

The reaction of northern Democrats to these developments varied. National and state officeholders applied pressure everywhere to force Democrats to accept the Kansas-Nebraska Act, and many grudgingly did so. Moreover, some Democrats who were furious about the measure, like Martin Van Buren, chose to contest southern political power from within the Democratic party. Other dissident Democrats joined the anti-Nebraska coalitions. Convinced that southerners controlled the Democracy and that they were purposely trying to drive out northern men of principle, Van Burenites like Preston S. King and David Wilmot, as well as many other Democrats who had not bolted in 1848, flocked to the new parties. By 1856, other Van Buren men like Francis P. Blair, Gideon Welles, and Hannibal Hamlin despaired of checking the Slave Power within the party, and they joined the early bolters in the incipient Republican party, campaigning for John C. Frémont, himself an erstwhile Democrat.

It is a mistake, however, to think that the Kansas-Nebraska Act alone caused the Democratic defections and the subsequent realignment of voters between 1854 and 1856. A combination of developments weakened the Democracy before 1854 and prepared men for revolt. The smoldering sources of division within the Democracy's lower-class coalition in the North that had flared up briefly in the 1830s and the 1840s were ignited again in the 1850s. By the middle of that decade, the Democratic party no longer answered the needs of many northern voters; indeed, it seemed to defend the interests of groups those voters could not tolerate.

The Pierce administration and the Democrats in Congress had failed to satisfy northwestern demands for economic measures. Democrats as well as Whigs in Ohio, Michigan, Illinois, Wisconsin, and Iowa wanted land grants to the states to aid railroad construction, federal rivers and harbors improvements, and a homestead act to encourage settlement. None of these measures became law during Pierce's administration despite western pressure and Democratic majorities in Congress. The president himself vetoed land grants and rivers and harbors bills in 1854 and 1855.

Impatience with the frustration of economic needs as well as outrage at the Kansas-Nebraska bill helped cause western defections from the Democrats in 1854 and the following years.

The endless factionalism within the party was equally debilitating. Perennial "outs" impatient with the monopoly of "ins" took the occasion provided by new opposition parties in which they might exercise leadership to bolt the Democracy. For example, opportunism seems the best way to explain the jump by Simon Cameron and his followers from a Pennsylvania Democratic party firmly controlled by his rival James Buchanan. In other areas, anger at appointments and the sheer delight in taking revenge on Democratic foes influenced the decision to switch.

Much more important, however, was the political reaction to the complex economic and social developments that were rapidly changing many communities in these years. Between 1846, when potato famines ravaged Ireland, and 1860, almost four million European immigrants, most Irishmen and Germans, inundated the United States. This tide swelled the Catholic Church. Between 1850 and 1854 the number of Catholic bishops jumped from 27 to 39, of priests, from 1,081 to 1,574, and of churches, from 1,073 to 1,712. Just when the rate of immigration was increasing, the completion of trunk-line railroads in the early 1850s produced disruptive changes in patterns of commerce, methods of manufacturing, and ways of life in many northern areas. Men lost jobs; merchants lost trade as railroads bypassed them. Relatively isolated and homogeneous communities were now brought into contact with men of different backgrounds as railroads increased communication between communities and as armies of immigrant railroad workers followed the tracks into area after area. The rapidity of these changes engendered feelings of dislocation among many Americans who attributed to the flood of aliens many evils that were probably caused by the whole panoply of economic, social, and intellectual forces disordering their lives. Cheap immigrant labor was blamed for pushing down wages and taking jobs from native-born workers. Immigrants were castigated for increasing the number of slums, crime, drunkenness, and pauperism. Politically, immigrants seemed to pervert the democratic process by voting in blocs that were easily manipulated by ward bosses and party wire pullers.

But it was the Catholicism of the newcomers that seemed most threatening to apprehensive native Protestants. Long warned of a papal plot to control America and long suspicious of the undemocratic hierarchical organization of the Catholic Church, anxious Protestants worried in the early 1850s, when the Catholic clergy began to agitate for ecclesiastical ownership of church property and when the Pope sent a special nuncio to the United States in 1853. Even more appalling, Catholic bishops and the Democratic politicians who represented them began to agitate for the cessation of Bible reading in public schools and for the division of school funds so that the taxes Catholics paid could be used to support parochial schools. The increasing political activity and influence of the Catholics was especially distressing. Because many states limited suffrage to citizens and naturalization required five years, immigrants who arrived in the late 1840s were only beginning to vote in the early 1850s. Their influence was seen in the additional Democratic vote in 1852 and Pierce's appointment of James Campbell, an Irish Catholic from Philadelphia, as postmaster general. In short, by the mid-1850s, some Americans believed that what the Catholic immigrants wanted and what they represented seemed to menace their most cherished values: political democracy, public education, and social order. And this menace could be identified precisely at a time when many Americans were bewildered by the rapidity and variety of change in their society.

The Democratic party had benefited in the 1830s and 1840s, when the growth of commercial capitalism threatened the values of many Americans. In the 1850s, when the menace seemed to spring from a group closely identified with the Democracy, the party suffered grievously. Political antipathy to the immigrants erupted in several forms. Middle-class Protestants of pietistical denominations agitated for prohibition, especially on Sundays, when to the horror of those groups the Germans and Irish flocked to grog shops and beer gardens. Nonpartisan temperance societies normally drew their members from both parties, but the issue was used against the Democratic party, which opposed such legislation. More powerful than the temperance movement of the "respectable" middle class was the emergence of the lower-class Know Nothing movement. Organized originally as a secret fraternal order whose membership was restricted to native-born Protestants, the Know Nothings entered politics in 1854 demanding the exclusion of foreigners and Catholics from political office and a lengthening of the naturalization period to keep them from voting. Both Know Nothings and temperance advocates joined the fusion coalitions that defeated the Democrats in 1854, and many entered the Republican ranks thereafter.

The social tensions that coincided with anti-Nebraska sentiment to reshape the opposition had a powerful influence within the Democratic party itself, although the working of these pressures was often very complex. Letters to Democratic leaders in the early 1850s indicate that some Protestant Democrats rankled at the patronage given Catholics and left the party because of it. Similarly, many Democratic temperance men may have defected to the opposition in the 1850s. One Democratic leader complained that prohibition laws had been "a curse to the Democratic party and produced a schism which puzzles the wisest heads to get rid of." The Know Nothing movement, with its lures of secret rituals and bold anti-Catholic programs, cut into Democratic strength among native-born workers who had long cherished the public school system. Baptists and Methodists, whose low social status had often brought them to the Democratic party, now joined the Know Nothings or the Republicans.

Although temperance and nativism engendered substantial defections among native-born Democrats, these issues tended to solidify immigrant and Catholic support for the Democratic party, which immigrants perceived as a shield against their enemies. Indeed, much of the increased political participation by immigrants in the early 1850s probably resulted from the new activism of temperance advocates on the state level after Maine passed its famous Liquor Law in 1851. Almost all immigrants hated the self-righteous temperance men.

But the social determinants of immigrant voting behavior were terribly complex. Anti-Catholicism, prohibitionism, nativism, and free-soilism were cross pressures affecting different groups in different ways. For example, there were small numbers of evangelical Protestant immigrants who favored temperance legislation and Sunday blue laws, and who were appalled by slavery. Normally, they would vote against the Democrats, but the nativism of the Know Nothings might drive them into the Democratic fold. Similarly, there were Protestant immigrants, Irishmen, Germans, and Welshmen, who along with the radical and anticlerical German "Forty-Eighters" feared the Catholic Church and despised their fellow countrymen who belonged to it. But these men could not abide the evangelical moralism behind the temperance and sabbatarian agitation or the antiforeign, as distinct from anti-Catholic, impetus of the Know

Nothings. Many German Lutherans who had no love for the Catholics could not tolerate the anticlericalism of the German Forty-Eighters, and the association of men like Carl Schurz with the Republicans was reason enough to keep thousands of Lutherans in the Democratic ranks.

The voting behavior of normally Democratic immigrants, then, varied from state to state and year to year. Often it depended on the local social structure and the presence or absence of groups other immigrants disliked. For example, German Lutherans crowded next to German Catholics in the city of Pittsburgh voted against the Democrats, the party associated with Catholics, in 1854, but in areas of Wisconsin and Michigan, where Catholics and Lutherans were not intermixed, Lutherans voted Democratic because pietistical Protestants were associated with the opposition parties. There was much fluctuation after 1854. Many Protestant Germans, who hated Catholics and staunchly opposed slavery extension and who had voted for the anti-Democratic coalitions in 1854 when the Know Nothings were still largely secret, scurried back to the Democrats in 1855 when the Know Nothings were running open campaigns and their nativism was as apparent as their anti-Catholicism. The absorption of most northern Know Nothings by the Republicans and the ease with which the nativist and prohibitionist stigma could be attached to that party were enough to keep the Germans and Dutch in many midwestern states firmly in the Democratic ranks for the rest of the decade, indeed for the remainder of the century. In other areas, however, the Republicans managed to drop nativism and soft-pedal the temperance issue, and by stressing their hostility to the Pope and the Slave Power they managed to win over some of the Protestant immigrants for good.

In the face of rising antagonism against southerners and Catholics in the North, the Democrats embraced both groups in the presidential election of 1856. The party nominated James Buchanan on a platform that endorsed the Kansas-Nebraska Act and popular sovereignty as the proper settlement of the slavery problem. The platform seemed to support the southern interpretation of that doctrine, because it vowed "non-interference by Congress with Slavery in States and Territories" and explicitly stated that the territorial decision on slavery should be made in the constitution when the population was large enough to apply for statehood. As in 1848, however, northerners denied this interpretation and insisted during the campaign that the decision would be made earlier, in the territorial stage. Apparently united, northern and southern Democrats were still deeply divided over the slavery issue, and that division would disrupt the party in the next four years. The Democrats also vigorously denounced the bigotry of the Know Nothings and defended religious liberty. They also argued that victory for the radical Republican party would provoke southern secession.

Buchanan won the election, but his constituency differed from that which had elected Pierce in 1852. The Democrats suffered defections in the North as the Republicans carried many traditionally Democratic areas, but the extent of those defections is difficult to gauge. Many who angrily bolted the party in 1854 had been persuaded to return by 1856, and the party actually gained 100,000 votes in the Midwest over 1852. Some of those votes, though, came from new sources. The party lost men angry at the Kansas-Nebraska Act and apparent southern aggressions in "Bleeding Kansas," westerners irate as well over the economic negativism of the party, dissident "outs" who saw political opportunities in the new parties, native-born Protestants from the middle and lower classes, and some anti-Catholic immigrants. Reasons for disliking the Democrats were not mutually exclusive, and a combination of grievances probably motivated most bolters. Sectional and ethnocultural tensions had split the large lower-class coalition the Democrats had built on economic issues. On the other hand, many conservative Whigs fearful for the Union now joined the Democrats in the North, as did many slaveholding Whigs in the South after the disintegration of their old party. Finally, the Know Nothing menace caused more Catholics and immigrants to vote, and the Democrats gained from their increased participation.

Although the party managed to retain considerable northern support in 1856, events during the hapless Buchanan administration completed the disruption of the Democracy. Like Pierce, Buchanan offended certain Democrats with his distribution of the patronage—especially the followers of Douglas, his longtime lieutenant in Pennsylvania John A. Forney, who would later organize the revolt against Buchanan in his home state, and the more radical southerners. Disclosures of corruption convinced southerners that the party was poisoned by the sordid Yankee lust for pelf. Simultaneously, northerners became more bitter than ever over southern control. Financial panic and then depression struck in the fall of 1857, and northerners clamored for a protective tariff. When such a bill came up in Congress, Pennsylvania and other northern Democrats voted for it, but southern Democratic votes blocked any action. Northwestern Democrats saw southerners continue to obstruct the passage of land-grant, homestead, and rivers and harbors legislation in Congress. Their anger was compounded when Buchanan vetoed land-grant college and homestead bills and thus attached forever the stigma of economic negativism to the Democracy. During Buchanan's last two years, party cohesion in Congress even shattered on general appropriation bills to fund government departments. Many vengeful northern Democrats determined as well to nominate Douglas in 1860 and strip control of the party from the Slave Power.

More damaging than economic issues and patronage squabbles to party unity was the disastrous handling of the slavery question. Buchanan hoped to save the country and his party by settling forever the disputes over slavery in the territories, especially Kansas. By doing so, he could rob the Republicans of their most effective issue. When, therefore, he learned that the Supreme Court had an opportunity to rule on the power of Congress over slavery in territories, he urged it to do so in a letter to one of the Democratic justices.

The resulting Dred Scott decision ruled that Congress could not constitutionally prohibit slavery in a territory. This helped drive a wedge between northern and southern wings of the party by ending the ambiguity of the popular sovereignty doctrine. Southerners who had stressed the noninterference part of it and argued that a territory's decision on slavery would be made when it entered as a state applauded the decision. If Congress could not bar slavery, they maintained, surely it could not delegate that power to a territorial legislature. Although the decision said nothing about territorial legislatures, it proved embarrassing to Douglas and northern Democrats, who had insisted that settlers could prohibit slavery early in the territorial stage. Douglas quickly searched for another formula to allow an early decision. In June, 1857, he said that the southerners' right to take slaves into territories was "barren and worthless" because slavery needed local laws to protect it. By refusing to pass such laws, he implied, the settlers could effectively prohibit slavery. The administration press printed and endorsed this speech, as did some southern Democratic papers. But the South was now warned that Douglas would not acquiesce entirely in its position.

More important in producing southern disenchantment with popular sovereignty was the fight over the Lecompton Constitution when Kansas applied for statehood in 1858. Because the free-state settlers in Kansas were largely excluded from a census of voters eligible to elect delegates to the constitutional convention at Lecompton in 1857, they had refused to participate in that election. As a result, proslavery men wrote a constitution that, among other things, protected the slaves already in Kansas and limited suffrage to citizens. Rather than submitting the constitution for popular approval in accord with Democratic dogma, the convention ordered that the voters could only choose between two versions of it: one with a clause allowing the entry of more slaves into the state and the other with a clause prohibiting future entry. Either way, they had to accept the constitution itself. Free-state settlers again refused to participate in the referendum on December 21, 1857, and the provision for future slavery passed 6,143 to 569. On January 4, 1858, however, the free-state men voted in another referendum called by the territorial legislature, which they controlled, and over 10,000 votes were cast against the entire constitution. Despite this evidence that the majority of Kansans opposed the Lecompton Constitution, the legalist Buchanan, who feared the ire of southern Democrats should he reject it, accepted the constitution and December referendum as legitimate and in early 1858 urged Congress to admit Kansas under it.

His decision ruptured the party. Even before the December vote, Douglas denounced the constitution as a fraud. Long a champion of self-determination by local majorities and faced with an election in Illinois, where that idea was popular, he could not accept the unrepresentative nature of the convention or the imposition of the Lecompton document on Kansans who had no chance to vote on it. Openly joining the Republicans in denouncing Lecompton, Douglas led an unsuccessful fight against it in the Senate; in the House his lieutenants organized a bloc of twenty-six anti-Lecompton Democrats who, along with the Republicans, prevented its passage. Almost every northern state delegation of Democrats was split between Douglas and administration supporters, with eastern states favoring Buchanan, and western states, Douglas. Eventually a compromise resubmitted the constitution to popular vote. It was roundly defeated. Kansas would remain a territory rather than become a slave state.

The struggle over Lecompton poisoned the relationship between Buchanan and Douglas. When Douglas denounced the Lecompton "swindle" in a speech in Chicago in July, 1858, all hope of reconciliation was gone. Buchanan and his friends removed Douglas' allies and other anti-Lecompton Democrats from office, worked for Douglas' defeat in the Illinois election of 1858, and vowed to prevent his nomination for president in 1860. On the state level, dissident leaders like Forney of Pennsylvania backed Douglas and helped form anti-Lecompton Democratic tickets that fought regular Democrats or aided Republicans throughout the North in the congressional elections of 1858. Many of these men supported Douglas in 1860, but others joined the Republicans.

Many northern voters who had supported Buchanan in 1856 were disillusioned by the Lecompton struggle. Promised that popular sovereignty would produce free soil, they found that the majority will could not prevent a proslavery constitution from being rammed down the throats of Kansans with the aid of the Democratic president. In the congressional and state elections of 1858 in the North, the Democrats were thrashed, losing eighteen seats and control of the House. Although these elections involved many issues, anti-Lecompton Democrats generally fared better than others, and it seems clear that Lecompton drove some voters into the arms of the opposition. Douglas and other northern Democrats knew they could make no more concessions to the South and survive politically.

The most important result of the Lecompton battle, however, was that it permanently soured southern Democrats on Douglas. Despite his long advocacy of local sovereignty, Douglas, when the chips were down, had refused to accept the "legal" December referendum on Lecompton. Moreover, he had joined the Republicans in preventing the entry of another slave state. Then, in August, 1858, during his debate with Abraham Lincoln at Freeport, Illinois, Douglas reiterated that "it matters not what way the Supreme Court may . . . decide as to the abstract question whether slavery may or may not go into a Territory. . . . [T]he people have the lawful means to introduce or exclude it as they please." Now furious at this so-called Freeport Doctrine, southern Democrats humiliated Douglas by stripping him of his chairmanship of the Senate Committee on Territories in 1859.

From early 1859 until the Democratic national convention in April,

1860, the rift between Douglas and the southerners widened. Southerners insisted that a territorial legislature could not bar slavery and that, if it refused to pass laws protecting the institution, it was the obligation of Congress to enact such protective legislation. In February, 1860, Jefferson Davis introduced resolutions to that effect into the Senate, and by that date the Alabama Democratic state convention had instructed its delegates to the national convention to withdraw if the platform did not call for a federal slave code. Southerners would no longer tolerate the ambiguities and double meanings of popular sovereignty; they called for an honest platform that protected their rights. Douglas, on the other hand, realized that the only viable political course in the North was defiance of the South. In public letters, articles, and speeches, he insisted that a territory could bar slavery, that he would not tolerate a slave code, and that the 1860 convention must reaffirm the Cincinnati platform of 1856. As the Charleston convention approached, very real differences of principle separated the leading candidate for the Democratic nomination from the influential southern leaders.

Accumulated personal grievances and political miscalculations as well as principle shaped the crucial decisions at Charleston. Before the convention even opened, the delegates from Alabama, Georgia, Mississippi, Florida, Louisiana, Texas, and Arkansas agreed to bolt if a provision for federal protection of slavery in the territories were not included in the platform. They knew that Douglas, whom they hated, could not accept such a platform, and they would stop him by imposing their will on the convention as southerners had so often before. A powerful group of Senators—Jesse Bright of Indiana, John A. Bayard of Delaware, and John Slidell of Louisiana—who were political allies of President Buchanan and who despised Douglas because of his feud with the president, encouraged this stop-Douglas strategy. Even if the southerners did withdraw and northern and southern Democrats nominated separate candidates, they calculated, no candidate could get an electoral majority or a majority of states in the badly divided House of Representatives. The securely Democratic Senate would then choose the vice-president, who would become president because of the House's inability to act. On the other hand, the free-state backers of Douglas were in the majority. They were willing to let some of the southern delegations stalk out of the convention, because such a bolt would reduce the size of the convention and make it easier to secure a two-thirds majority for Douglas. Moreover, they were determined that the majority rule within the Democracy and that the South acquiesce in their choice. Both principle and their political gamble prevented their compromising in order to defuse the southern menace.

Their overconfidence led the Douglas men to make a fatal decision. They agreed to have the platform voted on before nominations were made. Because the resolutions committee consisted of a delegate from each state, the fifteen slave states with their allies from California and Oregon had a one-vote edge, although the free states had the majority of delegates. The committee eventually reported three platforms to the convention—a majority platform that endorsed a slave code, a minority platform backed by the Douglas men that reaffirmed the Cincinnati platform and added a clause giving the decision on the power of Congress and territories over slavery to the Supreme Court, and another minority report merely reaffirming the 1856 platform. The Douglas men had sacrificed pure territorial self-determination, and their majority of delegates adopted the first minority report as the official platform. In a further effort of conciliation, the Douglasites then agreed to drop the clause referring squatter sovereignty to the Supreme Court, because some southerners feared future decisions might go against them.

The southern radicals were not appeased. The delegates from Alabama, Mississippi, Louisiana, South Carolina, Florida, and Texas marched out of the convention to the wild cheering of the Charlestonians packing the galleries. Later they were joined by delegates from Georgia, Arkansas, and other southern states. They did not march far, however, for many of them as well as the Buchanan managers hoped the withdrawal would coerce those who remained to drop Douglas and compromise with southern demands. But this calculation, like so many others, proved mistaken. Determined to assert their majority control of the party, the Douglas men insisted on their man and would make no further concessions. Their hope of an easier two-thirds majority, however, proved just as vain as the calculation of the southerners. More delegates had bolted than the Douglas managers had anticipated, and those who remained seemed to represent only the North and Upper South. The New York delegation was mainly concerned with finding a candidate who could unite the party and win in November so he might give them federal patronage. They did not want Douglas nominated by an unrepresentative rump, and they persuaded the convention to pass a rule requiring the nominee to have two-thirds of the original number of delegates, not just of those who remained. Douglas could not reach such a total, and the convention recessed until June, when it was to reassemble in Baltimore, where, the Douglas managers hoped, new delegates composed of Union Democrats would represent the Deep South states that had withdrawn at Charleston.

The division at Charleston proved irremediable. When the convention met at Baltimore, the Douglas men managed to exclude the original Alabama and Louisiana delegates and continued to insist that Douglas be the candidate, although the Little Giant himself was willing to step aside to save party unity. Thwarted again, southern delegations, along with those from California and Oregon, marched out of the convention, convened at another hall, and nominated John C. Breckinridge on the majority platform from Charleston. The other bolters from the Charleston convention who had reassembled at Richmond ratified this choice. Meanwhile, the regular convention in Baltimore nominated Douglas and changed the platform again to leave the decision over slavery in the territories to the Supreme Court.

The Democracy was split in two. Two separate Democratic national committees conducted the campaign from Washington. State organizations in the North, except Pennsylvania's, backed Douglas, whereas most in the South worked for Breckinridge. But each candidate wooed support throughout the country, thereby splitting the Democratic vote. When local politicians pushed for fusion electoral tickets in several northern states, the Douglas managers opposed the maneuver, but eventually some fusion was achieved. Many voters remained loyal to the Democracy despite, or perhaps because of, the division, and Douglas and Breckinridge together polled 280,000 more votes in the North than had Buchanan in 1856. But those votes were usually divided, and the leadership split may have kept Democrats at home. Lincoln won handily. Secession soon followed.

In a sense, the tribulations of the Democratic party after Charleston were anticlimactic. The southerners' loss of control of the Democratic party may have been as important in their decision to secede as Republican victory. Since the 1820s, southerners had remained in the Democratic party only so long as it seemed to protect slavery either by diverting attention from that issue or by championing a weak and noninterfering national government. By the 1840s, many southerners probably agreed with Calhoun that no party was safe that the South could not control, and southerners had indeed controlled the national party since 1844, even though their section was becoming more and more of a minority within the nation. Southern domination had provoked revolts by the northeastern Van Buren men in 1848 and after 1854, but at those times most northwestern Democrats had gone along with the southerners because they could defend the Democratic program as neutral or advantageous to their own section. By 1860, however, southerners were no longer satisfied with laissez faire in regard to slavery; they demanded positive congressional action on their behalf. Such an openly sectional policy could no longer be disguised as neutral. This southern demand tore the already frayed bonds of the party's North-South alliance. The Douglas wing faced political extinction at home unless it defied southern rule, seized control of the party, and ended the prosouthern policies so outrageous to the majority North. It was the Douglas men's insistence at Charleston that the northern majority rule that was intolerable to the southern minority. Unable to control the party, they no longer trusted it to protect southern interests. Rather than fight to regain control, they withdrew. This petulant refusal to allow the majority to rule within the party perfectly foreshadowed the southern reaction to the victory of the Republicans, a party determined to exercise the rule of the northern majority over the southern minority within the nation. Southerners would no longer rely on an alliance with northerners in a national party or the same government, and they turned to the Calhoun strategy of independent southern political action. But because neither northern Democrats nor Republicans could be bullied into concessions to the South any longer, that course now required the secession from the Union that Calhoun had hoped to forestall.

The Antimasonic and
Know Nothing Parties

By definition, third parties represent dissatisfaction with the two-party system. A diversity of reasons—intense concern with particular issues, factionalism within the major parties, and unorthodox ideological views, among others—have produced dissent from established parties and from the general consensus in which they have operated. In most cases, splinter or minority parties have attracted such small followings that their appearance has confirmed rather than threatened the health of the two-party system. By draining off the most disaffected, they have allowed the major parties to avoid divisive issues and to remain broad, heterogeneous coalitions. At certain times, however, third parties have achieved enough strength to weaken seriously or even destroy a major party and thereby reshape or realign the two-party system. The appearance of such powerful and influential third parties invites investigation, for the genius of the American party system has been its ability to absorb issues that generate widespread interest and convert them to a form manageable within that system. Massive defections to new parties that raise or exploit certain issues, therefore, indicate the failure of the system to integrate the emergent political demands of significant portions of the electorate.

The phenomenon of strong third parties, then, confronts the historian with basic questions about their origins and development. Why do they appear at some times and not at others? What accounts for the inability of existing parties to absorb certain kinds of issues that evoke popular enthusiasm? What kinds of people join third parties, and how do they differ from those who do not? What impact do these parties have on the established parties? Finally, if public concern was sufficient to produce a third party movement, how can one explain its collapse and the reassimilation of its supporters into a two-party matrix?

In seeking answers to these questions, one can profitably consider together the Antimasonic party, which mushroomed in the late 1820s, and the anti-Catholic, antiforeign Know Nothing party, which disrupted politics in the 1850s. On the surface, the Antimasonic crusade against secret societies differed sharply from the secretly organized Know Nothing order, yet they had much in common. Twenty years after the Antimasons helped shape the Whig party, the Know Nothings helped destroy it. Springing from grass-roots social, religious, and political anxieties caused by rapid social and economic change, both movements launched frenzied crusades against groups whose power and iniquity they exaggerated to monstrous proportions. Both imagined they were protecting vital American institutions from conspiracies that sought to undermine republican government. Fearing that these conspiracies had seized control of government from the people by manipulating the political process, both turned to political action and sought to restore sovereignty to the people by proscribing their opponents from public office and purging politics of their influence. Started as crusades to smite dragons and return power to the people, both were quickly taken over by professional politicians who rode the waves of popular excitement and changed the nature of the parties enough to erode their reasons for independent existence and to hasten the absorption of their supporters into a new two-party framework.

To understand the emergence of Antimasonry, one must look briefly at the nature of its target. Modern Freemasonry was a secret fraternal organization that began in England in the early part of the eighteenth century and was quickly imported to America. Drawing on ideals of the Enlightenment, the fraternity espoused the use of reason rather than religious faith in the achievement of philanthropy and reform. Organized in lodges, initiates learned secret rituals and passwords and took various oaths as they passed up the hierarchy of degrees of membership. With the higher degrees came elaborate titles and leadership in the society. The most important oath, though, was the vow to preserve the secrecy of the rituals of the fraternity. Many prominent Americans, including Benjamin Franklin, George Washington, Andrew Jackson, and Henry Clay, joined the Masons, and Masonry seems primarily to have been a social and charitable organization that by 1825 had lodges in almost every state. More research is necessary to establish the degree to which Masons favored fellow Masons in political and legal affairs, but it is clear that Masons often recruited members from local social and economic elites and that many officeholders and judges were Masons. The secret rituals of the fraternity and its stress on reason as opposed to religion had provoked charges of immorality and political conspiracy against the Masons as early as the 1790s, but these had quickly subsided. Masonry, then, was a familiar institution that continued to attract to its membership in the 1820s some of the foremost Americans. The newness of Masonry or its mere existence, that is, cannot explain the assaults on it in that decade. One must look elsewhere for the causes of Antimasonry.

Ostensibly, a single series of events in western New York engendered the Antimasonic crusade. In August and September, 1826, bands of Masons from several counties tried to stop the printing of an exposé of Freemasonry's secret rituals. Unsuccessful in their efforts to steal the manuscript and to burn the office of its publisher, they seized its author, a disgruntled Mason named William Morgan, from his home in Batavia, threw him into jail in another town, and then carried him over a hundred miles through Rochester to Fort Niagara. Balked when they attempted to hide Morgan in Canada, they apparently drowned him in the Niagara River for violating his oaths of secrecy. Indignant citizens in Genesee, Livingston, Monroe, and Orleans Counties launched investigations to find out what had happened to Morgan. Unearthing an apparent Masonic plot to suppress his book and identifying the men involved in the kidnapping, they asked Governor DeWitt Clinton to intervene, but he insisted that local law enforcement officials handle the matter.

Had investigations and prosecutions been pushed with vigor by such officials and had Masons cooperated fully with them, the episode might have ended with only local excitement. But it soon became evident that Masons sought to squelch the affair. Meetings of the fraternity pooh-poohed the matter, and Masons withdrew advertising from newspapers that dared publish anything about it. Masons refused to testify to committees or courts, grand juries handpicked by Masonic sheriffs failed to return indictments, and Masons found guilty in various trials received what seemed like remarkably light sentences. When local citizens' committees called on the state legislature in the spring of 1827 to undertake a special investigation, their resolutions met a crushing defeat. Official obstructionism convinced the incipient Antimasons that they faced not just the crime of a few zealous individuals but a gigantic conspiracy to subvert the rule of law through Masonic control of newspapers, the legislature, and the judiciary. No grand jury picked by Masonic sheriffs, no trial conducted by Masonic judges, no legislature dominated by Masonic officeholders could be trusted to bring Masonic murderers to justice, for Masons placed their oaths to protect each other before their duty to serve the people.

Such a seemingly thorough infiltration and corruption of government convinced early Antimasons that they must take political action to overthrow Masonry. In the summer of 1827, grass-roots Antimasonic groups held conventions throughout New York to nominate candidates for the legislature. Because "the masonic fraternity have outraged humanity and violated all law," declared Monroe County Antimasons, "considerations of imperious duty" demanded independent political action. "In the dark day of the investigation," that convention continued, "we supplicated the legislature to quicken her pace, and strengthen her arm, but it was a MASONIC LEGISLATURE, and we were coldly repulsed! We now appeal to the SOVEREIGN PEOPLE. Let *their* verdict be awarded upon the merits of the question." The people cast their verdict by electing fifteen Antimasonic assemblymen, primarily from the western part of the state where the excitement was most intense.

Encouraged by this local success, conventions in March, 1828, urged the calling of a state convention in August to represent the people and "to take measures for the destruction of the Masonic Institution, for sustaining the liberty of the press, and asserting the supremacy of the laws, for protecting the rights and privileges of the citizens against the vindictive persecutions of members of the Masonic society." Always the Antimasons trumpeted their desire to liberate newspapers and the government from the despotic control of Masonry, which considered itself above the laws and literally thought it could get away with murder. Their conviction was that action at the polls was the best way to destroy it, purify politics, and restore morality.

Despite a growing campaign carried on by newspapers and seceding Masons, and despite these early calls for a state convention and the creation of a state central committee in May, the decision to organize a new party depended on the positions taken by the established parties in the state. A third party crusade was not yet inevitable.

In the spring of 1828, a presidential election year, indeed, the inclusion of Antimasons within one of the major parties seemed more likely. Politics were in flux in the 1820s as the old Jeffersonian Republican party was disintegrating. As a result, party alignments on the state level often bore little relation to those on the national level, where new parties were only beginning to crystallize in 1827 and 1828. Since 1820, New York voters had been divided between the followers of Governor Clinton and of his opponent, Martin Van Buren. The Clintonians' program of rapid extension and completion of the Erie Canal, in contrast to Van Buren's opposition to extensive improvements, made them dominant in western New York, where Antimasonry first flourished. In 1827, Van Buren had thrown the support of his formidable Bucktail faction behind Andrew Jackson, whereas most Clintonians favored the incumbent John Quincy Adams, an ardent champion of internal improvements, even though Clinton himself backed Jackson. Adams had denounced secret societies, even promising to reveal the secrets of Phi Beta Kappa, whereas Jackson stoutly defended his Masonic membership. Because the Adams men had often cooperated with Antimasons in the 1827 assembly elections and because Masons were flocking to the Democrats as their best defense from Antimasonry, it seemed possible that Adams men could hold their support in western New York and channel Antimasonic outrage to their own advantage simply by citing Masonry as another reason to oppose Jackson and Van Buren's Albany Regency. One must ask, then, why a third party was ever formed.

The stubbornness of Masons among the New York Adams men and grass-roots Antimasonic demands for an unadulterated people's party best explain this failure to absorb the issue within the existing party framework. Some Antimasonic leaders like Thurlow Weed viewed the defeat of Jackson as the main priority in 1828, and they worked to effect an Adams-Antimasonic coalition by having the Adams state convention in July nominate Francis Granger, an ally of the Antimasons in the legislature, as their gubernatorial candidate against Van Buren. But the major Adams newspaper in the state, the Albany *Advertiser*, opposed any alliance, and the Adams convention, fearing Granger would alienate pro-

Adams Masons, nominated another man. They then nominated Granger for lieutenant governor, but this device failed to appease Antimasonic zealots who had already condemned "any attempt to render the honest indignation now existing against the [Masonic] institution subservient to the views of any of the political parties of the day" and renounced "all intentions of promoting political principles." Resolving at a later convention in August "to disregard the two great political parties, that at this time distract this state and the Union," they nominated Granger for governor on their own ticket. When he declined, they settled on Solomon Southwick in September, and three tickets were in the field. Blaming this split in the anti-Regency ranks on "the cunning of Freemasonry," Weed's *Antimasonic Enquirer* admitted, "Both political parties have contributed their exertions to cripple and embarrass the cause of the people. They have juggled us out of a candidate for governor." He went on to condemn the politicians from both parties for failing to take heed of Antimasonic demands.

> The violated laws of the country and the unavenged blood of a murdered citizen were not questions of sufficient importance to withdraw them from the pursuit of political honors. . . . The people were left to oppose Freemasonry without the aid of the laws and unsupported by the countenance of leading men. Indeed, so cautious were the prominent politicians, that none of them could be induced to identify their efforts and commit their fortunes to the hands of men devoted to the cause of civil liberty.

Weed's anger at the major parties was mild compared with that of other Antimasons who flayed Weed for his willingness to work with Adams men. That Southwick received only 12 percent of the popular vote in 1828 and that Antimasons did vote for Adams in the presidential contest were not as important as their declarations of war on both major parties.

Antimasons had won four senate and seventeen assembly seats in 1828, and in the legislature they pushed through a law stripping sheriffs of the power to select grand juries. This triumph increased their confidence. More important, Jackson's victory shattered the Adams organization in New York and elsewhere, and in the subsequent vacuum Antimasons became the major opposition party. In February, the Antimasonic state convention "disavow[ed] all connexion [*sic*] between Antimasons and any political party which has heretofore existed in the United States." To make sure the third party did not disappear for want of a national organization, it also called for a national convention in Philadelphia in 1830, the first national convention ever called.

While the party was establishing its separate identity in New York, it was also spreading to other states. Weed and other editors had distributed Antimasonic propaganda to Vermont, Connecticut, Massachusetts, Pennsylvania, Ohio, and Michigan Territory since 1827, and the movement was fanned in those areas and elsewhere by the renunciation of defecting Masons and by the assaults of Presbyterian, Baptist, and Methodist clergymen on the fraternity. The *Anti-Masonic Review* of New York circulated nationally. By 1830, Antimasons claimed they had established 124 "free" newspapers throughout the country. By that date as well, Antimasonry was a potent political force in most of those states, and it would grow more powerful. Antimasons ran local candidates in Pennsylvania as early as 1828, and in 1829 their gubernatorial candidate garnered 45 percent of the vote. In 1830, Antimasonic gubernatorial candidates drew 48 percent of the vote in New York and 35 percent in Vermont; in 1831, Antimasons carried 150 of Massachusetts' 490 assembly seats. All these states had Antimasonic state committees by 1830, and all sent delegates to the national convention that year, as did Rhode Island, Maryland, and Delaware. In most of these states, moreover, Antimasons adamantly opposed cooperation with either the Jacksonians or the National Republicans, the successors to the Adams party. Four years after the grass-roots indignation in western New York, an aggressive and influential third party flourished in ten states and was spreading to more.

Although it is relatively easy to trace the mushrooming of Antimasonry, it is more difficult to explain that phenomenon. Clearly, the party benefited from the inchoate political situation of the 1820s. The absence of two strong national parties organized at both the congressional and state levels had produced vacuums in some states and allowed Antimasonry to rise to potency on the basis of state politics alone. As long as the party did not have to confront the pressures of a national presidential campaign and did not worry about its negligible influence in Congress, it could function as an effective force in the arena of state politics, which in the 1820s and 1830s was more relevant to many voters than Congress. But even this favorable situation does not account for the remarkable appeal of Antimasonry on the grass-roots level. Earlier attacks on Masonry, as in the 1790s, had failed to provoke a mass political movement. What conditions sparked it at the end of the 1820s? Antimasonic conventions everywhere monotonously rehearsed the history of Morgan's abduction and constantly charged that the order condoned murder to protect its secrecy. Yet it seems clear that more than outrage at these events produced the popular frenzy that carried all before it in certain areas. Why would so many people in places far from western New York, or even people there, join the Antimasonic crusade?

Closer examination of Antimasonic rhetoric and voting support helps unravel this puzzle. As exaggerated and unfounded as the apocalyptic visions of Antimasons seem to the modern observer, they reveal fears and hopes about the course of American society. Imbued with values of individual liberty, the rule of law, equal rights and equal opportunity, and self-advancement restrained only by the dictates of a Christian conscience, Antimasons viewed Masonry as an unnatural power above the law—a "Monster," a "Beast with seven heads and ten horns," "an organized kingdom within the limits of the Republic," consisting of "irresponsible bodies, controlled by their own interest and, in effect, answerable to no tribunal." What awed and infuriated them most was Masonry's machinelike organization, its control of its members through "dreadful" oaths that could force them to act together in defiance of both conscience and law to the disadvantage and injury of law-abiding citizens. "These obligations," Antimasons warned constantly, "strike at the very existence of our government—at the very foundation of our rights—and at the impartial administration of our laws." Because of these oaths and its hierarchical structure, Masonry "like all corporations [was] a body without soul—selfish and monopolizing," "an aristocratic nobility, . . . a privileged order, claiming and securing to its members unequal advantages over their fellow citizens . . . and operating through our extended country at any time and on any subject, with all the efficacy of a perfect organization, controlled and directed by unseen and unknown hands." How, asked Antimasons, could an individual obeying the laws and his conscience compete or even coexist with this juggernaut?

Yet compete and coexist he must, for the conspiracy had "become widespread in its influence, extended in its operations, and . . . interwo-

ven with the very frame and fabric of society." "Every man's observation
and experience," complained a county meeting in New York, "will furnish instances of Masonic interference with almost all the transactions of
life." Antimasons in other states echoed this warning, and it is small
wonder that they accepted as accurate and constantly iterated as proof of
their charges the boast of a Mason in 1825:

> What is Masonry now? IT IS POWERFUL. It comprises men
> of RANK, wealth, office and talent, in power and out of power; and
> that in almost every place of power where POWER IS OF ANY IMPOR-
> TANCE; and it comprises among other CLASSES of the community,
> to the lowest, in large numbers, active men, united together, *and
> capable of being directed by the efforts of others,* so as to have the
> FORCE OF CONCERT, *throughout the civilized world!* They are distrib-
> uted too, with the means of knowing one another, and the means of
> keeping secret, and the means of co-operating, in the DESK—in
> the LEGISLATIVE HALL—on the BENCH—in every GATHERING OF
> BUSINESS—in every PARTY OF PLEASURE—in every ENTERPRISE
> OF GOVERNMENT—in every DOMESTIC CIRCLE—in PEACE and in
> WAR—among ENEMIES and FRIENDS—in ONE PLACE as well as in
> another!

As Alexis de Tocqueville noted, the relative equality of conditions
in America around 1830 made men intolerant of the slightest inequality
or privilege. Antimasons fervently expressed the fears of the average man
that he could not compete with organizations that pooled the resources
and energies of all their members against the limited means of the individual. New Yorkers complained that "our equal rights as citizens" were
assailed "by the concerted actions of numerous, wealthy, intelligent, and
powerful bodies of men; and the regular operations of our constituted
authorities is unable to protect us." Railing at the aristocratic trappings of
ritual and degrees, Antimasons declared that "the direct object of freemasonry is to benefit the *few* at the expense of the *many,* by creating a
privileged class, in the midst of a community entitled to enjoy equal rights
and privileges." Since Masonry "secures an undue, because unmerited
advantage to members of the fraternity over the honest and industrious
uninitiated farmer, mechanic, and laborer, in all the ordinary transactions
of life," as Thaddeus Stevens summarized in a speech to the Pennsylvania

legislature, "its whole tendency is to cherish a hatred of democracy, and a love of aristocratic and regal forms of power."

Although aristocratic pretensions and the power to obtain unfair advantage were obnoxious enough, Masonry had also, Antimasons charged, used its disciplined organization to infiltrate political parties and had "usurped" the government. Antimasons asserted that the "principal object" of Masonry was "the acquisition of political power." "A secret and self formed society avowedly acting to control the operations of government," Masonry "enters and corrupts our legislative halls, our executive affairs." "By hidden and unsuspected machinery" the order dominated elections and political parties. Because of oaths, members could "claim the vote of a brother for any elective office," and once elected, Masons "prefer[red] a corrupt 'brother' to honest citizens in appointments to office," warned Antimasons, "so that soon the Government in all its branches, must be controlled by members of the order."

The only way for men to expel this tyranny from government, to return power to the people, and to "restore equal rights, equal laws, and equal privileges to all men," the Antimasons made clear, was to vote and render "ineligible to office, the adherents of the bloodstained order." And the only party that represented the people and that could overthrow Masonry was the Antimasonic party, for Masons, aristocrats, and "unprincipled political leaders" controlled both the Jacksonians and the National Republicans. If Masons were aristocrats, Antimasons were the champions of the plain man. "The Antimasonic party is the organization of the people against a secret society—of republicans against grand kings," proclaimed a Pennsylvania county meeting. Antimasons came "from the people, they take their candidates, not from the exclusive circle of aristocracy, but from the people." Nor would these self-proclaimed farmers, mechanics, and laborers have anything to do with professional politicians who had sold the people out. One reason Antimasons stressed delegate conventions was that in these the people, and not crafty politicians, ostensibly made decisions. Their leaders were not old politicians, they boasted, but "new-made ·men . . . the made men of antimasonry." "Antimasonry has no use for any officeseeking, selfish, time serving politician." They were happy, declared Antimasons, to represent the "lower classes . . . for in this country the lower classes are the head of all. The PEOPLE are SOVEREIGN."

The real appeal of Antimasonry, indeed, probably lay not in its exposure of heinous conspiracies or in its egalitarian rhetoric but, at a time when suffrage was expanding, in its exaltation of what the people, the majority, could accomplish at the ballot box. If Antimasonry manifested fears about the loss of equal opportunity, it also represented the hopes of people by expressing perfectly what one historian has called a spirit of boundlessness that characterized America in the 1820s and 1830s. Americans then were optimistic about the perfectability of individuals and their ability to achieve anything if only artificial limits to their action were removed. By demanding the destruction of oaths, privilege, and aristocracy, and by lauding the power of the people once those limits were gone, Antimasonry vented the popular democratic faith of the age. If the government and the laws could not exterminate Masonry, the people could by voting. "In our country, is not Free Masonry subject to the mighty sovereignty of public opinion? Must it not surrender all its strongholds to the . . . will of the majority?" The majority, asserted Antimasons, could do anything it wanted. "There is a moral force in public opinion, which must, in this free country, crush everything, however powerful which is arrayed against it." The people, summarized a New York county convention, "are the proper judges of the evils which should be driven from among them, and the expediency and propriety of the means to be adapted for that purpose; . . . the ballot boxes afford a remedy peculiarly adapted to the removal of all evils which may be beyond the reach of judicial, executive, or legislative departments of government."

This populistic, antielitist appeal attracted men who were frustrated with economic and social developments and who despaired of action by government to redress their grievances. Antimasons not only voiced the anger of such men, but they identified a target that because of its pervasiveness could be blamed for all of society's wrongs. More than being a mere catchall for protests, Antimasons promised a solution by which the average man could regain control of government. It provided as well hope for those who wanted to perfect society by removing the limits from individual behavior.

Among the poor and the aggrieved, these arguments that the people could destroy privilege and effect reform by voting had potent appeal. Antimasonry was a protest of the discontented against the elite that ran both major parties. Proclaiming political participation a panacea, Antimasonry actually drew many new voters into the political arena, particularly in Vermont and Massachusetts, and most of these came from poor farmers who had previously been apathetic about politics or pessimistic about their ability to influence government.

In most places, Antimasonry began as a movement of poor farmers against the privileged rich whom they identified as Masons. In the birthplace of the movement in western New York, many farmers were tenants of the Holland Land Company or the Pulteney and Hornby Estates. They suffered from the high rents charged by their absentee landlords, and they responded enthusiastically to such Antimasonic demands as "Justice to the Old Settlers . . . opposed to the Aristocratic measures of the Agents of the Pulteney and Hornby Estates." Strong Antimasonic counties such as Chatauqua, Cattaraugus, and Allegany in southwestern New York, Windham and Tolland in Connecticut, Franklin and Hampshire in Massachusetts, and almost all of Vermont lacked access to economically viable transportation facilities, had no large towns to serve as local markets, and very often possessed poor soil. One or more of these liabilities doomed their inhabitants to subsistence farming. A careful study of Vermont, the state where Antimasons achieved their greatest success, found Antimasons strongest in the poorest towns, those with the lowest tax assessments and lowest values per acre and per dwelling, whereas the National Republicans, their major foes, tended to come from wealthier towns with more expensive homes.

The major exceptions to this pattern of bleak rural poverty were some relatively prosperous areas along the western part of the Erie Canal in New York and near cities in southeastern and southwestern Pennsylvania. Masonic lodges were primarily located in cities, and many farmers despised the cities themselves for their aristocratic pretensions, wealth, and cosmopolitanism. Although Antimasons could not carry Rochester, Pittsburgh, Harrisburg, and Lancaster, the surrounding counties were staunch Antimasonic areas.

To show that Antimasons initially were poor farmers who responded to the party's populistic and egalitarian rhetoric is, however, not to solve all the problems about the party's popularity. Most Americans in the 1820s were farmers; yet only a minority located in certain areas of certain states voted for the party. Egalitarianism, as Tocqueville pointed out, was a characteristic of the age. All parties appealed to it, and many people clearly channeled their resentment of the establishment through the Jacksonian party, the hated foes of Antimasonry. Jackson's popularity in the South on the Indian and slavery issues, for example, blocked the formation of any viable political opposition there, including political Antimasonry. Jealousy of the rich, moreover, probably was and still is a constant trait of the poor. Surely it existed before and after the appearance of Antimasonry. Simply demonstrating that poor farmers used the party as a vehicle for their protests and resentments does not explain why the movement attained such strength *when* it did or why some poor farmers and not others supported it.

To be sure, the Morgan affair in 1826 had much to do with the timing of the movement. Yet the frenzy of Antimasonry, the anguished fears about "usurpations" of government, and the subversion of republicanism suggest that more was involved. Developments in the 1820s aggravated the economic burdens of certain farmers, intensified their resentment of the rich, often increased their economic and cultural subordination to cities, and thereby heightened rural antagonisms toward urban arrogance and dominance. These changes and the subsequent dislocation contributed to Antimasonry's sudden strength in the late 1820s by allowing it to become the major voice of rural hostility to cities. Equally important, many of these developments were blamed on incumbent state administrations. Antimasonry's cries that Masons had stolen the government from the people gained enormous appeal precisely because so many people had specific grievances against state governments in the late 1820s. Economic and social developments exacerbated class, cultural, and regional antagonisms that Antimasons were in a unique position to exploit, because their charge that wealthy men controlled both National Republicans and Democrats was in fact true in most states.

In Vermont, depression ruined the lot of poor farmers who were already struggling unsuccessfully to scratch a living from the thin soil of their hilly farms. Between 1790 and 1810, people had flocked to the state with great expectations from its virgin lands, but lack of transportation had kept most of their farming at the subsistence level. By the 1820s, the soil was depleted, sources of timber were exhausted, and insect blights ravaged the wheat crop. Those who could afford to buy enough land turned to sheep raising, but this effort, like the English inclosures, forced many marginal farmers off the land. Newspapers in Antimasonic towns like Windsor warned poor farmers not to sell to their richer sheep-raising neighbors, but the process went on inexorably. These disastrous developments caused massive emigration from the state in the 1820s and 1830s, especially from the towns where wool raising was most heavily concentrated, and Antimasons tended to be strongest in those towns as well. Just when dislocation intensified the resentment of the poor against their rich neighbors, many Vermonters were complaining that their unrepresentative state government, which allowed "less than one fourth of the state [to make] laws for the whole, and have control of appointments," was unrepublican. Because nearly all the prominent legislators and lawyers in the state belonged to Masonic lodges, because rich men ran both the National Republican and Democratic parties, the poor directed their wrath against the establishment by flocking to the Antimasonic party, which promised to return government to the people and advance political democracy. A shrewd trio of political leaders built a thorough organization throughout the state, and beginning in 1831 the Antimasons elected the governor and controlled the legislature for the next five years.

The completion of the Erie Canal in 1825 gave products grown on the rich soils of upstate New York and beyond cheap access to eastern markets. This development seriously threatened Massachusetts farmers, who tilled exhausted land and could not compete with the influx of western goods. Declining incomes forced many farmers in Antimasonic counties like Franklin and Hampshire or Bristol along the Rhode Island border to mortgage their property to the hated banks and insurance companies of Boston. They were further outraged after 1825, when Boston and Worcester capitalists sought state support for a railroad between the two cities that would eventually run on to Albany. This would bypass them and result only in higher taxes and more western competition. Although farmers with aid from coastal towns and other areas not on the projected line defeated the scheme in the legislature and forced the chartering of a private road in 1831, this effort, as well as the action by National Republicans from those cities to defeat Antimasonic state senators in disputes over seats, increased mistrust of the urban bastions of National Republicanism. Antimasons were quick to exploit regional and cultural resentment. Their conventions constantly complained that the state legislature was under "the social influence of the aristocracy of Boston" while the National Republicans were "completely under the control of the ultra aristocracy, the ultra Federalism, and the ultra Freemasonry of Boston and Worcester."

If the Erie Canal imperiled New England farmers and benefited New York City, it proved a mixed blessing to upstate New York farmers. The canal increased the subordination of farmers to the merchants and lawyers of the canal towns, and Antimasons drew much more support from areas just removed from the canal than from those commercial centers. Those who shipped on the canal, moreover, feared that the Democratic legislature wanted to raise toll rates. Other farms in the central portion of the state around the Finger Lakes or in the southwestern counties had no outlets to the canal, and those landlocked regions resented the refusal of the Democratic legislature to build branch canals to serve them.

Because Antimasonry became the major anti-Democratic party in New York when the Adams organization collapsed after 1828, skillful leaders like Thurlow Weed, William Henry Seward, and Francis Granger seized on these and other grievances against the Democratic state administration to convert the party into a broad opposition coalition. Having already identified the Albany Regency with absentee landlords, Antimasons vowed to oppose higher tolls on the Erie Canal and demanded immediate construction of the Chenango Canal to help the central part of the state. To capture the vote of Workingmen's parties—anti-Regency parties that sprang up in 1829 and 1830 in eastern cities—Antimasons adopted some of their favorite measures like the abolition of the militia and of imprisonment for debt. When Thurlow Weed launched his Albany *Evening Journal* in March, 1830, he proclaimed not only his undying devotion to Antimasonry but his zealous advocacy of these additional measures. Before the state convention in 1830, Weed and Seward carefully arranged the nomination of a Workingman for lieutenant governor, and to the dismay of purists who hated manipulation of people's conventions pushed it through. Their platform called for internal improvements and "the securing of the rights of citizens by equal legislation," an appeal to the Workingmen's hatred of monopolies as well as to fears of Masonry's privileges. In 1831, Antimasons worked for the cessation of imprisonment for debt and denounced the privileged banking corporations chartered by the Regency. The main reason why the Antimasonic ticket received almost half the popular vote in 1830 was that the deft politicians who led the party had already constructed a heterogeneous opposition coalition on the framework of a spontaneous grass-roots movement. Their success meant that the party's voting support widened from its initial base of poor farmers to move into the urban middle class.

Similarly, efforts to compete with the Erie Canal in Pennsylvania after 1825 contributed to Antimasonic strength there by allowing the party to become the major antiurban, anti-Democratic force in the state. There, too, the party included more than just poor farmers. Under pressure from Philadelphia to tap the western market that New York was capturing, Democratic administrations began to build the Pennsylvania Canal System to link that metropolis with western waters. Although it was finally completed to Pittsburgh in 1834, its tortuously slow and expensive construction angered various groups who became the backbone of Antimasonic support in the state. Thrifty Germans in the southeast, especially those in Dauphin, Lebanon, Lancaster, and Chester Counties, whose trade flowed down the Susquehanna River to Baltimore and who therefore would not benefit from the canal, denounced it as an unnecessary expense that would raise their taxes to help wealthy Philadelphia merchants. Philadelphia's opposition in the legislature to a charter for a railroad from Lancaster to Baltimore further infuriated them. Taxpayers in other counties like Adams or Bedford, Somerset, Fayette, and Washington in the southwest, objected to the canal because it would bypass them and help others at their expense. At the same time, almost every western county from Allegheny north to Erie hoped that branches of the canal system would be built through it, for it was unclear whether the terminus would be on the Ohio River or Lake Erie. Competing with each other for construction funds, all these western counties chafed with impatience at the delay in construction, and they blamed that delay on the Democratic policy of building branch canals into the northeast before completing the main line. Whether they opposed all construction or thought that the west was being short-shrifted, all these areas proved fertile ground for Antimasonic recruitment. All could blame imperious Philadelphia and the bungling Democratic state administration for the disastrous canal policy, and rural delegates to the 1829 state Antimasonic convention vilified Philadelphia as "overweening, arrogant, and dictatorial." Although the sincerity of rural Antimasonic hostility to Philadelphia is undeniable, it is somewhat misleading, for on the complex canal issue Philadelphians were just as eager as westerners to complete the main line first and as eastern

Germans to stop wasting money and increasing the state debt by building branches. Ironically, the Antimasons received some votes from impatient Philadelphians themselves, whereas elsewhere Antimasonic strength came from areas on proposed western branches that hated Philadelphia for its opposition to those branches. The main point is that for different reasons people in southern and western Pennsylvania disliked Democratic economic policies. Antimasonic attacks on the Masonic usurpation and corruption of the legislature made the party the perfect vehicle for their protests against that policy. There were other reasons for Antimasonic antagonism to the Democrats, but, as in New York, because of the vacuum created by the defeat of Adams, Antimasonry by 1830 was not a single-issue crusade but a diverse, broad-based anti-Democratic coalition.

Economic developments in the 1820s thus help explain why Antimasonry emerged so strongly at the end of that decade and why some people supported it, but what most distinguished Antimasonic farmers from the agrarian adherents of other parties was their fervent desire to Christianize society and abolish immorality. Evangelical religious persuasions reinforced the agrarian antagonism to cities already aggravated by economic dislocations. Only if one understands that Antimasonry was at base a religious crusade against sin can one fathom the intensity of the movement. The birthplace of Antimasonry in western New York was called the Burned-over District because it had been singed by so many frenetic religious revivals. Among the sons of New England who settled there, millennialism, Mormonism, and all kinds of other isms flourished. In New England itself, Antimasons recruited from evangelical sects— Baptists, Methodists, and rural Congregationalists—that stressed the importance of individual conscience and of the conversion experience, and who thought that men should earn salvation by reforming themselves and society. In Ohio's Western Reserve and Michigan, Yankee Presbyterians and Baptists moved through Sabbatarian and temperance pressure groups to Antimasonry and then to Whiggery. The German sects that supported Antimasonry in southeastern Pennsylvania—Dunkards, Mennonites, German Reformed, and others—matched their abhorrence of taxation only with their abomination of secret societies, while elsewhere in the state Antimasons drew from Presbyterians who also despised secret societies and from Quakers.

Evangelical Antimasons condemned Masonry as "an infidel society at war with true Christianity" because it interposed oaths and pagan rituals between a man and his conscience, the only proper arbiter of his behavior. "All ceremonies and appendages of the Masonic Institution . . . lead on to . . . *blank Atheism,*" warned Antimasons. "The Institution . . . strikes at the basis of all morality and religion." Antimasons compared Masonic rituals and hierarchy to Roman Catholicism, which evangelical Protestants considered anathema. "Popery and Freemasonry [are] schemes equally inconsistent with republicanism," declared a Pennsylvania newspaper. Every escape from the "trammels of these horrible oath-binding systems" was an "emancipation from the very fangs of despotism." Other Antimasons in that state charged that the Democrats "for the last six years have priest-ridden the Commonwealth." Akin to the Illuminati, who had fomented the anticlerical and irreligious French Revolution, Masonry had to be destroyed to protect Protestantism and the moral order.

Just as specific events in the 1820s had heightened the economic resentment of poor farmers toward wealthy cities, so certain conditions and developments in that decade increased their religious antagonism toward Masonry and the urban establishment it was believed to represent. The aggressiveness of the evangelical sects sprang in part from their anxiety about the progressive secularization of American society. Antimasons abhorred the irreligion they associated with cities, and their antiurbanism, to an extent, was a defense of "that old time religion" against the forces of modernization and cosmopolitanism. Radical democrats in their political views, evangelicals were orthodox fundamentalists in their religious outlook. They despaired at the rise of deism and rationalism in American society, and they disliked the more liberal, less orthodox denominations like Unitarianism, which had such appeal to men of wealth in the cities. Much of the hatred of Boston and Worcester in Massachusetts sprang from the antipathy rural Baptists and Congregationalists felt toward the Unitarian elite of those cities and toward the National Republican party, which that elite dominated.

Probably crucial in fostering the Antimasonic crusade was the failure of the drive to stop Sunday mail service. In 1825, Congress extended postal and all other public services to Sunday. Horrified evangelicals regarded this "desecration" of the Sabbath as a symbol of the moral decline of American life. Presbyterian and Congregational clergymen organized a massive petition campaign in the late 1820s to stop the Sunday mails, but in 1829 a Democratically controlled Senate committee explicitly stated that declaring Sunday a day of rest would deprive non-Christians and irreligious people of their rights. This position, reiterated in 1830 by Senator Richard Johnson, gained enormous popularity among the urban poor who disliked any restraints on their Sunday activities. Evangelical Protestants, however, were furious. In areas like Michigan, evangelicals who had participated in the petition campaign moved into Antimasonry when it collapsed. In the East, its leaders probably did not because they were urban and wealthy, but many of the rural lower classes who sympathized with the campaign and signed petitions did. Certainly, Antimasonry was associated with the campaign, and its foes called it the Church and State party. In any case, the failure of the Sabbatarian drive made rural evangelicals respond all the more ardently to the Antimasonic appeal that people could purify society by going to the polls. The Senate's decision forever branded the Democratic party as the party of irreligion, whereas National Republicans seemed to be a party of snobbish aristocrats. The only recourse for rural Protestants who hoped to restore morality to American society was the Antimasonic crusade.

Antimasonry, then, presented a powerful appeal to frustrated voters. The Antimasons perceived "an insidious and dangerous enemy" so evil that "the safety of Government and Religion, the rights of citizens, and the impartial administration of justice required that this institution should be banished from our soil." The Antimasonic insistence that so long as Masonry existed the machinery of government would be corrupted struck a responsive chord among those who disliked government policies but who felt powerless to affect government decisions. Antimasons not only explained why government was so unresponsive and why so much inequity existed in a society dedicated to equal opportunity, but they also provided a method for people to right those wrongs. In the process, they vastly widened the horizons of what people would demand from government and politics. To be sure, the immediate target of the aroused majority was the Masonic order, but Antimasonry's populistic message had much broader implications. Poor farmers who hated the rich, especially the domineering city dweller, groups everywhere who were disenchanted with incumbent administrations, and evangelical Protestants horrified at the immorality of society all took comfort in the Antimasonic promise that the people could mend any fault by voting.

The very sources of Antimasonic strength help explain the third party's rapid demise. Their vehement assaults decimated Masonry's ranks as members resigned and lodge after lodge folded. Shrunken Masonic membership deprived Antimasonry of its original justification and hastened its adoption of new reform positions, as in New York and Pennsylvania. The popularity of the movement, moreover, attracted politicians who were more interested in building a new, winning anti-Jackson coalition than in fighting the Masons, and these men rapidly gained control of what had begun as a grass-roots, antipolitician movement.

The politicians who had converted Antimasonry in New York into a broad anti-Democratic coalition were determined to lead the national party in the same direction. At the national convention in September, 1830, New York delegates succeeded in calling the first presidential nominating convention to nominate a candidate in Baltimore the following September. When the National Republicans arranged for their own convention to meet in the same city shortly after the Antimasonic gathering, the way seemed open for a union of the opposition. Thurlow Weed and W. H. Seward now set out to find a candidate to facilitate that merger. They first asked Clay to renounce his Masonry, but he refused and denounced the Antimasons. Then they negotiated with other men, and when the Antimasonic convention met, John McLean of Ohio and former President Adams were the favorites. McLean withdrew, however, after it became clear that the National Republicans would nominate Clay no matter what the Antimasons did. The delegates then rejected Adams in favor of a new face. Weed and other New Yorkers pushed through the nomination of William Wirt of Maryland, who had been attorney general under Adams. Purist Antimasons were sufficiently strong to restrict the platform and address to standard criticisms of Masonry, but the selection of Wirt revealed the party's continuing shift to expediency. A Mason who had never renounced his oaths, Wirt made clear in his letter of acceptance that if elected he would not proscribe Masons from federal office. Thus, the Antimasonic presidential candidate repudiated one of the party's fundamental goals.

How far the party had drifted from its original purpose to become an eclectic coalition became clear in the campaign. Undaunted by the separate presidential candidates, Antimasonic and National Republican leaders in Ohio, Pennsylvania, and New York agreed to back common gubernatorial candidates, and Antimasons ran primarily on state and national economic issues, denouncing Jackson's bank veto and praising the American System. Of more importance, in all those states the two parties voted for the same slates of presidential electors, although they endorsed different candidates. In New York, Weed crafted a ticket equally divided between the two parties. Pennsylvania's National Republicans withdrew their slate and substituted the Antimasonic ticket, whereas in Ohio that process was reversed. It was carefully kept ambiguous whom the electors would vote for if they won, although many voters thought they would support the man with the best chance of beating Jackson. A minority of purist or radical Antimasons in these states protested these arrangements, and some refused to vote. Such gestures and defections, however, merely confirmed the fact that the purists had lost control of the party to politicians with other goals. In Pennsylvania, moreover, Germans in the southeastern counties continued to support the Antimasonic gubernatorial candidate Joseph Ritner, but they switched to Jackson or stayed home in the presidential contest. Only in New England did Antimasons reject coalition with the National Republicans and run separate Wirt tickets. Although they agreed with Clay's supporters on national issues like the tariff, the Bank, and internal improvements, Antimasons in Rhode Island, Connecticut, Massachusetts, and Vermont regarded the National Republicans as their major foes in state politics, and they refused to cooperate. The result of these confused arrangements is that it is impossible accurately to calculate Wirt's aggregate vote. Antimasons undoubtedly contributed significantly to the anti-Jackson vote in New York, Pennsylvania, Massachusetts, and Connecticut, but Vermont was the only state in the country that Wirt carried.

The 1832 election demonstrated the futility of Antimasonry as a national party and its inability to deliver all the support it could muster in state elections. The politicians who now ran the party and who were interested in defeating the Democrats, not just righteous crusading, realized that they could not attempt another national campaign. But there were four years until the next presidential election, and that hiatus allowed state Antimasonic parties to continue to flourish where they were strong, as in Vermont, Massachusetts, and Pennsylvania. As the presidential campaign of 1836 approached, however, pressures grew for assimilation of the Antimasons into the new Whig party, the successor to the National Republicans. By 1836, most Antimasonic organizations had at least formed alliances with the Whigs behind tickets pledged to William Henry Harrison. The reasons for this merger are clear. Most Antimasonic leaders had always opposed the national policies of Jackson, and the Democracy's stand on Sunday laws damned it with Antimasonry's evangelical supporters. The bitterness of the Antimasonic years, moreover, made lifelong anti-Democrats of many other voters. Not all Antimasonic voters joined the Whigs, however, and to trace the disintegration of the party and the destinations of its voters one must look briefly at the individual states.

The party disappeared first in Ohio, Michigan, and New York. Never very strong in the Buckeye State, it died there for all intents and purposes after the 1832 election. Antimasons there united immediately with the Whig party when it emerged. Evangelical religious attitudes caused Michigan's Antimasons to follow suit when the Whigs organized in that territory in 1835. Michigan's Antimasonic Presbyterians never forgave the Democrats for their insistence on Sunday mail deliveries, and they also identified them with popery. The Whigs, who had organized in Michigan primarily to prohibit alien Catholic voting, simply followed Antimasonry in that state as a vehicle of militant Presbyterianism. In New York, the Whig party existed in fact if not in name in the coalitions Weed arranged behind Francis Granger in 1830 and 1832. By the latter year, Antimasons were aiming their cries about subversion of the rule of law more at King Andrew's defiance of the people's representatives in Congress than at Masonry, and the banks chartered by the Albany Regency became the new monster they wished to slay. Antimasons disbanded their formal organization after their defeats in the legislative elections of 1833. In 1834, in response to Jackson's removal of federal deposits from the Bank of the United States, Weed lent his energies and the columns of the *Evening Journal* to building the Whig party. The state convention in September nominated Seward as the first Whig candidate for governor, and other erstwhile Antimasons like Granger, Weed, and Millard Fillmore became prominent Whig leaders.

The same pattern appeared in the two states where the party lasted longest, Vermont and Pennsylvania. Because Vermont Antimasons agreed with the Whigs on national questions and because their own party was so strong, they saw at first no advantage in disbanding their own organization. They continued therefore to elect a governor until 1836. In that year, the Whigs endorsed their state ticket and their slate of electors pledged to Harrison and Granger, and this action facilitated the final merger of the two parties in 1837. As in New York, Antimasons received major leadership roles in return for abandoning their separate organization. The Whig gubernatorial candidate in 1837 was an Antimason, as were two members of the new state central committee. Pennsylvania's Antimasons, like Vermont's, were much stronger than the Whigs at first, and they therefore maintained their independent organization until after 1840. A division among the Democrats allowed the Antimasons to elect Joseph Ritner governor for a three-year term in 1835, and that victory no doubt prolonged the life of the party. But the Antimasons were so successful in dictating terms to the Whigs that they saw no reason to abandon their party anyway. In 1836, for example, the Whigs meekly endorsed the Antimasonic nomination of Harrison for president. Finally, in September, 1839, Whigs and Antimasons met in a state anti-Van Buren convention and recommended the nomination of Harrison for president in 1840 as the best way to unite the opposition in Pennsylvania. Even after the Whigs became the dominant opposition party in the state, Antimasonic influence was so strong that in many areas the party called itself "Whig and Antimasonic" until the 1850s.

Only in some New England states did significant portions of Antimasonic voters, though not the leaders, join the Democratic party instead of the Whigs. In those states, National Republicans had constituted the main opposition to Antimasonry, and some Antimasons were reluctant to sign up with the Whigs. Although Antimasons formed coalitions with the Whigs in Connecticut and eventually joined that party after their poor showing in 1835, in Rhode Island they coalesced with the Democrats to elect an Antimasonic governor from 1833 to 1837. After 1833, however, more and more dissident Antimasons broke from this coalition, and by 1836 the original Antimasonic strength was evenly divided between Whigs and Democrats. The Whigs cemented their portion of that vote in 1838 when they nominated William Sprague, a one-time Antimason, for governor. Massachusetts' Antimasons never won a statewide election, coming closest in 1833 when they ran John Quincy Adams for governor. In 1835, they threw their support to the Whig candidate for governor, but at the same time they endorsed a Democrat for lieutenant governor and boomed Martin Van Buren for president. In 1836, most of their leaders marched into the Whig ranks, but the majority of voters apparently failed to follow and joined the Democrats instead. Van Buren won 45 percent of the vote that year, a proportion far higher than any other Democratic presidential candidate obtained before the Civil War, and in 1839 the Democrats won the governorship with the aid of rural voters whom the Antimasons had brought to the polls for the first time.

Although Antimasonry had a relatively brief existence as a separate political party, it made a lasting contribution to American politics and to the two-party system that succeeded it. Although Antimasons passed laws outlawing extrajudicial oaths and although they nearly annihilated Masonry, their most significant impact in the short run was shaping the northern Whig party. Antimasonry provided the bulk of Whig voters and leadership in Pennsylvania, New York, and Vermont and probably in Michigan, although the Antimason party disappeared there several years before the Whigs emerged as a state party. Certainly, in those states and others, Antimasonry left Whigs a legacy of egalitarianism and evangelism. Antimasonic leaders among the Whigs like Weed and Seward in New York or Stevens in Pennsylvania were much more willing to rabble-rouse and organize lower-class voters than patrician National Republicans had been. That Antimasons put forth Harrison in 1836 suggests that the Whig Log Cabin-Hard Cider campaign of 1840 owed as much to Antimasonic influence as to an imitation of Jacksonianism. Similarly, Antimasonic voters among the Whigs remained moralistic crusaders susceptible to isms, and they imparted to Whiggery a Sabbatarian, protemperance, and antislavery spirit in the North that shaped national and state campaigns and often did more than economic issues to define the Whig and Democratic electorates. Most important, Antimasonry raised the expectations of voters about politics and the role of "the people" in the governmental process. Much of the subsequent political debate in the 1830s revolved around widening the role of the common man in politics, driving the aristocratic establishment from power, and equalizing chances for economic gain. Both parties paralleled Antimasonic rhetoric. The Democrats emphasized the protection of individuals from monopolies and privilege, whereas the Whigs iterated Antimasonry's optimistic belief that government and legislation should be used to improve and perfect American society both morally and economically.

Antimasonry, then, was the first political movement to capture and exploit the feeling of boundlessness that seized Americans after the War of 1812. Because the privileged Masonic order seemed a major restraint on the aspirations of the people, they demanded its destruction to unleash true democracy and majority rule. By the 1850s, however, optimism about democracy and America's future had declined. Chaotic social and economic dislocations in that decade imperiled traditional values, and those who felt most threatened searched for ways to impose order and control on their changing society. Fears of displacement and ugly prejudice against Catholics and foreigners, widely blamed for society's ills, replaced the faith in complete democracy so characteristic of earlier decades. To apprehensive people as in the 1820s, government seemed unresponsive and politics beyond popular control, but this time they identified as the culprit, not a secret society, but the mechanisms of political parties themselves. To protest the control of regular parties by men who ignored their demands or fraternized with their enemies, impatient citizens created a secret society of their own that resembled Masonry in its oaths and hierarchical structure. By proscribing Catholics and immigrants from political participation either as officeholders or voters, this Know Nothing order entered politics to limit democracy rather than spread it, although Know Nothingism too acted in the name of preserving republican government. Denouncing politicians and championing the people, in a fashion similar to Antimasonry, Know Nothingism became so strong that it disrupted both the Whig and Democratic parties and forced a reorganization of politics that helped bring on the Civil War.

Like Antimasonry, Know Nothingism began in New York. In response to the increasing immigration of the 1840s, a New York City nativist named Charles Allen founded the secret Order of the Star Spangled Banner, a superpatriotic fraternal society with membership restricted to native-born Protestants. Participants learned rituals, grips, and passwords as they were initiated to different degrees of membership; when asked by outsiders about the order, they answered, "I know nothing," thereby giving the organization its popular name. Founded in 1849 as a social organization, the order from the start attempted to apply pressure to existing political parties to nominate only native-born American Protestants for public office. In 1852, the society, which was languishing with a small membership, was taken over by members of another nativist group, the Order of United Americans, which had been established by New York businessmen in 1844 and which had formerly eschewed political activity. Under the dynamic leadership of James W. Barker, the order now expanded its membership rapidly. Lodges blossomed throughout New York State in 1853 and 1854, and, as organizers fanned out from New York, lodges spread to other states as well until, in contrast to Antimasonry, Know Nothingism had organized throughout the country. As membership grew, an elaborate structure was created in pyramid fashion from local councils or lodges to city and county councils to state councils and finally to a grand national council composed of seven delegates from each state council. As early as June, 1854, the national council adopted a national constitution that defined membership requirements and postulated the oaths for various degrees. According to this plan, each state council had the responsibility for chartering new local councils and recruiting members.

Beginning in 1853, but especially in 1854, the order entered politics by secretly backing its members or other candidates from the tickets of existing parties who shared its desire to limit officeholding to native-born Protestants and to prevent immigrants from voting by lengthening the naturalization period for aliens. In these early elections, Know Nothings frequently astounded political observers by keeping their choices secret and electing men whom the opposition did not even know were in the race for various local offices. In 1855 and 1856, however, the Know Nothings abandoned total secrecy and held open conventions as the American party on the state and national level, although this process occurred at different rates in different states. By then, they had become a full-fledged third party whose avowed determination to reduce the political power of Catholics and foreigners attracted widespread support.

Indeed, between 1853 and 1856, Know Nothingism was the fastest growing political movement in the country, though these were also the years that the rival antislavery Republican party began. In an atmosphere of popular hysteria about Catholics, hundreds of thousands of men joined the lodges, including thousands who had never bothered to vote before. The precise membership is impossible to determine; contemporary estimates ranged from 800,000 to 1.5 million. But its political potency is clear. In 1854, Know Nothings captured the statehouse and almost every seat in the Massachusetts legislature, and they made impressive showings in Pennsylvania, New York, and elsewhere. By 1855, they controlled all the New England states except Vermont and Maine and were the major anti-Democratic party in the Middle Atlantic states, California, and such slave states as Maryland, Virginia, Kentucky, Tennessee, Georgia, Alabama, Mississippi, and Louisiana. In direct contests that year, they defeated the incipient Republican party in New York and Massachusetts and overwhelmed it in Pennsylvania. A discouraged Republican reported from the Bay State after the 1855 election, "The Election is most disastrous. . . . The people will not confront the issues at present. They want a Paddy hunt & on a Paddy hunt they will go." In other northeastern states, the party was so strong the Republicans could not even form, although in the Midwest Republicans became the major opposition party by absorbing the Know Nothings. Because of the party's national strength, many expected it to carry the presidential election in 1856. Millard Fillmore, the party's candidate that year, garnered 871,731 votes, over 21 percent of the total, even though by then, as will be shown, the majority of northern Know Nothings were supporting the Republican John C. Frémont. Only three years after the party began political activity, Fillmore received a larger share of the popular vote than any other third party candidate for president in our history except Theodore Roosevelt in 1912.

How can one explain this remarkable performance? What accounts for the extraordinary popularity of the Know Nothings and the strength of anti-Catholic prejudice at that particular time? Protestant propagandists had denounced the Roman Church since the birth of the nation, and ugly anti-Catholic riots had flared up in the 1830s and 1840s, but belief in a papal plot had never been so widespread nor anti-Catholicism so intense. Nativist parties had captured municipal elections in the 1840s, but their strength paled next to that of the Know Nothing eruption in the 1850s. One must explain why, even though immigration had been heavy since at least 1846, it was only after 1852 that reaction was so strong.

One wonders as well why the aroused bigotry that sparked Know Nothingism was not channeled through the regular parties. Just as with Antimasonry, it seemed possible that the major anti-Democratic party could have exploited the issues that gave birth to the new organization, for since the 1840s, in New York, Pennsylvania, Maryland, and elsewhere, the Whigs had been recognized as the party of temperance reform and nativism, issues on which the Know Nothings capitalized. In many elections, because Catholics were identified with the Democrats, anti-Catholic brickbats had been standard Whig ammunition. Why did the Whigs fail to benefit from the new salience of these issues in the 1850s? Why a new party?

Historians have traditionally answered these questions in terms of the sectional crisis of the 1850s. The Kansas-Nebraska Act of 1854 supposedly destroyed the Whig party. Outraged northerners readily deserted it for more militant antislavery coalitions, and southerners abandoned the party once its national power was broken. The Know Nothing order then arose in the vacuum created by the Whig party's disappearance. To it migrated opportunistic politicians, homeless voters with no place else to go, and especially conservative Whigs from the North and South who supported an issue that would bring slaveholders and abolitionists together and thus save the Union. Know Nothingism, then, according to the traditional wisdom, emerged in such strength only after the slavery issue had shattered the Whig party, and it gained as much from its availability to political refugees, especially unionists caught in a sectional crisis, as from its anti-Catholicism.

This picture contains much truth. Certainly, many conservatives voted for Millard Fillmore in 1856, and the desire to preserve the union was probably a major source of his strength in the South and the border states. Know Nothingism in many southern states was essentially a continuation of the Whig party under another name, a vehicle through which Whigs could contend with their longtime foes, the Democrats, for control of state governments and congressional seats. In northern cities such as New York and Philadelphia, as well, conservative fears for the Union aided Fillmore in the presidential election.

But there is much that this "political vacuum thesis" does not explain. Of most importance, the 1856 voting support of the Know Nothings was not always the same as their early support in 1854 and 1855. As in the case of Antimasonry, the nature of Know Nothingism changed very rapidly, and the unionism of 1856 does not necessarily explain the initial support for the party. For example, many northern Know Nothings of 1854 and 1855 voted Republican in 1856, and conservatism cannot account for their behavior. Nor were the Know Nothings simply refugees with no where else to go. In most areas of the North where the Know Nothings flourished, the Whigs had always opposed slavery extension, and there was no reason why voters had to leave the party to protest that act. The elections of 1854 and 1855 were local and state elections in which northern Whigs did not have to worry about defending their southern colleagues, and they could have run anti-Nebraska campaigns in those years. Indeed, in Pennsylvania, New York, and Massachusetts they tried to do precisely that, and in the spring and summer of 1854, Seward and other Whigs optimistically predicted that the Nebraska issue would produce smashing Whig victories in the fall. The Whig party, then, was very much alive in certain northern states in 1854. Yet voters still deserted it in droves for a new party that by and large ignored the slavery issue. Because the slavery issue, like temperance and nativism, should have helped the Whigs in 1854, one must explain why Know Nothingism ever emerged as a third party that attracted the bulk of the anti-Democratic vote away from the Whigs.

The reasons for Whig disintegration are complex, but the important point with regard to the Know Nothings is that the forces producing the movement did not result from Whig collapse but rather helped cause that collapse. Rapid social and economic change in the 1850s intensified anti-Catholicism among lower- and middle-class Protestants while it simultaneously created a hostility to politicians and an impatience with political parties. These sentiments gutted local Whig organizations and produced the initial Know Nothing triumphs. Almost as soon as it appeared, however, the party changed in leadership, support, and direction so that by 1856 it was quite different from the original people's crusade.

Basic to the emergence of Know Nothingism was the massive immigration that began in the 1840s. Between 1846 and 1855, over three million foreigners, mostly Irish and Germans fleeing famine and revolution, flooded our shores. To this alien invasion nativists attributed numerous evils, mentioned endlessly in platforms and pamphlets. Immigrants were alleged to swell the number of slums, violations of the Sabbath, drunkenness, pauperism, brawling, and crime. Know Nothings were wont to list statistics of poor houses and prisons to demonstrate the disproportionate numbers of immigrants found there, and they demanded federal legislation to prevent the dumping of European paupers and criminals on American shores. Furthermore, they blamed immigrant workers for driving wages down and the cost of food and rent up. "Are American *mechanics* to be borne down, crushed, or driven to western wilds?" complained a New York nativist. Politically, the immigrants were believed to subvert the democratic process by voting in blocs easily manipulated by ward bosses and party wire-pullers. Know Nothings, vowed the Virginia state platform in typical language, were "determined to preserve our political institutions in their original purity and vigor, and to keep them unadulterated and unimpaired by foreign influence, either civil or religious." Because of their apparently mindless voting, immigrants should be kept from the polls until they "shall have resided within the United States a sufficient length of time to have become acquainted with the principles and imbued with the spirit of our institutions." Until that time, native Americans should rule America. Like the Antimasons, then, Know Nothings viewed themselves as defending American institutions from a terrible menace.

Know Nothings particularly stressed the dangers to the American political system, and the sharp increase in the political participation of foreigners after 1851 was probably the major proximate cause of the formation of the Know Nothing order. Many states limited suffrage to citizens, and because naturalization required five years, immigrants who arrived in the late 1840s were only beginning to vote in the 1850s. To the dismay of nativists, however, some of the states allowed aliens to vote, and even where they could not, naturalization laws were frequently broken. The laws alone, that is, cannot account for the surge in immigrant voting in the 1850s. As important was the temperance campaign of those years. Maine passed a prohibition law in 1851, and temperance groups applied pressure in other states for similar legislation. Because almost all the immigrants opposed such laws, the prohibition campaign drew them into the political arena for the first time.

The Know Nothing demands for pure ballot boxes and longer naturalization periods reflected their horror at the visible signs of immigrant political strength. In some cities, if all foreigners voted, they could form a majority of the electorate. Between 1850 and 1855, for example, the number of naturalized citizens in Boston tripled, whereas the native-born electorate grew by only 14 percent. Especially galling was the seeming subserviency of both major parties to this emerging vote. Both wooed it by enlisting foreign speakers, lauding revolutionary efforts in Europe, and nominating and appointing foreign officeholders. The chief villain in this respect was the Democratic party, which since Jackson's day had attracted most of the foreign and Catholic vote. Even in the 1830s, Antimasons had denounced the Catholic influence among Democrats, and Franklin Pierce's appointment of James Campbell, an Irish Catholic from Philadelphia, as postmaster general in 1853 confirmed the worst fears of nativists about the political potency of foreigners within the Democratic organization. Not only nativists and Whigs but Protestant Democrats were appalled. In 1853, a Philadelphia Democrat warned Governor William Bigler that "the better part of the Democratic party . . . will not be led by the Irish vote, or contented with it either. If persisted in, the Party will, as large as it is, . . . *cave in.* This Irish influence must & will be put down."

What made this new political assertiveness so ominous to apprehensive nativists was that most of the immigrants were Catholics. American Protestants had long regarded the Catholic Church and its hierarchical organization as antithetical to democracy. Just when Catholic political influence was growing, the Church's clergy provided what some saw as concrete evidence of a long-warned-of papal plot to control the United States. Led by Archbishop John Hughes of New York, Catholic bishops around the country began in 1852 to demand ecclesiastical ownership of church property—that is, a transfer of the physical properties of Catholic churches from lay trustees to the clergy. Nativists viewed this effort as an attempt to increase the economic power of the Church. When the Pope sent a special nuncio named Gaetano Bedini to the United States to arbitrate some disputed claims in 1853, propagandists called Bedini the vanguard of the papal invasion. The most menacing action of the Church, however, was the effort by the Catholic clergy to agitate for, and by Democratic legislators who represented them to introduce, laws that would stop Bible reading in public schools and divide school funds so that the taxes Catholics paid would be used to support parochial schools rather than the common school system. Protestants viewed such efforts in Michigan, Ohio, Pennsylvania, Maryland, and New York after 1852 as an assault on public schools. And these actions especially angered middle- and working-class Protestants, who regarded education as the key to social mobility.

These apparent assaults on cherished American values and institutions helped foment an almost hysterical fear of and antagonism to Catholics. Rumors circulated that Irish Catholics planned to massacre Protestants on St. Patrick's Day and that friends of Irish maids threatened their employers with violence. The United States District Attorney reported to Caleb Cushing from Pittsburgh in 1854, in language reminiscent of Antimasonic acceptance of Mason boasting, that Jesuits crowed "that the Catholics number *four millions,* that they are, at the instrumentality of their Bishops and Priests entirely united, and that the visit of the Nuncio Bedini professedly to this Government is intended to form among them an organization so perfect that they will act as a unit in all coming [political] operations." Such fears spawned an anti-Catholicism that was, as observers in New York, Philadelphia, and elsewhere constantly testified, much more vehement than it had been in the 1840s. Even in isolated rural towns, Democrats worriedly reported, "Nearly everybody appears to have gone altogether deranged on Nativism here." "How people do hate Catholics," young Rutherford B. Hayes wrote his uncle after the 1854 elections in Cincinnati, "and what a happiness it was to thousands to show it in what seemed like a lawful manner." Or, as a New Yorker lamented after the 1854 election, "This election has demonstrated that, by a majority, Roman Catholicism is feared more than American slavery." To protect social order, political democracy, and public education, anxious Protestants turned to the Know Nothing party.

The specific grievances against the Catholics after 1852 help account for the intensity of anti-Catholicism and the timing of the Know Nothing movement. But the very ferocity of the bigotry suggests that more was disturbing these voters than the supposed transgressions of the Catholic Church. In many communities, the menace posed by Irish and German Catholics was identified just when rapid economic change was causing widespread dislocations. This dislocation certainly added to the feelings of malaise, disorientation, and frustration with politics as usual that motivated so many Know Nothings. By capturing the rage of these voters and promising a way for them to control the bewildering forces disrupting their lives and destroying their sense of community, Know Nothingism became a more powerful protest movement than Antimasonry had ever been.

The early 1850s were years of mercurial economic fluctuations.

Sharp slumps with subsequent unemployment in 1851 and 1854 accompanied rising prices caused by the California gold strikes. Compounding these problems was a sudden drought in the summer of 1854 that brought trade on the Ohio River to a standstill. Workers connected with the river trade in Pittsburgh, Cincinnati, Louisville, and St. Louis may have lost their jobs or had their wages lowered. Know Nothings were strong in the riverfront wards of those cities, and it seems reasonable that underemployed workingmen facing higher prices vented their wrath on immigrants, whom they blamed for their economic woes.

The major disruptive economic force in these years, however, was the massive railroad construction between 1849 and 1854, especially the opening of the trunk lines between the Atlantic Coast and the Midwest. The completion of the Erie, Baltimore and Ohio, Pennsylvania, and New York Central railroads between 1851 and 1854 abruptly transformed patterns of commerce, methods of manufacturing, and, as a New York State official put it, "the social conditions of our people." Relatively isolated and homogenous communities were now brought into contact with men of different backgrounds as railroads and the telegraph increased communication among towns and as armies of immigrant railroad workers arrived with the tracks. From Pennsylvania, Virginia, Illinois, New York, and elsewhere poured complaints that the immigrant working force on railroads provided the Democrats with a powerful and illegal floating vote. Railroads, moreover, caused food prices to soar in eastern and especially midwestern cities. Because farmers now had easy access to New York and the foreign market by railroad, they could and did raise prices elsewhere.

Faced with inflation and increasing competition, many workers probably lost their jobs as railroads began to take trade away from water routes and to alter manufacturing and commercial relationships. Some towns along rivers and canals were bypassed entirely, and communities that suffered from a lack of railroad transportation may have turned to nativism. But railroads proved mixed blessings to the communities they came to as well. Through lines destroyed the jobs of men in former transshipment centers. Midwestern manufacturers and merchants faced increasing competition from the East, and in certain cities like Pittsburgh and Cincinnati, forwarding and commission merchants and the workers they employed were displaced by the railroads themselves, which provided that service free of charge. In the face of a deluge of eastern goods, those manufacturers who could centralized and enlarged their enterprises; but many could not, and those enlarged businesses simply added to the plight of small manufacturers and artisans whose competitive advantage in local communities was destroyed by the railroads. Indeed, just as the Erie Canal had given new economic leverage to the cities along it and thus increased rural resentment in the 1820s, so railroads drew many communities into the economic nexus of larger cities. By linking towns and increasing the economic domination of larger communities, railroads and the telegraph thus undermined the economic and social security of those who lived in smaller places. In both small towns and larger cities, artisans and the employees of small firms that were shut down or had to lower wages because of the increased competition could easily blame cheap immigrant labor for their plight, especially because many of the new factories employed skilled immigrants. In some small communities as well, like the towns of southern Illinois, local merchants and lawyers joined the Know Nothings to express their resentment at their new subordination to the elites of larger cities. In sum, railroads during the 1850s produced wrenching structural changes in the economies of many communities, either by displacing men employed in the old businesses—whether they be river and canal men or artisans not employed in the new factories—or by eliminating the geographical advantages certain groups had enjoyed. Such disorientation increased prejudice and frustration and caused men to lash out at Catholic immigrants and at the established parties.

Railroads had an equally disruptive impact on the East. Agricultural regions suffered from western competition, and small towns connected to larger cities increasingly fell under their economic sway. By opening up fast, all-weather transportation to the Midwest, moreover, the trunk lines allowed manufacturers to mechanize their factories and use interchangeable parts on a large scale in the 1850s—developments that caused technological unemployment among skilled workmen or at least threatened to reduce them to wage-earner status. Sam Bass Warner has pointed out that the dislocation caused by industrialization and mechanization in Philadelphia drove some workers to nativist politics, and it is likely that the same process occurred in Baltimore, New York, and the New England strongholds of Know Nothingism as well. Studies of the membership of various Massachusetts lodges reveal that Know Nothings came disproportionately from manual workers and artisans—shoemakers, carpenters, wheelwrights, and so forth—who may have suffered displacement or lower wages just as they faced higher prices.

What quantitative and qualitative evidence we have about Know Nothing membership in New England, New York, Pennsylvania, Ohio, Virginia, and elsewhere indicates that Know Nothingism was overwhelmingly a movement of the poor and middling classes. Friends of Know Nothings described the membership as honest and poor workingmen and mechanics, whereas their foes often dismissed them as rabble or thugs. In cities, workers and many from the huge floating population, men who suffered most from the traumatic economic changes of the decade, flocked to Know Nothingism. Along with farmers who feared the cultural menace of alien groups and with the residents of small towns suddenly swamped by outside forces, these disoriented groups struck out at Catholic immigrants upon whom much of the disorder in society could be blamed. Many Democrats joined the movement, but at least three-fifths of its membership, and probably more, were former Whigs.

The suddenness and coincidence of unsettling economic, political, and cultural changes in the early 1850s, then, produced the widespread desire for political action against Catholics and immigrants. But in and of themselves they do not explain why a third party was formed, why the traditional party system and especially the Whigs failed to respond to this demand when the Democracy became an obvious target. Equally crucial to the emergence of Know Nothingism was a hostility to the established parties and politicians because of their refusal to heed the will of the people and take action against their foes. Confronted with the new salience of prohibitionism and nativism, the leaders of the established parties hedged and stalled, for these issues were internally divisive for both organizations. Fearful of alienating certain elements of their coalitions, party leaders did nothing.

This intransigence sparked a voters' revolt against the established party system. As a New York Whig remarked in 1852: "The temperance question, however, will govern not only a large share of the Whig votes but many of the Democrats have pledged themselves to vote for temperance men only, let the consequences be what they will for the two Political

Parties. They think the Temperance question is of far more importance to the people of this state than any other that agitates the public mind." In the face of such pressures, party discipline, which had been remarkably strong in the 1840s, broke down at the grass-roots level in the 1850s. Independent temperance and anti-Catholic splinter parties mushroomed in Boston, Philadelphia, Pittsburgh, Cincinnati, Detroit, and elsewhere. From Maryland, where Independent tickets opposed Democrats and Whigs in 1851 and 1853, an observer lamented to Caleb Cushing, "I was mortified to find so much disorganization." In most cases, these issue-oriented parties sprang from the people and not the professional politicians.

In the specific case of the early anti-Catholic parties and of the Know Nothings in 1854, many who were violently prejudiced against Catholics considered Whig leadership too passive or too moderate on this issue. Although the Whigs often made nativist appeals, the party rarely did anything against Catholics. Even more than the Democrats, the Whigs were usually led by the elite of a community, men who did not feel the pressures from poor Catholic immigrants that were so unsettling to the common man. Important Whig leaders like Seward, moreover, were friendly toward Catholics. Bigots wanted more militant parties.

After 1852, some considered the Whigs not only too passive but actively pro-Catholic. Their presidential candidate that year, Winfield Scott, alienated nativists within and outside the party. Scott had respected Catholic churches in the Mexican War and educated his daughters in convents. A disgusted Ohio Whig wrote even before his nomination that Scott had "compelled the American Armies to prostrate themselves in mud whenever a *crucifix*, or an idolatrous *Doll Baby* passed along." The Order of United Americans bitterly opposed Scott, and the leader of Pennsylvania's separate Native American party reported that "the feelings among my friends is intense—intense hostility to the Whigs." Other observers from the Keystone State wrote Franklin Pierce before the election: "Many honest Protestants among the Whigs are disgusted at the course Scott has taken to secure the Catholic vote and will vote against him." Four years later, the vitriolic Know Nothing Parson Brownlow of Tennessee condemned both parties for their efforts to seek the Catholic vote. Associated with Catholic priests and bishops to woo the Catholic vote, he asserted, were "the worst class of American politicians, designing dema-gogues, selfish office-seekers, and bad men, calling themselves Democrats and 'Old-Line Whigs!' "

Brownlow's attack on politicians was significant, for especially im-portant in causing the revolt against parties and the initial strength of the Know Nothings was a pervasive loss of faith in and animosity toward politicians and the mechanisms of party politics, especially conventions. Rutherford B. Hayes attributed Know Nothing triumphs in Cincinnati in 1854 to, among other things, "a general disgust with the powers that be." From Maryland, St. Louis, Philadelphia, Connecticut, Ohio, and elsewhere came frequent complaints that the people had lost control of the political process because "professional tacticians and wirepullers," "cliques" of corrupt party bosses, and "selfish office-seekers" managed conventions, chose unpopular candidates, and generally frustrated the popular will. Young James A. Garfield recorded in his diary during 1852, "I am exceedingly disgusted with the wire-pulling of politicians and the total disregard for truth in all their operations." A comprehensive statement of the combination of grievances producing Know Nothingism appeared in a letter from a Detroit judge to Justice John McLean in 1855.

> You know that for the last quarter of a century political traders and gamesters have so manufactured public opinion, and so directed party organization, that our Union has been endangered, and bad men elevated to place and power, contrary to the true sentiment of the People. . . . Both parties courted what was called the foreign vote; and the highest aspirants of the Senate, to ensure success, strove which could pay more homage to a foreign Prince, whose ecclesias-tical subjects, constituted so large a portion of this imperium in im-perio. The Papal Power at Rome, apprised fully of this state of things, gave direction to her vassal priesthood, to use their supposed power for the propaganda files, and hence the attack upon our school systems in Cincinnati, New York, Baltimore and Detroit. I give thanks to God, that they commenced the warfare at the time they did, and that their plan was discerned and defeated.

After condemning Whigs and Democrats for fearing to offend the Pope during this crisis, he rejoiced that good men had united secretly so "that *secret* jesuitism in America might be triumphantly met by a *secret Ameri-*

can movement—the leading object of which—is good and competent men for public stations, and the preservation of the freedom of conscience and the right of private interpretation of the scriptures."

This hostility to old parties and politicians helped destroy the Whig party and prevented its resurgence on the basis of the new issues of 1854. Even when the Whigs denounced "papal aggressions" and the Kansas-Nebraska Act, many people were too suspicious of old political chieftains, the aura of corruption and expediency around Whig officeholders of all ranks, and especially the lack of popular control to remain in the party. Gideon Welles of Connecticut perceptively explained the failure of northern Whigs to capitalize on anti-Nebraska sentiment: "The truth is there is a general feeling to throw off both the old organizations and their intrigues and machinery."

This impatience with the old political system and desire for new leadership provided a powerful impetus to the early growth of the Know Nothings. Welles was again acute when he observed of the order: "Many people were justly tired of the old party combinations and discipline, and many, I apprehend, have entered into this new movement with a view of relieving themselves of fetters that they could not otherwise easily cast off." With unusual pith, Charles Sumner explained Know Nothing victories in Massachusetts in 1854: "You will observe the curious course of things in Mass. The explanation is simply this. The people were tired of old parties and they have made a new channel." Much of the appeal of the order was its clearly expressed purpose to destroy the old parties, drive hack politicians from office, and return power to the people. "We are determined to give old party lines and old party hacks a glorious drubbing this fall," vowed a New York Know Nothing in 1854. The correspondence of Know Nothings in that state makes clear that many Silver Greys and other Whigs joined the order explicitly to overthrow the Seward-Weed "dynasty" in their party. "Sewardism and Political Catholicism" were labeled the party's major targets there. Seward's one-time ally Horace Greeley legitimately complained to Schuyler Colfax, "In this state, Know-Nothingism is notoriously a conspiracy to overthrow Seward, Weed, and Greeley, and particularly to defeat Mr. Seward's reelection to the Senate." These disgruntled Whigs objected to the tyrannical power of Weed's machine and to Seward's pro-Catholic proclivities, but the effort to reform politics and break up machines prevailed elsewhere. A Virginian rejoiced to William C. Rives in 1854: "This new and mysterious party called 'Know Nothings' may, and I think will, do good in ridding the country of the trading and trafficking politicians who have had controul [*sic*] of its affairs for years past!" In Pittsburgh, a Know Nothing editor attributed the phenomenal growth of Know Nothingism to "the profound disgust every right-thinking man entertained for the corrupt manner in which the machinery of party had been perverted to suit the base purpose of party wireworkers—an evil they honestly believed the orders would remedy." Even the American national platform of 1855 pledged "hostility to the corrupt means by which the leaders of party have hitherto forced on us our rulers and our political creeds [and] Implacable enmity against the prevalent demoralizing system of rewards for political subserviency, and of punishment for political independence."

One way the Know Nothings promised to return power to the people was to provide a kind of direct primary system by choosing the party's nominees by majority vote in the local lodges or councils. Historians disagree about the extent of popular control in the party, and many contend that state or national councils could dictate the selection of candidates to local lodges. But the correspondence of party leaders makes it amply clear that local lodges made their own decisions despite the selections of state councils. One result of this practice was that the nominal candidate of the Know Nothings for a state office often did not receive the full Know Nothing vote. It is fallacious, therefore, to estimate the order's membership simply by looking at election returns.

Like the Antimasons, the Know Nothings also represented themselves as being the people's party, and they endeavored to make sure their candidates represented the people and not the political machine. In the Midwest, the fusion parties that Know Nothings joined and dominated in states like Indiana referred to themselves as People's parties. Everywhere, though, the Know Nothing rank and file demanded candidates who came from the people, and they often called their nominees "People's Candidates." A Bostonian wrote that one of the Know Nothings' "cardinal principles is to send Representatives 'fresh from the people'—no professional, no politician or any office seeker can have part or lot with them." Pittsburgh's Know Nothings demanded that Pennsylvania's United States senator "should be a new man, fresh from the ranks of the people—clad in American raiment, and not the cast off garments of Whiggery or Democracy." A Know Nothing from western New York summarized the party's appeal to frustrated and rebellious voters in December, 1854:

> There is a prestige surrounding new measures and particularly new men which it is worth our while to concentrate and secure. Under this we have shook off the yoke of political bondage. Under it more than all else we are indebted for our success. Our acts must tally with our throng. Let it be generally understood during the coming presidential campaign that new men are to be the leaders and all the offices filled from the ranks, and I care little by what name we are known, success is sure—but once by our own acts disipate [*sic*] this impression and half our prospects are gone.

Perhaps there is no better proof that rank-and-file Know Nothings demanded a genuine people's party than the fawning letter of that perpetual presidential aspirant Justice John McLean to a member of the order who had suggested him as a presidential nominee. "Suffer not the political hacks of any party to enter into your organization or to control your action. You are the party of the people; make your own candidates from the highest to the lowest, and give no countenance to those who endeavor to make themselves candidates. This should be the work of the people, and they can do it better, than the politicians can do it for them, as has been the practice for years past."

In its early years the Know Nothing party did select most of its local leaders from new men, men who were younger and poorer than most political leaders. Of a sample of Know Nothing leaders in Pittsburgh, over half were younger than thirty-five, 60 percent owned property worth less than $5,000, a proportion much larger than that of the contemporary Whig and Republican parties, and 48 percent were artisans or clerks. Know Nothings in the Massachusetts legislature elected in 1854 were predominantly artisans from the building trades and shop industries, clerks, and rural clergymen, not the farmers and lawyers who had been prominent in former legislatures. A New Haven, Connecticut, resident noted that Know Nothings there would "put an entire set of new men in office who are very little known in any way." "Some of them [are] young men only four years from College and others quite uneducated and as it now appears unfitted for their places." One of the major complaints about Know Nothings who took office concerned their inexperience and incompetence, and these suggest that most of the initial Know Nothing office-holders were political novices.

Know Nothingism, then, generated a powerful reform appeal to voters who felt powerless to control their government. Not only would they take action against immigrants and Catholics, but they would clean up politics, cast aside corrupt wire-workers and party hacks, and put common men in places of political power. Such a reform movement had particular appeal to the young. Everywhere observers noted that young men were especially attracted to the order, and Know Nothingism should be understood in part as a generational revolt of the young against their elders, a revolt that helped break down both major parties. "Whig young men will not follow the lead of King Weed and Co.," explained a New Yorker, and a Philadelphia Democrat lamented to James Buchanan that "there are too many of our young men in it, sons of Democrats, that dont care, have no idea of the rong [*sic*] that they are doing to the country. . . ." In some areas, Know Nothingism allowed the revolt of regions against the dominance of rival towns in their states. In Connecticut, for example, residents of the eastern counties of New London and Windham and of rural Litchfield, areas with few immigrants, flocked to Know Nothingism to protest the control of both major parties and the state government by Hartford and New Haven interests. Much of early Massachusetts Know Nothingism, like Antimasonry there, reflected a protest of the rest of the state against Boston. To all who abhorred the course of American society, who resented their lack of political power to change or halt that course, Know Nothingism provided an attractive channel of protest.

As in the case of Antimasonry, however, the Know Nothings were in part ruined by the very sources of their success. The early triumphs and the growing membership of the order attracted to it, in the words of an indignant nativist, "a set of selfish politicians who cared not a straw about its principles [but] were trying to *use* the order for the promotion of their heartless and sordid aims." The very inexperience of the first Know Nothing leaders allowed these shrewd politicians to achieve dominance in statewide offices. Henry Wilson and a small band of Free Soilers, for example, rose quickly to leadership in Massachusetts, and they supported Henry Gardner for governor in return for Wilson's subsequent election to the United States Senate. Wilson's adeptness in manipulating Massachusetts Know Nothings has caused some historians to view the movement there simply as an extension of the Free Soil antislavery and reform drive; but there is no denying the intensity of anti-Catholic sentiment in the state, especially in view of Know Nothing victories over a separate Republican party in state elections in 1855 and 1856. Similarly, the rapid rise of the erstwhile Democrat Simon Cameron in the Pennsylvania party or of Daniel Ullmann and other office-seeking Silver Grey Whigs in the leadership of the New York Know Nothings does not mean that the prejudice and antiparty sentiment that motivated the vast majority of Know Nothing voters was any less real. Know Nothings in Pennsylvania denounced those legislators who voted for the crafty Cameron, and Ullmann's voluminous correspondence contains scores of letters warning against open alliance with the Silver Greys because it would offend so many Know Nothings. Indeed, the eminence of seasoned politicians in the party by 1855 disillusioned thousands who joined the order to escape the rule of politicos and return power to the people. A North Carolinian complained in 1855 about developments in Pennsylvania and New Hampshire, where the order helped reelect John P. Hale to the Senate: "This struggling and scrambling for office and promotion was one of the very great evils it was the object of our organization to remedy—and yet our success is likely to be jeoparded by the very same evil. The masses are sound but the old party leaders and political hacks, who have come into the order, from selfish purposes, will ruin us, if we are not strictly on our guard."

Additional problems combined with disillusionment to sap Know Nothing strength in some areas as early as 1855. Internal disagreements over the order's secrecy divided its members. Although it is clear that the rituals and passwords attracted the curious, Know Nothingism's secrecy also alienated many voters, including one-time Antimasons, who shared the order's antipathy to Catholics. In the summer of 1855, a Buffalo Know Nothing reported, "There are a great many men in every section of the State who adopt the principles of our party and desire to act with us but are opposed to secret political societies and decline to be with us and of us solely on this ground." From Delaware, a Know Nothing complained, "Men are now daily leaving us, because the K.N.'s have not met their expectations" by dropping secrecy and amalgamating "with the whole mass concurring with them in sentiment." Southerners were especially eager to end secrecy, and many southern state councils decided to do so in 1855. In response to these pressures, Know Nothings held mass meetings and open conventions in some states, but these offended those who favored secrecy and often drove them to separate splinter organizations.

Also offensive to many sincerely interested in political reform and in purifying the ballot boxes was the increasing violence associated with the Know Nothings. In cities, it is clear that Know Nothings did attract gangs of thugs who used force to prevent immigrants from voting. Large bands of armed men literally controlled certain sections of cities on election days, and such tactics led to bloody riots in Louisville, Cincinnati, Baltimore, and New Orleans, among other cities.

Almost as debilitating was the sorry performance of Know Nothing legislatures in 1855. Not only did they support established politicos like Hale, Wilson, and Cameron for the Senate, but in New York Thurlow Weed continued to exercise enough control to persuade some Know Nothing legislators to help reelect the hated Seward to the Senate. Know Nothing efforts to pass stern temperance laws as in Pennsylvania also angered some who had been willing to go along with the party in 1854. More important, the Know Nothings failed to do much against Catholics and foreigners, often because of legislative inexperience. In Massachusetts, attempts to amend the constitution to restrict voting to those who had resided in the country for twenty-one years aborted. Know Nothings succeeded in passing only a literacy test for voting and appointing a committee to investigate Catholic schools and convents. This farcical witch-hunt scandalized the voters because of the excessive imbibing by members as they toured the state. In other states, too, bills on naturalization, voting rights, and officeholding qualifications died in committee or were never brought to a vote on the floor. Efforts by Know Nothings in Congress in 1854 and early 1855 also came to naught as bills to stem immigration never emerged from committee. Although action on economic and political reform legislation was often respectable and although several states passed laws prohibiting the clergy from owning church property, these did not matter to many voters. One of the major attractions of the Know Nothings was their promise to take action against the Catholics and immigrants when the major parties had been unresponsive to popular demands. Once in office, however, they too failed to produce, and thousands of nativists quickly became disillusioned with them.

The emergence of the party into the open in 1855 and the clarification of its principles also destroyed its amorphousness, which had aided it so much in 1854. Because the party was clandestine at first, few people outside the order knew which candidates it was backing. As a result, those men received votes from nonmembers. Often unsuspecting voters were handed a Know Nothing ballot at the polls by men whom they assumed to be regular Whigs or Democrats, and they voted for Americans without even knowing it. More important, widespread evidence from contemporaries indicates that thousands of Irish and German Protestants who hated Catholics initially voted with the Know Nothings. If correspondents from Buffalo can be believed, even some German Catholics who were resisting the efforts of bishops to gain control of church property supported the nativists. In 1855, however, when the bigotry of the Know Nothings against all immigrants and Catholics became clear, these elements were driven to the Democrats in self-defense.

Another result of the identification of parties and clarification of party positions out of the flux and confusion of 1854 was the emergence of the Republican party as a serious competitor of the Know Nothings for the northern anti-Democratic vote. The internal impact of the slavery issue on the American party will be discussed below. The point here is that another party stressing a different issue provided a real challenge to the independent existence of the Know Nothings. In 1855, Republicans were strongest, excluding the Pacific Coast, in the states west of Pennsylvania, in part because they formed alliances with the Know Nothings in most of them. In Ohio, for example, Salmon P. Chase headed the Republican ticket for governor, but all the under offices went to the Know Nothings. Chase and other western Republicans were solicitous not to offend the nativists, and their very adroitness doomed the separate existence of the party, especially when events in Kansas intensified antisouthernism. As a Democrat noted of the 1855 Republican coalition in another state, "Know Nothingism as a *distinct creed* is among the things that *were* in Indiana." In most states east of Ohio, Know Nothings held the upper hand primarily because many voters continued to hate Catholics, whereas incipient Republican leaders there were openly hostile to Know Nothingism and spurned coalition. Weed and Seward started the Republican party in New York, and extremist antislavery men began it in Massachusetts and thus infuriated free-soil Know Nothings like Governor Gardner. In western Pennsylvania, old Antimasons who despised Know Nothingism's secrecy even when approving its anti-Catholicism joined the Republicans, and the open antagonism between Republicans and Know Nothings in other eastern states where the Antimasons had flourished suggests that Antimasonic repugnance at secret societies may have influenced other Republican parties. Although this feuding prevented the absorption of Know Nothing organizations in 1855, the emergence of the Republicans provided an alternative for anti-Democratic voters who disliked Catholics *and* Know Nothings and who increasingly worried about the slavery extension issue as violence flared in Kansas.

The Republicans proved especially embarrassing to northern Know Nothings after the Know Nothing national council met in Philadelphia in June, 1855, and issued a platform whose twelfth section accepted as final the existing legislation on slavery (*i.e.*, the Fugitive Slave and Kansas-Nebraska acts), recommended against congressional interference in the territories, and condemned further agitation of the slavery question. Even though Henry Wilson and Henry Gardner of Massachusetts and Thomas Ford of Ohio had led most northern delegates out of the meeting in a bolt of protest and even though almost every state council in the North endorsed that bolt and reaffirmed its antislavery credentials, the issue proved a trying one for northern Know Nothings. Almost everyone in the North disliked the Nebraska Act, and Know Nothings were no exception. The action of the national council not only split some northern organizations but also gave additional reasons for voters to leave the nativist crusade, which they had joined in such a frenzy. Some of the bolters formed rival Know Something parties that combined antislavery and anti-Catholicism in many northern states, but in most cases these became stepping-stones to the Republican party, which posed the real threat to Know Nothingism.

The result of the infiltration of politicos, defections of immigrant voters, disagreements over secrecy, and the Republican challenge was a significant shift in the bases of Know Nothing support as early as 1855. It is a great error to conceive of the Know Nothings as a monolithic bloc that emerged in 1854 and disappeared after 1856. Support for and membership in the order was constantly fluctuating. A careful and elaborate statistical study of voting by township in fifteen New York counties and by ward in New York, Brooklyn, Albany, and Buffalo, for example, reveals little relationship between the 1854 and 1855 Know Nothing votes. The major changes occurred in the rural townships as the vote shifted from areas with rapidly changing populations to relatively wealthy areas with stable populations. Commenting on the rural support of the Know Nothings, an observer noted in 1855: "There is one thing about this contest quite discernible—that where they were strong last year they have now lost and where they were weak now they are strong." Much of this shift apparently reflected an exodus of antislavery voters to the Republicans and an influx of conservative Whigs to the Know Nothings. A Democrat reported to William L. Marcy after the election, "This hurricane of Know Nothingism has been contributed to largely by the 'straight out Whigs' who rushed blindly in, to defeat 'republicanism.' "

Similarly, students of Massachusetts Know Nothingism have detected a change in its support after 1854, when almost everyone voted for the order. Rural voters deserted the party, and it concentrated in conservative areas such as Boston. A close statistical study of Worcester County found blue-collar defections to the Republicans in mill towns, whereas conservatives shifted to Know Nothingism in other areas. Henry Wilson wrote Salmon Chase that many conservative Whigs joined the party in 1855 "to crush out the Republican movement." But reactions to the slavery issue alone do not explain the change in Know Nothing support. For one thing, many antislavery Know Nothings did not change but remained loyal to Gardner. In addition, an examination of the membership of a single lodge in the city of Worcester shows a sharp drop in the original membership from 1,120 in 1854 to 200 in 1855, with 214 new men belonging to the order at the later date. This change in an area where the state council had adopted a new antislavery constitution in August, 1855, as well as the New York evidence, suggests that many men joined the order because of its newness and mystery but quickly left it when their curiosity was sated or they were disillusioned. The shifting support, that is, suggests that Know Nothingism would only grow where it was new, that the order was more successful in attracting initiates than in retaining members once they discovered what it was really like.

Although many reasons produced defections from the Know Nothings as early as 1855, the portentous problem for the future was the slavery question or, more precisely, the problem of dealing with the southern wing of the party as the presidential election of 1856 and the subsequent pressures for national cooperation approached. Like Antimasonry, Know Nothingism was essentially a grass-roots protest movement, and the party did best in local and state elections unconfused by national issues and free of the necessity of national coordination. The early Know Nothing victories and the spread of the order to the South, however, had encouraged its leaders to try to build a national organization to contest the presidential election of 1856. Southerners had entered the party for a variety of reasons, some very different from those that motivated northern voters, and to understand the perplexing situation of the party it is necessary to take a closer look at the American party in the South.

In some parts of Dixie, many of the same forces that fostered Know Nothingism in the North contributed to the strength of the party. Maryland, Kentucky, Louisiana, and Missouri had relatively heavy foreign populations, and Know Nothingism appeared first in their local and municipal elections. Know Nothings organized in 1853 in Maryland, for example, stimulated by the efforts of Catholics in the legislature to pass a bill giving public aid to parochial schools. Their first Know Nothing political activity was to back an independent Temperance slate of legislators in Baltimore the fall of that year. Know Nothings appeared next in New Orleans, where they backed an Independent ticket in the municipal elections in the spring of 1854 to seize control of the city from a corrupt Democratic machine that fraudulently naturalized immigrants. Many southerners, moreover, favored limitations on immigration to slow the growth of northern states and territories and preserve southern political power in the national government. If anti-Catholicism, nativism, and desires for political reform engendered some of the state organizations, it is also likely that antiparty sentiments played a role in these and other southern states. Southerners had always displayed a suspicion of the trappings and mechanisms of political parties like conventions and patronage, and these sentiments may have propelled them toward Know Nothingism. A Tennessee Know Nothing in 1854, for example, complained, "Nothing is more evident than that our political parties have become sadly, deplorably corrupt." Whigs in Mississippi had tried to revive their party in 1853 by denouncing the corruption of party caucuses and conventions, condemning the tyrannical "*spirit of party*" that had ruled the state, and endorsing candidates already in the field as the "choice of the people." Although expediency dictated this tactic, many of these Mississippi Whigs joined the Know Nothing order within a year. In Virginia, an editor informed William C. Rives, "I have joined the American order to aid in breaking up the senseless prejudices of party which have so long distracted Virginia."

If the same motivations that produced Know Nothingism in the North appeared here and there in the South, it seems clear that other forces must have contributed to its emergence. Outside of the border states and Louisiana, immigrants and Catholics constituted a tiny fraction of the southern population. Many rural Protestants, if the Know Nothing Kennedy Rayner of North Carolina was correct, hated Catholics, but for most of them popery and immigration were distant, not immediate, threats. The major impetus to Know Nothingism in the South was rather the political vacuum left by the collapse of the national Whig party.

Southern Whig parties were in trouble as early as 1850, when divisions over the Compromise of 1850 produced a realignment of parties along Union and southern rights lines in Georgia, Alabama, and Mississippi. Although Union parties prevailed, voters and leaders proved reluctant to return to the Whig organization in 1852, especially when the Whigs nominated Scott, whom southerners regarded as a tool of the hated Seward. Moribund in some Deep South states by 1852, the Whig party was shattered in others in 1854, when the northern wing of the party vehemently opposed the Kansas-Nebraska Act. Political survival in the South depended on stalwart devotion to southern rights, and many Whig politicians correctly recognized that continuing as Whigs was suicidal because the northern wing of the party had become so odious to southern voters. By the summer of 1854, Whig leaders and editors were anxiously looking for other parties in which they could save their livelihood. Many, like Senator Archibald Dixon of Kentucky and Robert Toombs and Alexander Stephens of Georgia, shifted directly to the Democrats. But other Whigs, such as Rayner of North Carolina, John J. Crittenden of Kentucky, and John Bell of Tennessee, declining to align with their old foes, drifted to the American party, not only to prolong their careers but also to preserve the Union. Southern Democratic parties were moving toward an increasingly proslavery stance, and Whigs who in desperation had often referred to themselves as Conservative or Union parties in 1853 looked on Know Nothingism, with its glorification of the nation, as the best way to continue this conservative tradition. Especially ardent in extolling the virtues of Know Nothingism in 1854 was the Whig press in small towns and large. Their need for political patronage for financial survival and the unlikelihood they could get it from the Democrats played no small part in their decision to endorse the new party.

Along with these leaders went the vast bulk of Whig voters. Contemporary letter writers and newspapers make it clear that Know Nothingism was not solely a continuation of Whiggery; many Democrats joined the order. Many large Whig planters, moreover, moved directly to the Democrats as the best way to protect slavery. But the party competition between Democrats and Whigs had been especially fierce in the South, and most Whig voters resisted the idea of cooperating with the Democrats. As a result, they quickly accepted Know Nothingism as the best way to continue their antagonism to their longtime foes. In Louisiana, for example, New Orleans was the core of Know Nothing strength, and even large Whig sugar and cotton planters became Americans. Similarly in Georgia, Know Nothings flourished in Black Belt Whig counties and in those counties containing large towns, where Georgia's foreign population was concentrated. Comparisons of Whig and Know Nothing voting support in Florida, North Carolina, Virginia, Kentucky, Tennessee, and Mississippi reveal them to be located largely in the same counties, although throughout the South those counties containing foreigners tended to go more strongly Know Nothing than other Whig counties. In Tennessee, for example, twenty-eight of thirty-nine counties the Whigs carried in 1853 went Know Nothing in 1855. Only five other counties went over to the Know Nothing column the latter year. Basically the southern American party, despite the Democratic infusions and the shift of some Whigs directly to the Democrats, was a continuation of the old Whig party's opposition to the Democracy and sectional extremism.

The emergence of southern Know Nothingism and the concomitant attempts to absorb them into the national organization created certain problems for national Know Nothing leaders. As has been mentioned, southerners chafed at the clandestinity of the order, and many southern councils decided to open the organization as early as 1855. Southerners were certainly instrumental in the recommendation of the national council to abolish secrecy in June, 1855. Another thorny issue was the provision of the national constitution barring Catholics from membership. Outside of Tennessee, Kentucky, North Carolina, and Texas, southern Know Nothings soft-pedaled anti-Catholicism and emphasized antiforeignism.

In 1855 and early 1856, state councils in Louisiana, Mississippi, Virginia, Alabama, Maryland, and Missouri, like that in California, rejected the religious test and admitted Catholics who swore they gave no temporal allegiance to the Pope. The issue had arisen when a Creole Catholic Charles Gayarré led the Louisiana delegation to the national council meeting in June, 1855. When Gayarré was refused a seat, he returned to Louisiana, and in July the state council there repudiated the part of the 1855 platform that proscribed Catholics. Indeed, the Know Nothing candidate for governor in 1855 in Louisiana was a Catholic. To the dismay of rabid Protestants like Kenneth Rayner, a Catholic delegation from Louisiana was seated at the national council meeting in 1856, which in turn sharply moderated the party's religious test for membership.

The most serious problem posed by southerners concerned slavery. Although Know Nothings eschewed the extremism of southern Democrats on this issue, they insisted that northern Know Nothings drop any criticism of the South. Indeed, one of the main attractions of the American party to southerners was its claim to be a national, conservative organization once the national Whig party had disappeared. Southern Know Nothings could only make that assertion if northern Know Nothings were neutral, if not prosouthern, on the slavery issue. From the inception of the national council in June, 1854, when sectional animosities over the Kansas-Nebraska Act were heating up, therefore, southerners endeavored to commit the party at least to neutrality and, if possible, to a calculated policy of ignoring the slavery question and stressing unionism. Rayner achieved the first victory of this effort when the national council in November, 1854, adopted the third degree of membership, the so-called Union Degree. On taking this oath, members pledged to uphold the Union, to oppose all threats to it, and to vote against any candidate who menaced the Union. Indeed, all American candidates for office were to have taken the Union Degree.

Northerners were willing to go along with neutrality in November, 1854, after most of the elections were over, but sectional differences over slavery proved more intractable as the 1855 elections approached. By then, northern Know Nothings faced the competition of the Republicans, and most in any case deplored the repeal of the Missouri Compromise. Thus, when Rayner introduced a resolution at the June, 1855, meeting that "we do therefore declare . . . that the question of slavery does not come within the purview of the objects of this organization," Henry Wilson, Thomas Ford, and other northerners defeated it. The adoption of Section 12 by that meeting, even though it failed to satisfy some southerners because it was not proslavery enough, provoked the bolt of northerners who refused to be silenced on the slavery extension issue. At a Know Something convention in Cleveland, some of these bolters blamed the South for forcing the slavery issue on them, pledged opposition to the admission of more slave states, and continued to abhor "every politico ecclesiastical reference in political affairs by potentate, pontiff, or priest, or their abettors."

Although some northerners like Wilson left the party in the summer of 1855 to become Republicans and although most northern state councils repudiated Section 12, the vast majority of northern Know Nothings were still, in Wilson's words of condemnation, "willing to unite again with the South on some basis" to preserve the national organization to contest the presidency in 1856. Their continued bias against Catholics was evident in the bolters' and the Know Something resolutions. All they wanted was a slavery plank they could live with. Toward that end, delegates from eight northern states attended another meeting in November in Cincinnati. Thomas Ford of Ohio, elected lieutenant governor only weeks earlier on the same ticket with Republican Salmon Chase, chaired the meeting and called for harmony among northern and southern Know Nothings. In that spirit, the meeting invited the president of the national council, E. B. Bartlett of nearby Covington, Kentucky, to attend. Rejecting a stiff antislavery platform, the convention passed resolutions recommending that the national council meet in Philadelphia in February before the scheduled national nominating convention and substitute for Section 12 a plank demanding the restoration of the Missouri Compromise. Should that effort fail, "Congress should refuse to admit into the Union, any State tolerating slavery, which shall be formed out of any portion of the territory from which that institution was excluded by that Compromise." To sweeten this insistence on repeal of the Nebraska Act, the northerners protested "against coalescing with any party which demands the postponement or abandonment of American principles or the disorganization of the American party." Anti-Nebraska Know Nothings, that is, abjured coalition with the Republicans and pledged to remain in the party and to cooperate with the southerners, so long as they helped restore the Missouri Compromise.

Others northerners feared these terms would shatter the party, and they hoped to delay the national convention to avoid a sectional confrontation. Leading this group were Daniel Ullmann and the Silver Greys who headed the party in New York. More conservative than other northerners, New Yorkers had not bolted the June convention. Nor had their local councils repudiated the national platform; rather, they had added moderately free-soil resolutions to it. Nor had they attended the Cincinnati meeting. These men were especially concerned that George Law, an erstwhile antislavery Democrat from their state, had gathered enough votes through bribery and other expenditures to make a strong run for the American presidential nomination. Backers of Millard Fillmore, they feared that a Law candidacy would drive southerners out of the party and dash their hopes for a new national conservative coalition. Aiding Ullmann in the attempt to stall the convention was Vesparian Ellis, editor of the Know Nothing newspaper in Washington, the *American Organ*. Hoping to patch up the damage done in Philadelphia in June, Ellis called a meeting of the party's leaders in Washington in December to reschedule the convention and to persuade Know Nothing congressmen to combine behind a program forbidding alien suffrage in Kansas but dropping efforts to repeal the Nebraska law.

All of these efforts failed. Bartlett called a national council meeting in Philadelphia on February 18 as the Cincinnati group had requested, and the nominating convention would still meet four days later. Nor did Know Nothing congressmen coalesce into a workable coalition for the new session beginning that December. Divisions immediately appeared in the protracted battle to elect the Speaker of the House, which lasted from December to February, 1856. The exact number of Know Nothings in this Congress is difficult to determine. Many northern Know Nothings had been elected in 1854 on Anti-Nebraska fusion tickets, and by December, 1855, some were apparently ready to drop the party and become Republicans because of the increasing sectional tension over Kansas. It seems clear there were 43 out-and-out Know Nothings, and of the 108 Anti-Nebraska men, it has been estimated 70 were Know Nothings. Had all the nativists cooperated, then, they probably could have organized the

House; but whereas conservatives wanted a Speaker unoffensive to the South, many northerners insisted on an Anti-Nebraska man. After a scattering of votes, the former supported first Humphrey Marshall of Kentucky and then Henry M. Fuller of Pennsylvania, whereas most of the latter backed Nathaniel P. Banks of Massachusetts, who was converting to Republicanism. Because of the split in the American strength and the stubborn refusal of Democrats to vote for a Know Nothing, the vote remained deadlocked for weeks. Finally, a rule to pick the Speaker by a plurality passed, and Banks was elected by a narrow margin over William Aiken of South Carolina. Know Nothings, as a Republican observer in Washington pointed out, played a crucial role in this victory. Banks was, after all, a member of the order, and Washington Know Nothings were determined to elect a Speaker who could parcel out the House jobs to Americans. When, therefore, it appeared that Aiken might triumph with the support of southern and conservative northern Know Nothings, the local Americans persuaded three northerners to throw their votes away on Fuller and others to abstain, and with the subsequent reduction in Aiken's total, Banks won. Know Nothings then attended the antiadministration caucus with Republicans and demanded jobs such as doorkeeper and sergeant-at-arms. Gamiel Bailey, the Republican observer, deplored these arrangements and the fact that of Banks's 103 votes about 70 came from Know Nothings.

Despite the crucial Know Nothing influence in electing the Speaker, the main fact of this contest had been the division between northern and southern Know Nothings. This division reappeared when the national council met in Philadelphia before the national convention. The anti-Nebraska northerners immediately took command when they succeeded in seating the Edie Council from Pennsylvania, opponents of Section 12, rather than the more conservative council from that state. Successfully pushing through a rule giving each state a vote equal to its representation in Congress, rather than the seven each held on the council, the northerners repealed Section 12. All the southerners except one voted to keep it, as did two from California and fifteen of thirty-five in the New York delegation. The council then adopted the so-called Washington Platform, which Ellis had first formulated, but since it did not call for the restoration of the Missouri Compromise and still seemed to condone popular sovereignty, even though it denounced the Nebraska Act, it failed to satisfy the northerners, who determined to bolt the national convention should any nomination be made. Led by Ford and the Ohio delegation, they wanted to wait and see whom the Republicans chose.

The nominating convention itself furthered the disruption of the party. Southerners who wanted to defy the antislavery northerners and northern conservatives who feared the absorption of the party by the Republicans insisted on an immediate nomination. Sam Houston, George Law, and Millard Fillmore, who had joined the order in the spring of 1855 and then sailed for Europe, were the main contenders, and Fillmore won on the second ballot with support from the South, New York, Pennsylvania, and Illinois. Andrew Jackson Donelson of Tennessee was then chosen as his running mate. The selection of Fillmore, who had signed the hated Fugitive Slave Law and who was hardly the new face so many Know Nothings were looking for, confirmed the previous decision of northerners to bolt. Seventy-one men representing New England, the Midwest, and part of Pennsylvania withdrew, demanded restoration of the Missouri Compromise, and called for a new nominating convention of North Americans, as they called themselves, to meet in New York on June 12 to select a candidate satisfactory to northern voters.

After February, the Know Nothing campaign of 1856 must be viewed in two separate parts. Southerners and a minority of Know Nothings in the North fell in behind Fillmore, strove to woo the northern bolters back to the party, and searched for a strategy to elect their man. They called for the national council to meet again in New York before the North American convention to prevent a separate nomination, but that effort aborted. After that point, their campaign focused on the South, the border states, and conservative strongholds in the North, and stressed the theme of unionism rather than nativism. Symbolizing this emphasis was Fillmore's endorsement by the remnants of Whig organizations in the South and by a Whig national convention in September. The sincerity of anguished Whig leaders who feared a disruption of the Union is beyond doubt, but their capacity to influence many voters by 1856 was certainly questionable. The Americans, however, moved to facilitate this support, and in many southern states Fillmore-Donelson clubs, not American parties, led the campaign. The Fillmore men also tried to use patronage in certain northern states like New York to force Know Nothings to vote for him, and Fillmore received an important vote in some northern states from die-hard nativists like the Order of United Americans and from conservatives. This part of the campaign, however, was primarily a southern one.

More interesting were the maneuverings of the northern Know Nothings who had rejected Fillmore's nomination. Eager to preserve an independent existence or at least to ensure that they obtained a large share of the offices at stake in the election, they also were determined to back a free-soil man for president. Inevitably, therefore, their activities became intertwined with the efforts of the Republican party to build a united northern party to oppose southern aggressions.

Many North Americans initially had no intention of playing second fiddle to the Republicans and hoped to impose their choice on them. Because the Republicans would hold their nominating convention in Philadelphia on June 17, the Americans hoped that their earlier gathering in New York could pick a candidate whom the Republicans would be forced to endorse. Toward this end, some tried to persuade Fillmore to decline the American nomination, but he accepted shortly before they were to assemble in June. Others worked before the convention to form an alliance between Republicans and North Americans on platforms combining their principles. Correspondents from Massachusetts, for example, informed Banks, the Know Nothing–Republican Speaker of the House, that they were forming clubs whose constitutions "oppose malign foreign and ecclesiastical influence" and favored "securing Freedom to all the Territories." The purpose of these men and others was to secure the North American nomination for Banks, whose antislavery reputation could win support from the Republicans. To further this plan, some areas sent the same delegates to the North American and Republican conventions in June.

If some northern Know Nothings sincerely expected to impose their own candidate on the Republicans, others plotted a North American surrender to the Republicans. Ironically, Banks himself was a leader of this group. An early backer of John C. Frémont, Banks agreed to be a stalking horse. The plot was for Banks to win the North American nomination, delay acceptance until after the Republicans chose Frémont, and then withdraw, urging support for the Pathfinder. To mollify the nativists, the Republican schemers also planned that the Republican convention would accept the North American vice-presidential nominee. As delegates gathered in New York in early June, they grew suspicious of such a deal, but Banks's managers assured them that he was in the race to stay and would never withdraw. It is unclear from their letters whether many of these men understood what Banks was up to, but the plan went off with only a single significant discrepancy. The New York convention selected Banks and William F. Johnston of Pennsylvania for vice-president and waited to see what the Republicans would do. The latter party nominated Frémont but spurned Johnston in favor of William L. Dayton of New Jersey. Then Banks withdrew. The North Americans were furious, and only the persuasiveness of Banks's friends and the personal assurances of Frémont that Dayton would withdraw to allow Johnston to run convinced them to endorse the Republican. Some refused to be appeased, and they made a separate nomination of Robert F. Stockton of New Jersey and Rayner, but this effort proved stillborn.

This formal alliance of the two parties behind the same candidate did not complete the merger. Dayton refused to withdraw, and obstinate state councils in Massachusetts and Connecticut as well as local councils in western Pennsylvania ran Frémont-Johnston tickets against the Republican Frémont-Dayton tickets. If the numerous complaints of Republican leaders can be believed, Know Nothings in these and other states bitterly resented the dominance of the Republicans and refused to surrender their separate organizations. To save Know Nothing pride, Frémont clubs rather than Republican parties ran the campaign in many states. Johnston's tardy withdrawal in August smoothed the way for fusion, as did the careful construction of electoral tickets evenly divided between Republicans and North Americans in some states. Even then, however, Know Nothing insistence on independence and, perhaps, their antiparty sentiment forced these state coalitions to eschew the name Republican for innocuous titles like "Union," "Fusion," or "People's" parties. These often divided the tickets for state offices between Know Nothings and Republicans, or, as in Massachusetts, most Republicans supported the Know Nothing gubernatorial candidate in return for support for Frémont.

Even these efforts on the state level failed to swing all the northern Know Nothings behind Frémont. The Democrats and Fillmore men quickly raised false charges that Frémont was a Catholic, and these caused many local councils to support Fillmore, especially in southeastern Pennsylvania. In that state and elsewhere, the Democrats financed Fillmore newspapers in order to split the opposition vote, and these tactics worked.

In Pennsylvania, Illinois, and Indiana, the crucial states in the contest, the Fillmore men, as distinct from the North Americans, refused to form joint tickets with the Republicans, often deserting the Fusion or Union tickets in the state elections in October. In Massachusetts and New York, Fillmore Know Nothings ran separate candidates for state offices. Conservative unionism and nativist fanaticism both contributed to this intransigence, as did loyalty to Fillmore on the part of many New York Silver Greys. Whatever the reasons, Fillmore received about 395,000 votes in the free states, enough to deny Frémont the election. The combined Fillmore and Frémont totals in Illinois, New Jersey, and California surpassed Buchanan's and almost equaled the Democratic vote in Pennsylvania and Indiana.

With the aid of Whigs who had never joined the order, Fillmore also ran very well in the slave states. Although Maryland was the only state he carried, he trailed Buchanan by only 479,000 to 609,000 in the South as a whole, and he came very close in Florida, Kentucky, Louisiana, and Tennessee. A shift of some 8,800 votes out of 322,000 cast could have given him these states.

It is erroneous to assume that everyone who cast his ballot for Fillmore was a Know Nothing, but, even if one did, it is evident that the bulk of northern Know Nothings had defected to Frémont and the Republicans. In New England, except for Maine, where there are no comparative figures, Fillmore's vote was only about 25,000 compared to a Know Nothing total of 127,000 in the off-year state elections of 1855. In New York, the drop was only 24,000 and in Pennsylvania, 67,000 out of 150,000, but turnouts were always higher in presidential years; therefore, these figures might not reflect the true extent of defections. Because some Know Nothings in these eastern states had switched to the Republicans in 1855 and almost all of them had in the Midwest, the majority of original Know Nothings in the North, except perhaps in New York and Pennsylvania, must have backed Frémont.

Clearly, the concrete events of 1856 that intensified northern animosity toward the South did most to hasten the absorption of northern Know Nothings by the Republicans. Violence in Kansas and the caning of Senator Charles Sumner increased demands for a united northern party to resist southern aggressions. An astute Virginian complained to Daniel Ullmann, "Recent events in Kansas and Washington seem to be driving the masses of your people into the arms of the Republican party and forcing a coalition between them and the Americans who disapprove of Mr. F[illmore]'s nomination." Scores of northerners concurred in this analysis.

Almost as vital to the merger was the care Republicans took on the state level to woo Know Nothings. Not only did they drop the name Republican where it was offensive to Know Nothings, but, as noted above, they skillfully divided state and local tickets with the Know Nothings or backed Know Nothings like Gardner. Nor were Republicans averse to making anti-Catholic and nativist appeals in state platforms and local newspapers, although they tried to avoid offending immigrant Protestants where possible. The Union state platform in Pennsylvania, for example, was equally divided between antislavery and Know Nothing planks. The latter resolutions censured the interference "of foreign influence of every kind" in American government, castigated "the pandering of any party to foreign influence as fraught with manifold evils to the country," and pledged to defend the common school system from any attempts "from whatever quarter" to convert it to sectarian purposes. Indiana's Republican platform in 1856 contained a clause condemning alien suffrage before the five-year naturalization period required by Congress. Michigan's Republicans endorsed a book because it demonstrated "the antagonism of Romanism to Freedom and true Progress."

Republican National Chairman Edwin D. Morgan, recognizing the importance of the anti-Catholic issue, recruited nativist speakers to tour Pennsylvania and New Jersey and worked assiduously to bring James W. Barker, the original Know Nothing organizer, into the party in New York. Morgan also assured a correspondent in Syracuse that "the anti-Catholic tract is to be out soon." Indeed, even the Republican national platform written in June before final merger was effected contained indirect appeals to Know Nothings. The last plank of the platform stated that "believing that the spirit of our institutions as well as the Constitution of our country, guarantees liberty of conscience and equality of rights among citizens, we oppose all legislation impairing their security." This clause is normally interpreted as a victory of the German element of the party over the proscriptiveness of Know Nothingism, but one should note that it spoke of "citizens," not aliens, and that "liberty of conscience" was standard Know Nothing rhetoric when arguing for Bible reading in public schools. To them it meant protection from the priesthood and the right to individual interpretation of the scriptures. Democrats understood the anti-Catholicism of Republicans, and it remained a Republican staple for the remainder of the century.

Finally, the Republicans managed to capitalize on the antiparty, antipolitician sentiment that had brought so many of the early initiates to the Know Nothing order. In a sense, the Republicans evinced the image of newness, of being the people's party, just as the infiltration of the party by established politicos destroyed this for the Know Nothings. From the inception of Republicanism, its leaders had recognized and profited from the popular mood of protest against the party system. Early anti-Nebraska coalitions in Ohio and Indiana were called People's parties, and Republicans employed that name in Connecticut in 1856 and later in Pennsylvania and New Jersey. In other places like Michigan, they often took the name Independent. Republicans clearly needed an inoffensive title that could attract mutually suspicious Whigs, Democrats, and Free Soilers, but they also hoped to appeal to the public demand for popularly controlled parties.

In 1856, the Republicans also took advantage of the old-fashioned, machine-controlled aura around the American and Democratic parties. Fillmore's nomination "fell flat" among northern Know Nothings who demanded, as one informed Banks, a candidate "fresh from the loins of the people—a mechanic—able and jealous of the hierarchy of Rome." Others warned Banks that the nomination should emanate from the people and not merely be the choice of a convention. Although Frémont was selected by a convention, at age forty-three he seemed a much fresher face than the shopworn Fillmore, who was fifty-six, or the old wire-puller Buchanan, who was sixty-five. Republican editorialists shrewdly presented the Pathfinder as a "new man, fresh from the people and one of themselves . . . [who] has been singled out by the people themselves to retrieve the government from maladministration." Too new to have an electoral machine, the Republicans formed Wide Awake clubs, marching societies whose members paraded the streets. Many of the original Know Nothing lodges had been called Wide Awakes, and these militaristic societies attracted the young and the poor, workingmen and mechanics, precisely the kind of men who had rushed to Know Nothing lodges in 1854 and 1855. Through their candidate, appeals, and imitative campaign paraphernalia, the Republicans could lure those Know Nothings who resented southern aggressions, found nothing new in Millard Fillmore, and yearned for a genuine people's party.

The election of 1856 was the last great effort of Know Nothingism. National defeat doomed the party as it had the Antimasons. After the election, some demanded a return to total secrecy to preserve the order. When the national council met in Louisville in June, 1857, it authorized each state council to adopt the rules of organization it thought best for its locality. It then adjourned sine die, never to meet again, and after that date the party only survived at the state level.

Know Nothingism did not disappear abruptly after 1856, but limitations of space prevent a detailed analysis of its disintegration in individual states. Certain patterns are clear. In northern states like Massachusetts, Connecticut, New York, New Jersey, Pennsylvania, and Ohio, the party continued as a dwindling minority; most of its supporters were gradually absorbed by the Republicans. This was a long and thorny procedure, for in all these states Know Nothings wanted an equal hearing for their principles and, more important, a large share of leadership positions in the opposition coalition. In Massachusetts, merger was facilitated when Banks ran for governor in 1857 and 1858 against both Republican and Know Nothing extremists. In Pennsylvania, after an independent American nomination had denied the Republicans the governorship in 1857, the opposition elements fused as the People's party in 1858, which, among other things, pledged to preserve the purity of the ballot box and demanded laws to stop the immigration of foreign criminals. New Jersey also formed a People's party. In these years as well, the Republican press continued to fire anti-Catholic salvos at the Democrats. The influence of Know Nothingism can also be seen in the nativist actions of Republican legislatures, the most important of which was an 1859 Massachusetts law denying suffrage to immigrants until two years after their naturalization.

It is a great error to think that with the disappearance of Know Nothingism as a separate party anti-Catholicism and nativism evaporated in the North. These sentiments continued to find expression in the Republican party, and the assimilation of those issues played a central role in the rise of the Republicans as the major anti-Democratic party in the country. Abraham Lincoln received the Republican nomination in 1860 rather than Seward in large part because Seward was so offensive to the Know

Nothings. Nonetheless, Lincoln was a strong, if less notorious, opponent of Know Nothingism. "I am not a Know-Nothing," he had written privately in 1855.

> How could I be? How can any one who abhors the oppression of negroes, be in favor of degrading classes of white people? Our progress in degeneracy appears to me pretty rapid. As a nation, we began by declaring that "*all men are created equal.*" We now practically read it "all men are created equal, *except negroes.*" When the Know-Nothings get control, it will read "all men are created equal, except negroes, *and foreigners, and catholics.*" When it comes to this I should prefer emigrating to some country where they make no pretense of loving liberty—to Russia, for example, where despotism can be taken pure, and without the base alloy of hypocracy [*sic*].

Despite this, the difference between Frémont's defeat in 1856 and Lincoln's victory in 1860 came about to a large extent because by the later date the Republicans had attracted almost all of the northern Know Nothings who had been divided in 1856. Capturing the Fillmore vote in the North allowed Lincoln to sweep that section.

The party also waned very rapidly in the South except for pockets of strength such as Maryland or New Orleans, which the party dominated until 1862. Although it maintained its separate organization in some states until 1859, almost everywhere in the South it disappeared into amorphous "Whig and American" or "Opposition" coalitions, in which many old Whig voters prolonged their hostility to Democracy. Most of them would back the Constitutional Union candidate John Bell in 1860. Traditional voting alignments and intrastate hostilities had counted for much of the Know Nothing power in the South, and these voters readily abandoned the party when other coalitions provided a better vehicle to carry on the fight. Some Americans joined the Democrats to protect southern rights as the sectional issue intensified, among these Whigs who passed through Know Nothingism to the Democrats. What most strikes an observer of southern voting behavior, however, is the persistence of the voting alignments formed in the 1830s, no matter what the name of the anti-Democratic party. Southern Know Nothingism was but a phase of that opposition.

As third parties, both Antimasonry and Know Nothingism emerged initially as grass-roots protest movements against the unresponsiveness of government to the felt needs of voters. Both movements singled out targets that could plausibly be blamed for disorienting social and economic developments. Both, moreover, decidedly influenced the new anti-Democratic parties they helped form. Yet in a crucial respect, the impact of Antimasonry and Know Nothingism on the American political system was different.

Antimasonry arose at a time when there was no distinct two-party system. In the 1820s, the one-party era that had succeeded the Jeffersonian-Federalist competition was ending, but two new national parties had not yet replaced it. Thus, many voters had no strong political loyalties to party, and the most significant long-run impact of Antimasonry was to form such loyalties, or more precisely, to imbue Antimasons with a life-long hostility to Democrats. Even when Masonry disappeared and when the Antimasonic party collapsed, that antagonism persisted.

Know Nothingism, on the other hand, arose in part as a protest against a stultifying two-party system of Whigs and Democrats that refused to address seriously issues of concern to the people and whose discipline and mechanisms denied them an adequate role in political decision making. One of its purposes and one of its major effects was to erode loyalty to the old parties. By doing this, Know Nothingism, like Antimasonry, became an important transition to a new party system. For many, it provided a halfway house to new affiliations. In the North, for example, many Democratic leaders like Simon Cameron and Nathaniel Banks as well as thousands of Democratic voters moved through Know Nothingism to Republicanism. They could not or would not jump directly to anti-Nebraska coalitions controlled by their longtime Whig foes, and the presence of the amorphous Know Nothing party in which they could attain leadership positions certainly made easier their decision to abandon the Democracy. Similarly, in the South, many old Whigs moved through Know Nothingism into the Democratic party in a search for the best way to defend both southern rights and the Union.

Despite this significant difference, both Antimasonry and Know Nothingism instilled in many voters certain views, biases, or principles that they carried for a lifetime. Just as Antimasonry turned many evangelical Protestants against Democracy forever, so the anti-Catholicism that spawned Know Nothingism aligned urban working-class Protestants and other rural voters against that party. It was the singular feat of the Republican party to combine many of the principles of both of these third parties. Not only did the Republicans mouth a moralistic antagonism to slavery that appealed to old Antimasons, but their determination that the majority—the northern majority—should rule the nation in part reflected the Antimasonic creed that the majority could do as it wished. At the same time, the Republicans inherited from the Know Nothings a virulent anti-Catholicism and, initially, an insistence on representing the people. The very skill of Republicans in combining these themes helped elect Abraham Lincoln. And because the last thing the South would accept was naked majority rule of the people in the nation, that triumph provoked the Civil War.

The Election of 1840, Voter Mobilization, and the Emergence of the Second American Party System: A Reappraisal of Jacksonian Voting Behavior

In 1840, the Whig party won the presidency for the first time in a campaign famous for log cabins and hard cider, a memorable slogan, "Tippecanoe and Tyler, Too," and delightful ditties such as "Van, Van, Van—Van's a Used Up Man." Historians have long mined that colorful election for sprightly lecture material, but the research of Richard P. McCormick has demonstrated that it had substantive significance as well. Voter turnout reached unprecedented heights, jumping from 57.8 percent in 1836 to 80.2 percent in 1840, and the figure was even higher than that in fifteen of twenty-five states. In absolute numbers, the total vote increased from 1,505,290 to 2,408,630, or 60 percent. New voters thus cast 37.5 percent of the ballots in the 1840 presidential election, a share never again equaled in American history.[1]

More important, that election was the culmination of the long process during which the second American party system emerged between 1824 and 1840. Since the publication in 1966 of McCormick's pathbreaking account of that process, a number of historians have confirmed even while revising his seminal insight that the Jacksonian party system of Whigs and Democrats did not fully stabilize until 1840, four years after Andrew Jackson left the White House. Recently, excellent studies by Harry L. Watson, William G. Shade, and Ronald P. Formisano,

---

1. Richard P. McCormick, "New Perspectives on Jacksonian Politics," *American Historical Review*, LXV (1960), 288–301. I have used the figures on turnout gathered by Walter Dean Burnham in U.S. Bureau of the Census, *Historical Statistics of the United States: Colonial Times to 1970* (2 vols.; Washington, D.C., 1975), II, 1072.

among others, have explicitly argued that the years between the presidential elections of 1836 and 1840 marked a crucial transitional stage in that party system, a shift from what might be called a fluctuating or realigning phase from 1824 to 1836, when voter allegiances had not yet crystallized, to a stable phase from 1840 to 1852, when voter loyalty to the rival organizations was fixed and fierce.[2]

The transition between 1836 and 1840 that ended in the election of the first Whig president involved far more than the hardening of voters' partisan identities and the mobilization of new voters. It was also marked by the elaboration of party machinery and by the emergence of impressively high levels of internal party cohesion and interparty disagreement or conflict on roll-call votes in both Congress and the state legislatures. For the first time, moreover, the parties articulated coherent and contrasting platforms regarding proper governmental policy at the state and national levels. Both the formulation of platforms and the emergence of party-oriented voting in legislative bodies, in turn, primarily reflected the parties' divergent responses to the Panic of 1837 and the subsequent depression that gripped the country for most of the period between 1837 and 1844.[3]

Here those responses can be summarized only briefly. The incumbent Democrats denied culpability for the depression and blamed it instead on bankers, paper money, and excessive credit. Explicitly rejecting any governmental responsibility to provide economic aid to those suffering hardship, they condemned governmental intervention in society as inimical to a moral economic order, equal rights, and personal freedom. Their negative state doctrines were perfectly encapsulated in the Independent Treasury plan of Martin Van Buren that occupied Congress from

2. Richard P. McCormick, *The Second American Party System: Party Formation in the Jacksonian Era* (Chapel Hill, 1966); Harry L. Watson, *Jacksonian Politics and Community Conflict: The Emergence of the Second American Party System in Cumberland County, North Carolina* (Baton Rouge, 1981); William G. Shade, "Political Pluralism and Party Development: The Creation of a Modern Party System, 1815–1852," in *The Evolution of American Electoral Systems*, ed. Paul Kleppner (Westport, Conn., 1982), 77–111; Ronald P. Formisano, *The Transformation of Political Culture: Massachusetts Parties, 1790s–1840s* (New York, 1983).

3. The literature on these developments is extensive, and I will not attempt to cite it all here. For a succinct summary, see Shade, "Political Pluralism and Party Development," in *The Evolution of American Electoral Systems*, ed. Kleppner; see also Michael F. Holt, *The Political Crisis of the 1850s* (New York, 1978), 17–38.

September, 1837, until July, 1840, when it finally became law in the midst of the presidential campaign. In contrast, the Whigs blasted the Democrats both for causing the depression and for refusing actively to end it, and they demanded positive governmental action to spur economic recovery and promote growth. Thus, at the state and national levels, sharp interparty legislative battles developed over specific economic policies concerning banking and currency, corporate rights, tariffs, distribution of land revenues to the states, and subsidies for internal improvements. Debates over state and national economic policies, moreover, dominated state and congressional election campaigns from 1837 until 1844. Rarely if ever in American history have political parties provided to the electorate such clear and contrasting alternatives on both concrete policies and general orientations toward the economic role of government.[4]

The concurrence of these developments is significant. In terms of an intensification of voter interest, a widening of issue differences between rival parties, and an increase in ideological polarization, the years between 1836 and 1840 shared most of the characteristics historians and political scientists ascribe to periods of critical voter realignment, such as the 1850s, the 1890s, and the 1930s.[5] Just as severe economic crises sparked the latter two realignments, so apparently did depression and the contrasting party responses to it in the 1830s produce a swing of previous voters and a surge of new voters against the incumbent Democrats, thus accounting for the Whig victory of 1840. Yet few if any historians ana-

4. On economic issues in state campaigns after 1837, see James Roger Sharp, *The Jacksonians Versus the Banks: Politics in the States After the Panic of 1837* (New York, 1967); William G. Shade, *Banks or No Banks: The Money Issue in Western Politics, 1832–1865* (Detroit, 1972), 1–111; Herbert Ershkowitz and William G. Shade, "Consensus or Conflict? Political Behavior in the State Legislatures During the Jacksonian Era," *Journal of American History*, LVIII (1971), 591–622; and William J. Cooper, Jr., *The South and the Politics of Slavery, 1828–1856* (Baton Rouge, 1978), 102, 155–66.

5. Shade makes the same point in "Political Pluralism and Party Development," in *The Evolution of American Electoral Systems*, ed. Kleppner, 104. On realignment theory, see Walter Dean Burnham, *Critical Elections and the Mainsprings of American Politics* (New York, 1970); James L. Sundquist, *Dynamics of the Party System: Alignment and Realignment of Political Parties in the United States* (Washington, D.C., 1973); Jerome M. Clubb, William H. Flanigan, and Nancy H. Zingale, *Partisan Realignment: Voters, Parties, and Government in American History* (Beverly Hills, 1980); and Paul Kleppner, "Critical Realignments and Electoral Systems," in *The Evolution of American Electoral Systems*, ed. Kleppner, 3–32.

lyze those years in terms of voter realignment. More surprising, most historians make no connection between the emergence of sharp partisan conflict over economic issues after 1836 and the stabilization of voter loyalties to the respective parties, the mobilization of 900,000 new voters, or the Whig victory of 1840. The central purpose of this essay, therefore, is to argue that previous interpretations of the election of 1840, the emergence of the second party system, and Jacksonian voting behavior have seriously erred in minimizing the role of economic issues and economic conditions. My contention is that they were the most important forces shaping American political development between 1836 and 1844.[6]

Even Shade and Formisano, who argue so perceptively that the second-party system reached full flower only between 1836 and 1840, are unwilling to admit that economic issues explain *why* it matured at that time. Formisano, for example, notes that in the first half of the 1830s, Massachusetts was shaken by populistic protest movements that worked outside of and against the major parties. After 1836, however, the energies of those protestors as well as of additional voters were channeled "into two mass parties, whose almost ritualized electoral warfare replaced the creative chaos of the early 1830s." He offers no explicit explanation of how the once repudiated major parties managed to incorporate this support, although he argues that the means of communication upon which mass organization depended had improved and that the parties adopted a crusading style of campaigning that tapped "hopes and fears of public salvation." He admits that the depression after 1837 helped Whigs to mobilize voters, but the partisan polarization over economic issues is largely peripheral to his analysis. In short, he seems more impressed by the style than the objectives of the partisan crusades in those years.[7]

6. Watson, *Jacksonian Politics and Community Conflict*, 245–81, is a decided exception to this generalization, for he not only stresses the centrality of the panic and the economic issues it generated to voting patterns between 1836 and 1840 and to the election of 1840 itself, he sees divergent responses to the evolution of the economy as the key to party formation in the entire period from 1824 to 1840. A more recent study also stresses the centrality of economic issues to political developments after 1837. See Marc W. Kruman, *Parties and Politics in North Carolina, 1836–1865* (Baton Rouge, 1983), 3–28, 55–63. In a sense, therefore, this essay contends that their interpretation of events in North Carolina is applicable to the entire United States. William R. Brock, *Parties and Political Conscience: American Dilemmas, 1840–1850* (Millbrook, N.Y., 1979), 3–70, also recognizes that issue conflict caused the voter mobilization between 1836 and 1840.

7. Formisano, *The Transformation of Political Culture*, 173–320 (quotations on 245).

Shade is more candid about his uncertainty. "At present," he asserts, "it is nearly impossible for the historian to explain with any precision why Phase II—the 'normal' or stable phase of the second party system—appeared when it did." He too admits that the decisive transition coincided with the Panic of 1837, but because he believes that attempts to establish economic sources of voting behavior have been fruitless for the South and refuted for the North, he deems the depression only a background condition, not a cause of party development. In the end, he also cites improvements in communications as the major reason the party system crystallized in the late 1830s.[8]

Like much of the stimulating recent work on the emergence of the second party system, almost all previous interpretations of the presidential election of 1840 ignore or emphatically deny the role of economic issues in that contest. Most, indeed, argue that "issues [of any kind] counted for little in the 1840 campaign." Even historians like Daniel W. Howe and William J. Cooper, Jr., who correctly stress the importance of the executive tyranny and slavery issues in the presidential race that year, give short shrift to economic issues, and Cooper baldly asserts that they had no impact in the South.[9]

Other historians attribute the Whigs' victory in 1840 to the legendary "Log Cabin—Hard Cider" campaign they ran on behalf of General William Henry Harrison, a military hero of great renown and minimal identification with Whig policies. According to this view, pragmatic Whig politicos, intent on winning at any cost, engineered the nomination of the aged Indian fighter rather than their most prominent congressional leader Henry Clay because they believed they could not win on their issues. Refusing to write a national platform and carefully avoiding any mention of issues during the campaign, they instead lubricated voters with generous amounts of strong drink, stirred them with ingenious slogans, songs, and symbols, and roused them to a frenzy through the bril-

---

8. Shade, "Political Pluralism and Party Development," in *The Evolution of American Electoral Systems*, ed. Kleppner, 102–105.

9. Paul Murray, *The Whig Party in Georgia, 1825–1853* (Chapel Hill, 1948), 94; Daniel Walker Howe, *The Political Culture of the American Whigs* (Chicago, 1979), 7–8, 90–92; Cooper, *The South and the Politics of Slavery*, 121–48, esp. 132–33. It should be pointed out that Cooper argues that economic issues were important in state elections and local races between 1837 and 1844, but he specifically denies their significance in the presidential campaign of 1840.

liant imitation of Jacksonian techniques such as parades, mass rallies, and log cabin-raisings. Excited, dazzled, and befuddled, voters poured out in record numbers to carry Harrison into office. Thus both the unprecedented turnout and the Whig triumph are explained by Whig hoopla.[10]

This analysis possesses a certain logic. After all, if the Whigs thought they could win by advocating their economic policies, why did they nominate Harrison rather than Clay? It also comports with the facts—or at least some of them. Before the Whig nominating convention, many strategists did believe the party could win only by shunning a platform and nominating a military hero whose fame might rally the electorate. As one proponent of General Winfield Scott argued, "Scott's name will bring out the hurra boys. The Whig party were broken down by the popularity and non-committal character of old Jackson, and it is but fair to turn upon and prostrate our opponents, with the weapons . . . with which they beat us. . . . The General's lips must be hermetically sealed, and our shouts and hurras long and loud." After Harrison's nomination, the Whigs appeared to follow this scenario to the letter. They employed flummery and mummery with astonishing effectiveness, and one of their notorious campaign songs openly advised:

> Mum is the word boys,
> Brag is the game;
> Cooney is the emblem
> of Old Tip's fame.[11]

Yet there are defects in the logic of this interpretation and obvious facts that it ignores. It assumes that the reasons why Harrison was nominated are identical with the reasons why he won. It does not explain how

10. For examples, see Robert G. Gunderson, *The Log-Cabin Campaign* (Lexington, Ky., 1957), 28, 73–74, 96, 115; Walter Dean Burnham, *Presidential Ballots 1836–1892* (Baltimore, 1955), 21–22; and Arthur M. Schlesinger, Jr., *The Age of Jackson* (Boston, 1945), 283–305. Schlesinger asserts that the 1840 election forced the Whigs "to a concrete choice. Should the campaign be fought once more with the issues and leaders with which the Whigs had repeatedly gone down to defeat? Or should the past be forgotten, and the party enter the canvass unencumbered by its former issues and leaders?" (289).

11. M. Bradley to Thurlow Weed, August 29, 1839, quoted in Gunderson, *The Log-Cabin Campaign*, 52; for the ditty, see *ibid.*, 115.

the carnivallike Whig campaign could have caused the substantial increase in the Democratic vote between 1836 and 1840. It takes the absence of a national platform as evidence of an absence of issues and does not consider other forums in which Whigs articulated differences from the Democrats. Similarly, it drastically minimizes the impact Democratic actions and rhetoric had on defining the choices before the electorate. Proponents of this view, moreover, generally ignore the considerable evidence from Whig sources during and especially after the campaign that Whigs believed they won because of economic issues. Even the supposedly obtuse Harrison noted in the spring of 1840 that "we have many recruits in our ranks from the pressure of the times." Four years later, an Indiana editor who anticipated a rematch against Van Buren declared that "the Harrison boys of Hoosierdom will prove in a way that they consider pretty conclusive to Mr. Van Buren that they were neither 'drunk' nor 'mad' in 1840. . . . They will show him that they cast him out because they were opposed to his Sub Treasury—his profligate expenditures—his disregard of the petitions of the people." [12]

Much more important, those who explain the results of 1840 solely in terms of the theatrical Whig campaign for Harrison, or even Van Buren's personal unpopularity, ignore the performance of the Whigs in congressional, gubernatorial, and state legislative races, how that performance varied over time, and how it related to changing economic conditions. Once one adopts a broader and longer perspective, the crucial role of economic conditions and economic issues in causing both voter mobilization and the outcome of the 1840 election becomes palpable.

Proponents of the McCormick thesis do adopt such a perspective, but they are equally emphatic in their rejection of economic causation. According to McCormick, the system was formed "in the successive contests for the presidency between 1824 and 1840. It did not emerge from cleavages within Congress, nor from any polarization of attitudes on specific public issues." Equally important, "the rate at which voters participated was directly related to the closeness of interparty competition rather than to the presumed charismatic effect of candidates or the urgency of particular issues." Specifically, McCormick and others argue that voter

---

12. William Henry Harrison to Nathaniel P. Tallmadge, February 22, 1840, quoted *ibid.*, 12; report of Schuyler Colfax in New York *Tribune*, April 8, 1844.

turnout jumped in 1840 because highly competitive party organizations that were "for the first time . . . truly national in scope . . . exerted every effort to arouse popular excitement. . . . The result of this competitive situation was an unprecedented outpouring of the electorate." [13]

Party organization did become more extensive after 1836, and it is plausible to contend that the turnout of previous party identifiers was a function of the closeness of party competition—that is, they were more likely to vote if they thought their party needed every vote to win. It is less plausible, however, to maintain that former nonvoters could be automatically mobilized simply because parties now competed for their votes. If so, the drop-off in turnout rates after 1840 is inexplicable. Nor does this rather mechanistic behavioral model adequately explain why the Whigs rather than the Democrats captured three-fifths of the 900,000 new voters mobilized between 1836 and 1840. Was it a case, as McCormick asserts, of "the Whigs leading the way in inventiveness and enthusiasm"? It was, after all, the lopsided surge of new voters to the Whigs, not the close balance between the parties, that produced the Whig victory in 1840. In the states with the largest increase in turnout, moreover, competitive balance was a product not a cause of that voter surge. Because it focuses only on presidential elections, finally, this interpretation, like the traditional accounts of the log cabin campaign, neglects the crucial role of events and elections *between* November, 1836, and November, 1840, in producing the unprecedented voter turnout, forging lasting voter allegiances, and building the coalition that brought the Whigs victory in 1840. [14]

Even more surprising, most analysts of Jacksonian voting behavior also underestimate how much the economic crisis of the late 1830s and

13. McCormick, *The Second American Party System*, 13, 16, 341–42, and "New Perspectives on Jacksonian Politics," 299–301; William N. Chambers and Paul C. Davis, "Party, Competition, and Mass Participation: The Case of the Democratizing Party System, 1824–1852," in *The History of American Electoral Behavior*, ed. Joel H. Silbey, Allan G. Bogue, and William H. Flanigan (Princeton, 1978), 174–97.

14. McCormick, *The Second American Party System*, 341. For evidence that close party balance was a result rather than a cause of voter turnout, see Table 5.1 in Chambers and Davis, "Party, Competition, and Mass Participation," in *The History of American Electoral Behavior*, ed. Silbey, Bogue, and Flanigan, 176–77, and note especially the figures for New Hampshire, Maine, Illinois, Michigan, Arkansas, and Tennessee.

the contrasting party responses to it determined who voted for whom. This error is especially true of the so-called ethnocultural interpretation of voting, which was first applied to New York in Lee Benson's *Concept of Jacksonian Democracy* and has since been extended to Michigan by Formisano, to Illinois and Pennsylvania by Shade, and to Ohio by Stephen C. Fox. Indeed, I think it accurate to say that for the last twenty years this has been the dominant interpretation of northern voting throughout the nineteenth century. According to this model, ethnic and religious differences were more important determinants of voter cleavages than were the economic characteristics of voters or economic issues.[15]

Virtually all proponents of this interpretation admit that people sometimes have economic reasons for voting. Yet they tend to posit a narrow or rigorous set of conditions that in effect equates economic motivations with class or interest group motivations. They insist that only if one can prove that specific occupational groups or economic interests voted for a particular party because of a specific plank in its platform can a historian speak of economic issues motivating voters. As Formisano says, "Let it be granted that economic policy divided the parties. It must then be shown that parties conveyed these contrasts to voters, that campaigning and communications efficiently disseminated information on formal issues, and that voters saw and acted as members of economic groups. At least all these inferences are necessary if voting is to be seen as motivated by economic interest." Or, as Formisano's mentor Benson argues, "Historians must try . . . to specify the conditions under which different types of economic factors are most likely to exercise determining influence upon the voting behavior of specific classes or groups of men."[16]

15. Lee Benson, *The Concept of Jacksonian Democracy: New York as a Test Case* (Princeton, 1961); Ronald P. Formisano, *The Birth of Mass Political Parties: Michigan, 1827–1861* (Princeton, 1971); Shade, *Banks or No Banks*, 18–19, 158–67, and "Pennsylvania Politics in the Jacksonian Period: A Case Study, Northampton County, 1824–1844," *Pennsylvania History*, XXXIX (1972), 313–33; Stephen C. Fox, "Politicians, Issues, and Voter Preference in Jacksonian Ohio: A Critique of an Interpretation," *Ohio History*, LXXXVI (1977), 155–70, and "The Bank Wars, the Idea of 'Party,' and the Division of the Electorate in Jacksonian Ohio," *Ohio History*, LXXXVIII (1979), 253–76.

16. Ronald P. Formisano, "Toward a Reorientation of Jacksonian Politics: A Review of the Literature, 1959–1975," *Journal of American History*, LXIII (1976), 61; Benson, *The Concept of Jacksonian Democracy*, 156.

Largely because of this narrow conceptualization of economic motivation and economic issues and also because they apparently could find no correlation between occupational and class variables and voting behavior, virtually all of the ethnoculturalists insist that economic factors had little or no influence on voting behavior in the 1830s and 1840s. Benson, for example, contends that New York's voting pattern solidified in 1832 and remained the same until 1853. Hence, "party differences over *socioeconomic* issues did not have sufficient impact to alter voting patterns already fixed in 1832; some localized, minor shifts and temporary fluctuations occurred, but the pattern remained essentially unchanged." Fox, who like Shade argues that banking issues often resonated with contrasting cultural values, still asserts that in Ohio "the financial crisis of 1837 and the banking issues of the early 1840s caused no discernible change in voting habits." Formisano emphatically denies that voters had any issue orientation at all. Economic conflicts, he declares, did not bring Michigan's parties into being in the 1830s or cause different voters to align behind one party or the other in the hard times after 1837. Moreover, he apparently believes that economic issues were insignificant outside of Michigan as well, for elsewhere he maintains that "economic issues at times became quite salient in nineteenth-century politics, though far more in the 1890s than in the 1830s." [17]

Let us grant that in the elections the ethnoculturalists have studied, they have demonstrated that there were no clear distinctions between the voting support of the two parties in terms of wealth or occupation. An absence of class polarization, however, is not proof that economic conditions and economic issues do not shape voting behavior. First, one cannot assume that the rich and the poor or bankers and workers react in opposite ways to economic issues. There could be, during a depression, an across-the-board surge toward one party without any correlation between the party's vote and occupational groups or classes appearing. Second, studies of the twentieth-century electorate by political scientists have found that real income, particularly change in real income, is the most salient economic variable influencing voting. Yet this is not measured in any of the

17. Benson, *The Concept of Jacksonian Democracy*, 292; Fox, "Politicians, Issues, and Voter Preference in Jacksonian Ohio," 161; Formisano, *The Birth of Mass Political Parties*, 11–12, 31, 48, 55, and "Toward a Reorientation of Jacksonian Politics," 61–62.

economic indexes devised by historians of the nineteenth century.[18] Instead, they measure occupation or wealth as signified by the value of real or personal property. Most important, by focusing on individual or group voting behavior, historians have normally ignored fluctuations in party strength or success *over time,* which is what must be used to test the impact of economic variables. Put differently, the ethnoculturalists have little concern for the results of elections—for who won and who lost—and how the pattern of party victory fluctuated over time.

By using time-series analysis, political scientists have generated compelling evidence that economic conditions, as distinguished from individual economic status, do shape changes in voting behavior. More precisely, declining economic conditions depress the vote of the incumbent party and increase that of its rival. Improving economic conditions, on the other hand, have little discernible impact on the vote. Yet historians normally correlate variables from a particular census or tax year with voting returns from a single year or with average party strength over a series of elections. In short, they employ static rather than dynamic variables. If they consider economic change at all, it is usually change over a considerable period of time—the ten years between census returns or the four years between presidential elections. Modern research indicates, however, that only change within the year immediately preceding an election affects voting behavior. Thus, in the way they construct both their independent and dependent variables, most historians have made it impossible to measure the impact of changing economic conditions.[19]

18. Howard S. Bloom and H. Douglas Price, "Voter Response to Short-Run Economic Conditions: The Asymmetric Effect of Prosperity and Recession," *American Political Science Review,* LXIX (1975), 1240–54, esp. 1243.

19. I have relied heavily on the article by Bloom and Price cited above, but in addition I have used Francisco Arcelus and Allan H. Meltzer, "The Effect of Aggregate Economic Variables on Congressional Elections," Saul Goodman and Gerald H. Kramer, "Comments on Arcelus and Meltzer: The Effect of Aggregate Economic Conditions on Congressional Elections," and Arcelus and Meltzer, "Aggregate Economic Variables and Votes for Congress: A Rejoinder," *American Political Science Review,* LXIX (1975), 1232–69; John R. Hibbing and John R. Alford, "The Electoral Impact of Economic Conditions: Who Is Held Responsible?" *American Journal of Political Science,* XXV (1981), 423–39; and Stephen J. Rosenstone, "Economic Adversity and Voter Turnout," *American Journal of Political Science,* XXVI (1982), 25–46. It should come as no surprise that political scientists do not agree about these matters. I have found the Bloom and Price and the Hibbing and Alford articles the most persuasive.

To compound matters, the years that most historians have used to test the relative impact of economic versus ethnic and religious variables have been years in which economic conditions were improving rather than declining. They have focused on those times, that is, when modern research suggests that economic factors would have had the least impact on voting behavior. To identify the parties' voting bases in New York between 1832 and 1853, for example, Benson studies 1844. Yet 1844 was not only a year of economic recovery but also one in which ethnic and religious tensions were unusually salient because of anti-Catholic riots in Philadelphia, the appearance of the American Republican party, and the presence on the Whig national ticket of Theodore Frelinghuysen, a man who personified evangelical Protestantism and who was consequently anathema to Catholics. Similarly, Formisano examines an average of the party vote for 1848 and 1852. Fox runs most of his tests on returns for 1848; Shade utilizes an Illinois referendum in 1851, when the gold rush and foreign investment were spurring an economic boom. We have, in fact, few close statistical studies of voting in the depression years from 1837 to 1843.[20]

The realignment model adopted by these historians also obfuscates the impact of economic issues on both old and new voters. According to this framework, cleavages in the electorate form during the fluctuating stage of a voting cycle when voters polarize over certain issues. During the following stable phase, those alignments remain constant. Antagonisms engendered by the original polarizing issue persist even after it is resolved, and rival party loyalties themselves become sources of voting behavior. Issues count in the realigning stage, in short, but have minimal

---

20. This point about the unusual intensity of ethnic tensions in 1844 is also made in Donald J. Ratcliffe, "Politics in Jacksonian Ohio: Reflections on the Ethnocultural Interpretation," *Ohio History*, LXXXVIII (1979), 5–35, esp. 10–16, which is a superb critique of the ethnocultural analysis. Both Ratcliffe in this article and Fox in "Politicians, Issues, and Voter Preference in Jacksonian Ohio" do run correlations between economic indexes and returns from 1840. However, Fox found no relation between wealth and voting, and Ratcliffe (29–31) found that Whigs were stronger in wealthier, more commercially oriented counties, while Democrats were stronger in poorer, less commercially oriented counties. Even James Roger Sharp, who attempts to establish an economic division in the electorate in his *Jacksonians Versus the Banks*, distorts the impact of the depression, for he uses as his dependent variable an average of the Democratic vote in the presidential elections of 1836, 1840, and 1844. Economic conditions in the first and last were far different from those in 1840.

impact during stable phases. Instead, voters habitually refight old battles. To bolster this interpretation, historians cite two kinds of evidence: high interyear correlations of a party's vote that suggest the same men voted for the same party for the same reasons year after year, and research based on survey data from the 1950s that indicates a low issue awareness among voters and the overwhelming importance of party identification in voting behavior.[21]

This notion of a "standing decision" among voters in most elections is beguiling but dubious. The realignment model ignores new voters who enter the electorate after the realigning stage. At most, it assumes that they chose one party or another for the same reasons that motivated those whose allegiance crystallized in the realigning phase. If the years between 1836 and 1840, when the electorate expanded by 60 percent, were considered as part of the realignment, this tendency would not be so harmful. But most historians insist that voting patterns froze prior to the Panic of 1837 and the articulation of contrasting economic programs. Thus Benson argues that the alignments and motivations of New York's voters remained essentially the same from 1832 to 1853, although the vote increased from 305,649 to 441,692, or 44.5 percent, between 1836 and 1840. Thus Formisano contends that Michigan's cleavage was fixed by battles over alien suffrage between 1835 and 1837, even though turnout jumped by 47 percent between 1837 and 1840.[22]

High interyear correlations do not necessarily prove stability in voting patterns. Instead, they mask the movements of the voters into and out of the participating electorate. Correlation and regression coefficients, like the party percentages on which they are based, conceal changes in the size of the vote and the fact that new voters may have been attracted to a party for reasons that differ from those of its previous supporters. In Ohio, for

21. See, for example, Formisano, "Toward a Reorientation of Jacksonian Politics," 61–62. One of the most frequently cited pieces by a political scientist is Philip E. Converse, "The Nature of Belief Systems in Mass Publics," in *Ideology and Discontent*, ed. David Apter (Glencoe, Ill., 1964), 206–61.

22. More recently, Benson has argued more accurately that New York's voting patterns stabilized in 1839 rather than 1832, though he does not credit either economic conditions or economic issues for causing that crystallization. See Lee Benson, Joel H. Silbey, and Phyllis F. Field, "Toward a Theory of Stability and Change in American Voting Patterns: New York State, 1792–1970," in *The History of American Electoral Behavior*, ed. Silbey, Bogue, and Flanigan, 87–91; and Formisano, *The Birth of Mass Political Parties*, 134.

example, the Whig proportion of the vote increased only from 52.1 to 54.2 percent between 1836 and 1840, and the interyear correlation was +.888. In Pennsylvania, the arithmetic increment in the Whig proportion of the vote was a microscopic 1.3 percent, and the correlation between the 1836 and 1840 returns was approximately +.95.[23] Yet 70,000 more men in Ohio and 109,000 in Pennsylvania voted in 1840 than in 1836. How can one assume that habits acquired before 1836 account for the massive mobilization of votes in those two states, New York, and elsewhere, or explain why most of those new voters, quite unlike the majority of voters in 1836, preferred the Whigs to the Democrats?

Recent research by political scientists on both aggregate and survey data, moreover, is quite at odds with earlier work based on data from the complacent 1950s. It indicates that voters do respond to issues, especially those who have no previous party identity or low levels of identification with a particular party. In short, new voters are precisely the ones most likely to respond to the issues extant when they cast their first ballot. At the least, people who do not yet identify with a party, those who today might be termed independents, are the most likely citizens to be mobilized to cast a vote against an incumbent party if they form a negative judgment of its performance.[24]

This research has received its most powerful and sophisticated formulation in Morris P. Fiorina's *Retrospective Voting in American National Elections*. Fiorina demonstrates that voter allegiance to a party depends upon evaluations of the party's record in office. "Citizens monitor party promises and performances over time, encapsulate their observations in a summary judgment termed 'party identification,' and rely on this core of previous experience when they assign responsibility for current societal conditions and evaluate ambiguous platforms designed to deal with uncertain futures." More important, "retrospective evaluations" of what a party does in office can change the intensity of party loyalty. "Party ID waxes and wanes in accord with a citizen's evaluations of the recent performance of the party in power . . . with his/her perception of societal conditions, political events, and the performance of incumbent officehold-

23. The Ohio correlation is given in Ratcliffe, "Politics in Jacksonian Ohio," 14, and that for Pennsylvania in Shade, "Political Pluralism and Party Development," in *The Evolution of American Electoral Systems*, ed. Kleppner, 85.

24. Bloom and Price, "Voter Response to Short-Run Economic Conditions," 1240–41.

ers." A positive evaluation can reinforce identification with a party, but a negative evaluation will weaken it. Negative evaluations may not change the voting behavior of those whose loyalty to a party is strong, but for those with weak partisan identifications—and new voters, of course, have the weakest attachment of all—such evaluations are likely to cause a conversion to its opponent.[25]

Research by Samuel Kernell on voting in midterm congressional elections supplements Fiorina's findings. He has found that voters with a negative judgment of an incumbent president are far more likely to turn out in such congressional elections than are those who approve his performance, and they will cast their vote against candidates of the president's party. This differential, moreover, is especially true of independents. Members of the president's own party who disapprove of his record support that party's candidates less strongly than do those who approve of his record. Sometimes such disapprovers defect to the opposition, but more often they simply abstain. Across all categories, however, disapproval of a party's record has far more impact than does approval in determining whether a potential voter goes to the polls and how he casts his vote once he is there.[26]

These findings, especially those concerning independents or weak party identifiers, are surely relevant to the late 1830s and early 1840s, when a fundamental condition—the depression—affected evaluations of incumbent parties. Moreover, the large minority if not the majority of the electorate in 1840 probably had weak party identities. Three-eighths of those voters had not voted in 1836, and, as Shade's research shows, many of the others who entered the electorate prior to 1836 could have developed only a tenuous party identification. That identification might easily have been swayed by the coherent and contrasting party records on economic policy that appeared only after 1836, records that had much greater salience then because economic conditions had changed. Not only were there shifts in party allegiance by previous voters between 1836 and 1840, but vast numbers of new voters were mobilized by both parties

25. Morris P. Fiorina, *Retrospective Voting in American National Elections* (New Haven, 1981), 83, 96, 102.

26. Samuel Kernell, "Presidential Popularity and Negative Voting: An Alternative Explanation of the Midterm Congressional Decline of the President's Party," *American Political Science Review*, LXXI (1977), 44–66.

during those years. To understand why voters switched parties, why new voters were mobilized, and why most chose the Whigs so that the Whig party triumphed in 1840, therefore, one must look at the party performances and economic and social conditions that shaped voter judgments between 1836 and 1840.

The parties did in fact establish clear records that voters could judge after 1836. Thus the contention that there were no issues in the 1840 election is untenable. In 1837–1838 and again in 1840, the rival parties took sharply contrasting stands on virtually every economic issue that came to a vote in Congress. Attention focused primarily on the Independent Treasury bill, which Democrats backed and Whigs opposed, and when Van Buren signed it into law on July 4, 1840, Democrats proudly called it a second Declaration of Independence. Since 1837, Whigs had denounced this measure as precisely the wrong kind of economic remedy. Withdrawing government monies from private banks, they predicted, would reduce bank-note circulation, strangle credit, and thereby drive prices down. That it was passed when prices were already plummeting could only have given these warnings greater resonance among the electorate. The rival parties in Congress and the Democratic president had thus given voters a clear record to evaluate on a concrete issue. The party lines were in fact more sharply drawn than on other issues that historians have traditionally seen as central to elections, such as, say, the Kansas-Nebraska Act of 1854.[27]

Fascination with the folderol of the 1840 Whig campaign has similarly obscured the extent to which its intent was to draw a contrast between the parties, to remind voters of the Democrats' responsibility for the panic and their refusal to do anything to remedy it, and to convince them that

27. Schlesinger, *The Age of Jackson*, 261–65. For a particularly good example of a detailed Whig attack on the Independent Treasury bill, see the speech Abraham Lincoln delivered on December 26, 1839, in Springfield, Illinois, in *The Collected Works of Abraham Lincoln*, ed. Roy P. Basler (9 vols.; New Brunswick, N.J., 1953), I, 159–79. For the partisan dimensions of voting patterns in Congress, see Thomas B. Alexander, *Sectional Stress and Party Strength: A Study of Roll-Call Voting Patterns in the United States House of Representatives, 1836–1860* (Nashville, 1967), 24–36, 137–52. When the House passed the Subtreasury bill in 1840, 97 percent of the Democrats supported the measure, and 95 percent of the Whigs opposed it. In contrast, in 1854 only 68 percent of the Democrats supported the Kansas-Nebraska Act, whereas 78 percent of the Whigs opposed it. Even in the North, where all Whigs voted against the act, the Democrats were evenly divided for and against it.

only the Whig program of positive governmental action could restore prosperity. Even that notorious piece of demagoguery "The Regal Splendor of the Presidential Palace," a widely publicized speech in which a Pennsylvania Whig congressman denounced the luxury in which Van Buren supposedly lived, had a more serious purpose than arousing the resentment of the poor or proving that Van Buren was a pampered aristocrat compared to Harrison, the fabricated frontiersman with his coonskin cap. In addition, it was meant to remind voters that the president who had announced that the government could do nothing to help its suffering citizenry was living like a king off the largesse of that same government. So, too, Whig pamphlets such as *The Contrast: William Henry Harrison Versus Martin Van Buren, Harrison and Prosperity or Van Buren and Ruin*, and *The Crisis of the Country* underlined the differences between the results of a Democratic administration and what the results of a Whig administration might be. When Whig speakers announced that wheat would be a dollar a bushel under Harrison and forty cents a bushel under Van Buren, when in many places they promised to repeal the Independent Treasury Act, charter a new national bank, and raise the tariffs, voters learned what the alternatives were, just as they did when Democrats inveighed that the central issue of the election was, "Shall the banks or the people rule?"[28]

Much more important than voting records in Congress and campaign rhetoric in framing the issues before the electorate in 1840 were the performances of the two parties at the state level after 1836. Modern political scientists focus almost exclusively on the impact of economic issues on national elections for congressmen and president, perhaps because they assume that only the actions of the national government today can affect economic conditions. In the nineteenth century, however, state governments intervened in the private economy much more frequently and actively than authorities in Washington did, and after 1836 most of the battles over banks, paper money, corporate rights, and governmental subsidies occurred in state legislatures rather than in Congress. Because Democrats controlled Congress and the White House between 1836 and 1840, moreover, the only place that Whigs could establish a record for

---

28. Gunderson, *The Log-Cabin Campaign*, 101–105, 149, 194, 211, 228–29; Howe, *The Political Culture of the American Whigs*, 7–8.

voters to evaluate, other than opposition to Democratic measures, was in the states they controlled. The policies Whigs enacted when in power at the state level, that is, gave voters a clear record to contrast with Democratic actions in Washington and in the states. As a result, people knew what kinds of policies, if not exactly the precise legislation, they could expect should either party win the 1840 election. They hardly needed a national platform to tell where the parties stood as regards the issues. Reactions to state policies, in other words, were as important as, if not more important than, reactions to national issues or to the rhetoric and hoopla of the 1840 campaign in forging voters' allegiances that were reflected in the presidential balloting of 1840.

In most states between 1836 and 1840, indeed, voters were not only presented with sharp differences in the voting records and rhetoric of rival parties. They also gained experience with the actual policies of the two parties as control of state government seesawed back and forth. When the Democrats were in power, they tried to punish banks that had suspended specie payments by forcing them to resume, placing stringent restrictions on note issue, or banning paper money altogether. In addition, they often curtailed expenditures on internal improvements and blocked charters for new corporations. Conversely, when the Whigs came to power, they repealed the antibanking legislation of Democrats, attempted to expand banking facilities and the supply of paper money and credit, and voted state subsidies for beleaguered internal improvement projects on the grounds that their completion would promote prosperity.

Constraints of space preclude the systematic state-by-state survey necessary to prove this contention, but illustrations from three states suggest the ways in which issue conflict defined choices for the electorate in 1840. In Kentucky, Democrats in 1839 and 1840 attacked the dominant Whig party for incompetence and extravagance in its management of slack-water navigation projects the state had begun in the early 1830s, and demanded an immediate cessation of expenditures on those projects. In reply, the Whigs called for an increase in state taxes to pay for their completion and ran on that issue in the 1840 state election. In Massachusetts, where the Democrats had come to power for the first time in November, 1839, Democratic governor Marcus Morton attacked the previous Whig record in his message to the legislature in 1840 and outlined a sweeping plan to impose restrictions on banks, corporate rights, and state subsidies to railroads. Whig legislators vilified the governor's proposals as dangerous to the economic health of the commonwealth in a point-by-point rebuttal. In Pennsylvania, the Democrats also gained firm control of the state legislature in 1839, and in 1840 they passed harsh antibanking measures while the Democratic governor was forced to ask for new taxes, which Whigs had eliminated in 1836. At the end of the legislative session in March, 1840, the Whigs issued an address denouncing the tax proposal as evidence of Democratic incompetence and the antibanking measures as evidence of Democratic radicalism. The Democrats, Whigs charged, were "breathing nothing but destruction to the banking and credit systems of the Commonwealth." They were "men of no practical experience in the affairs of life—bearded enthusiasts, full of crude and chimerical notions of reform and with no better idea of a banking institution than such as might be picked up in the various but unmeaning vocabulary of a village newspaper." Whigs, they assured the electorate, would succor the banking system to promote prosperity. Apparently, voters responded to that message, for the Whigs made substantial gains in the state legislative elections held in 1840, as they also did in Kentucky and Massachusetts.[29]

Throughout the nation, in fact, the Whigs enjoyed sweeping success in the issue-oriented state and congressional elections of 1840, whereas they had suffered defeats in the equally issue-oriented state and congressional contests of 1839. The reason for this reversal of fortune was not that in the latter year Whig candidates could cling to the coattails of Harrison, for whom the party was conducting such a frenzied campaign. Most state and congressional elections were not held on the same day as the presidential balloting but instead took place earlier in the year. The reason was simply that economic conditions had changed dramatically;

29. The details of many of these state battles are given in the works listed in note 4. In addition, I have relied on Harry A. Volz III, "Party, State, and Nation: Kentucky and the Coming of the American Civil War" (Ph.D. dissertation, University of Virginia, 1982), 22–25; Arthur B. Darling, *Political Changes in Massachusetts, 1824–1848* (New Haven, 1925), 202–43; Charles McCool Snyder, *The Jacksonian Heritage: Pennsylvania Politics, 1833–1848* (Harrisburg, 1958), 112–50; and Henry R. Mueller, *The Whig Party in Pennsylvania* (New York, 1922), 43–66 (quotation on 63).

1839 was a year of relative prosperity, and 1840 was a year of deep depression. Voters' reactions to the contrasting party programs and records varied with changing economic conditions.

Throughout the period from 1836 to 1840, party fortunes fluctuated in relationship to oscillating economic conditions. After a period of soaring prosperity from the summer of 1834 to February, 1837, prices began to drop in March and April, and financial panic struck in May, 1837, when banks throughout the nation suspended specie payments. By the end of May, prices had plunged 22 percent from their boom-time high in February, and they remained low for over a year. Then, from about September, 1838, to October, 1839, a period of price and economic recovery set in. In October, 1839, however, prices began to plummet once again after a renewed round of bank suspensions, and they continued to drop throughout 1840, 1841, and 1842, with the next recovery beginning only at the end of 1843.[30]

Changes in wholesale prices come closer to approximating changes in real disposable income than do indexes measuring wealth. In the Jacksonian period, the vast majority of Americans were producers who sold the goods they grew, mined, or made, and were not simply wage-earning consumers. Sudden price changes affected the difference between production costs and selling prices. When prices rose, prosperity prevailed; when prices dropped, most people's income dropped.

Fortunately, moreover, price changes can be compared to political trends rather easily. Price data are available by the month. So are election returns because different states held state and congressional elections in different months. Therefore, one can plot the relationship between politi-

30. Peter Temin, *The Jacksonian Economy* (New York, 1969), offers the best discussion of economic fluctuations in those years. For the data on monthly wholesale prices, see his Table 3.2 (p. 69). Temin argues that although there was a price deflation after 1837, there was no depression. In the minds of contemporaries, however, the economic hardship was very real. It is difficult to be precise about the date that recovery set in because price figures were for the nation as a whole, and there could have been regional and local variations. Whereas most of the nation's banks did not resume specie payments until August 13, 1838, for example, New York City's had done so in May of that year. I have used September as the start of the recovery not only because most banks did not resume until August but because of price trends. From a bottom of 98 in September, 1837, the wholesale price index reached 100 in May, 1838, 102 in July and August, 107 in September, and 113 in October.

cal results and economic conditions over time, without employing the sophisticated multiple regression techniques used by political scientists in time-series analysis. The analysis I have made is not multivariate. I have examined only the relationship between changing price levels and changes in party votes and success in winning office. I recognize that local issues and local constituency characteristics obviously influence voting behavior. Certainly, I believe that some voters in all elections are motivated primarily by ethnic and religious or other noneconomic influences. Yet I also assume that if there is a systematic relationship between economic factors and a party's vote across units of widely varying socioeconomic and ethnocultural composition, then economic factors do shape voting behavior and the results of elections. In other words, if slaveholding, staple-crop-producing southern states as well as New England, if the Middle Atlantic and midwestern states, all seemed to respond in the same way to changing economic conditions and issues, those conditions and issues must have had a crucial impact on political behavior.

Between 1836 and the summer of 1841, when the Whigs took control of the presidency and Congress, the parties' fortunes clearly fluctuated with economic conditions. When prices dropped, the Whig vote and the number of offices won by Whigs rose dramatically. When prices climbed, on the other hand, the Whig share of the vote dropped, the Democratic vote grew, and the Whigs lost some but not all of the offices they had won during hard times. Table 1 lists the proportion of congressional and gubernatorial seats won by Whigs in different economic conditions from the start of 1836 to the end of 1844, and Table 2 presents the proportion of seats won by Whigs in the lower house of state legislatures from 1836 through 1843.[31] States are listed in the chronological order in which they held elections, and periods of economic decline are enclosed in blocks. Figure 1 presents a computer-constructed graph of legislative returns in eight states between 1836 and 1840 whose elections were held at different times of the year and whose economies and demographic composition differed widely, and compares the political trend lines with price trends

---

31. Virginia's congressional and legislative elections of May, 1837, are included in the boom period in both tables because they were held prior to the bank suspension that month. Even though prices began to drop before May, that is, the most dramatic slump came only after mid-May.

Table 1 Whig Proportion of Congressional and Gubernatorial Seats, 1836–1844

Date of Election and Economic Condition	Congressional Seats	Gubernatorial Seats
January–December, 1836 (boom)	40.4% (N = 151)	46.1% (N = 13)
January–May, 1837 (boom)	23.5% (N = 34)	0% (N = 3)
June–December, 1837 (panic)	67.2% (N = 61)	66.7% (N = 9)
January–August, 1838 (panic)	50% (N = 8)	66.7% (N = 6)
September–December, 1838 (recovery)	50% (N = 130)	42.8% (N = 7)
January–October, 1839 (recovery)	48.4% (N = 93)	14.2% (N = 7)
November–December, 1839 (depression)	0% (N = 2)	33.3% (N = 3)
January–December, 1840 (depression)	62.2% (N = 136)	85.7% (N = 14)
January–December, 1841 (depression)	60.2% (N = 103)	38.5% (N = 13)
January–December, 1842 (depression)	29.2% (N = 65)	27.2% (N = 11)
January–September, 1843 (depression)	28.9% (N = 97)	42.9% (N = 7)
October–December, 1843 (recovery)	48.5% (N = 66)	50% (N = 4)
January–December, 1844 (recovery)	37.9% (N = 145)	58.8% (N = 17)

SOURCES: Congressional Quarterly, *Guide to U.S. Elections* (Washington, D.C., 1975), 556–81; and Joseph E. Kallenbach and Jessamine S. Kallenbach, eds., *American State Governors, 1776–1976* (3 vols.; Dobbs Ferry, N.Y., 1977–82), I, which lists both the results of elections and the date on which state elections were held.

NOTE: I have included both special and regular congressional elections, so the number of total seats contested occasionally exceeds the number of seats in the House.

Table 2 Whig Share of Seats Won in the Lower House of State Legislatures, 1836–1843

State and Month of Election	1836	1837	1838	1839	1840	1841	1842	1843
New Hampshire (Mar.)	23%	N.A.	46%	37%	38%	35%	27%	36%
Connecticut (Apr.)	35%	35%	73%	59%	66%	67%	32%	41%
Rhode Island (Apr.)	44%	42%	60%	44%	87%	76%	N.A.	73%
Virginia (May)	43%	35%	54%	52%	55%	51%	37%	43%
Louisiana (July)	N.A.	N.A.	35%		46%		57%	
Alabama (Aug.)	51%	51%	41%	33%	49%	45%	33%	38%
Illinois (Aug.)	31%		52%		45%		31%	
Indiana (Aug.)	56%	68%	62%	39%	78%	47%	45%	45%
Kentucky (Aug.)	59%	71%	68%	58%	77%	77%	57%	62%
Missouri (Aug.)	29%		40%		45%		26%	
North Carolina (Aug.)	49%		55%		61%		44%	
Tennessee (Aug.)		64%		44%		52%		53%
Maine (Sept.)	35%	50.5%	39%	39%	54%	30%	22%	34%
Vermont (Sept.)	73%	57%	68%	N.A.	75%	58%	56%	51.5%
Arkansas (Oct.)	25%		44%		34%		30%	
Georgia (Oct.)	44%	N.A.	50%	43%	57%	42.5%	44%	61%
Maryland (Oct.)	76%	60%	53%	41%	76%	47%	43%	58%
New Jersey (Oct.)	38%	68%	62%	62%	77%	60%	55%	40%
Ohio (Oct.)	49%	56%	47%	32%	71%	49%	42%	54%
Pennsylvania (Oct.)	28%	44%	44%	32%	52%	36%	40%	42%
Delaware (Nov.)	67%		67%		100%		67%	
Massachusetts (Nov.)	69%	87%	70%	52%	70%	62%	50%	58%
Michigan (Nov.)		44%	40%	71%	61%	11%	11%	11%
Mississippi (Nov.)	37.5%	50%	52.3%	40%	54%	39%	33%	33%
New York (Nov.)	26%	78%	64%	55%	52%	26%	27%	29%

SOURCES: With the exception of Alabama and Mississippi, these data on the partisan division of state legislatures were made available by the Inter-University Consortium for Political and Social Research. They were originally collected by Walter Dean Burnham. Neither the original source or collectors of the data nor the Consortium bears any responsibility for the analyses or interpretations presented here. For Alabama, I supplemented Burnham's data with information from *Niles' Weekly Register*, LI (1837), 19, and J. Mills Thornton III, *Politics and Power in a Slave Society: Alabama, 1800–1860* (Baton Rouge, 1978), 34–36. For Mississippi, I utilized what I consider the more reliable data in Table III of Melvin Philip Lucas, "The Period of Political Alchemy: Party in the Mississippi Legislature, 1835–1846" (M.A. thesis, Cornell University, 1981).

NOTES: N.A. indicates that Burnham found no data available.

Periods of economic decline are enclosed in blocks.

In 1836 the Antimasonic and Whig parties in Vermont still ran separate candidates. Thus the figure given represents the combined total of Antimasonic and Whig seats and helps explain the curious fact that the Whig share of seats in Vermont appears to have declined after the outbreak of panic.

Figure 1   Wholesale Price Trend and Whig Legislative Strength

Wholesale Price Trend

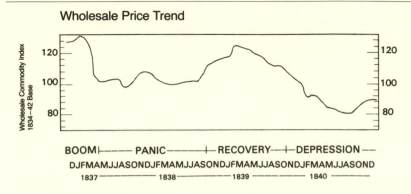

Percentage Whig Seats in Eight Legislatures

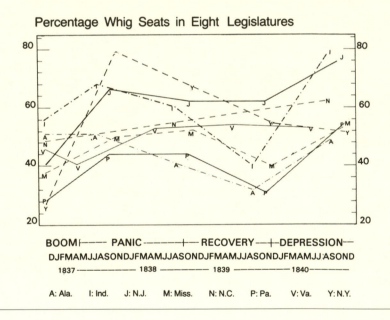

A: Ala.   I: Ind.   J: N.J.   M: Miss.   N: N.C.   P: Pa.   V: Va.   Y: N.Y.

based on the monthly wholesale price index. Table 3, which is constructed in the same way as Table 2, gives the Whig share of the popular vote in gubernatorial and congressional elections between 1836 and 1840. Figure 2 plots the average Whig vote in different months compared to price trends. To clarify the trends still further, Table 4 groups the states by the month or months in which elections were held and shows the mean Whig vote over time. Figure 3 charts those trend lines graphically. Such grouping is undoubtedly artificial. States with vastly different political complexions and economies were grouped together. Yet it is precisely those differences that make the general trend so compelling.

Despite the wide variation in the political preferences, economic structures, and ethnic and religious composition of these states, the figures indicate that with few exceptions the Whigs did substantially better in hard times than during prosperous times. Even the apparent anomalies, moreover, can in large part be accounted for by a more precise economic analysis.[32]

Yet it would be a mistake to infer from these figures that voters reacted to economic conditions alone rather than to the parties' contrasting responses to the economic crisis. If that had been the case, one might expect angry voters to have swung to the Whigs in order to punish the incumbent Democrats in hard times and then during the recovery either to have returned to the Democrats or abstained. Yet such was not usually the case. Unlike most off-year elections in the twentieth century and most in the nineteenth century after 1840, voter turnout in fact continued to increase with each subsequent state or congressional election between 1836 and 1840.

Table 5 presents the change in the absolute vote of each party after the presidential election of 1836. It also indicates the proportion of each state's increase in turnout, between the presidential elections of 1836 and

32. To give but one example, Whigs in many southern states did better in the fall of 1838 than in 1837, yet far worse in 1839 than one would predict from the wholesale price trends. Mississippi and Georgia are good examples. One reason for this may have been that cotton prices at New Orleans followed an idiosyncratic pattern. In 1837 they did not fall as fast as the general wholesale price index, yet were considerably lower in 1838 than 1837, even though other prices started to rise. In the autumn of 1839, in contrast, cotton prices were high, even though other prices had started to plummet. Compare Tables 3.2 and 3.6 in Temin, *The Jacksonian Economy*, 69, 103, and see his analysis of cotton prices, pp. 152–54.

Table 3 Whig Proportion of the Popular Vote Related to Economic Condition, 1836–1840

State and Month of Election	1836 P	1837	1838	1839	1840	1840 P
New Hampshire (Mar.)	25.0%	2.2% G	46.9% G	43.9% G	40.8% G	44.5%
Connecticut (Apr.)	49.3%	47.5% G	54.1% G	52.6% G	53.9% G	55.5%
Rhode Island (Apr.)	47.2%	56.8% C		52.5% C	58.4% G[1]	61.3%
Virginia (May)	43.6%	N.R.		48.2% C		49.4%
Louisiana (July)	48.3%		52.8% G		56.5% C	59.7%
Alabama (Aug.)	44.7%	46.3% G		49.6% C[2]		45.6%
				10.0% G		
Illinois (Aug.)	45.2%		49.2% G			48.9%
			40.7%			
Indiana (Aug.)	55.9%	55.5% G		49.3% C	53.7% G	55.8%
Kentucky (Aug.)	53.0%	63.9% C		N.R. C	57.2% G	64.3%
Missouri (Aug.)	39.4%		42.3% C		42.8% G	43.2%
North Carolina (Aug.)	46.9%	44.1% C[3]	64.2%	45.5% C[3]	55.0% G	57.5%
	53.1% G					
Tennessee (Aug.)	58.0%	60.7% G		49.0% G		55.7%
		68.9% C		51.5% C		
Maine (Sept.)	39.9%	50.1% G	47.9% G	45.9% G	49.9% G	50.1%
Vermont (Sept.)	60.0%	55.7% G	56.4% G	52.5% G	62.7% G	63.9%
	55.7% G		54.7% C			
Arkansas (Oct.)	36.0%		39.0% C		42.4% C	43.7%
Georgia (Oct.)	51.8%	50.6% G	51.5% C	48.5% G	52.2% C	55.8%
Maryland (Oct.)	53.7%	53.8% C[4]	49.7% G	48.8% C		53.8%
New Jersey (Oct.)	50.5%		49.9% C		51.7% C	51.8%
Ohio (Oct.)	52.1%		48.6% G		52.9% G	54.2%
Pennsylvania (Oct.)	48.8%		48.9% G		46.0% C[5]	50.1%
Delaware (Nov.)	53.2%		49.7% C		53.8% G	55.0%
Massachusetts (Nov.)	54.4%	60.3% G	54.9% G	49.7% G	55.6% G	57.6%
Michigan (Nov.)	45.6%	48.8% G	49.6% C	51.8% G	51.2% C	52.1%
Mississippi (Nov.)	48.2%	53.6% G[6]		45.7% G		53.4%
		68.8% C		45.7% C		
New York (Nov.)	45.4%	52.6% L[7]	51.4% G	50.6% L[7]	50.3% G	51.2%

Continued

1840, achieved in state and congressional elections. These figures indicate, among other things, that the remarkable turnout in 1840 was not simply a product of the Whigs' log cabin campaign or of the fact that party organizations competed for the first time on a national scale. Prior to 1840, at least two-thirds of the total increase in turnout had been achieved in ten states, and Pennsylvania almost reached that mark in 1838. Although the excitement engendered by the presidential campaign surely contributed to the additional turnout in 1840, moreover, the size of the vote in the state and congressional races in the spring, summer, and early fall of that year often exceeded the total in November. It is equally noteworthy that in most states that held elections prior to November in 1840, the Whigs gained the majority of their total increment that year in the issue-oriented congressional and gubernatorial elections, not in the presidential balloting. Something more than hard cider and hoopla was

Table 3 (*Continued*)

SOURCES: Walter Dean Burnham, *Presidential Ballots, 1836–1892* (Baltimore, 1955); Kallenbach and Kallenbach, eds., *American State Governors, 1776–1976*; and Congressional Quarterly, *Guide to U.S. Elections.*
NOTES: Those returns contained in lined blocks represent elections held during times of depression.

The initials *C* (congressional), *G* (gubernatorial), and *L* (legislative) denote the type of election.

¹Although Rhode Island held gubernatorial elections annually, 1840 is the first year for which the Kallenbachs list the party affiliation of candidates.

²The percentage for the Alabama congressional elections of 1839 is based on the popular vote in only three of five districts. It inflates Whig strength statewide, for the Whigs did not contest the other two races.

³These percentages are based on the popular vote in only nine of thirteen congressional districts in 1837 and eleven of thirteen in 1839. In 1837 the Whigs elected six of thirteen congressmen, as they had in 1835, and four of thirteen in 1839. In these elections, the *Guide* lists Augustine H. Shepperd as a Whig. I have considered him a Democrat, for he was a Conservative Democrat who only converted to the Whig party after the 1838 session of Congress. In 1839 he ran as a Whig and lost. See Jean E. Friedman, *The Revolt of the Conservative Democrats* (Ann Arbor, 1979), 131.

⁴The percentage in the Maryland congressional elections of 1837 is based on popular returns for six of seven districts.

⁵This percentage is based on the popular vote in only twenty-one of twenty-five districts. It was not reported in the other four. Two of these were multimember districts in which the Whigs elected a total of five members. The Democrats carried the other two.

⁶This represents the combined share of the vote polled by two Whig candidates. Their division of the Whig vote allowed the Democrat Alexander G. McNutt to win the Mississippi governorship in 1837.

⁷The New York returns for 1837 and 1839 are for statewide totals of the votes for state legislative candidates. The returns can be found in the *Tribune Almanac*.

Figure 2   Wholesale Price Trend and Whig Percentage of Popular Vote

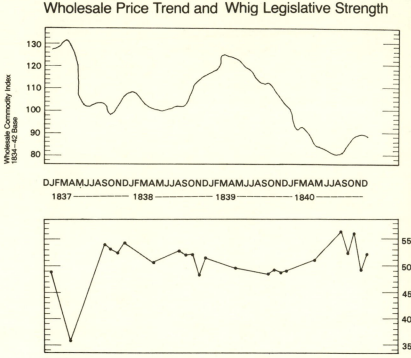

Wholesale Price Trend and Whig Legislative Strength

The Whig percentage of the vote in the lower graph represents the mean vote for states in which elections were held in the different months. The price trend is based on the monthly wholesale price index in Temin, *The Jacksonian Economy*, Table 3.2, p. 69.

bringing these voters to the polls to elect Whig legislators, Whig congressmen, and Whig governors.

The figures on the change in each party's vote between successive elections also suggest that different voters were responding to the parties' contrasting programs in different ways during different economic conditions. Although there were some defections and abstentions from the Democrats during depression periods and from the Whigs during the recovery of 1838–1839, the fluctuation in the party vote and success rate over time was caused primarily by a kind of leapfrogging pattern of voter mobilization. In the panic period of 1837–1838, that is, the Whigs gained the larger share of new voters joining the electorate. Then, in the recovery elections of 1838–1839, they retained most of those new voters and even added more newcomers to their ranks. Still, their share of the vote and of offices declined because the Democrats brought out even more new voters than the Whigs had earlier mobilized. Finally, in 1840, the pattern reversed again, and considerably more new voters swung to the Whigs than to the Democrats in most states.

Table 4 Mean Whig Share of the Vote in State and Congressional Elections, 1836–1840

Month	1836 P	1837	1838	1839	1840	1840 P
March–April (N.H., Conn., R.I.)	40.5%	35.5%	50.5%	49.6%	51.0%	53.8%
July–August (La., Ala., Ill., Ind., Ky., Mo., N.C., Tenn.)	48.9%	54.1%	52.1%	48.3%	53.1%	53.8%
September (Maine, Vermont)	50.0%	52.9%	52.1%	49.2%	56.3%	57.0%
October (Ark., Ga., Md., N.J., Ohio, Pa.)	48.8%	52.2%	47.9%	48.7%	49.0%	51.6%
November* (Del., Mass., Mich., Miss., N.Y.)	49.4%	54.2%	51.4%	49.1%	52.7%	53.9%

SOURCES: Burnham, *Presidential Ballots;* Kallenbach and Kallenbach, eds., *American State Governors, 1776–1976;* and Congressional Quarterly, *Guide to U.S. Elections.*

NOTES: Where gubernatorial and congressional returns existed for the same year, I used the gubernatorial return, unless the turnout in the congressional election was bigger. The figures represent averages of the Whig percentage of the vote in different states, not the raw vote. Thus they are not weighted by population. Clearly, states of widely varying political complexions are grouped together, but the mean does allow a clearer picture of the impact of economic fluctuations on Whig fortunes.

Those figures enclosed within blocks again represent returns from elections when the economy was slumping.

Virginia, the lone state to hold elections in May, is not included because of insufficient data, but the figures on the proportion of legislative seats won there are generally congruent.

* Neither this table nor the chart computed from it includes the New York Whig percentages in 1837 and 1839, which I discovered after constructing the graph on the computer. Inclusion of those figures would change the November average for 1837 to 53.8 percent and that for 1839 to 49.4 percent.

Figure 3   Wholesale Price Trend and Whig Popularity

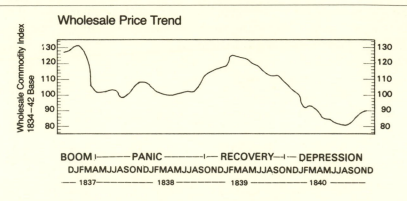

Wholesale Price Trend

BOOM ⊢———— PANIC —————⊣— RECOVERY—⊣— DEPRESSION
DJFMAMJJASONDJFMAMJJASONDJFMAMJJASONDJFMAMJJASOND
—— 1837———————— 1838 ————————— 1839 —————————1840 ————

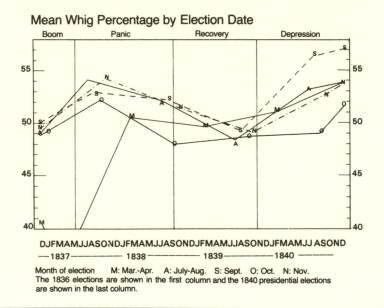

Mean Whig Percentage by Election Date

DJFMAMJJASONDJFMAMJJASONDJFMAMJJASONDJFMAMJJ ASOND
—1837——————— 1838————————— 1839————————1840 ————
Month of election   M: Mar.-Apr.   A: July-Aug.   S: Sept.   O: Oct.   N: Nov.
The 1836 elections are shown in the first column and the 1840 presidential elections
are shown in the last column.

Contemporary research by political scientists helps explain this pattern. They have found that bad economic conditions hurt an incumbent party far more than good conditions help it. People who disapprove of a party's record are more likely to vote against it than people who approve of that record are likely to vote for it, especially among independents, who for our purposes can be equated with previous nonvoters. Finally, those most directly hurt by bad economic conditions are more likely to turn against the party they blame than are voters less affected by hard times.

If this modern research is applicable, it seems likely that during the panic period of 1837–1838 those voters who suffered most from declining prices, who blamed them on Democratic hard-money programs, and who found the Whig program more likely to restore economic recovery, swung to the Whigs. During the recovery period, most of those men continued to vote Whig because they attributed the recovery to Whig actions in the states. Still, the Democrats rebounded because they mobilized tens of thousands of new voters who regarded the Whigs' probanking legislation of 1838 and 1839 as a threat to equal rights. At the same time, during that brief period of relative prosperity, many potential new voters who approved of the Whig effort did not vote because the Whig program did not seem as necessary to them as it once had. Once prices plummeted in 1840, however, the Whigs again attracted tens of thousands of additional supporters from men who suffered economic hardship, who resented the refusal of Democrats to help them, and who found the Whig program of governmental activism once again necessary in changed economic conditions.

Such a scenario is consistent with the growing evidence that Whigs and Democrats attracted supporters from different kinds of economic constituencies, if not from different classes. That is, the Whigs were far stronger than Democrats in areas that were closely involved in the commercial economy. Because these areas were most likely to be hurt by financial stringency, bank suspensions, and price declines, their residents would respond most positively to the Whig message. In contrast, Democrats received their strongest support from groups and areas that were at once most immune from price fluctuations, most impervious to Whig promises of economic recovery, and most likely to respond instead to Democratic warnings that Whig programs would create a privileged aristocracy subversive of republicanism. In much of the nation, Democratic voting strength was concentrated among subsistence farmers in the most remote and economically underdeveloped regions of states and counties. Such voters feared becoming ensnared in precisely the kind of commercial-monetary network the Whigs hoped to foster. New Democratic vot-

Table 5 Change in the Whig and Democratic Vote, 1836–1840

State		1836 P	1837	1838	1839	1840	1840 P
New Hampshire (Mar.)	W	6,228	−5,671	+25,008	−1,640	−3,225	+5,597
	D	18,697	+3,664	+6,380	+1,725	−997	+3,332
	T		−1.5% G	86.0% G	86.0% G	75.5% C	
Connecticut (Apr.)	W	18,798	+7,819	+498	+3,589	−344	+1,238
	D	19,294	+10,075	−7,880	+6,156	−1,863	−499
	T		95.0% C	63.7% G	107.5% C	96.9% G	
Rhode Island (Apr.)	W	2,711	+1,571	N.A.	−232	+747	+416
	D	3,036	+225		+399	−242	−155
	T		65.0% C		71.0% C	89.0% G	
Virginia (May)	W	23,361	N.A.	N.A.	+7,284	N.A.	+11,992
	D	30,263			+2,542		+10,952
	T				30.0% C		
Louisiana (July)	W	3,583		+4,005		+1,561	+2,147
	D	3,842		+2,934		+267	+573
	T			60.4% G		76.3% C	
Alabama (Aug.)	W	16,658	+3,947		−7,767	+8,718	+6,959
	D	20,638	+3,264		−1,221	+13,056	+4,894
	T		28.6% G		−30.6% C*	53.0% L	
Illinois (Aug.)	W	15,240		+14,482		+8,580	+7,274
	D	18,459		+12,209		+12,904	+3,871
	T			44.8% G		81.0% L	

Indiana (Aug.)	W	41,221	+4,846		+3,569	+13,334	+2,337
	D	32,478	4,437		+14,136	+3,246	-6,567
	T		21.0% G		62.0% C	100.4% G	
Kentucky (Aug.)	W	36,762	+8,195		N.A.	+9,945	-3,705
	D	32,762	-7,410			+13,808	-6,567
	T		4.6% C*			117.6% G	
Missouri (Aug.)	W	7,377		+9,814		+5,014	+671
	D	11,342		+12,068		+6,246	+373
	T			64.0% C		96.9% G	
North Carolina (Aug.)	W	23,643	-5,524	+20,000	-11,405	+17,800	+1,015
	D	26,810	-3,869	-1,786	+10,806	+4,819	+615
	T		-18.6% C*	47.0% G	43.1% C*	105.0% G	
Tennessee (Aug.)	W	36,058	+19,404		-3,672		+8,404
	D	26,120	+9,789		+18,268		-6,231
	T		55.0% G		94.0% G		
Maine (Sept.)	W	15,239	+19,119	+8,539	-8,148	+10,848	+1,015
	D	22,990	+10,889	+12,337	-5,448	+4,819	+615
	T		55.0% G	94.0% G	68.0% G	96.8% G	
Vermont (Sept.)	W	20,951	+1,306	+1,489	+875	+9,032	-1,208
	D	13,962	+3,760	+1,913	+2,621	+744	-4,991
	T		32.0% G	53.4% G	75.4% G	118.0% G	
Arkansas (Oct.)	W	1,339		+2,989		+1,469	-628
	D	2,380		+4,391		+1,105	-1,220
	T			91.0% C		122.8% C	

Continued

Table 5 (*Continued*)

State		1836 P	1837	1838	1839	1840	1840 P
Georgia (Oct.)	W	24,481	+9,697	−900	−563	+6,584	+1,045
	D	22,778	+10,639	−2,147	+3,418	+1,291	−3,996
	T		81.0% G	69.1% C	80.3% G	111.8% C	
Maryland (Oct.)	W	25,853	−5,902	+7,458	−2,679		+8,803
	D	22,269	−5,173	+10,626	−1,765		+2,802
	T		−23.0% C*	49.0% G	18.0% C		
New Jersey (Oct.)	W	26,137		+2,289		+4,916	+9
	D	25,592		+2,900		+2,646	−97
	T			41.0% C		100.7% C	
Ohio (Oct.)	W	105,809		−3,663		+43,298	+2,599
	D	97,122		+10,762		+21,428	−5,368
	T			10.0% G		102.7% G	
Pennsylvania (Oct.)	W	87,233		+35,088		N.A.	+21,702
	D	91,233		+36,592			+15,848
	T			65.5% G			
Delaware (Nov.)	W	4,736		−337		+1,446	+122
	D	4,154		+297		+633	−212
	T			−0.5% C		100.9% C	
Massachusetts (Nov.)	W	42,247	+8,318	+1,077	−917	+20,159	+1,990
	D	35,721	−2,734	+8,808	+9,239	+4,135	−3,215
	T		12.5% G	33.0% G	50.0% G	101.8% G	
Michigan (Nov.)	W	5,545	+9,339	+1,215	+2,970	+3,772	+92
	D	6,607	+8,711	+1,042	+1,350	+3,754	−368
	T		58.0% G	64.0% G	77.0% G	100.9% C	

		1836 P					1840 P
Mississippi (Nov.)	W	9,820	+4,992	+1,074			+3,629
	D	10,294	+2,529	+6,057			−1,870
	T		46.0% G	89.0% G			
New York (Nov.)	W	138,765	+17,340	+37,042	−9,287	+38,416	+1,002
	D	166,884	−26,355	+42,422	−3,182	+37,447	−3,990
	T		−2.9% L	51.0% G	49.7% L	99.8% G	

SOURCES: Congressional Quarterly, *Guide to U.S. Elections*; Burnham, *Presidential Ballots*; Kallenbach and Kallenbach, eds., *American State Governors, 1776–1976*; and the *Tribune Almanac*.

NOTES: The figures listed in the left column, 1836 P, are the totals for each party in the presidential election of 1836. Other columns list the change in the popular vote measured from the total in the immediately preceding election. For 1840, the figures under the presidential election column represent changes from the state and congressional elections held earlier in the year. For states that held congressional and gubernatorial elections in November simultaneously with the presidential election, the figures in column 1840 P represent the difference between the presidential vote and the gubernatorial or congressional vote.

The initials C (congressional), G (gubernatorial), and L (legislative) denote the type of election used in the table.

Where more than one election was available, I used the returns for the election with the highest voter turnout.

The row marked T for each state gives the proportion of the total increase in turnout between the presidential elections of 1836 and 1840 achieved in the state or congressional elections. For example, if the presidential vote increased by 100,000 in a state between those two years and the vote for governor in 1838 in that state was 60,000 larger than the presidential vote in 1836, then the T for that state in 1838 would be 60 percent.

*These are incomplete congressional returns—that is, where the popular vote was given for some but not all congressional districts; hence the statewide total was usually smaller than votes for governor or president. In most cases, the reasons for partial returns was that some congressional seats were uncontested by one party or the other.

ers, that is, were not responding to economic conditions. They came to the polls to punish the Whigs for their actions at the state level.[33]

It is possible, in sum, that the parties recruited their new voters between 1836 and 1840 from different economic constituencies and that, as economic conditions changed, new voters were more likely to turn out in one kind of constituency than the other. It is beyond my purpose here to attempt to test that hypothesis. Preliminary research on Ohio, Mississippi, and Virginia, however, demonstrates that Whigs significantly outpaced Democrats among new voters in wealthy, commercially oriented counties between 1836 and 1840 and that a far larger proportion of new Democratic voters than of new Whig voters came from the poorest counties in those states.

Whatever the source of the parties' new voters, the tables and especially the graphs presented here clearly refute the notion that the Whigs won the election of 1840 because of hullabaloo and snappy slogans. Whig strength surged during the panic period of 1837–1838, they retained most of those gains during the recovery of 1838–1839, and their fortunes soared once again almost as soon as depression set in at the end of 1839. Their striking gains in the spring and summer of 1840 before the presidential election simply repeated the pattern set in 1837–1838. Presidential coattails cannot account for triumphs that occurred months before the presidential balloting. Once prices fell again, Whig victory in 1840

---

33. Watson, *Jacksonian Politics and Community Conflict*, 246–81, makes this point explicitly and even provides statistical evidence (p. 279) that the two parties' votes in Cumberland County grew in different areas—the Whigs' in wealthier, more commercially oriented sections and the Democrats' in the remote areas hostile to the urban commercial sector. For additional evidence on this difference in the economic orientation of Whig and Democratic constituencies, see Ratcliffe, "Politics in Jacksonian Ohio," 29–31; Kruman, *Parties and Politics in North Carolina*, 16–17; J. Mills Thornton III, *Politics and Power in a Slave Society: Alabama, 1800–1861* (Baton Rouge, 1978), 39–45; Thomas B. Alexander *et al.*, "The Basis of Alabama's Antebellum Two-Party System," *Alabama Review*, XIX (1966), 243–76; Donald B. Cole, *Jacksonian Democracy in New Hampshire, 1800–1851* (Cambridge, Mass., 1970); Charles G. Sellers, *James K. Polk, Jacksonian, 1795–1843* (Princeton, 1957), 374; and Shade, *Banks or No Banks*, 158–63. That concrete probanking measures by Whigs could incite Democratic voters was demonstrated in Pennsylvania in 1836. In 1835 the Whigs won sixty-eight of the one hundred seats in the Pennsylvania house, and in 1836 they used that power to give a state charter to the Bank of the United States. Attacking that action, Democrats won seventy-two of the one hundred seats in the house in October, 1836, even though Van Buren won only 51 percent of the state's vote a month later.

was assured because depression made their program salient and attractive to new voters who yearned for recovery. Their victory in 1840, moreover, was emphatically a triumph of the Whig party as a whole—legislators, gubernatorial candidates, and congressmen—and not just of "Tippecanoe and Tyler, Too." In short, Henry Clay's famous lament when he learned that he had been denied the Whig nomination for 1840—that he was "always run by my friends when sure to be defeated, and now betrayed for a nomination when I, or any one, would be sure of an election"—was correct. No matter whom the Whigs ran for president in 1840, he was going to win because the presidential victory was simply a single facet of a genuinely sweeping party victory.[34]

Why, then, did the Whigs nominate Harrison instead of Clay? The answer to that question lies largely, though not exclusively, in the timing of the Whig national convention that met in early December, 1839. Since 1836, Clay's prospects for the nomination had risen and fallen with the record of the Whig party in off-year elections, that is, inversely with economic trends. Prior to the panic, many Whig strategists believed the party needed Harrison to win, but during the Whig surge of 1837–1838 Clay became the front-runner because it seemed that the party could triumph with the economic issues that Clay championed. When the Whigs suffered reverses at the end of 1838 and in 1839, however, Clay's chances were crippled. A military hero who might lure voters away from the Democrats once again seemed necessary.

The Whig convention met after economic recovery had dealt the Whigs a series of losses in the summer and fall of 1839 and before the real impact of the price slump that began late in 1839 had been felt.[35] Hence the Whigs shunned a national platform, opted for a military hero, and planned a "hurra" campaign. Even they, however, could not have anticipated that the disdainful Democratic response to Harrison's nomination would give them their most memorable symbols, log cabins and hard cider. Had the Whigs convened in May, 1840, when the Democratic national convention met, the results would probably have been very

34. The statement was originally attributed to Clay by Henry Wise in his memoirs, *Seven Decades of the Union*, and is quoted in Gunderson, *The Log-Cabin Campaign*, 68.

35. In 1839 the Whigs lost state or congressional elections in Maine, Ohio, Indiana, Pennsylvania, Massachusetts, Maryland, Georgia, North Carolina, Tennessee, Mississippi, and Alabama, and their hold on New York was precarious.

different. Then prices would have been 16 percent lower than they were in December. Then the Whigs would have been coming off a string of victories in Rhode Island, Connecticut, and Virginia, which pointed as they surely did to triumph in the fall. In those conditions, Clay, who had considerable support even in December, might well have received the prize he so hungered for. By May, 1840, in sum, it would have been clear that the Whigs did not need a noncommittal general to win.

Why Harrison received the Whig nomination and why he won the election, therefore, are different questions that have different answers. Yet, ironically, changing economic conditions explain his triumph in both cases.

The economic roller-coaster ride between 1837 and 1843, indeed, was clearly the predominant influence shaping American political development in those years. Not only did it spur the parties for the first time to formulate clear and contrasting economic policies, but it also molded officeholders in the respective parties into disciplined phalanxes who supported their rival programs in state and national legislative bodies in order to establish contrasting records to take to the electorate.[36] Because economic conditions gave salience to those records, moreover, men with different levels of involvement in and attitudes toward the commercial economy joined the electorate in record numbers and gave their respective allegiance to the rival parties. Hence it was in the state and congressional elections between November, 1836, and November, 1840, that voter loyalties crystallized, new voters were mobilized, and the Whigs built a

---

36. Referring to Congress, Donald Stokes has argued that the solidarity of a party behind its program is partially a function of the members' "perception of forces on their constituents' voting behavior. . . . If the member of the legislature believes, on the one hand, that it is the national party and its leaders which are salient and that his own electoral prospects depend upon the legislative record of the party as a whole, his bonds to the legislative party will be relatively strong. . . . But if the legislator believes, on the other hand, that the public is dominated by constituency influences and that his prospects depend on his own or his opponent's appeal or on other factors distinctive to the constituency, his bonds to the legislative party will be relatively weak" (Donald E. Stokes, "Parties and the Nationalization of Electoral Forces," in *The American Party Systems: Stages of Political Development*, ed. William N. Chambers and Walter Dean Burnham [New York, 1967], 184). In other words, party became a much more important determinant of roll-call voting behavior after 1836, because Whig and Democratic officeholders believed voters responded to the parties' records on specific issues.

coalition that gave them control of most state governments, both houses of Congress, and the White House in 1840.

The period between 1836 and 1840, in short, witnessed a realignment that should have made the Whigs the majority party during the stable phase of the second party system. Yet, as recent research has made clear, permanent realignments are not simply products of the voter movements that replace one party in power with another. Rather, they are products of the policies passed by the new "in" party once it gains power.[37] To cement the allegiance of the new voters gained in 1840 and effect a permanent realignment, the Whigs had to pass the programs for economic recovery they had promised, just as they had at the state level in 1838 and 1839. After 1840, however, state legislation would not be enough to hold those voters, for the Whigs now controlled the White House and Congress, and expectant Whig voters looked to Washington for action. For that reason, the Whigs failed to remain the majority party during the stable phase of the party system. As is well known, John Tyler, who succeeded Harrison a month after his inauguration, vetoed crucial parts of the Whig program in the summer of 1841 during a special session of Congress and again in the summer of 1842. As a result, disillusioned and frustrated Whig voters dropped out of the electorate almost as fast as they had joined it in 1840. They could not support the Democrats, but neither would they turn out for a party that had so disappointed them. The upshot was that the majority that the Whigs had built in the off-year elections between 1836 and 1840 melted away in the off-year elections between 1840 and 1844.

Perhaps no better evidence exists that voters responded to issues and party records, indeed, than what happened to the Whigs in the elections of 1841, 1842, and 1843. The congressional and gubernatorial results set forth in Table 1, for example, reveal not only a dramatic decline in Whig fortunes in 1842 and 1843, at least while the depression lasted, but a striking disparity between Whig fortunes in congressional and gubernatorial elections in 1841. The reason for that disparity is that all elections for Congress in 1841 were held before May 31, when a special session of Congress convened, and many of the gubernatorial elections were held in

37. See Clubb, Flanigan, and Zingale, *Partisan Realignment*, 11–45.

the fall of the year, after Tyler had wrecked Whig plans for a new national bank. The special session of Congress lasted from May 31 to September 13, 1841, and Tyler cast his major vetoes on August 16 and September 9. Of the five gubernatorial elections held before the first veto, the Whigs won three; of the eight held between September and November, when the extent of the Whigs' programmatic failure had become clear, they lost six. To a remarkable extent, indeed, even the results of the state legislative elections listed in Table 2 reflect the impact of the Whigs' failure in Washington. In 1841, with the exception of Indiana, the Whigs did as well in states voting before September as they had in 1840. Beginning with the elections of September, 1841, on the other hand, the Whigs suffered disastrous declines in their legislative strength everywhere, and those declines continued in 1842 and 1843.

The reason for this reversal of Whig fortunes was clear to Whigs and Democrats alike. Prior to September, 1841, voters responded to the promise that the Whig program would bring economic recovery just as they had in 1840. In the words of a defeated Democrat, before September "the people acted in view of the liberal promises of *relief and reform* which had been made to them." Once Congress adjourned, however, they were "disappointed and dissatisfied. They now find that they have been deceived." Throughout 1841 and 1842, indeed, both Whig congressmen and their constituents warned that people had elected Whigs because of their program. If they did not enact it in its entirety, the Whigs would suffer disaster at the polls because disillusioned voters would no longer support them. It was fear of such a reaction that caused congressional Whigs to pass measures they knew that Tyler might veto. The consequences of those vetoes and the ruin of the Whig program were precisely what they had predicted—substantial and one-sided abstentions that allowed the Democrats to recover the offices they had lost in 1840 and the first half of 1841.[38]

Thus the Whigs failed to remain the majority party during the stable phase of the second party system. They failed, not because of antiparty sentiment among the voters or defections to the Liberty party, as

38. James K. Polk to John C. Calhoun, February 23, 1842, in J. Franklin Jameson, ed., "Correspondence of John C. Calhoun," *Annual Report of the American Historical Association for 1899* (Washington, D.C., 1900), II, 844–45.

some historians have maintained. Rather, they failed because the new voters they mobilized by promising to pass an economic program before
1841 stayed at home once they did not enact it.[39] Between 1841 and 1843,
in sum, economic issues and contrasting party records were the central
determinants of voting behavior just as they had been between 1836 and
1840 when the electorate expanded, the party system crystallized, and the
Whigs won their first presidential election.

39. Benson, *The Concept of Jacksonian Democracy,* 133, states that the Whigs failed to remain
the majority party in New York because of defections to the Liberty party; Formisano, *The Birth of
Mass Political Parties,* 57–58, says that antiparty sentiment and vulnerability to the Liberty party
explain why Whigs became the minority party in Michigan after 1840. Yet abstentions far outnumbered defections to the Liberty party in the North, and they wrecked the Whig party in the South as
well. I have found popular voting returns from forty-nine state and congressional elections in twenty-
five states in 1841, 1842, and 1843. Of those forty-nine elections, the Whigs suffered drop-off in
forty-seven, and in all but three of those forty-seven Whig drop-off was greater than Democratic
drop-off and usually substantially greater.

Winding Roads to Recovery:
The Whig Party from 1844 to 1848

T he Whig party won the presidency for the second and last time in November, 1848, when General Zachary Taylor, a Mexican War hero and Louisiana slaveholder was elected to the White House. Four years earlier, many Whigs would have found this triumph inconceivable. In 1844 they had run Henry Clay, "the embodyment and polar star of Whig *principles*," as one had called him, against the Democrat James K. Polk, and the Whigs had been convinced that they had both the superior candidate and the superior position on the issues of the day. They would win in 1844, or else, many thought, they could never win. Thus one Whig paper had proclaimed on the eve of the election, "If J. K. Polk prevails over Henry Clay, the WHIG PARTY IS NO MORE." Clay's narrow loss to Polk, therefore, filled Whigs with "gloom and consternation" and shattered their faith in popular government. "The people have been appealed to and have elected a mere *Tom Tit* over the old Eagle," protested one Kentuckian. "Our strongest man has been beaten by a mere John Doe." Or, as Millard Fillmore, who himself lost the 1844 gubernatorial election in New York, wrote in despondency, "If with such *issues* and such *candidates* as the national contest presented we can be beaten, what may we not expect. A cloud of gloom hangs over the future. May God save the country, for it is evident the people will not." An equally dismayed Virginian evinced more anger: "With a most emphatic by God, I do say it is a disgrace, a lasting disgrace to our God Almighty—God damn—raggedy arse—hyena-made Republic to have elected over H. Clay that infernal poke of all pokes James K. Polk of Tenn." Gauged against this background of defeat and demoralization, the election of Taylor in 1848 marked a dramatic recovery for the Whig party.[1]

Rather than stressing the Whig's resiliency, however, many historians portray that very nomination of Taylor as a sign of the party's bankruptcy and a portent of its impending demise. By this interpretation, Taylor's victory in a campaign in which the Whigs refused to adopt a national platform, like that of William Henry Harrison in 1840, demonstrated that the Whigs could prevail only when they ran a military hero and fudged the issues. They could not win on their policies and principles. Actually, Taylor was even more apolitical than Harrison. He had never voted before 1848, and, as in the case of Dwight D. Eisenhower a century later, he was initially considered by both major parties as a potential presidential candidate. Since 1847, Taylor had been presented as a "no party" or "people's" candidate for president and had frequently vowed that he would never accept a regular party nomination from a convention or run a party administration. In the spring of 1848, he had threatened to remain in the race even if the Whigs nominated someone else, and only shortly before the Whig convention had he publicly admitted that he was a Whig, though not, he emphasized, an "ultra Whig." Patently, as both Whig and Democratic contemporaries were quick to point out, Taylor was not a devoted champion of traditional Whig programs.[2]

Because of Taylor's fame and popularity, he also appealed to many outside the ranks of normal Whig voters. The Whigs needed precisely

1. J. W. Mighels to Henry Clay, November 11, 1844, in Henry Clay Papers, Library of Congress; Richmond *Whig*, November 1, 1844, quoted in William J. Cooper, Jr., *The South and the Politics of Slavery, 1828–1856* (Baton Rouge, 1978), 225; Richard W. Thompson to Millard Fillmore, January 8, 1845, in Millard Fillmore Papers, State University of New York, Oswego; Leslie Combs to John M. Clayton, November 20, 1844, in John M. Clayton Papers, Library of Congress; Fillmore to Clay, November 11, 1844, in Clay Papers; William Cooke to William C. Rives, December 14, 1844, in William C. Rives Papers, Library of Congress.

2. The "no party" campaign for Taylor is described in Holman Hamilton, *Zachary Taylor: Soldier in the White House* (Hamden, Conn., 1966), 38–81; George R. Poage, *Henry Clay and the Whig Party* (Gloucester, Mass., 1966), 154–58; and Michael F. Holt, *The Political Crisis of the 1850s* (New York, 1978), 62, 72–73. The public avowal of being a Whig but not an ultra Whig came in the first Allison letter, April 22, 1848.

such a candidate in 1848, many historians argue, because their policies were sterile and obsolete. A campaign on those issues would have been hopeless. By 1848, according to Allan Nevins, the Whigs had lost their ideas and integrity. "They lacked any vital doctrine to give them real cohesion. They had been beaten on the tariff, on the United States Bank, and on generous national appropriations for internal improvements; it was plain that national sentiment was against their main ideas." In his splendid study of Abraham Lincoln's economic thought, Gabor S. Boritt also contends that the Whig strategy in 1848 "sadly implied that the Whigs had failed to get their message across, that their policies were not viable enough to be carried to victory by party regulars, at least in 1848." By backing Taylor, Lincoln joined other Whigs in "attempting to bring their principles to triumph through the back door." Similarly, William R. Brock has written that by August, 1846, the Whig program was "dead beyond the hope of recovery" and that the Whigs were "intellectually barren." Whig economic policies "were an inevitable casualty when the economy flourished without their adoption and prophecies of doom went unfulfilled." Taylor had been adopted in desperation. When he reached the White House, "the Whigs became a party without a head . . . [and] the heady stimulant of Taylor's popularity would leave the party too weak for survival."[3]

There is considerable evidence, however, that the Whig party was more robust and that its issues were more vital than this interpretation indicates. The superb quantitative studies of roll-call voting in Congress by Thomas B. Alexander and Joel H. Silbey, for example, demonstrate that Whigs did remain internally cohesive and sharply divided from Democrats on most issues through the summer of 1848, despite sectional rifts over the Wilmot Proviso. Elsewhere, I have argued that the economic and expansionistic policies of the Polk Administration and Democratic Congress, including the Mexican War, sharpened party lines in the states in 1846 and 1847 and enabled the Whigs to conduct successful campaigns in the off-year state and congressional elections as well as in

3. Allan Nevins, *Ordeal of the Union: Fruits of Manifest Destiny, 1847–1852* (New York, 1947), 194; Gabor S. Boritt, *Lincoln and the Economics of the American Dream* (Memphis, 1978), 145; William R. Brock, *Parties and Political Conscience: American Dilemmas, 1840–1850* (Millwood, N.Y., 1979), 151–52, 188. See also David M. Potter, *The Impending Crisis, 1848–1861*, edited and completed by Don E. Fehrenbacher (New York, 1976), 181.

the presidential election of 1848.[4] Certainly, the results of those crucial elections between 1844 and 1848 belie the notion of a bankrupt party. If Whig issues were so defunct that the party needed a military hero to win in 1848, one would expect the party to have sustained drubbings in those off-year elections when it lacked the coattails of such a leader. Yet in the congressional elections of 1846–1847 the Whigs picked up 38 new seats in the House while the Democrats lost 35 seats. Put another way, in the Twenty-ninth Congress, which enacted Polk's policies in 1846, the Democrats had a majority over the Whigs of 143 to 77. In the next Congress, the Whigs would have a majority of 115 to 108 and control of the House for the first time since 1841. More important, 30 of those new seats came from states Clay had lost in 1844. The Whig gains in New York, Pennsylvania, Virginia, and Indiana were especially significant. Nor was that all. Between 1844 and 1848, Whigs won the governorship in Georgia, New York, and New Hampshire and control of the legislatures in New York, Georgia, Louisiana, and Indiana—all states that Clay had lost. Over the same period, they maintained control of the state governments of such Whig strongholds as Massachusetts, Vermont, Connecticut, Kentucky, Tennessee, North Carolina, and Ohio.[5]

By these measures, surely, the Whig party was hardly an invalid as the election of 1848 approached. Since 1844, it had bounced back strongly at virtually all levels of the federal system and seemed to be flourishing. Why, then, did the Whig party find it necessary to select a candidate in 1848 whose very nomination signaled to Whigs and Democrats alike an abdication of Whig principles?

One answer has been offered by those historians who stress the centrality of the slavery issue in 1848 and the sectional nature of Taylor's support. Whatever the reasons for Whig gains after 1844, they argue, by 1847 and 1848, slavery expansion, crystallized by sectional divisions in both parties over the Wilmot Proviso, had become the major political issue of the day. The Polk administration may have revived economic

4. Thomas B. Alexander, *Sectional Stress and Party Strength: A Study of Roll-Call Voting Patterns in the United States House of Representatives, 1836–1860* (Nashville, 1967); Joel H. Silbey, *The Shrine of Party: Congressional Voting Behavior, 1841–1852* (Pittsburgh, 1967); Holt, *Political Crisis of the 1850s*, 39–66.

5. Figures on party strength are in U.S. Bureau of the Census, *Historical Statistics of the United States: Colonial Times to 1970* (2 vols.; Washington, D.C., 1975), II, 1083.

issues in northern states. But in the South, where slavery monopolized political attention and where each party jockeyed to prove itself a better proslavery party than its opponent, economic issues were dead by 1846. In this view, southern Whigs were in an especially desperate position. Democratic state parties vowed to reject any Democratic presidential candidate who was not pledged against the proviso, and John C. Calhoun was calling on all southerners to abandon the major parties and form a new Southern Rights party to resist northern aggressions. Pressed by the need to prove that the Whig party was safe on the proviso issue, southern Whigs seized on the candidacy of Taylor not only because he was a military hero but also because they could argue that his status as a large slaveholder guaranteed that southern rights would be protected in the controversy over slavery extension. Thus, according to this interpretation, southern Whigs were the driving force behind the Taylor candidacy. Southern Whig congressmen formed the core of his initial support and orchestrated the Taylor boom. Southern Whigs provided the votes for Taylor at the Whig National Convention, and Taylor's nomination should be regarded as a victory of the southern wing of the party over its northern leaders, virtually all of whom opposed slavery extension and many of whom publicly advocated passage of the Wilmot Proviso.[6]

There is much to be said for this interpretation. Southerners were integral to the initial Taylor movement, and southerners did back him solidly at the Whig convention. Three-fourths of the slave-state delegates cast votes for Taylor on the first ballot, and they constituted over three-fourths of his total. On the fourth and final ballot, 106 of 110 southerners supported Taylor. Moreover, the Whig party *was* divided over the slavery issue, and many northern Whigs, especially in Massachusetts and Ohio, did perceive Taylor's nomination as a triumph of the South and an insult to the North. In 1847, a Massachusetts Whig had warned, "The southern Whigs want to go for Taylor on the ground of slavery, even if they knew it would break up the Whig party." After the convention, another angrily fulminated that the southern Whigs "have trampled on the rights and just claims of the North sufficiently long, and have fairly shit upon all our Northern statesmen and are now trying to rub it in and

6. For a forceful restatement of this argument, see Cooper, *The South and the Politics of Slavery*, 225–68. See esp. 228–31 for the disappearance of economic issues in southern states.

I think now is the time and just the time for the North to take a stand and maintain it till they have brought the South to their proper level."[7]

Yet there is much that this thesis fails to explain. For one thing, the implication that all southern Whigs wanted Taylor only to neutralize or capitalize on the slavery issue oversimplifies their motivation; a variety of circumstances pointed southerners in that direction. For another, Taylor had northern support for the nomination from the time his name was first mentioned in 1846, and that support was clearly not based on his being a safe proslavery candidate. For example, New York's Whig boss Thurlow Weed was attracted to Taylor in 1846, a year in which he had tried to court antislavery voters in New York by pushing for black suffrage in the new state constitution. Two of the so-called Young Indians, the initial congressional supporters of Taylor, were northerners, and one of these was the influential Truman Smith of Connecticut, who came closer to being the equivalent of a modern national party chairman than any other Whig of the day. By March, 1848, Abraham Lincoln, then a Whig congressman from Illinois, wrote that not only he and Smith but also two Whig representatives from Indiana, three from Ohio, five from Pennsylvania, and four from New Jersey supported Taylor. Like Lincoln, all of these men had been elected in the Whig sweep of 1846–1847. Most important, of course, solid southern support alone did not secure Taylor's nomination at the Whig National Convention in June, 1848. One-fourth of Taylor's votes on the first ballot and almost two-fifths of his support on the final ballot came from free-state delegates.[8]

Taylor's northern supporters on that final ballot constituted 38 percent of the free-state delegates. By the final ballot, another 37 percent of the northern delegates voted for General Winfield Scott, the other hero of the Mexican War and a man whose credentials as a champion of Whig

7. Charles Hudson to William Schouler, June 28, 1847, in William Schouler Papers, Massachusetts Historical Society, Boston; William H. Howe to Roger Sherman Baldwin, Jr., July 25, 1848, in Baldwin Family Papers, Sterling Library, Yale University.

8. On Weed, see Robert F. Dalzell, Jr., *Daniel Webster and the Trial of American Nationalism, 1843–1852* (Boston, 1973), 125–26; Abraham Lincoln to Usher F. Linder, March 22, 1848, in Roy P. Basler, ed., *The Collected Works of Abraham Lincoln* (9 vols.; New Brunswick, N.J., 1953), I, 45. For voting on the different ballots, I have used the report of the Whig convention printed in the appendix of Glyndon G. Van Deusen, "The Whig Party," in *History of U.S. Political Parties*, ed. Arthur M. Schlesinger, Jr. (4 vols.; New York, 1973), I, 433–44.

policies were almost as negligible as those of Taylor. In sum, not only did virtually all southern Whigs support a military hero rather than a known advocate of Whig programs, but so too did fully three-fourths of the northern Whigs. On the final ballot, Henry Clay and Daniel Webster, the two contenders for the nomination who were prominent proponents of Whig measures, together garnered a meager 25 percent of the northern delegates and 16 percent of the total vote.[9]

One of the reasons some northern Whigs supported Scott and Taylor was indeed the divisiveness of the Wilmot Proviso. Early in the spring of 1848, several shrewd Whigs like Thurlow Weed recognized that the party would need a malleable candidate who had taken no public position on the proviso so that the party could conduct a two-faced campaign in 1848, running as a free-soil, pro-proviso party in the North and as an antiproviso, pro–southern rights party in the South.[10] But there were orthodox civilian Whig politicians who met that need and still had a record on Whig policies. Moreover, it is difficult to believe that most northern delegates who backed Taylor or Scott did so because they calculated on this two-faced strategy to salvage the election. It is much more likely that those delegates were primarily attracted to the generals' appeal as military heroes and by the promise, especially in Taylor's case, that they could lure thousands who had never voted Whig.

Thus the questions arise again. If the Whigs had done so well in the off-year elections between 1844 and 1848, if they had already made a dramatic recovery from the narrow yet psychologically crushing defeat of 1844, why did so many apparently believe in 1848 that they couldn't win on traditional issues with an orthodox Whig politician? Why did so many think, as the evidence makes abundantly clear they did think, that they required a military hero not only to capture the White House but also to help the Whigs win the congressional and state elections that were simultaneously being conducted that year?

Why the Whigs thought they needed a military candidate in 1848 and why Taylor won the Whig nomination are related but separate questions. The latter involves delineation of complex considerations, such as

9. On the first ballot, Clay and Webster together won 42.6 percent of the total vote and 58 percent of the northern vote. Even then, military heroes attracted the support of the majority of the convention and of a large minority of northern delegates.

10. Holt, *Political Crisis of the 1850s*, 61–62.

intraparty factional maneuvering for advantage in virtually every state, that are beyond the scope of this essay. My concern here is with the first question, and the best way to answer it is to take a closer look at the nature of, and the reasons for, the apparent Whig recovery in the off-year elections between 1844 and 1848. Such an examination reveals that there was no single road to Whig recovery after 1844. Rather, the fortunes of the party and the strategies it pursued varied both geographically and chronologically, from state to state and from year to year. The winding paths Whigs followed after 1844 and the changing fortunes that befell them along those roads greatly help to explain why many Whigs believed that yet another route was necessary to achieve victory in 1848.

Theoretically, the Whigs could have traveled several different roads as they sought recovery after 1844, but in essence these narrowed to three alternatives, which they could pursue singly or in some combination. The choice depended upon their answer to the following question: could they win by emphasizing and clarifying traditional differences with the Democrats or would they have to change the party's image and broaden its appeal? In other words, should they work to retain majorities where they already had them or attempt to build new ones where they did not? The first possible course was to abandon national issues in favor of state and local concerns in the hope of forging statewide majorities in off-year elections that could be retained on the basis of party loyalty in the next presidential election. Most Whigs and Democrats in this period considered control of state governments to be as important as control of the national government anyway, and a resort to state issues often seemed an efficient way to capture statehouses. A second possibility was to attack the Democrats on national issues in off-year elections. These issues could be old ones like the tariff and territorial expansion that had dominated the 1844 campaign or new ones generated by the Polk administration and the Democratically controlled Congress that would meet in December, 1845. Finally, they could resort to nominating a presidential candidate in 1848 who had broader appeal than Clay had had in 1844.

The attractiveness of these alternatives or the necessity of employing them depended upon a number of factors. These included varying Whig perceptions of why they had lost in 1844, the availability of viable state issues that could be separated from national issues, and the presence or absence of minor parties that threatened to siphon off crucial Whig votes.

But the most important variable by far was the competitiveness of a state's Whig party with the Democratic opposition. It is fruitful, accordingly, to divide the states into three groups: (I) states Whigs carried for Clay in 1844, however closely; (II) states they lost narrowly in 1844; and (III) states they lost decisively, that is, where the margin between the Democrats and Whigs exceeded ten percentage points (Table 1).

The behavior of Whigs in the states composing Group III is easiest to understand. For all practical purposes, Whig prospects in these states— Illinois, Mississippi, Maine, Missouri, Alabama, New Hampshire, and Arkansas—were hopeless. To this group should be added Texas, which entered the Union in 1845, a state where the Whig party bore the crippling stigma of having opposed Texas' admission in the first place. True, the Whigs picked up three extra congressional seats from Mississippi, Alabama, and New Hampshire in 1847, and they won the New Hampshire gubernatorial election in 1846. But those gains were ephemeral and exceptional. In New Hampshire, for example, the Whigs won only because of a coalition with the Liberty party and dissident antislavery Democrats led by John P. Hale. In 1846, when no candidate received a popular majority in a three-way gubernatorial race, this coalition in the legislature elected a Whig governor. Yet his own share of the popular vote was less than 32 percent, and in 1847, when turnout was higher than in 1844 and the Whigs picked up a congressional seat, they received only 35 percent of the statewide vote. Similarly, the telling fact in Alabama, Mississippi, and Arkansas was the Whigs' decision not even to contest gubernatorial elections during most of these years and to write off a number of congressional seats as well. The Whigs were so weak in Missouri, finally, that their historian argues that they constituted more of a pressure group than a viable political party.[11]

Whigs and Democrats alike commented on the bleak Whig position in these states. In 1845, for example, Mississippi's Whigs moaned in despair, "We have no hope as a party in this state—you know we are in the egyptian darkness of Locofocism." Similarly, a Mississippi Democrat confidently predicted victory in the 1847 gubernatorial election because

---

11. John Vollmer Mering, *The Whig Party in Missouri* (Columbia, Mo., 1967). Data from uncontested elections, as well as the data on most off-year elections in this essay, come from the voting returns listed annually in the *Whig Tribune Almanac*.

Table 1 The Strength of Whig State Parties Ranked by the Percentage of the 1844 Vote

	Whig	Democratic	Liberty	Major Party Margin*
Group I				
Rhode Island	60.0	39.9	0.0	+20.1
Vermont	55.0	37.0	8.0	+18.0
Kentucky	53.9	46.1	0.0	+7.8
North Carolina	52.7	47.3	0.0	+5.3
Maryland	52.4	47.6	0.0	+4.8
Massachusetts	51.7	40.0	8.3	+11.7
Delaware	51.2	48.7	0.0	+2.5
Connecticut	50.8	46.2	3.0	+4.6
New Jersey	50.4	49.3	0.2	+1.1
Tennessee	50.1	49.9	0.0	+0.2
Ohio	49.6	47.7	2.6	+1.9
Group II				
Georgia	48.8	51.2	0.0	−2.4
Louisiana	48.7	51.3	0.0	−2.6
Pennsylvania	48.5	50.6	0.9	−2.1
Indiana	48.4	50.1	1.5	−1.7
New York	47.8	48.9	3.3	−1.1
Virginia	47.0	53.0	0.0	−6.0
Michigan	43.5	49.9	6.5	−6.4
Group III				
Mississippi	43.4	56.6	0.0	−13.2
Missouri	43.0	57.0	0.0	−14.0
Illinois	42.4	54.4	3.2	−12.0
Alabama	41.0	59.0	0.0	−18.0
Maine	40.4	53.8	5.7	−13.4
Arkansas	37.0	63.0	0.0	−26.0
New Hampshire	36.3	55.2	8.5	−18.9

*A plus sign indicates that the Whigs carried the state; a minus sign indicates that the Democrats carried the state.

"the Whigs offer no organized opposition to our state candidates," and he ridiculed as well the refusal of Whigs to accept congressional nominations because their cause was futile.[12] In Illinois, a prominent Whig legislator lamented in early 1845, "I have hardly the faintest hope of this State ever being Whig." By the end of that year, he had determined to leave politics for private business because "there is precious little use for any Whig in Illinois to be wasting his time and efforts. This state cannot be redeemed. I should as leave think of seeing one rise from the dead." He was right. The Whigs, who had won pathetic 42 percent of the popular vote in 1844, did even worse in the congressional and gubernatorial elections of 1846, elections in which Whigs elsewhere were making a comeback (Table 2).[13]

In short, however much new state and national issues might help Whigs elsewhere, they were simply not enough to generate Whig recovery in these states. Here Whigs could not win on their program; here they needed a presidential candidate who could cut into the Democratic vote. It is no wonder, then, that Whigs from these states favored Taylor's candidacy overwhelmingly. Historians have long pointed out the delicious irony that Lincoln, the future Republican president, was an original member of the "Young Indians," the small group of congressmen who began the boom for the slaveholder Taylor in early 1847. Lincoln, in fact, was not one of Taylor's earliest congressional supporters, for he did not arrive in Congress until December, 1847, long after the Taylor bandwagon was rolling.[14] Still he was an ardent Taylor booster, as were other

12. Duncan McKenzie to Duncan McLaurin, November 2, 1845, in Duncan McLaurin Papers, Perkins Library, Duke University; B. F. Dill to John A. Quitman, September 7, 1847, in John F. H. Claiborne Papers, Mississippi Department of Archives and History, Jackson. See also P. B. Barringer to Daniel M. Barringer, June 26, 1845, in Daniel M. Barringer Papers, Southern Historical Collection, University of North Carolina, and John P. Stewart to Duncan McLaurin, July 11, 1845, in McLaurin Papers.

13. David Davis to John Henry, February 11, 1845, Davis to John Rockwell, December 17, 1845, and Davis to William P. Walker, December 6, 1846, in David Davis Papers, Chicago Historical Society.

14. Among the historians who repeat the error that Lincoln was one of Taylor's earliest congressional supporters are Hamilton, *Zachary Taylor*, 63; Poage, *Henry Clay and the Whig Party*, 157–58; Cooper, *The South and the Politics of Slavery*, 245; and Joseph G. Rayback, *Free Soil: The Election of 1848* (Lexington, Ky., 1970), 38. More precisely, all of these historians mistakenly date the formation of the "Young Indians" in the winter of 1846–1847. The group was not organized until December, 1847, and Lincoln was one of its original seven members.

Illinois Whigs who publicly endorsed Rough and Ready in the summer of 1847. He was well aware that he was the lone Whig congressman from Illinois and that the Whigs had to reach far beyond their own ranks to carry the state. Only Taylor could win the presidency for the Whigs, Lincoln insisted over and over, and only Taylor could help the Whigs in Illinois: "In Illinois, his being our candidate, would *certainly* give us an additional member of Congress, if not more, and *probably* would give us the electoral vote of the state. That with him, we can, in that state, make great inroads among the rank and file of the democrats, to my mind is certain; but the majority against us there, is so great, that I can no more than express my *belief* that we can carry the state.[15] To Lincoln, the slavery issue was irrelevant in 1848. He backed Taylor because Taylor was a winner, because Taylor was the only hope Whigs in states like Illinois had.

This same consideration motivated Whigs from other states where the party had been badly defeated in 1844, most of which were slave states. It is true that by 1848 southern Whigs needed a candidate to neutralize Democratic and Calhounite positions on the proviso issue. But Whigs from Texas, Arkansas, Missouri, Mississippi, and Alabama would have needed an ostensibly nonpartisan and enormously popular candidate like Taylor even without the slavery issue. Only with such a presidential candidate could they hope to broaden their voting base sufficiently to triumph. Thus delegates from these states to the Whig National Convention in 1848 provided Taylor with his most solid support. Fully 71 percent of those delegates backed Taylor on the first ballot and 85 percent on the final ballot. The totals for Scott and Taylor together were even higher. Indeed, there was an almost perfect correlation between the competitiveness of Whig parties in different states and the level of support those states gave Taylor at the convention (Table 3).[16] Where the Whig party was weakest, it needed a military hero to have a fighting chance.

15. Lincoln to T. S. Flournoy, February 17, 1848, in Basler, ed., *Collected Works,* I, 452; see also Lincoln to Taylor Committee, February 9, 1848, Lincoln to Usher F. Linden, February 20, March 22, 1848, and Lincoln to Jesse Lynch, April 10, 1848, *ibid.,* 449, 453, 457–58, 463–64.

16. Without New Hampshire, the total for Taylor on the first ballot would have been 81 percent. New Hampshire was unusual in that Whigs there depended on coalitions with antislavery Democrats and the Liberty party for the meager success they enjoyed; hence, New Hampshire delegates were especially unlikely to back a slaveholding candidate. In addition, Webster had immense personal influence among the Whigs of his native state.

Table 2 Fluctuations in the Major Party Proportions of the Vote

	1844		1845		1846		1847	
	Whig	Democrat	Whig	Democrat	Whig	Democrat	Whig	Democrat
Group I								
Rhode Island	60	39.9	49.1	50.4[1]	49.8	49.2[1]	57.4	36.3
Vermont	55	37	47.9	39.1	49.1	36.5	48.7	36.7
					47	32.4[2]		
Massachusetts	51.7	40	48.8	35.3	53.9	32.7	50.8	37.5
					55.4	32.9[2]		
Kentucky	53.9	46.1	51.6	48.4[2]	—	—	53.1	44.3[2]
North Carolina	52.7	47.3	42.9	57.1[2]	54	46	52.4	47.6[2]
Maryland	52.4	47.6	43.3	54.6[2]	—	—	49.5	50.5
							50	50[2]
Connecticut	50.8	46.2	51	45.3	48.6	47.5	50.5	45.9
			51	44.8[2]			50.8	46.1[2]
Delaware	51.2	48.7	—	—	49.4	50.6	—	—
					50.6	49.4[2]		
Ohio	49.6	47.7	—	—	48.3	47.3	—	—
New Jersey	50.4	49.3	—	—	51.4	46[2]	48.1	51.9
Tennessee	50.1	49.9	49.4	50.6	—	—	50.4	49.6
Group II								
New York	47.8	48.9	—	—	51.5	48.5	53.6	41.7[3]
Indiana	48.4	50.1	46.8	51.8[2]	48.3	51.7	50.1	49.9[2]
Pennsylvania	48.5	50.6	38.1	51.1[4]	51.3	48.7[2]	44.6	50.8
					47.9	43.5[4]		
Georgia	48.8	51.2	51.1	48.9	46.9	53.1[2]	49.1	50.9
Louisiana	48.7	51.3	N.A.		44.1	53.2	47.2	52.8[2]
Virginia	47	53	N.A.		—	—	48.8	51.2[2]
Michigan	43.5	49.9	41.2	50.8	43.8	50.1	41	53.1
Iowa	—	—	—	—	48.9	51.1	48	52[2]
Florida	—	—	49.6	51.1[2]	50.8	49.2[2]	—	—

Continued

Table 2 (*Continued*)

	1844		1845		1846		1847	
	Whig	*Democrat*	*Whig*	*Democrat*	*Whig*	*Democrat*	*Whig*	*Democrat*
Group III								
Illinois	42.4	54.4	—	—	36.7	58.2	—	—
					40.3	54.4[2]		
Mississippi	43.4	56.6	35.2	64.8	—	—	33.6	64.7[5]
Maine	40.4	53.8	40.2	50.7	40.1	46.9	37.2	51.3
Missouri	43	57	N.A.		N.A.		N.A.	
Alabama	41	59	Two Dems.		—	—	44.7	55.3
New Hampshire	36.3	55.2	34	51.2	31.8	48.7	34.9	51
Arkansas	37	63	—	—	No Contest		—	—

[1] I have listed the Law and Order percentage under the Whigs and the Liberation party percentage under the Democrats.

[2] These are returns from congressional races. All other returns after 1844 are for gubernatorial races except where otherwise indicated.

[3] The returns in New York in 1847 are for comptroller.

[4] These returns in Pennsylvania are for canal commissioner.

[5] In this Mississippi election, the Whig candidate was a volunteer. The party made no official nomination.

However logical and important was the Whig support for Taylor from these normally Democratic states, it provides only a partial answer to the puzzle raised at the beginning of this essay. The Whigs' comeback in off-year elections did not center on those states; rather, it occurred in the states the Whigs had carried in 1844 and especially in the states they had lost narrowly like New York, Pennsylvania, Indiana, and Georgia. To solve the riddle of why an apparently robust party needed a military candidate who was not associated with its principles, one must examine the performance of the Whigs in those states after 1844. Such an examination reveals a predictable variety in the strategies and fortunes of Whig parties in different states. More important it also shows that the Whig comeback in off-year elections was not as substantial as a mere count of congressional seats and statehouses won seems to indicate. Rather, those victories were based on razor-thin margins, idiosyncratic conditions that could not be re-created, or issues whose salience and appeal proved

Table 3 Proportions of Votes Cast for
Military Candidates by Group
at the Whig Convention

Percentage for Taylor

	First Ballot	Final Ballot
Group I	29.5	56
Group II	37	56
Group III	70.8	85

Percentage for Taylor and Scott Combined

	First Ballot	Final Ballot
Group I	48.5	80
Group II	55.5	86
Group III	73	92

NOTE: Groups are those defined by Table 1.
Group II includes Iowa and Florida as based on
margins in 1846. Group III includes Texas.

ephemeral. The result was that even where the Whig party had flourished in 1845, 1846, or 1847, many Whigs believed by the spring of 1848 that nominating a Mexican War hero was necessary to win in the state, congressional, and presidential elections of that year.

For year or so after Clay's defeat, stunned Whigs experimented with several different routes toward recovery, but most of these proved to be dead ends. By the spring of 1846, the party was generally in worse shape than it had been in November, 1844—listless, worried, and internally divided. In the South, the major Whig priority in 1845, a year of important congressional and gubernatorial elections, was to bury the national issues that Whigs thought had hurt them in 1844—the tariff and especially Texas annexation. As one Georgia Whig wrote of the Texas issue, "This question was in our way last year, it is in our way now, and will be a thorn in our side until it is . . . put to rest in some way." Thus Whigs in Virginia, Tennessee, and Georgia urged their congressmen and senators to support annexation by joint resolution in February, 1845, to prevent Democrats from "making party capital" of the Texas issue in gubernatorial elections. And even though a number of Whig senators from the

South opposed annexation by that measure, its passage did resolve the issue. At the same time, the lack of concrete tariff proposals in 1845 allowed the Whigs to dodge the tariff issue where they wanted to.[17]

Problems remained for southern Whigs, however. When they did manage to bury the supposedly deleterious national issues of 1844, they usually found that they then had nothing else to run on. In Georgia, they clung to the coattails of the popular incumbent Governor George W. Crawford, whose management of state finances was universally praised. They also went out of their way to prevent the Democrats from focusing the campaign on the record of Whig Senator John M. Berrien, who had resolutely defended the Whig tariff of 1842 and opposed Texas annexation and who was up for reelection in 1845.[18] In this way, Georgia's Whigs captured the governorship and one house of the legislature in a key southern state that Clay had lost. But this stratagem clearly could not be repeated in future Georgia elections; Crawford, indeed, had been very reluctant even to run for reelection.

Elsewhere in the South, the Whigs apparently had no viable state issues, and as a result their performance was dismal. They lost the governorship in Tennessee, a state Clay had carried, even though their candidate, Ephraim Foster, had supported Texas annexation in the United States Senate. In Virginia, where internal regional rivalries prevented a coherent stand on any state issues, they unexpectedly lost the legislative elections of 1845 and one U.S. Senate seat, and elected just one of fifteen

17. For the quotations, see N. C. Barnett to John M. Berrien, February 18, 1845, in John M. Berrien Papers, Southern Historical Collection, University of North Carolina, and Joseph H. Peyton to William B. Campbell, February 16, 1845, in Campbell Family Papers, Perkins Library, Duke University. On the general desire to bury the Texas and tariff issues, see, on Virginia, W. E. Sutton to William C. Rives, January 31, 1845, J. J. Fry to Rives, January 23, 1845, James F. Strother to Rives, November 17, 1844, February 2, 1845, all in Rives Papers; on Tennessee, Arthur Campbell to David Campbell, November 17, 1844, in Campbell Family Papers; on Alabama, H. M. Cunningham to Alexander H. Stephens, December 21, 1844, in Alexander H. Stephens Papers, Library of Congress; and on Georgia, David S. Anderson to Alexander H. Stephens, February 16, 1845, in Ulrich B. Phillips, ed., *The Correspondence of Robert Toombs, Alexander H. Stephens, and Howell Cobb* (Washington, D.C., 1913), 60–64, and Charles J. Jenkins to John M. Berrien, February 3, 15, 1845, Robert Toombs to Berrien, February 13, 1845, in Berrien Papers.

18. See the sources on Georgia in the previous note and Charles J. Jenkins to John M. Berrien, April 22, 1845, C. B. Strong to Berrien, May 9, 1845, J. R. A. Merriwether to Berrien, May 10, 1845, and Francis S. Bartow to Berrien, July 30, August 3, 1845, all in Berrien Papers.

congressmen.[19] North Carolina's Whigs captured only three of nine House seats, and two of those were not contested by the Democrats. Moreover in the districts the Democrats did contest, the Whig share of the vote dropped from 46.3 percent in 1844 to 42.9 percent in 1845. In Kentucky, the Whigs gained an additional congressional seat but suffered a drop in their proportion of the vote. They also lost a special gubernatorial election in Louisiana in January, 1846, with a smaller share of the vote than Clay had attracted in 1844. Worst of all was the Whig experience in Maryland, a state Clay had carried handily. Controlling all six of the state's congressional seats going into the 1845 election, the Whigs lost four of those seats and saw their share of the vote plummet from 52.4 to 43.3 percent. Despair, apathy, and a lack of viable issues obviously contributed to these reverses, for in every southern state except Georgia the Whig drop-off in voter turnout since 1844 was significantly higher than Democratic drop-off (Table 4). By early 1846, the Whig party in the South was clearly in trouble.

In sharp contrast to their southern brethren, northern Whigs initially tried to keep the issues growing out of the 1844 campaign alive as long as possible. They thought they could profit from them, even in the northern states they had lost. Thus the influential New York *Tribune* argued shortly after Clay's defeat that Whig principles were "approved by a large majority of the American people . . . We are beaten not because we were in favor of Protection and opposed to Annexation, but because our opponents concealed or mystified these vital issues throughout two-thirds of the Union." The road to Whig victory, editor Horace Greeley concluded, lay in clarifying the real differences between the two parties on those issues as sharply as possible.[20] Such a tack might galvanize the loyalty of Whig voters and convert people who had supported Polk because they had been hoodwinked by the Democratic campaign. It also might win back the crucial Liberty party vote in closely divided states like Connecticut, New York, Pennsylvania, Ohio, Indiana, and Michigan. Holding this belief, Whigs kept up a steady drumfire against Texas annexation in editorials, party platforms, and legislative resolutions, even

19. For the Whig expectations and disappointment in Virginia, see J. J. Fry to William C. Rives, January 23, 1845, and John Pendleton to Rives, May 1, 1845, in Rives Papers.
20. New York *Tribune*, November 16, 1844.

Table 4 Drop-off Rates of Major Parties in Selected States after 1844

	1845		1846		1847	
	Whig	*Democrat*	*Whig*	*Democrat*	*Whig*	*Democrat*
Vermont	22.6	5.8	14.5	5.4	10.6	− 0.4
Massachusetts	23.5	28.2	18.8	36.3	20.4	23.9
Rhode Island	− 5.1	− 62.3	− 2.1	− 51.8	6.3	10.7
Connecticut	10.1	12	15.2	8.8	8.2	8.2
New York	—	—	14.4	21.1	24.8	42.7
Pennsylvania	44.4	28.6	39	46.8	20.1	12.7
Ohio	—	—	24.6	23.2	—	—
Indiana	13.3	7.1	15.2	12.4	0.5	4.2
Maryland	33.8	8.3	—	—	6.4	− 5
Virginia		N.A.	—	—	17.1	24.4
North Carolina	17	4.7	7.2	12.1	22.6	21.9
Georgia	13.7	21.4	34.5	29.4	0.4	1.8
Kentucky	7.7	− 14.3	—	—	− 6.2	− 3.8
Tennessee	5.6	2.7	—	—	− 2.1	0.9
Louisiana	—	—	15.1	2.9	0.4	1.8

NOTE: This table is based on the same returns as Table 2. When congressional and statewide elections were held in the same year, I used the statewide return to calculate drop-off. On Rhode Island, I again put the Law and Order party in the Whig column and the Liberation party in the Democratic column. A negative drop-off indicates that a party drew more votes in that election than it had in the presidential election of 1844.

after Congress offered and Texas accepted annexation in 1845.[21] While the issue remained salient, it clearly helped the Whigs. In April, 1845, the Whigs swept to victory in Connecticut, winning the governorship and replacing the entire congressional delegation of Democrats with Whigs.

21. See, for example, Daniel Webster to Robert C. Winthrop, January 10, 1845, in Robert C. Winthrop Papers, Massachusetts Historical Society; Daniel Webster to Samuel Hurd, March 8, 1845, in Daniel Webster Papers, Dartmouth College; copy of anti-Texas resolution passed by the Massachusetts legislature, March 31, 1845, in Adams Family Papers, Massachusetts Historical Society; New York *Tribune*, February 6, September 27, 1845; D. T. Disney to William Allen, December 3, 1844, and C. B. Flood to Allen, December 3, 1844, January 16, 1845, in William Allen Papers, Library of Congress; Samuel Sample to Schuyler Colfax, June 8, 1845, in Schuyler Colfax Papers, Northern Indiana Historical Society, South Bend; and Holt, *Political Crisis of the 1850s*, 44–45.

The Democrats' support of annexation by joint resolution, the triumphant Whigs explained, accounted for this rout.[22]

Yet the Texas issue was severely limited so far as northern Whigs were concerned. It was finite. Once Texas accepted annexation to the Union in July, 1845, and its admission by the impending session of Congress seemed assured, the issue lost impact. Indeed, further agitation of it only divided Whigs in states like Massachusetts. Nor could they find different strategies for wooing Liberty party voters that did not also fragment the party. In New York, for example, the Weed-Seward-Greeley wing of the Party bid for antislavery voters by pushing for revision of the state constitution to broaden black suffrage. Conservative New York Whigs, however, vehemently opposed such a change, and their hostility neutralized any lure the Whig party as such had for political abolitionists in the state legislative elections of 1845.[23]

Without a powerful unifying national issue like Texas, in fact, the Whig party fragmented almost everywhere in the North in 1845 and early 1846. Ohio was an exception. There the party was in sharp conflict with the Democrats over state banking policy, and it scored impressive gains in the October legislative elections. Pennsylvania was more typical. Whigs from the eastern and western ends of the state, like Democrats, were dividing over the rival claims of the Baltimore & Ohio and Pennsylvania railroads for chartered routes to Pittsburgh. This battle would completely disrupt Whig cohesion in the legislative session that began in January, 1846. Similarly, Indiana's Whigs split over issues like slavery, state internal improvements, and the repudiation of state bonds issued for construction of the Wabash & Erie Canal, and those divisions apparently contributed to the party's defeat in the congressional and legislative elections of August, 1845.[24]

22. William Ellsworth to Roger Sherman Baldwin, April 9, 1845, and Baldwin to S. C. Phillips *et al.*, July 3, 1845, in Baldwin Family Papers.

23. On Massachusetts, see Kinley J. Brauer, *Cotton Versus Conscience: Massachusetts Whig Politics and Southwestern Expansion* (Lexington, Ky., 1967). On New York, see New York *Tribune*, January 13, April 26, May 17, July 2, 1845; Horace Greeley to Schuyler Colfax, January 26, 1846, in Greeley-Colfax Papers, New York Public Library.

24. On Ohio, see Stephen Maizlish, "The Triumph of Sectionalism: The Transformation of Antebellum Politics in the North, Ohio, 1844–1860" (Ph.D. dissertation, University of California at Berkeley, 1978), 74–95; on Pennsylvania, see Holt, *Political Crisis of the 1850s*, 112, and

Rhode Island provides yet another example of Whig vulnerability to divisive state issues following the settlement of unifying national questions. In 1844 the Whigs had rolled up a higher percentage of the vote in Rhode Island than in any other state, but in the April gubernatorial elections of 1845 and 1846 the Whig coalition virtually disintegrated. Legacies of the Dorr Rebellion, those campaigns were conducted by state-oriented parties called the Law and Order and the Liberation parties, each of which ran a Whig as its candidate. The party fractured so badly that in March, 1846, a furious Whig berated the folly of his party's newspapers for making so much of the law and order issue. They should make clear, he advised, that the tariff was at stake in the 1846 legislative elections. Whig Senator James F. Simmons, a stalwart on the matter, was up for reelection, and intraparty squabbles over state issues endangered his seat. Only by focusing attention on national issues, in short, could the Whig party be saved from its suicidal internal bloodletting.[25]

Perhaps the most dramatic evidence of how a lack of salient national issues damaged the Whigs came in Connecticut, the state the Whigs had swept so impressively in April, 1845, on the tariff and Texas issues. In the absence of concrete action from the new Congress, Democrats managed to focus the state election of April, 1846, on a state issue, temperance, which divided the Whigs internally and cost them votes among the foes of liquor laws. As a result, the Whigs lost their statewide majority, and the Democrats captured the legislature, which then elected a Democratic governor. Almost concurrently, both the Whig and Democratic parties were splitting internally over the question of bridging the Connecticut River at Middletown to build a railroad from New Haven to Boston. New Haven and Hartford Whigs, along with their respective regional allies, would war with each other over this disruptive issue for two years.[26]

Henry R. Mueller, *The Whig Party in Pennsylvania* (New York, 1922), 131–32; on Indiana, see Godlove Orth to Schuyler Colfax, August 16, 1845, in Godlove Orth Papers, Indiana State Library, Indianapolis.

25. Thomas J. Stead to Samuel F. Man, March 18, 1846, in Thomas Jenckes Papers, Library of Congress. Without statistical analysis, it is impossible to say precisely how the Whig vote divided, but see Table 2 for the apparent divisions of the Whigs' 1844 vote between the two parties.

26. Roger Sherman Baldwin to S. D. Hubbard, March 28, 1846, Emily Baldwin to Edward Baldwin, April 12, 1846, in Baldwin Family Papers; A. E. Burr to Gideon Welles,

Adding to the disarray caused by intrastate regional divisions and damaging issues in specific states was a more general legacy of the 1844 campaign—the existence of independent nativist or anti-immigrant parties. To the Whigs, such parties posed both a problem and an opportunity. They might drain off Whig voters, and yet they might help broaden the party's base. Many angry Whigs blamed Clay's defeat on a large and illegal immigrant vote for Polk, and some even wanted to merge with the Native American or American Republican party, as it was called in different places. The threat such a development posed for Whig fortunes became clear soon after the presidential election. In December, 1844, an independent nativist party defeated both Democrats and Whigs in the Boston mayoral election. A few months later in the spring of 1845, there were other disturbing signs—many Whigs continued to back the American Republican party in New York City's municipal election, and nativist parties made overtures to Whig voters in other cities such as Philadelphia, Baltimore, and Richmond. The threat to Whiggery intensified when natives nominated their own state tickets in Massachusetts, Louisiana, and Pennsylvania.[27]

In the face of this growing challenge, Whig politicians opposed formal mergers that entailed abandoning the Whig name and did what they could to offset the minor parties' appeal to their voters. For example, in order to establish their own nativist credentials, Whigs made a concerted attack on illegal immigrant voting. In November, 1844, Webster made a strong speech in Boston calling for reform of the naturalization laws, and Whigs in the Massachusetts legislature passed a resolution to the same effect the following March. Whig governors in Kentucky and Maryland demanded new registration laws to stop illegal immigrant voting in January, 1845, and Whig newspapers and meetings in Virginia

---

June 17, 1846, in Gideon Welles Papers, New York Public Library; Gideon Welles to Isaac Toucey, June 23, 1846, in Gideon Welles Papers, Library of Congress. Emily Baldwin wrote to Edward Baldwin on May 12, 1847, that there were so many divisions in the state over the question of bridging rivers that "sectional feelings overcome party lines" (Baldwin Family Papers).

27. L. Saltonstall to Henry Clay, December 10, 1844, in Clay Papers; George William Boyd to John Quincy Adams, April 7, 1845, in Adams Family Papers; New York *Tribune*, November 28, 1844, April 10, 1845; S. M. Troutman to James M. Bell, November 13, 1844, in James M. Bell Papers, Perkins Library, Duke University; J. J. Fry to William C. Rives, November 13, 1844, in Rives Papers.

and Connecticut called on Congress for action. One result of this pressure was that the Whig-controlled Senate Judiciary Committee undertook a well-publicized, if futile, investigation of illegal naturalization and reported a bill to remedy it during the second session of the Twenty-eighth Congress (December, 1844—March, 1845).[28]

None of these measures stopped the hemorrhaging of Whig voters toward nativist ranks. Separate nativist and temperance tickets cost the Whigs a congressional seat in Baltimore in October, 1845, even though their own candidate had called for reform of the naturalization laws. As the Massachusetts gubernatorial election approached, Whigs there despaired of holding their support. Frantically they tried to portray their familiar candidate, George N. Briggs, as a foe of immigrants, but to no avail.[29] In November, a Native American candidate drew 8 percent of the vote, as large a share as the Liberty candidate, and the Whigs lost their absolute statewide majority. A month earlier, the Whigs had been smashed in the race for canal commissioner in Pennsylvania. Their vote plummeted from 48.5 percent to 38.1 percent while the Native American candidate attracted 9.6 percent of the vote. Worse still from the Whig point of view, overt attempts to woo nativists were counterproductive in two regards. They bitterly divided the party, especially in New York where the Seward-Weed-Greeley wing vehemently opposed that strategy, and they probably drove immigrants toward the Democratic party in large numbers. Certainly, this tactic did not prevent Democratic victories in New York and Pennsylvania in 1845, any more than in Maryland or Virginia. Recognizing the futility of this path, Whigs abandoned it in 1846. In Congress and in the states, Whig spokesmen renounced any

28. New York *Tribune*, November 11, 26, 1844, January 7, 9, 1845; Daniel Webster to David P. Hall, November 16, 1844, and Webster to Robert C. Winthrop, December 13, 29, 1844, in Webster Papers; copy of the Massachusetts legislative resolutions, March 31, 1845, in Adams Family Papers; John H. Pleasants to William C. Rives, December 23, 1844, in Rives Papers; the pressure on the Senate Judiciary Committee can be followed in the papers of its chairman, John M. Berrien.

29. On Maryland, see New York *Tribune*, September 26, 1845; John P. Kennedy to Philip C. Pendleton, October 9, 1845, in John P. Kennedy Papers, George Peabody Division of the Enoch Pratt Free Library, Baltimore. On Massachusetts, see Abbott Lawrence to William C. Rives, January 17, 1845, in Rives Papers; Robert C. Winthrop to John P. Kennedy, September 30, October 9, 1845, in Kennedy Papers; and Boston *Courier*, quoted in *Pennsylvania Telegraph* (Harrisburg), October 29, 1845.

plans to merge with nativists or change naturalization laws.[30] Broadening the party's base by a direct appeal to nativists had proved another dead end. The Whigs would have to find a different road to recovery.

By the spring of 1846, in sum, northern Whigs, like their southern colleagues, had made a series of false starts. Routes that had seemed like shortcuts to power turned out to be blind alleys. In the few states they carried, they had either exploited ephemeral issues or suffered serious erosion of their voting support. They had failed to come back in the key states of New York, Pennsylvania, and Indiana, and seemed in danger in former strongholds like Rhode Island, Connecticut, and Maryland. To pull back apathetic and defecting voters, the Whigs clearly had to look elsewhere for winning issues. An indication of where most would look came from a discouraged Indiana Whig in January, 1846. Pessimistic about capturing the state's impending gubernatorial election on state issues that divided the party internally, he wistfully yet accurately predicted, "Congress may kick up some deviltry out of which we can make something to put in our pipes."[31]

The actions of the Polk administration and of the Democratic Congress in 1846 and 1847 indeed provided the basis for the Whig party's dramatic comeback in the congressional and state elections of those years. Polk negotiated and the Senate ratified a treaty establishing the northern boundary of Oregon at the forty-ninth parallel, a treaty viewed as a betrayal by both Whigs and Democrats in the Midwest. Polk initiated and Congress declared war against Mexico, a war that dragged on until the spring of 1848 and became increasingly unpopular. Whigs throughout the nation denounced the war itself as an immoral aggression, Polk's management of it as partisan and inept, and the prospect of territorial annexation from it as dangerous to North and South alike. At Polk's urging as well, Congress enacted three important economic measures in the summer of 1846 that together marked a frontal assault on the Whig economic program: the Independent Treasury Act, which removed government

30. On the splits in New York, see New York *Tribune, passim* for 1845; for the changes in 1846, see William Henry Seward to Thurlow Weed, January 1, 1846, and John Tayler Hall to Weed, February 17, 1846, in Thurlow Weed Papers, Rush Rhees Library, Rochester University.

31. Godlove Orth to Schuyler Colfax, January 27, 1846, in J. Herman Schauinger, ed., "The Letters of Godlove S. Orth: Hoosier Whig," *Indiana Magazine of History,* XXXIX (1943), 378–80.

revenues from private banks and required the government to deal exclusively in specie; the Walker tariff, which lowered most rates on manufactured goods, raised rates on a number of raw materials imported by American manufacturers, and substituted *ad valorem* for specific duties; and the Public Warehouse Act, which in effect gave government credit to importers and foreign manufacturers by allowing them to deposit imports in government warehouses for up to a year before paying customs duties rather than paying the tariff immediately upon the arrival of the goods. To compound matters, Congress defied Polk's wishes and passed a massive rivers and harbors improvement bill, which Polk vetoed. Polk's veto, of course, offended all the intended recipients of government aid.

All of these actions provided the Whigs with something they could put in their pipes, but initially the Democratic economic program formed the chief target. Almost as soon as the election of 1844 was over, Whigs had predicted that Democratic ascendancy meant economic disaster for the country. Yet some Whigs were prepared to let the Democrats have their way on the tariff and subtreasury because the inevitable depression would spark a Whig comeback. Clay himself confidently forecast that "errors" by the Polk administration would offer "abundant cause of public dissatisfaction." So hopeful were the Whigs of the tariff issue that as early as April, 1846, Truman Smith, who was trying to organize a central Whig congressional committee to coordinate state and congressional campaigns in 1846, planned to send Whig tariff speeches to every congressional district in the country. By June, as the Walker bill progressed through the House, Georgia's Whigs were said to anticipate the final law "with the eagerness of hyenas and jackals waiting only for the final onslaught to be over to rush on to the work of mutilation" because the bill included new duties on coffee and tea, while Whigs in Pennsylvania and New York declared that passage of the tariff would doom the Democrats in the ensuing elections.[32]

32. New York *Tribune*, December 20, 1844, January 7, 17, 18, August 14, 1845; Thurlow Weed to Francis Granger, February 12, 1845, in Francis Granger Papers, Library of Congress; Henry Clay to John J. Crittenden, November 28, 1844, in Clay Papers; Henry Clay to John M. Clayton, December 2, 1844, in Clayton Papers; Truman Smith to Nathan Appleton, April 9, 1846, in Nathan Appleton Papers, Massachusetts Historical Society; John B. Lamar to Howell Cobb, June 24, 1846, in Phillips, ed., *Correspondence*, 82–84; H. King to Thomas Butler King, June 22,

Lest they lose such a potent issue at the last moment, congressional Whigs put the construction of a winning platform ahead of the economic interests of their constituents. They had no hope of stopping the Democratic steamroller in the House, but the Senate was closely divided and contained a number of protariff Democrats. Businessmen therefore beseeched Whigs to modify the Walker bill in the Senate to offer them more protection and to save specific duties at all costs. Daniel Webster, after extensive consultation with businessmen in the Northeast, prepared a compromise tariff as an amendment to Walker's bill, one that would lower rates more gradually and preserve specific duties. Webster was confident he had the votes to adopt the substitute in the Senate and kill the whole bill when it returned to the House. But he never even offered the amendment because other Whigs would not support him. They wanted the Walker tariff passed, regardless of businessmen's pleas. The worst tariff possible would make the best platform possible. As Webster himself put it, Whigs opposed his amendment because they preferred "the continuance of the controversy to a reasonable and safe settlement of it." Similarly, a bitter manufacturer concluded with perfect accuracy that Whig politicians were "striving to make political capital to overthrow the present administration at whatever cost to the country."[33]

Once the Democratic program passed Congress, Whigs gleefully seized it as an invincible combination of issues. A Massachusetts Whig attempted to console Webster by suggesting that the party could sweep northern congressional elections and secure the next president on the tariff issue. "It is an ill wind that blows no one any good," he wrote. Agreeing, Thomas Corwin of Ohio predicted that Whigs could carry the entire Midwest by attacking the tariff, the subtreasury, and Polk's veto of the rivers and harbors bill. William Bebb, Ohio's Whig gubernatorial candidate, was exultant: "If the repeal of the Tariff, the passage of the Sub Treasury, the veto of the river and harbor bill and other measures of this

---

1846, in Thomas Butler King Papers, Southern Historical Collection, University of North Carolina; James Bowen to Thurlow Weed, July 21, 1846, in Weed Papers.

33. The negotiations over the aborted attempt at amending the Walker bill can be followed in great detail in the Daniel Webster Papers for July, 1846. For the quotations, see Daniel Webster to Fletcher Webster, July 27, 29, 1846, and Joseph Balch to Webster, July 25, 1846, in Webster Papers.

administration added to our *state issues* fail to 'stir up the very stones to meeting' we may as well hereafter hang our harps on the willows." At last, Whigs everywhere believed, they had discovered the long-sought road to recovery.[34]

The Whigs, in fact, made extraordinary progress in the 1846 elections. They picked up fourteen additional congressional seats in New York, one in New Jersey, five in Pennsylvania, three in Ohio, and one in Georgia. They held all their seats in other northern states, including the entire Massachusetts delegation, and they won governorships in New York, Ohio, North Carolina, and Massachusetts, where they did much better than in 1845. Although they narrowly lost the gubernatorial election in Indiana in August, they won control of the legislature. More important for the future, the Whigs won a larger proportion of the vote in the fall elections of 1846 than they had in 1844 in every state except Delaware, Georgia, and Ohio and Vermont, two states where the Liberty party cut into their ranks.

Nevertheless, perceptive Whigs might have found cause for concern even in the midst of this truly impressive performance. Attacks on the Polk record by themselves did not give the Whigs control of the crucial states they would need to carry the presidency in 1848. In Georgia, for example, reapportionment of the congressional districts by the Whig legislature was probably more responsible for the Whigs' success in carrying four of eight seats than the Walker tariff, which in its final form did not contain the tea and coffee duties Georgia's Whigs had anticipated so eagerly.[35] Even so, Whigs won only 47 percent of the popular vote, evidence of both the effectiveness of their gerrymander and how hazardous their position in a statewide race remained. Pennsylvania's Whigs won the statewide election for canal commissioner in 1846, but with less than a majority of the vote. The Native American candidate still drew 7.5 percent, and Democrats suffered a significantly larger drop-off than the Whigs. Manifestly, Pennsylvania's Whigs were still vulnerable to a full

34. Moses Stuart to Daniel Webster, August 3, 1846, in Webster Papers; Thomas Corwin to Thomas Ewing, August 1, 1846, and William Bebb to Ewing, August 10, 1846, in Ewing Family Papers, Library of Congress. See also R. Fisher to Thomas Butler King, August 3, 1846, and S. Jardin to King, August 6, 1846, in King Papers.

35. On the Whigs' delight with the reapportionment, see Robert Toombs to Alexander H. Stephens, January 1, 1844, in Phillips, ed., *Correspondence*, 52–53.

Democratic turnout. Even in New York, where Whigs scored their biggest gains, they depended in 1846 on conditions that went beyond their platform. According to editor Horace Greeley, they had elected the governor and as many as five congressmen only by capturing the Anti-Rent vote and exploiting the growing division between Hunker and Barnburner Democrats.[36]

New York provides a marvelous microcosm of the trial and error method by which Whigs tried to find a winning strategy between 1844 and 1848. Until late in the spring of 1846, the dominant wing of the party, led by Greeley, Weed, and William Henry Seward, had attempted to broaden the Whig coalition by adding antislavery, black, and even immigrant voters to it. To accomplish that goal, they had focused on the state constitutional convention that was to meet in the summer of 1846 and had pushed for the adoption of alien suffrage and broader black suffrage in the new constitution. When it became apparent by late spring that both measures would fail and that both seriously divided the party and might alienate more old Whig voters than attract new ones, the Whig leadership jettisoned that strategy for a different one. They recognized that Hunkers and Barnburners were deeply split over provisions of the new constitution and over control of the state Democratic machine. The Seward Whigs had previously cooperated informally with the Barnburners to call the convention, but now they turned to the Hunkers. Hunker Democrats privately assured them that, if the Whigs chose an acceptable gubernatorial candidate, the Hunkers would sit the election out and allow the Whigs to win. Their main goal was to strip Barnburners of the state patronage controlled by incumbent governor and Democratic candidate Silas Wright. With Democrats and hence Barnburners out of power, the Hunkers believed their chances of winning control of Democratic party machinery would be enhanced. At the same time, the Whigs perceived a bloc of voters other than immigrants and the Liberty party that might be up for grabs—the Anti-Renters, who despised Democratic candidate Wright. To appease the Hunkers and lure the Anti-Renters, the Whigs nominated John Young for governor in 1846. Democratic abstentions and additional Anti-Rent voters provided him with a narrow margin over Wright and made him the only Whig to

36. Horace Greeley to Henry Clay, November 15, 1846, in Clay Papers.

win on the statewide ticket. Significantly, it was precisely the summer of 1846 when the cagey Thurlow Weed, who had been forced to abandon his blatant bid for antislavery votes, embraced Taylor as the Whig nominee in 1848. He may have realized even then that exploiting Young's popularity among Anti-Renters was a temporary expedient at best, a tactic that could not be repeated in the future. In any event, because Young alienated virtually every important faction of the Whig party once he took office, it was soon clear that the Whigs would not renominate him for governor in 1848. They would then have to pursue some other course to win the state, congressional, and presidential elections in New York.[37]

Despite these indications that their comeback in 1846 was less solid and more evanescent than it first appeared, most Whigs believed that they had won by attacking the Polk administration's record and that they could continue to ride those issues into the White House in 1848. As one Whig proclaimed of the results in New York, "Whiggism ascends. The present administration are your best recruiting officers, tho' rather expensive." Marveling at the Whig capture of Congress, a Georgian gushed to his congressman: "Did you ever see such a rapid and tremendous revolution . . . I congratulate you on the signs of the times, for I cannot now have a doubt of your receiving in 1849 [from a new Whig president] some distinguished post." Ohio's Whigs explicitly interpreted their victory as a repudiation of Polk's policies and predicted triumph in 1848 on those issues. No better statement of Whig faith that they could disdain evasive tactics and win on substantive issues can be found than that of Massachusetts Senator John Davis to Henry Clay. The tariff, he asserted, explained the Whig sweep: "We have at length reached an open palpable issue which all can understand, and the policy of the administration is

37. The complex machinations in New York can be followed in Horace Greeley to Schuyler Colfax, April 22, 1846, in Greeley-Colfax Papers; John Bush to Millard Fillmore, March 11, 1846, in Fillmore Papers, State University of New York, Oswego; William Henry Seward to John McLean, March 20, 1846, in William Henry Seward Papers, Library of Congress; and Benson Rose to Thurlow Weed, February 6, 1846, Greeley to Weed, March 13, 1846, Charles Boynton to Weed, March 17, 1846, Seward to Alvah Worden, March 22, 1846, Washington Hunt to Weed, April 4, 1846, Seward to Weed, April 5, August 10, 1846, Greeley to Weed, May 14, 1846, and Seth Hawley to Weed, August 24, 1846, all in Weed Papers. On divisions over the black suffrage issue and the eventual Whig abandonment of it, see also John L. Stanley, "Majority Tyranny in Tocqueville's America: The Failure of Negro Suffrage in 1846," *Political Science Quarterly*, LXXXIV (1969), 412–35.

enough to excite alarm without coonskins, hard cider, or even a song or a hurrah. As far as my observation has extended the revolution has been accomplished without any argument or effort. The sense of the public is manifestly opposed to the doings of Congress. The war is daily becoming unpopular and the revenue act meets with condemnation everywhere."[38]

Utterly convinced that they could win the next presidential election on economic issues. Whigs worried only that Webster might derail their express by reintroducing his compromise tariff proposal when Congress met in December, 1846. Across the North, nervous Whigs wrote that Webster must be stopped in order to retain their trump card. His plan "is regarded by the most eminent statesmen in the Whig ranks as calculated to produce the overthrow of that ascendancy which we are now gaining with the country and ought to preserve in 1848," wrote a Whig newspaper correspondent. Pennsylvania's Whigs would oppose Webster because they had "secured positive superiority in Pennsylvania through the influence of the Tariff issue, as contrasted with the present impotent scheme & to maintain it we cannot afford to surrender any of the ground." Senator Davis assured Clay that he and other Massachusetts Whigs would not support Webster if he reintroduced the bill. Even Massachusetts manufacturers, who liked Webster's plan, would back a Whig platform demanding a complete return to the tariff of 1842. "If this is the best issue to keep before the public and the great end which we have in view can be obtained by it then it is our best policy to adhere to it and I have no doubt Mass. will acquiesce in that policy." By the end of November, Whigs rejoiced that Webster had abandoned his scheme: their winning issue had been kept intact.[39]

Buoyed by the results of the 1846 elections and the apparent power of their new issues. Whigs who faced congressional and gubernatorial campaigns in 1847 were convinced at the end of 1846 that they could

38. John Couper to Thomas Butler King, November 17, 1846, R. R. Cuyler to King, November 12, 1846, circular of the Whig State Central Committee of Ohio, October 17, 1846, and Robert C. Schenck to King, October 26, 1846, all in King Papers; John Davis to Henry Clay, November 13, 1846, in Clay Papers.

39. James E. Harvey to William Hayden, November 6, 29, 1846, in Schouler Papers; John Davis to Henry Clay, November 13, 1846, with Abbott Lawrence to Davis, November 12, 1846, enclosed, in Clay Papers; see also Walter Forward to Millard Fillmore, October 26, 1846, in Fillmore Papers, State University of New York, Oswego.

maintain the party's momentum. Virginia Congressman John Pendleton exulted, "For my part, I have never doubted since the new Tariff and the war, that the Whigs must carry the election the next time." Whoever the presidential candidate might be in the 1848, moreover, "we shall beat them and beat them badly." Even long-time Virginia Democratic boss Thomas Ritchie agreed, at least, that the tariff would be the dominant issue through 1848. As early as August, 1846, a jubilant Tennessee Whig had predicted that "from the signs of the times . . . the canvass next year will be the easiest one for the Whigs since 1840. We have them on the defensive now." By the end of the year, other Tennessee Whigs confidently anticipated victory in 1847 and 1848 because of disgust with Polk. A North Carolina congressman argued as well that anger at the war, hostility to territorial acquisition from Mexico, and the virtual certainty that the tariff and subtreasury measures would bankrupt the government ensured Whig victories in that state's impending congressional elections. Finally, Indiana's long-suffering Whigs, who had searched in vain for popular issues they could use against the Democrats since 1844, believed that they had at last found them. As late as July, 1847, for example, Whig congressional candidate Richard. W. Thompson was urged to "attack the Administration at every vulnerable point—upon the Oregon question—the veto of the River and Harbor bill—the subtreasury with a raking fire at the Mexican War, and the attempts of the Administration to prostrate Gen. Taylor." Thompson, who directed his campaign primarily against the war and territorial acquisition, himself declared, "If we can't sustain the issues on which we now stand—we are gone."[40]

Despite the volume and sincerity of the Whigs' bravado, their optimistic belief that they could recapture the presidency on the basis of economic issues and antiwar sentiment soon proved unfounded. Once again they had chosen a pathway to power that would lead them away from their goal. Whig momentum did continue into the spring and summer of

40. John C. Pendleton to William C. Rives, November 3, 1846, January 31, 1847, in Rives Papers; Thomas Ritchie to Edmund Burke, October 21, 1846, in Edmund Burke Papers, Library of Congress; Sam W. Fite to William B. Campbell, August 13, November 24, 1846, John Bell to Campbell, November 22, 1846, in Campbell Family Papers; Alfred Dockery to Duncan McLaurin, January 9, 1847, in McLaurin Papers; T. H. Nelson to Richard W. Thompson, July 5, 1847, in Richard W. Thompson Papers, Indiana State Library; Richard W. Thompson to H. J. Hilton, July 16, 1847, in Richard W. Thompson Papers, Lilly Library, Indiana University.

1847. In April, they rebounded strongly in Connecticut, where once again they swept the state and congressional elections on the tariff and antiwar issues, and in Rhode Island, where the new national issues allowed them to campaign for governor as Whigs for the first time in three years and to amass 57 percent of the vote.[41] That month, as well, they picked up five additional congressional seats in Virginia and made gains in the state legislature for their strongest showing in the Old Dominion in years. In August, they captured two new congressional seats in Indiana, winning a statewide majority of the vote, added three new seats in North Carolina, and recaptured the governorship of Tennessee.

The Whig tide crested in August, however, and it ebbed markedly by the fall of 1847. Although Whigs were victorious, their vote was down in Massachusetts and Ohio, where their margin in the legislature was narrower than in either 1845 or 1846. They carried the state officers in New York, but only because of massive Democratic abstentions stemming from the Hunker-Barnburner feud. As the Whigs in New York well knew, their future there depended upon preventing the Democrats from reuniting.[42] On the other hand, Georgia's Whigs continued to stumble in 1847. They lost the governorship because they could not match the growing Democratic vote among nonslaveholders in north Georgia. Worst of all were the results from the Middle Atlantic states, where the Whigs continued to campaign hard on the tariff. They lost governorships in Maryland, New Jersey, and Pennsylvania, where the Native American party still siphoned off vital voters from them. Thus, in the fall of 1847, Whig prospects sagged most dramatically in precisely those states where one year earlier they had boasted that economic issues could carry them to the White House.

Economic issues in fact probably did not contribute much to earlier Whig triumphs in the spring and summer, except in New England. In

<hr>

41. On the impact of the war and tariff issues in Connecticut, see John M. Niles to Gideon Welles, April 11, 1847, and William G. Pomeroy to Welles, May 11, 1847, in Welles Papers, New York Public Library; A. E. Burr to Gideon Welles, April 13, 1847, in Gideon Welles Papers, Connecticut Historical Society, Hartford.

42. For example, the Whig margin in the Ohio state assembly fell from twenty-six seats in 1845 to six seats in 1847; in the state senate the margin dropped from six seats in 1845 to two seats in 1847. On the New York Whigs' recognition of their dependence on Democratic factionalism, see Horace Greeley to Schuyler Colfax, September 18, 1847, in Greeley-Colfax Papers.

other states, Whigs campaigned primarily against the war, against any absorption of Mexican territory, and against Polk's partisan mistreatment of Generals Taylor and Scott. Even so, they probably gained congressional seats in North Carolina in 1847, as they had in Georgia in 1846, more because of a Whig-engineered reapportionment of districts than because of the issues they raised.[43] In four of the six districts they carried, their share of the vote was lower than it had been in 1844. However impressive their performance in Virginia, moreover, it still left them with only six of fifteen congressional seats and less than a statewide majority in an election where the Democrats suffered a much heavier drop-off than the Whigs. Even in victory, Virginia Whigs had to doubt their ability to carry the state in 1848. The fact that Whig candidates tried to ride on the coattails of Taylor's popularity by endorsing him for president in Virginia, Maryland, Tennessee, and Georgia indicated that those southern Whigs believed that they could not win in 1847, let alone 1848, on the basis of issues alone.[44] To be sure, one motive for this action was the southern Whigs' fear of the slavery issue and their perceived need to offset it. But the tactic demonstrated as well, just as did election results in the North, that campaigning against the Democratic economic record had lost its punch. Back in November, 1846, even as he exuberantly cheered the "tremendous revolution" in Whig fortunes, a Georgia Whig had worried, "The only fear is that the revolution has come too early, and that its effects may wear out before the next Presidential election." Unfortunately for the Whigs, he was right.[45]

43. On North Carolina's reapportionment, see Alfred Dockery to Duncan McLaurin, January 9, 1847, in McLaurin Papers; David Outlaw to Emily Outlaw, February 24, 1848, in David Outlaw Papers, Southern Historical Collection, University of North Carolina; and Marc Wayne Kruman, "Parties and Politics in North Carolina, 1846–1865" (Ph.D. dissertation, Yale University, 1978), 6–7.

44. On Virginia, see John C. Pendleton to William C. Rives, November 3, 1846, William Ballard Preston to Rives, February 28, 1847, in Rives Papers; on Tennessee, Meredith P. Gentry to William B. Campbell, February 20, 1847, William B. Campbell to David Campbell, January 23, 1848, in Campbell Family Papers; on Georgia, Iverson S. Harris to John M. Berrien, May 9, 1847, in Berrien Papers, and Berrien to Daniel Webster, June 21, 1847, in Webster Papers. See also Cooper, *The South and the Politics of Slavery*, 246–47; and Rayback, *Free Soil*, 41–44.

45. R. R. Cuyler to Thomas Butler King, November 12, 1846, in King Papers. Another index of the disappearance of the Whigs' advantage on economic issues by the fall of 1847 is the way the two parties handled those issues in party platforms and newspaper appeals. In Pennsylvania, for

What, we must ask, had happened? Whig campaigns in 1846 and early 1847 in fact had been based on predictions of what would happen to the economy under the Democratic program, not on the actual impact of that program. Most of their triumphs and most of their boasting occurred before that economic legislation even went into effect. The Walker tariff did not begin operation until December 1, 1846, and the Independent Treasury Act until January 1, 1847. Indeed, the requirement of the latter law that the government pay out only specie or treasury notes didn't take effect until April 1, 1847. What happened, simply, was that most Whig predictions turned out to be wrong. Despite the authentic conviction of Whig politicians and businessmen alike that the economy would be plunged into disaster, the nation instead prospered in 1847, and the Democrats reaped the benefits. They could and did say, in effect, "I told you so."

In the Whig scenario, the tariff and subtreasury would drain the country of specie and hence dry up credit for commercial transactions. Lowering the tariff would increase imports and cause specie to flow to Europe to pay for them. Democrats argued that the concurrent reduction of Britain's Corn Laws in 1846 would allow increased grain sales to England and therefore America would enjoy a favorable balance of trade. The Whigs responded that under the Corn Laws American farmers already enjoyed favored-nation status in British grain markets vis-à-vis Russian and other European competitors and still didn't sell enough grain

---

example, although the Whigs continued to attack the Walker tariff in 1847, the Democrats were defending it in 1847 and 1848 as "the most judicious and equitable that has ever been established." Democratic state platforms can be found in the Philadelphia *Pennsylvanian*, March 8, 1847, September 8, 1848. The quotation is from the resolution of the Allegheny County Democratic Convention, Pittsburgh *Morning Post*, January 13, 1848. In New York, Whigs abandoned economic issues entirely in their official address to voters in 1847, whereas Democrats continued to boast of the tariff and subtreasury. In 1846, 42 percent of the Whig address had been devoted to economic issues, whereas in 1847 it focused entirely on the war and slavery extension issues. The Democrats, in contrast, devoted 26 percent of their 1846 address to a defense of the Polk economic measures, but 35 percent of their 1847 address to that defense. These figures are based on a content analysis in Gillis Harp, "The Character of Party Dialogue: Democrats and Whigs in New York State, 1844–1852" (seminar paper, University of Virginia, 1980), 30–32. North Carolina's Whig state platform of February, 1848, similarly tried to shift attention from economic issues to the Mexican War. It can be found in the Washington *National Intelligencer*, March 2, 1848.

to balance payments. Hence the repeal of the Corn Laws would only increase European grain sales to England, not American profits. Farmers would suffer from the new tariff, indeed, because the purchasing power of American workers would drop, thereby forcing farm prices down. While the lower tariff would propel specie out of the country, according to Whigs, the subtreasury would suck what was left from the private economy. Under that bill, the government would require all payments for tariff duties, land sales, and excise taxes in gold, and then, rather than recirculating that gold through the economy by depositing it in private banks that could issue bank notes based on it, the government would simply hoard its gold in public vaults. Given the low levels of federal expenditure in the nineteenth century, such a critique was plausible, especially because it had been standard Whig fare since Martin Van Buren first introduced the subtreasury idea in 1837. Even Democratic businessmen had constantly denounced the scheme's deflationary implications. The result would be disaster. Depleted of gold by unfavorable foreign trade balances and governmental accumulation, the economy would see its bank note circulation and commercial credit shrink, and eventually it would grind to a complete halt.[46]

If the economy in general would suffer from Democratic programs, argued the Whigs, the lower tariff and warehousing act would inflict a one-two punch on manufacturers in particular. Three aspects of the Walker tariff were especially pernicious. First, those manufacturers who used imported raw materials complained that, because of higher rates on raw materials and reduced differentials between duties on raw materials and those on finished goods, their production costs would increase to the point where they could not compete with foreign manufacturers. Second, the general reduction of rates would expose all manufacturers to cheap foreign competition, drive them out of business, and throw hundreds of thousands of workers out of their jobs. It was a calamity, Whigs iterated and reiterated, to expose American labor to the competition of European pauper labor. Finally, the *ad valorem* rates would encourage fraud that would reduce the protective barrier of the tariff still further. Importers

46. The summary of the Whig case against the Democratic economic program is based on a reading of speeches in the *Congressional Globe*, 29th Cong. 1st Sess., the extensive correspondence of businessmen to Daniel Webster in the summer of 1846, and other correspondence such as Abbott Lawrence to William C. Rives, January 17, 26, 1846, in Rives Papers.

and foreign manufacturers would undervalue imports because the tariff duty was a fixed percentage of the invoice price. Even if they didn't cheat, *ad valorem* duties would drop as the price of foreign imports dropped, thus providing less protection than specific duties on precisely the goods that were most dangerous to American manufacturers.

As if this weren't bad enough, Whigs complained, the warehousing act in effect subsidized foreign competitors by allowing them to accumulate large inventories in government warehouses before paying any duty and then to sell only when prices were high enough that even with the cost of tariff duties added to their goods they could undersell American manufacturers. Put another way, Whigs charged that the warehousing act would allow foreigners to sell only when profitable rather than run the risk of paying duties immediately and carrying an inventory they could not sell at a profit. The law, that is, permitted foreigners to build up inventories in anticipation of sales, ample enough to meet all demand. Thus it negated the advantages American manufacturers gained by their proximity to customers and by their ability to fill orders before foreign goods could be ordered and shipped from abroad. Under the Public Warehouse Act, according to the Whigs, cheap foreign goods would always be readily at hand in government warehouses.

American businessmen, workers, and farmers would be ruined, and so would the government, Whigs predicted. It was suicidal to lower the tariff after declaring war on Mexico, they argued, because lower tariff rates, even with increased imports, would mean lower government revenue just when the government needed more money to pay for the war. Nor would the government be able to sell bonds, for banks would have no gold with which to buy them. The Independent Treasury Act would require the government to accept only gold for bonds, and what little gold banks had left after the removal of government deposits and shipments of specie aboard would quickly be used up as they physically transferred their gold to government vaults to pay for early bond issues. Lest this augury seem too farfetched, Bray Hammond has pointed out that precisely such a dilemma paralyzed bond sales during the first year of the Civil War.[47]

47. Bray Hammond, *Sovereignty and an Empty Purse: Banks and Politics in the Civil War* (Princeton, 1970), 37–163.

In 1847, however, almost every one of these predictions proved fallacious. Because of the Irish potato famine and crop failures in Europe, foreign demand for American grain soared. Secretary of the Treasury Walker's rosy analysis of the impact of the reduction of the Corn Laws on American farmers misidentified the source, but grain exports did increase enormously in 1847. As a result, the nation enjoyed its most favorable balance of trade in years. Gold and silver flowed into the economy from abroad in record amounts, eastern cities were awash in specie, and farmers enjoyed unprecedented profits. Nor in a time of war could the government sit on its revenues. It had to spend its money on war contracts, thus providing a stimulus to war-related industries. Further to help manufacturers and give a more protective edge to his own tariff, Walker ordered customs collectors to add the cost of shipping, insurance, and exchange to the invoice price of goods when they calculated the *ad valorem* duties. Commerce, agriculture, and industry all flourished.

The forecast of government bankruptcy also went awry. Government revenues did decline just as Whigs said they would, and so did the circulation of state bank notes. But Walker ingeniously financed the war in a way that replaced bank note circulation and increased the general prosperity. He had to borrow money to pay for the war, but instead of issuing long-term bonds in large denominations, which would suck money from the private sector, he relied primarily on short-term treasury notes in small denominations, which could be used as currency. Moreover, to facilitate funding of this debt by bankers, he waived provisions of the Independent Treasury Act and accepted installment payments in certified checks rather than in gold. Because treasury notes earned interest and could be used to pay tariff duties, there was a huge demand for them by businessmen. Bankers, sensing the large profits to be made from the sale of treasury notes, scrambled to handle the loans. The government, in short, pumped much more money into the economy than it took out of it. Instead of the shrunken money supply and deflation Whigs had dreaded, the amount of circulating currency jumped sharply in 1847 even though the number of bank notes declined, wholesale prices rose, and prosperity prevailed.[48]

48. Virtually every economic statistic available bears out this portrait. Exports in merchandise and grain exceeded imports, but imports of gold and silver dramatically exceeded exports in

Both Whigs and Democrats were well aware of these developments. As early as November, 1846, a Boston Democrat had argued that the Polk economic program was eminently defensible, even in Whiggish Massachusetts. The Warehouse Act was a boon to importing merchants, he said, and any deflationary impact of the subtreasury system would be offset by the flow of English and French gold and by treasury notes, which would be in large demand because they could be used to pay tariff duties. In December of that year, Webster was puzzled by the equanimity of New York's business community, which seemed to welcome rather than dread the advent of the independent treasury because of the rush of foreign specie, the circulation of treasury notes, and the increased wartime demand for government expenditure. By February, 1847, a Tennessee Whig congressman was warning that Whig prospects in his state's gubernatorial election were not so bright as others had predicted just months earlier, because improved economic conditions resulting from the grain trade helped the Democrats. "Money will be plenty—the Banks easy— Treasury notes in demand and the people prosperous. All these will be claimed as the natural effects of Locofoco measures and the people you know when prosperous, are prone to attribute their prosperity to the direct action of the Administration in power for the time being. Hence I conclude that the Whigs will have heavy work in Tennessee next summer." Significantly, he also concluded that in this situation Taylor was the only man whom the Whigs could possibly elect president in 1848.[49]

As the year progressed, Whig hopes of exploiting economic issues dimmed perceptibly. In July, a worried New Yorker on a business trip to Pennsylvania aptly summarized the party's dilemma:

1847. The value of wheat exports jumped 300 percent in 1847 over 1846. Circulating currency expanded by 15.7 percent in 1847, even though state bank note circulation dropped slightly that year. Government receipts were down and deficits up, but the wholesale price index rose from 83 in 1845 and 1846 to 90 in 1847. For the relevant tables, see *Historical Statistics of the United States*, I, 201, II, 886, 899, 993, 995, 1104, and 1106. For Walker's financing of the war, see James P. Shenton, *Robert John Walker: A Politician from Jackson to Lincoln* (New York, 1961), 87–98, and Henry Cohen, *Business and Politics in America from the Age of Jackson to the Civil War: The Career Biography of W. W. Corcoran* (Westport, Conn., 1971), 40–62.

49. Sidney Homer to Edmund Burke, November 23, 1846, in Burke Papers; Daniel Webster to Robert C. Winthrop, December 18, 1846, in Webster Papers; Meredith P. Gentry to William B. Campbell, February 20, 1847, in Campbell Family Papers.

It will be necessary to handle the question of the Tariffs of 42 & 46. It is somewhat difficult to meet our opponents before the farmers when wheat is ranging from $1.25 to $2 per bushel. The famine in Europe has produced such an enormous rise in all grains and specie has flowed in on us to such an extent that they have drowned the effects of the Tariff of 46 and somewhat neutralized the effects of the Sub-Try. Besides the mania for Railways in Europe and this country has kept up the price of iron; and the war has called for such enormous supplies of all its materials, and such immense expenditure of money that almost every branch of business has been greatly stimulated. Thus, to the great mass, the country appears to be eminently prosperous.

Only bumper crops in Europe and a prolongation of the war until the government went bankrupt, he concluded, would allow the Whigs to exploit economic issues in the future. In April, 1848, Congressman Meredith Gentry of Tennessee flatly told Webster that it would be a mistake for the Whigs to attempt to repeal the Walker tariff because "a combination of circumstances at home and abroad has made it eminently successful as a revenue measure and less destructive to our home manufacturers than was anticipated." Action against the tariff should be avoided in Congress, he maintained, because it would allow the Democrats themselves to utilize the tariff issue in 1848. They could "insist (plausibly) that the large exports and consequent prosperity of the country combined with heavy receipts at the Customs Houses of the Republick were produced by the Tariff of 1846." Because the Whigs now would be hurt rather than helped by economic issues, running Taylor for president was their only hope in 1848.[50]

It is true that many Whigs in late 1847 accurately predicted in private that the economy would turn downward in 1848 as exports declined, imports increased, and specie flowed outward, and that the Whigs might once again use economic issues. But those trends took time to de-

---

50. Daniel Ullmann to Henry Clay, July 12, 1847, in Clay Papers; Meredith P. Gentry to Daniel Webster, April 13, 1848, in Webster Papers. For an analysis similar to Ullmann's of what happened in 1847, with a similar prediction that the continuation of the war and improved economic circumstances in Europe might allow the Whigs to make effective use of economic issues in 1848, see Thomas Wren Ward to Webster, January 10, 1848, in Webster Papers.

velop and continued to be disguised during the first months of 1848 by the injection of treasury notes into the economy. Certainly, the economy had not flagged sufficiently by June, 1848, when the Whig National Convention met, for Whigs to be sanguine about their prospects of running a traditional champion of Whig economic policies on economic issues.[51]

It is little wonder, then, that Whig delegates from northern states like Connecticut, Rhode Island, Pennsylvania, New Jersey, Ohio, and Indiana, where running against Democratic measures had once seemed such a clear track to the White House, would turn to Taylor and Scott in large numbers at that gathering.

Actually, in the summer of 1847 when the effectiveness of economic issues had already waned, the Whigs still retained one compelling issue that unified the party and that might, many thought, bring them victory in 1848. This was opposition to the Mexican War and to any territorial acquisition from it. Antiwar and antiexpansion sentiment was strong among Whig voters everywhere, but especially in the North. Equally important, perceptive Whig politicians like Thomas Corwin of Ohio, Richard W. Thompson of Indiana, Robert C. Winthrop of Massachusetts, William B. Campbell of Tennessee, and John M. Berrien of Georgia realized that the Whigs' "no territory" program offered the best way to hold the party together on the divisive slavery extension issue.[52] By blocking the annexation of any new territory, they could avoid the sectionally rupturing issue of the Wilmot Proviso. One indication of the strength of antiwar, antiextension sentiment was that many Whigs ini-

51. See the statistical tables cited in n. 48. A different chart, "American Business Activity Since 1970" (17th ed.; Cleveland Trust Company, 1966), shows that indexes of growth increased for every month in 1847 and the first six months of 1848. Beginning in July, 1848, however, the economy declined for the remainder of the year so that by the fall of 1848 economic issues seemed much more viable than they had in the spring of 1848 before Taylor was nominated.

52. C. B. Lewis to Roger Sherman Baldwin, January 19, 1848, in Baldwin Family Papers; Thomas Corwin to Thomas B. Stevenson, December 10, 1847, in Thomas B. Stevenson Papers, Indiana Historical Society Library, Indianapolis; Thomas Corwin to John J. Crittenden, September 2, 1847, in Thomas Corwin Papers, Ohio Historical Society, Columbus; Richard W. Thompson to (?), June 8, 1847, draft, Thompson Papers, Indiana State Library; Robert C. Winthrop to John P. Kennedy, January 24, 1848, in Winthrop Papers; William B. Campbell to David Campbell, November 20, 1847, in Campbell Family Papers; William H. Underwood to John M. Berrien, December 19, 1847, in Berrien Papers.

tially opposed Taylor's nomination because he had not publicly committed himself to a quick end of the war with no territorial indemnity. Another was the fact that Henry Clay chose to launch his public bid for the 1848 nomination by denouncing the war and territorial expansion in a major speech at Lexington, Kentucky, in November, 1847. As Congress met in December, 1847, therefore, Whigs hoped to unite against the war and expansion and to run on that platform during the presidential campaign. A Virginia Whig predicted early in February, 1848, that the war would not be terminated "until the issue of 'Conquest' or 'no conquest' is fairly made and tried at the polls in the next presidential election."[53]

Once again the Whigs were to be disappointed. As in the case of the Texas issue in 1845 and economic issues in 1846, the antiwar issue ran out of steam before it could carry them into power. Polk reluctantly accepted peace with the Mexicans, and the Senate's ratification of the Treaty of Guadalupe-Hidalgo on March 10, 1848, effectively killed the war itself as an issue. Antiwar sentiment remained strong enough to contribute to Whig victories in Connecticut and Rhode Island in April, but the Whigs had been stripped of their last substantive issue. Peace, one Whig congressman had lamented in late February, endangered his party's chances in 1848; nevertheless, Whigs dared not oppose the treaty.[54] Even worse, the actual cession of Mexican territory in the treaty negated the Whigs' "no territory" policy and created an urgent necessity to find some other way to deal with the divisive Wilmot Proviso question. As virtually everyone in the party recognized by the spring of 1848, the party would simply be shattered if it were forced to take a concrete stand for or against the proviso at the national convention.

Time was of the essence. The Whig National Convention was scheduled to meet almost exactly three months after Congress ratified the

53. The Lexington speech is reproduced in the *Whig Tribune Almanac for 1848*, 7–16; Alexander H. H. Stuart to Richard W. Thompson, February 9, 1848, in Richard W. Thompson Papers, Lincoln National Life Foundation, Fort Wayne.

54. On Connecticut, see James F. Babcock to Roger Sherman Baldwin, March 22, 1848, in Baldwin Family Papers; Mark Howard to James M. Barnard, April 5, 1848, in Mark Howard Papers, Connecticut Historical Society. The congressman who was alarmed that peace would hurt the Whigs was Nathan K. Hall of Buffalo. See Hall to Millard Fillmore, February 23, 1848, in Fillmore Papers, State University of New York, Oswego.

treaty with Mexico. The Whigs seemed to be stranded in a cul-de-sac. Every trail they had followed since 1844 had veered away from their goal rather than leading them to it. Trying to keep Texas alive or trying to bury it in 1845, openly courting the nativists, attacking Democratic economic policies, and running against the war had all left them short of the mark by March, 1848. And the only substantive route that remained open that spring—exploitation of the slavery extension issue—seemed too hazardous to attempt by a clear party stand. In these circumstances, Whigs from states where they were competitive just like those from states where Whig prospects had always been hopeless turned to the nomination of a military hero for president as the only road to victory in 1848.

Many southern Whigs, of course, and been pushing Taylor's nomination since the spring of 1847 as the best way to neutralize the slavery issue. As on Georgian put it at the end of that year. "Nothing can keep us together & save us but Genl. Taylor—nothing can destroy the Democracy but General Taylor. Under his flag we can give them a Buena Vista drubbing." Some southerners were also attracted to Taylor by the populistic image he had cultivated with his "no party" or "people's" campaign. Georgia's Whigs, for example, desperately needed a weapon to counter the growing Democratic strength among nonslaveholders in the Cherokee District, where the very name Whig was anathema because of its aristocratic connotation. Taylor, and Taylor alone, seemed to provide that weapon. In Kentucky, Maryland, and Virginia, Whigs were accused of being aristocratic foes of the people because they opposed Democratic reforms that would democratize those states' constitutions. Taylor's reputation provided a shield to ward off such charges in all these states. Even in the stronghold of North Carolina, some Whigs feared in early 1848 that the party would need Taylor's coattails to carry the state election in August. The Democrats, they worried, might run a populistic campaign against them in that election, and Democratic gubernatorial candidate David Reid took precisely that tack in May, when he called for eliminating suffrage restrictions in elections for the state senate.[55] Hence in North

55. Iverson L. Harris to John M. Berrien, December 15, 1847, in Berrien Papers. The argument about the Whig attempt to neutralize attacks on their opposition to constitutional reform is inferred from descriptions of the Democratic exploitation of that issue in Harry A. Volz III, "Party,

Carolina, as in other southern states, Whigs wanted Taylor's nomination in part to offset their disadvantage on a state issue that had little to do with the slavery question. With Taylor as a candidate, Whigs everywhere could run as the true people's party, regardless of their stand on specific issues. As with their handling of the slavery issue in the South, they could counter the concrete platform proposals of their foes with their presidential candidate's image.

It was in the North, however, that the swing of Whig opinion toward a military candidate became most marked in the spring of 1848. Some northern Whigs, of course, had boomed Taylor since 1846, and more joined them after Whig defeats in the fall of 1847. But the predicament that developed after the ratification of the treaty with Mexico transformed the movement toward military candidates into a stampede. For one thing, the end of the war and the acquisition of territory removed one of the major objections to Taylor and Scott. In addition, Taylor's Allison letter of April 22, 1848, mitigated the fears of other Whigs that he did not even belong to their party. Most important, the combined impact of the apparent resolution of traditional issues that might have aided orthodox candidates like Clay and Webster, the fact that Democrats could claim the benefits of a successful war while the Whigs themselves could no longer promise to stop it or expansion, and the naked confrontation with the proviso question simply convinced large numbers of northern Whigs that now only a military hero would do.

Thus it was only nine days after the Senate ratified the Treaty of Guadalupe-Hidalgo that New York Whig Congressman Washington Hunt wrote Thurlow Weed that he, Corwin, John M. Clayton of Dela-

---

State, and Nation: Kentucky and the Coming of the Civil War" (Ph.D. dissertation in progress, University of Virginia), Chap. 1; Stephen Green, "The Collapse of the Whig Party in Maryland" (seminar paper, Yale College, 1973); and Stephen White, "The Partisan Political Elements in the Virginia Constitutional Convention of 1850–51" (seminar paper, University of Virginia, 1980). On North Carolina, see E. J. Hale to Daniel M. Barringer, January 21, 1848, in Barringer Papers; David Outlaw to Emily Outlaw, February 22, 1848, in Outlaw Papers; Alex Fleming to M. B. Fleming, June 22, 1848, in M. B. Fleming Papers, Perkins Library, Duke University; Alfred Dockery to Robert L. Caruthers, July 25, 1848, in Robert L. Caruthers Papers, Southern Historical Collection, University of North Carolina; and Kruman, "Parties and Politics in North Carolina," 116–24.

ware, and others now wanted as a candidate a general who had been and could remain mum on the proviso so that the Whigs could run one way in the North and another way in the South on the slavery extension issue.[56] Similarly, Ohio Whig Congressman Robert Schenck, who in 1846 had declared confidently that the Whigs could easily win the presidency on the tariff issue, became a Scott proponent in the spring of 1848. Pennsylvania's Andrew Stewart, a famous exponent of protective tariff doctrine, had moved into the Taylor camp even earlier.[57] Other Pennsylvania Whigs pleaded for the nomination of Taylor because he was the only man who could combine the Native American and Whig forces against the Democrats. Taylor had already accepted the Native American nomination in 1847, and his name on the ticket could therefore cement an alliance with the Native Americans for the October state elections. Such a combination could be achieved, moreover, without overt appeals to nativists, which might alienate immigrants whom Pennsylvania's Whigs were also courting in that election. "With Gen. Taylor as the Whig candidate we gain 15000 Native American voters without being connected with Nativism politically," wrote a frantic Philadelphian in May. "With Gen. Taylor we shall carry the Gen. Assembly and the State Senate we have and thus we shall secure the U.S. Senator to be chosen in place of Mr. Sturgeon." Without Taylor, on the other hand, "the Whig party of this state will be broken up into helpless confusion."[58]

56. Washington Hunt to Thurlow Weed, March 19, April 17, 1848, in Weed Papers. Although New York Whigs like Hunt and Weed wanted a military candidate because of intrastate factionalism and calculations of the national results, the majority of Whigs in the state steadfastly supported Henry Clay. Almost alone among northern states, New York resisted the rush toward military candidates after March. The reason for this atypical loyalty to Clay was, ironically, that New York Whigs by 1848 believed that the rift between the Hunkers and Barnburners was so severe that any Whig would carry the state. By 1848, even a Clay candidacy could not reunite the feuding Democracy.

57. On Schenck, see John McLean to Salmon P. Chase, May 19, 1848, in Salmon P. Chase Papers, Historical Society of Pennsylvania; on Stewart, see N. K. Hall to Millard Fillmore, December 23, 1847, in Fillmore Papers, State University of New York, Oswego.

58. E. Joy Morris to John P. Kennedy, May 6, 1848, in Kennedy Papers. For additional evidence of how the need to combine with the Native Americans influenced Pennsylvania Whig support for Taylor, see George C. Collins to Henry Clay, June 10, 1848, in Clay Papers; William J. S. Birken to Millard Fillmore, December 25, 1850, E. G. Lindsey to Fillmore, January 28, 1851, April 7, 1851, in Millard Fillmore Papers, Buffalo Historical Society. For evidence that

Elsewhere, too, Whigs who had seen their bid to build a permanent majority on the issues of 1846 and 1847 fall short now abandoned former Whig champions and turned to military heroes who alone could draw the additional votes Whigs needed to win. Furious at Clay's last-minute grasp for the nomination in April, an Indiana Whig explained, "The Locos never can be brought into the support of Mr. Clay. We must have a new man, and where can we get a more acceptable man than Gen. Taylor." Fearful that Clay's ambition would disrupt the party and prevent it from rallying behind Taylor, he later complained, "Mr. Clay has been looked on as the embodiment of the Whig party. And if we are defeated again, he will be looked on as the demolisher of the same." Five days after the treaty with Mexico was ratified, another Indiana Whig warned, "The Whigs will have to run either Scott or Taylor or be defeated so badly that you will hardly know we run a candidate. To talk of Clay or [Supreme Court Justice John] McLean is worse than madness." No one, indeed, captured the desperate mood of many Whigs by the eve of their convention better than this same former congressman when, in late May, he again disparaged the thought of a McLean candidacy. "The Whig party would be so dead in a month after his nomination that a galvanic battery could not move a muscle in the whole body. . . . We must have the aid of gunpowder—the fortress of Locofocoism cannot be taken without it."[59]

At the beginning of 1848, the notorious Thomas Dorr of Rhode Island, a Democrat, observed: "The Whigs admit that it was proved in 1844, that it is next to impossible for them to succeed in their own unassisted strength, and that they must come into power, if at all, with the aid of Democratic votes as in 1840. Hence the importance to them of a *taking* candidate. A brave old soldier they think is the man for them."[60] Dorr would prove correct about the eventual decision of the Whig party in 1848, but he was wrong about the process by which they reached it. Not

---

Pennsylvania's Whigs tried to court immigrants as well as Native Americans in the 1848 state elections, see Michael F. Holt, *Forging a Majority: The Formation of the Republican Party in Pittsburgh, 1848–1860* (New Haven, 1969), 62–63.

59. John Edwards to George Dunn, April 3, 27, 1848, in George Dunn Papers, Lilly Library, Indiana University; E. W. McGaughey to Caleb B. Smith, March 15, 1848, in Caleb B. Smith Papers, Library of Congress; McGaughey to George Dunn, May 23, 1848, in Dunn Papers.

60. Thomas Dorr to Edmund Burke, January 13, 1848, in Burke Papers.

all Whigs had believed that a *"taking* candidate" provided the only route to power after 1844. Whigs in heavily Democratic states quickly gravitated in that direction, but elsewhere the Whigs essayed a number of different roads to recovery. Only when those various sallies failed to reach the target did Whigs in most states adopt a different strategy to defeat the Democratic foe in 1848. Most southern Whigs did indeed turn to Taylor in 1847, largely but not exclusively, because of the slavery issue. But it was only the disappointing results of 1847 and the apparent issue vacuum following the end of the Mexican War in March, 1848, at a time when the economy still flourished, that shifted the majority of northern delegates toward Taylor and Scott. But just as some Whigs had predicted, that issue vacuum proved to be only temporary. By the fall of 1848, after Taylor had already been nominated, the economy had soured sufficiently that Whigs could once again hammer away at the Walker tariff, at the subtreasury, and at large government deficits in key northern states. Those attacks on traditional issues would reinforce the loyalty of most Whig voters in the North to their party. In combination with Taylor's palpable appeal beyond Whig ranks to Democrats, Native Americans, and first-time voters, with his malleability on the proviso issue that allowed the Whigs to run a two-faced campaign on the slavery extension issue, and with the aggravation of the rupture in the New York Democratic party, they would help to give the Whigs their second, and last, chance to occupy the White House.

The Mysterious Disappearance
of the American Whig Party

T his essay briefly examines one of the most fascinating puzzles in American political history: namely, what explains the death or total disappearance of the Whig party in the 1850s? Between 1834 and 1848, the Whigs battled the Democrats on even terms if one considers the number of popular votes and of local, state, and national offices won. After winning control of the House of Representatives in the elections of 1846–1847, they captured the presidency, 57 percent of the seats in the House, and 71 percent of the governors elected in 1848.[1] By the end of 1856, eight years after this genuinely impressive performance, the Whigs had ceased to exist as a functioning political organization.

The essay's primary goal is to argue that the collapse of the Whig party should indeed be regarded as a riddle by pointing out how unusual

---

1. After the 1848 elections, the Whigs also controlled the legislatures in fifteen of thirty states. All figures on percentages of House seats or governorships won in a specific year are taken from Congressional Quarterly, *Guide to U.S. Elections* (Washington, D.C., 1975). Figures on the partisan share of seats in any particular Congress, in contrast, are taken from U.S. Bureau of the Census, *Historical Statistics of the United States: Colonial Times to 1970* (2 vols.; Washington, D.C., 1975), II, 1083. The figures differ because prior to 1876 congressional elections were held at different times in different states in both odd- and even-numbered years. For example, although Whigs won 57 percent of the House seats in 1848, they lacked a majority in the next Congress because they did so poorly in 1849. Figures on party strength in state legislatures refer only to the lower house and were aggregated by Walter Dean Burnham for the Inter-University Consortium for Political and Social Research. Neither Professor Burnham nor the consortium is responsible for the use I make of them.

the utter evaporation of a major political party is. But it also explores a fruitful way to begin to solve the mystery of the party's disappearance. The method it employs both to demonstrate and to unravel this puzzle is to make a few brief forays into comparative history.

Most historians have found nothing very mysterious about the expiration of the Whig party, and they have offered a host of explanations for it. Among others, these include the death of the Whigs' two great leaders, Henry Clay and Daniel Webster, internal factionalism, the obsolescence of Whig issues, sectional disruption over the slavery issue, and the incursion of the nativist Know Nothing party into Whig voting support.[2] All of these factors contributed to the party's demise, but the problem is that one can easily think of examples of other major political parties that survived the death of founding leaders, internal division, the loss of old issues, and the threat of third party incursions. Individually or in combination, that is, these weaknesses need not prove fatal to the life of a political institution. Simply put, the mystery is this: Why did the Whig party succumb to these pressures when other major parties at other times and places did not? To give two brief examples of what I mean: the Republican party still exists today long after the death of its founders and the obsolescence of the sectional issues on which it was originally built; and the Dixiecrat revolt from the Democratic party in 1948 was a far more severe sectional rupture than the Whigs ever suffered, yet the Democratic party continues to thrive in both the North and South. Once one invokes a comparative perspective, in short, the reasons for the death of the Whig party are less transparent than historians have thought.

Nineteenth-century Americans who lived through the party's demise also offered a host of explanations for its disappearance. Here let me focus on one that differs somewhat from the list proffered by later historians.

2. One could cite numerous examples of these interpretations, but see: Allan Nevins, *Ordeal of the Union* (2 vols.; New York, 1947), I, 194, II, 28–42; William R. Brock, *Parties and Political Conscience: American Dilemmas, 1840–1850* (Millwood, N.Y., 1979), 151–52, 188; Albert D. Kirwan, *John J. Crittenden: The Struggle for the Union* (Lexington, Ky., 1962), 279–92; Eric Foner, *Free Soil, Free Labor, Free Men: The Ideology of the Republican Party Before the Civil War* (New York, 1970), 9, 193–94; Richard P. McCormick, *The Second American Party System: Party Formation in the Jacksonian Era* (Chapel Hill, 1966), 353; Michael F. Holt, "The Politics of Impatience: The Origins of Know Nothingism," *Journal of American History*, LX (1973), 309–31; David M. Potter, *The Impending Crisis, 1848–1861*, completed and edited by Don E. Fehrenbacher (New York, 1976), 240–52.

In 1870 a newspaper editor from Jackson, Mississippi, named Edward Stafford wrote this wonderfully pithy epitaph for the Whigs: "The Whig party died of too much respectability and not enough people."[3] Although this breezy diagnosis may strike some as flippant, it is as trenchant as it is succinct.

First, note what Stafford omitted from his postmortem. Although he wrote only five years after the close of the Civil War and although Mississippi ranked next to South Carolina in terms of fire-eating southern sectional extremism during the antebellum period, he did *not* cite sectional disruption over slavery as *the* or even *a* cause of the Whigs' death. Many historians would probably reject Stafford's analysis peremptorily because of this omission, for surely the most widely accepted explanation of the Whig party's disappearance is that it was a casualty of the sectional conflict that ultimately eventuated in civil war. Yet Stafford in 1870 undoubtedly remembered what later historians who advance this interpretation conveniently forget. The Democratic party was far more rancorously divided along sectional lines in 1860, to say nothing of the next five years when hundreds of thousands of northern and southern Democrats were literally trying to kill each other, than the Whig party ever had been. Yet it had recovered by 1870 and still flourishes today, 135 years after the Whig party descended to its grave. Patently, sectional division need not be fatal to a political party. Northern and southern Whigs, in fact, had been at odds over the slavery issue since the party's founding in 1834, yet despite that internal split it contested and won elections for twenty years. It was only when the Whigs ceased to hold conventions, nominate candidates, and contest elections under the Whig label that we can speak of its death, and the division of the party along sectional lines does not explain its collapse as an effective political force within the rival sections.[4]

3. Jackson *Pilot*, July 30, 1870.

4. For evidence of the persistent division between northern and southern Whigs over slavery, see Thomas B. Alexander, *Sectional Stress and Party Strength: A Study of Roll-Call Voting Patterns in the United States House of Representatives, 1836–1860* (Nashville, 1967); and Michael F. Holt, *The Political Crisis of the 1850s* (New York, 1978). Potter, *The Impending Crisis*, 240–52, argues that it is a mistake to equate sectional division in a national party with its collapse within the respective sections and that nativism, not anti-Nebraska sentiment, best explains the disintegration of the northern Whigs, who tried to exploit anti-Nebraska sentiment. I made the same point earlier in "The Politics of Impatience," and it has recently been conclusively demonstrated in William E. Gienapp, *The Origins of the Republican Party, 1852–1856* (New York, 1987).

If we turn from what Stafford omitted to what he wrote, his assertion that the Whig party died of too few people points to a crucial fact about American political parties in the nineteenth century. They were not primarily legislative or parliamentary organizations. Rather, they were mass parties whose continued existence was determined by the allegiance of voters to them. In some states, leaders were the first to abandon the Whig organization, but in most places only the previous and massive loss of voter allegiance to the party convinced regretful Whig politicians that they must jettison a party they loved. Stafford, in short, was on the mark. Whig leaders gave up the ghost and the party dissolved when it no longer retained enough voting support to have a chance of winning office.

This last statement, of course, is a truism, and ultimately it is as unsatisfactory an explanation of the Whigs' disappearance as is Stafford's otherwise astute analysis. For one thing, we need to know why, not just whether, the Whigs lacked sufficient voter support. Stafford himself provides no explicit answer to that question, but his implicit thrust is that the Whigs were an elitist party that could not attract enough nonelite voters to win elections and quite possibly drove the majority of them into opposition precisely because it was elitist. If that is what Stafford meant, it is no help at all in explaining why the Whigs died in the 1850s. In most places, the great majority of the wealthy, silk-stocking set supported the Whigs, some Whigs always possessed an aristocratic or antidemocratic ideology, and Whigs did self-consciously present themselves as the party of the sober, church-going, educated, respectable classes, if not of the elite, while simultaneously disparaging Democratic voters as a mindless, feckless, and dangerous rabble. Stafford's characterization of the Whigs, and certainly the Whigs of Mississippi, then, was accurate. The problem is that the Whig party always had a patrician, smugly self-righteous image, yet it still won enough votes and offices to remain an effective opponent of the Democrats for twenty years.[5] Whig elitism cannot explain why the party flourished for a number of years and then vanished.

5. The studies that show the preference of wealthy classes in northern cities as well as southern black-belts for the Whigs are too numerous to list. On the Whigs' aristocratic ideology and self-consciously adopted image of respectability, see John Ashworth, *"Agrarians" & "Aristocrats": Party Ideology in the United States, 1837–1846* (London, 1983), esp. 52–84, 111–31; Daniel Walker Howe, *The Political Culture of the American Whigs* (Chicago, 1979); and Paul E. Johnson, *A Shopkeepers' Millennium: Society and Revivals in Rochester, New York, 1815–1837* (New York,

More important, Stafford's reference to "not enough people" is too vague to be helpful. The crucial issue is exactly how small does a major party's share of the electorate have to be before its leaders decide to throw in the towel and abandon the party entirely. Let me be as precise as possible about this point, for it is central to my analysis. The question before us is not why one party loses to another in an election or even over a series of elections. In any two-party system, one will be the normal majority party and the other the normal minority party, and there is no doubt that during the life of the second party system the Whigs were the weaker of the two major parties. The question is why a major party that may have languished in the minority for a period of years disappears altogether rather than remaining in place as an outlet for those voters, however small their numbers, who dislike the majority party. Why a party dies, in sum, is much more puzzling than why it loses.

Some concrete numbers help illustrate this point. Aside from strong showings in the presidential elections of 1840 and 1848, the Whig record in Mississippi, Stafford's home state, was dismal. Whigs never won the governorship and averaged only two-fifths of the vote in six such elections between 1839 and 1849. Of a total of twenty-two Mississippi seats in the U.S. House of Representatives filled between 1837 and 1849, the Whigs won a grand total of two. Finally, during the decade of the 1840s, the Whigs' share of seats in the state legislature averaged a paltry 32.8 percent. If ever a party had too few people to compete for control of government, the Mississippi Whig party appeared to be it. "We have no hope as a party in this state," one Whig moaned in 1845. "You know we are in the egyptian darkness of Locofocoism."[6]

Despite this palpable futility, the party endured until 1854, long after Mississippi Whigs had every reason to abandon it as a certain loser. One could point out as well that for most of the twentieth century the Republican party was far weaker in most southern states than Whigs ever were and that it survived if only to serve as a broker for federal patronage

---

1978). For particularly vivid examples of the Whig tendency to disparage the Democratic electorate as a drunken, illiterate, and irresponsible rabble, see Horace Greeley's election postmortems in the New York *Tribune* in November and December, 1844.

    6. Duncan McKenzie to Duncan McLaurin, November 2, 1845, in Duncan McLaurin Papers, Perkins Library, Duke University.

when Republicans controlled the White House. Constant defeat at the polls, that is, need not result in utter disappearance.

As this last example suggests, the real measure of a party's competitiveness, if that determines its ability to survive, is not how it does in any single state but its performance nationwide. Even that, however, leaves the Whigs' disappearance a mystery. True, after the party's exemplary electoral record between 1846 and 1848, it went into a sudden tailspin. In 1849, for example, Whigs won only 30 percent of the House seats and 27 percent of the governorships contested. In the election cycle of 1850–1851, the Whigs captured only 38.5 percent of the seats in the House of Representatives, and in 1852–1853 their share dipped still further to 31 percent. During the same years, Whigs lost control of many state legislatures, and consequently their representation in the United States Senate also dropped from 41.6 percent in the Thirty-first Congress (1849–1851) to 39 percent in the Thirty-second and 35.5 percent in the Thirty-third, the Congress that passed the Kansas-Nebraska Act. Finally, even though Winfield Scott, the Whig presidential candidate in 1852, won more popular votes than any Whig ever had, he garnered only 43.8 percent of the popular vote and 14 percent of the electoral vote, whereas the victorious Zachary Taylor had received 47.3 percent of the popular and 56 percent of the electoral count in 1848.

This demoralizing trend, especially the rout in the presidential election, did engender a fatalistic defeatism among many Whigs, who became convinced that the party could never win again and must be abandoned. Manuscript evidence indicates, however, that by the end of 1853 most Whigs had no intention of deserting the party, particularly in states where it had traditionally been most competitive. Moreover, in the North the passage of the Kansas-Nebraska Act in the spring of 1854 kindled enormous optimism among Whigs and pessimism among Democrats that the Whigs were destined to recapture control of Congress and the White House. That act, groaned a New York Democrat in a typical lament, "must throw most if not all the free states into the hands of the Whigs . . . and secure to them the next President."[7]

---

7. J. J. Jones to William L. Marcy, March 21, 1854, in William L. Marcy Papers, Library of Congress. For additional evidence of Whig optimism and Democratic pessimism in the spring of 1854 because of the Kansas-Nebraska bill, see Holt, *Political Crisis of the 1850s*, 149–50.

Whatever the plight of the Whigs between 1849 and 1853, indeed, it pales in comparison with the abyss into which the still-flourishing Republican party was plunged in the 1930s. Although the Whigs were routed in the electoral vote in 1852, the margin between their share of the popular vote and that of the Democrats was only 7.1 percent, and that defeat followed a victory four years earlier. In contrast, Republicans lost the presidential election of 1932, and four years later they lost again with a disastrous 36.5 percent of the popular vote and 1.5 percent of the electoral count.[8] At their lowest ebb, the Whigs still controlled 31 percent of the seats in the House and 35.5 percent of those in the Senate. After the 1936 elections, the Republicans held a pathetic 20.5 percent of House seats and 16.6 percent of those in the Senate. Viewed somewhat differently, the Whigs disappeared only three years after they lost control of the White House and seven years after losing their majority in the House of Representatives. In contrast, Republicans were a minority in the House between 1930 and 1946, and after 1932 it would be twenty years before they again won the presidency.[9] Yet the Republicans, unlike the Whigs, obviously survived to fight and win another day.

By this point, it should be clear that the disappearance of the Whig party is more mysterious than most historians have admitted. The question is, Why were the Whigs the only mass major party in all of American history to die?[10] One way to answer that question is chronologically to reconstruct the history of the party and its death throes in order to identify the reasons why voters and politicians eventually deserted it. I have advanced such an interpretation in a previous book, and I am now engaged

8. The previously dominant Republicans lost control of the House as early as 1930, in 1932 Democrats captured control of the Senate as well, and in 1934 Democrats increased their majorities in both. The point is that the Republicans' record of defeat in the 1930s was longer and more severe than that of the Whigs after 1848.

9. Democrats also controlled the Senate from 1932 to 1946.

10. The Federalist party, of course, also died, but although the Federalists were the major rival of the Jeffersonian Republicans between 1792 and 1815, they were not a mass party like the Whigs. They never developed the electoral organization or elicited the passionate loyalty that the Whigs did, and most certainly they never mobilized anywhere near the number of voters that the Whigs did. The same could be said for the short-lived National Republican party, which appeared prior to the emergence of truly mass parties, never developed a credible base in the South, and failed even to combine all the opponents of the Democrats in the North. Hence it seems accurate to say that the Whigs were the only mass major party in American history to disappear.

in writing a much more detailed full-scale history of the party's birth, life, and death. Here I can give only a brief summary of my argument, one that will be familiar to readers of my *Political Crisis of the 1850s*.

The Whig party formed in the winter of 1833–1834 as an opponent of the Jacksonian Democrats, and it continued to exist only so long as it remained a credible opposition party, that is, only so long as it provided clear alternatives to the Democrats on matters of local, state, and national public policy and was perceived as being in conflict with the Democrats. Between 1849 and 1853, a series of developments both within and outside of the political system and of decisions by both Whig and Democratic political leaders narrowed or eliminated the issue conflicts between the parties and created a widespread public conviction that they were more alike, than different from, each other. Of these manifold and complex developments three were most important.[11]

First, in 1852 the national platforms of both major parties committed them to accepting the Compromise of 1850 as a final settlement of the slavery issue. This congruence, which came over the bitter protests of many northern Whigs who wanted to run against the compromise, not only erased partisan differences over slavery but also destroyed the ability of Whigs to campaign one way on the slavery issue in the North and another in the South, an ability that had allowed the Whigs to survive sectional differences over slavery since the party's founding.

Second, whereas the Whigs had traditionally been the party of native-born evangelical Protestants who were most infected with anti-Catholic, anti-immigrant, and prohibitionist sentiments, in 1852 the Whigs attempted to outbid the Democrats for the support of Catholics and immigrants, a tactical shift that required Whigs to disavow any sympathy for prohibitionism as well.[12] In the short run, this about-face proved futile, and it is now clear that a major reason the Democrats won the presidency in 1852 was a massive outpouring of new immigrant vot-

11. Documentation for this argument can be found in Holt, *Political Crisis of the 1850s*, 90–138.

12. On the traditional support of evangelical Protestants for the Whigs, see Johnson, *A Shopkeepers' Millennium*; Howe, *Political Culture of the American Whigs*, 9–38, 150–80; Lee Benson, *The Concept of Jacksonian Democracy: New York as a Test Case* (Princeton, 1961); and Ronald P. Formisano, *The Birth of Mass Political Parties: Michigan, 1827–1861* (Princeton, 1971).

ers into their column.[13] In the long run, the decision proved disastrous, for it permanently alienated nativists and prohibitionists from the Whig party just when they were about to become the fastest-growing voting blocs in the nation.

Third, and most significant of all, a series of state constitutional revisions and an economic boom fueled by the California gold strikes and unprecedentedly massive British investment erased partisan divisions on a host of economic issues that Whigs and Democrats had fought over since the Panic of 1837. This sudden prosperity proved especially pernicious to the Whigs, for the basic rationale behind their economic programs had been that the dearth of private capital required active governmental interventionism to promote economic growth. The abundance of private funds after 1849 not only seemed to render government activism unnecessary, but it also seemed to confirm the wisdom of the Democrats' negative state doctrines.

Whigs themselves were well aware that the economic mission of their party had suddenly become obsolete. A Baltimore Whig wrote his brother in 1853, for example, that because of the abundance of gold in private hands "the great dividing lines between the two old parties are fast melting away and such changes are taking place in the world that issues formerly momentous are now of comparatively trifling importance." Similarly, a Cincinnati Whig concluded in 1852: "The real grounds of difference upon important political questions no longer correspond with party lines. . . . Politics is no longer the topic of this country. Its important questions are settled. . . . Government no longer has its ancient importance. Its duties and powers no longer reach to the happiness of the people. The people's progress, progress of every sort, no longer depends on government." As important as what Whigs said is what they did. In 1852, 1853, and 1854, scores of leading Whig politicians reacted to their perception that government had become irrelevant by

13. Gienapp, *Origins of the Republican Party*, 31–35 and Tables 1.1–1.10 (pp. 482–86); Robert William Fogel, *Without Consent or Contract: The Rise and Fall of American Slavery* (New York, 1989), 319, and Paper 69 in the forthcoming second volume of Fogel's work, to be entitled *Evidence and Methods*. I possess a manuscript copy of this lengthy statistical paper, which stresses the increasing share that naturalized immigrants and American-born sons of immigrants formed of the participating electorate in the 1850s.

retiring from political life altogether in order to devote themselves exclusively to business activities to exploit the boom.[14]

The perceived congruence between Democrats and Whigs fostered widespread public apathy and alienation from *both* parties. The proportion of eligible voters participating in the presidential election of 1852 was lower than it had been in sixteen years.[15] Turnout plummeted still further in the state elections of 1853, but, more important, antipathy toward both parties as corrupt, spoils-oriented machines led by selfish, wire-pulling hacks who impeded popular self-government mushroomed. Party "controversy is continued not for measures, but for men—not for the public good, but for public office," complained a Baltimore newspaper in 1851, while a Philadelphian groused in 1853 that "without any present questions of political importance to preserve the old lines of parties, parties yet preserve the old names which prove convenient vehicles to convey certain individuals to places of trust & distinction & emolument."[16] The concomitant of these complaints that major party politicians were interested only in public pelf rather than redressing public grievances was the appearance in 1852 and especially 1853 of a host of third or splinter parties in local and state legislative elections. Seeking clean government, action against Catholics, prohibition, or simply political reform, these parties, like abstention, severed the moorings that had previously tied tens, if not hundreds, of thousands of voters to the Whig and Democratic parties.

14. Charles Barringer to Daniel M. Barringer, February 4, 1853, in Daniel M. Barringer Papers, Southern Historical Collection, University of North Carolina; diary entry for September 24, 1852, in Charles R. Williams, ed., *Diary and Letters of Rutherford Birchard Hayes, Nineteenth President of the United States* (5 vols.; Columbus, Ohio, 1922), I, 421–22. I will document this assertion about prominent Whig politicians retiring from political life in my forthcoming book, but I have in mind men like William B. Campbell, who left the governorship of Tennessee in 1853 to become a cotton factor in New Orleans, and Connecticut's Truman Smith, who resigned his Senate seat in May, 1854, before his term expired, in order to practice law in New York City.

15. Estimates of voter turnout can be found in U.S. Bureau of the Census, *Historical Statistics of the United States*, II, 1072. The tables in Gienapp, *Origins of the Republican Party*, 482–86, indicate that the turnout rate in the North would would have been even lower had not first-time voters and previous abstainers replaced former voters who now stayed home. Everywhere except Massachusetts and Connecticut, moreover, Democrats captured the preponderance of that new vote.

16. Baltimore *Clipper*, January 6, 1851, quoted in William Evitts, *A Matter of Allegiances: Maryland from 1850 to 1861* (Baltimore, 1974), 45; William Pettit to John M. Niles, December 8, 1853, in Gideon Welles Papers, Library of Congress.

Hence, when powerful new issues—namely, anti-Nebraskaism, anti-Catholicism, and prohibitionism—emerged in 1854 and 1855 and produced a realignment against the Democrats, most anti-Democratic voters wanted nothing to do with the Whig party. Its credibility as an authentic opponent of the Democrats and representative of the people had already been destroyed. Instead, anti-Democratic voters chose populistic new parties, the Republicans and the Know Nothings, through which they could punish the Democrats and the despised political hacks who commanded both old parties. As a New York Know Nothing paper explained that party's appeal in 1854, the people "saw [the Whig and Democratic] parties without any apparent difference contending for power, for the sake of power. They saw politics made a profession, and public plunder an employment." [17] At the same time, however, the very ferocity of Republican and Know Nothing assaults on the Democrats gave the targets of those parties—southerners, Catholics, immigrants, and wets—a new appreciation of the Democracy, thus sparing it from the utter disintegration suffered by the Whigs.

If one can describe what happened to the Whig party—and I fully realize that not everyone will agree with my interpretation—that description still does not fully answer the question of why the Whig party was the only mass major party in American history to disappear. As previously suggested, other major parties have withstood defeat, division, voter apathy and alienation, and third party threats. Put differently, the danger of chronologically reconstructing the demise of the Whig party is that one gets so immersed in the trees that he fails to see the forest, that one becomes so familiar with the details of the story that he remains blind to what differentiated the political structure and political ideology of the 1850s from other times when major parties managed to survive similar disabilities.

In other words, we must alter the question from what *caused* the death of the Whig party to what in the political context of the 1850s *allowed* the party to vanish at that time. If we think of the issues and

17. Livingston *Republican*, October 11, 1855. Although I name only Republicans and Know Nothings as new parties that emerged in 1854 and 1855, the situation in those turbulent years was not simple. Literally dozens of splinter parties with a wide variety of names mushroomed then to challenge the Whigs and Democrats, and it took time before Know Nothings and Republicans emerged from that confusion as the two major challengers.

developments of the 1850s as a chemical reaction, what in the chemical solution acted as the catalyst to cause the mix of elements to produce a specific result when, absent that catalyst, the reaction would not have occurred? To isolate and identify those distinctive catalytic agents, the best approach is to examine other major parties at other times and places that suffered similar degrees of duress but did not disappear.

Reasonable people will always disagree about the appropriateness of the two things being juxtaposed in any comparative analysis, but two major parties, the American Republican party in the 1970s and the British Conservative party in the 1840s and 1850s, so closely approximated the condition of the Whig party in the 1850s that extended comparison is justified. Together, these comparisons yield vital clues as to why the Whigs disappeared.

Given Republican control of the White House throughout the 1980s, it is easy to forget the striking similarities between the condition of the Whig party in the 1850s and that of the Republicans in the 1970s. The Whigs elected Zachary Taylor president in 1848, yet Taylor died in July, 1850, the second summer of his term, in the midst of scandals that tarred his administration as corrupt. His successor, Millard Fillmore, immediately alienated a substantial fraction of his party by supporting the Compromise of 1850, and in the following congressional and state elections of 1850–1851 the Whigs were reduced to 38 percent of the seats in the House, 39 percent in the Senate, and 20 percent of the governorships. Worse still, the party was deeply divided along sectional and ideological lines going into the national convention in 1852, and its outcome failed to unite the party as northerners repudiated the platform while southerners denounced the candidate. As many Whigs predicted, they lost the election that year when turnout plunged to its lowest level in sixteen years. Then, in 1853, 1854, and 1855, the party disintegrated because of the apathy, alienation, and voter defection I have already described, despite the fact that the actions of the new Democratic administration, both in its endorsement of the Kansas-Nebraska Act and in its blatant solicitation of Catholic immigrant support, handed the Whigs golden issues that should have allowed a comeback like the one that the actions of the Polk administration generated in 1846–1847.

Now look at the Republicans' story. After his overwhelming reelection in 1972, Richard Nixon was forced to resign the presidency in August, 1974, the summer of the second year of his new term, because of the Watergate scandal. His successor, Gerald Ford, immediately alienated a large portion of the electorate, including many Republicans, by pardoning Nixon. Watergate also helped spawn a widespread sense of unresponsiveness and pervasive corruption in the political system, just as existed in the 1850s, and in part because of this the Republicans were crushed in the midterm elections of 1974. That year they were reduced to a third of the seats in the House and 38 percent in the Senate, slightly worse than the Whig showing in 1850–1851, and they controlled only 26 percent of governorships compared with the Whigs' 20 percent in 1850–1851.[18] Like the Whigs, the Republicans were also sharply divided along sectional and ideological lines going into their next national convention, with conservatives and southerners supporting Ronald Reagan for the nomination and moderates and northerners supporting Ford. As in 1852, moreover, the favorite of the southerners lost.

Other aspects of the politics of the 1970s are also eerily akin to those of the 1850s. Every index available—ranging from the deplorably low level of voter turnout, to the declining rates of partisan identification in the electorate, to public opinion polls, to the scholarship of political scientists like Walter Dean Burnham, to the comments of pundits, most notably the astute David Broder of the Washington *Post*—indicated massive popular disgust with and disaffection from both major political parties and a despairing sense of political inefficacy. Indeed, because of this lack of public confidence and because of demonstrable institutional weaknesses, political parties by the 1970s barely resembled the formidable organizations that dominated nineteenth-century political life.[19]

More intriguing, between 1974 and 1976 there were widespread predictions from both within and without the Republican party that it would disappear and be replaced by a new party, most likely a new conservative party, unless it won the presidential election of 1976. Moderate

18. The figures on Republican strength come from an illuminating article by David Broder and Lou Cannon, "The Future of the GOP in Question," Washington *Post*, June 28, 1976.

19. The literature on the loss of confidence in political institutions, the waning of partisan loyalty, and and the disintegration of modern political parties is too vast to be cited, but much of it is conveniently summarized and annotated in Richard Jensen, "The Last Party System: Decay and Consensus, 1932–1980," in *The Evolution of American Electoral Systems*, ed. Paul Kleppner (Westport, Conn., 1981), 203–41.

Republicans expressed fright at this possibility. In contrast, many conservatives, angered by the me-tooism of the Ford administration, enthusiastically welcomed it. In 1975, for example, House Minority Leader John Rhodes actually circulated a document asking the 144 House Republicans to pledge that they would never desert the party for a new organization. Only 111 signed the pledge, and the others said they would welcome a new party. In the spring of 1976, national party chairman Mary Louise Smith called herself "terribly worried" about the future of the party because of "apathy and indifference and the drift to independence," while Republican political consultant John Deardorf bluntly declared, "Nationally, the Republican party is finished—it is saddled with too many problems, some current and some historic." Moderate Minnesota Republican congressman Bill Frenzel predicted that Reagan's nomination that year would put "the stake in the heart of the corpse . . . but I don't believe there's much life left in the party in [any] case." The widely respected moderate Republican senator from Maryland, Charles Mathias, echoed that sentiment when he stated on several occasions in 1976 that unless the Republicans broadened their base, they would "go the way of the Whigs."[20]

Although the Republicans lost the presidential election of 1976, which just like 1852 evoked the lowest level of turnout in sixteen years, and remained decided minorities in the House, Senate, statehouses, and state legislatures, the party palpably did not "go the way of the Whigs" by disappearing entirely during the next four years.[21] Rather than start a new party to challenge Republicans for the anti-Democratic vote, conservatives simply seized control of the Republican party, which remained in place to benefit from public exasperation with the blundering Carter administration. Nor did anyone else start a new party to replace the Republicans. The vast majority of moderates remained in the GOP despite the Reaganite takeover and used it, not a new organization, to punish the

20. "111 on Hill Vow GOP Loyalty," Washington *Post*, March 14, 1975; "The Future of the GOP in Question," *ibid.*, June 28, 1976. All of the quotations, except that by Senator Mathias, come from the latter article. I have not bothered to find newspaper citations for the Mathias statement, but I am absolutely certain that he made it and have personally talked to him about it.

21. On Republican weakness at the state level and in Congress throughout the 1970s, see Table 6.9 in Jensen, "The Last Party System," in *Evolution of American Electoral Systems*, ed. Kleppner, 221.

offending Democrats. Aside from preexisting and hopeless minor parties like the Libertarians and Socialists or principled abstention, the only other alternative available for voters who disliked the choice presented to them in 1980 was the forlorn independent candidacy of John Anderson, who with approximately 8 percent of the popular vote amassed a total akin to that won by John P. Hale, the Free Soil candidate, in 1852.

Given the similarity in the political atmosphere of the 1850s and 1970s, and given the fact that the Democratic Pierce administration between 1853 and 1856 generated even more opposition than did the Carter administration, why didn't the Whigs replicate the Republicans' performance? Why couldn't the party remain in place long enough to exploit a voter backlash against the incumbent Democrats?

This contrast illuminates an absolutely crucial point. It was both far more necessary and, paradoxically, more easy for those who wished to challenge the major parties' dominance of political life to start new parties in the nineteenth century than in the twentieth century. The vital fact is so obvious that it can easily be overlooked, but the Whig party did not disappear simply because its supporters became temporarily disillusioned with it. Had that alone been the case, the Whigs could have rebounded once voters' wrath turned against the Democrats, just as the Republicans did in 1980. Rather, it disappeared because new parties suddenly emerged and won away the allegiance of former Whig voters. Unlike the 1970s, when the only realistic choice was between Democrats and Republicans, after 1853 voters had a choice among Democrats, Whigs, Republicans, and Know Nothings. In sum, unlike the modern Republicans, the Whig party could not monopolize opposition to the Democrats, and, more than anything else, that simple fact explains its disappearance.

As so many scholars and observers have demonstrated, in contemporary politics those who are dissatisfied with the leadership or agendas of both major parties need not attempt to start a new party to challenge them. The parties' control of the nominating process is so attenuated that any outsider who has enough money to purchase television time can announce his or her candidacy for either party's nomination for congressman, senator, or governor and try, in effect, to buy the nomination by a media campaign. Because the existing major parties are so vulnerable to outside penetration, beginning a new party seems unnecessary except to ideologically inspired fringe groups.[22] In the nineteenth century, in contrast, the absence of electronic media through which one might reach the electorate over the heads of established party leaders, the partisan control of the existing means of communication, decentralized party organization, and the clout of established leaders in local, state, and national party conventions rendered such incursions by complete party outsiders virtually impossible. To win public office, an ambitious or disgruntled aspirant or group of voters either had to build an organization within one of the major parties to capture its nomination or to build a new party organization outside the existing ones.

If nineteenth-century parties were less vulnerable to internal challenges from outsiders than they are today, they were far more susceptible to external competition from new parties. Launching a new party to contest the major parties was simply far easier for most of the last century than it is today. In turn, the ability of new parties to lure away Whig voters and thus displace the Whigs as the most effective anti-Democratic party, perhaps more than anything else, provides the key to explaining the party's disappearance. The contrast between the 1970s and 1850s is again instructive.

In 1980 the most plausible alternative for those dissatisfied with the choice between Republicans and Democrats was the isolated candidacy of John Anderson in the presidential race, not a *party* that ran candidates for other offices as well. In fact, since the Progressive party of the 1910s and 1920s, all significant challenges to the major parties, except in occasional local or state contests, have come in presidential elections from men who ran on their own without support further down the ticket—Strom Thurmond and Henry Wallace in 1948 and George Wallace in 1968. It is almost inconceivable to think of a new party today building from the bottom up, running candidates simultaneously in a number of states for local, state, and congressional offices *before* mounting a campaign for the presidency.

Yet that kind of ground-up political movement is precisely what displaced the Whig party. True, Whigs faced challenges from the Liberty and Free Soil parties in presidential elections between 1840 and 1852,

---

22. Again, Jensen, "The Last Party System," in *Evolution of American Electoral Systems*, ed. Kleppner, 219–20, summarizes much of the literature on this point.

but those antislavery parties caused the Whigs far more harm because they also contested congressional and especially state legislative elections than because they ran presidential candidates.[23] More important, the Whig party disintegrated because its voters defected to new parties in local, state, and congressional elections in 1853, 1854, and 1855, not in a presidential election. By the next presidential election of 1856, it had already been so weakened that it was moribund.

The operative question then becomes, Why have challengers to the major parties since the 1920s focused almost exclusively on the presidency, whereas new parties in the 1850s, and for most of the nineteenth century, for that matter, were launched in subpresidential and especially in local and state races? In part, the timing of events explains this discrepancy, for the local, state, and congressional elections of 1854 and 1855, and not a presidential election, were the first to be held after the passage of the Kansas-Nebraska Act in May, 1854, and the emergence of the Know Nothing movement. Those who wanted to exploit anti-Nebraska sentiment and nativism when they were most powerful had to focus on the elections at hand. They could not wait until 1856, particularly because a conscious purpose of both Republican and Know Nothing leaders was to displace the Whig party.

Yet I would suggest that a more fundamental difference between the 1850s and contemporary politics has been the shift of effective governmental power within the American federal system. Since the beginning of the twentieth century and especially since the New Deal, more and more power has been concentrated in the national government at the expense of state and local governments. Within the elective branches of the national government, moreover, the tendency has been for power to concentrate in the hands of the executive at the expense of Congress, because the president has the initiative in conducting foreign policy and in staffing regulatory and other administrative agencies as well as the federal judiciary. Because of that trend and because of the apparent invulnerability of congressional incumbents, I suspect, the perception exists that the only

23. Some will question this assertion, for the Whigs' loss in the presidential election of 1844 is often attributed to the defection of northern Whigs to the Liberty party, especially in New York. Close statistical examination, however, reveals that most former Whig defectors to the Liberty party returned to vote for Clay in 1844 and that the growth of the Democratic vote after 1840, not the loss of Whig votes since that date, was the primary reason for Clay's defeat.

way to change the direction of the national government is to capture control of the White House. Hence the sporadic Lone Ranger independent campaigns for the presidency alone.

In the 1850s, in contrast, the federal system was far more vibrant in that local and state governmental jurisdictions possessed more effective power over matters of vital importance to voters than they do today. Hence, gaining control of local and state governments was every bit as important to them as winning control of Congress or the presidency. Look briefly at the issues that fueled the party reorganization and voter realignment of the mid-1850s, for example. Prohibition was a matter of state and local, not national, jurisdiction. It required control of state legislatures and governorships to pass prohibition laws, but enforcement of those laws was primarily the responsibility of county and municipal officials. Hence prohibitionists focused on local and state races. Know Nothings wanted to bar Catholics and immigrants from voting and holding public office, and state legislatures (or state constitutional conventions), not Congress, established those requirements. State and local governments also had direct jurisdiction over the three chief menaces angry Protestants identified with the Catholic Church: the transfer of legal title to the physical properties of Catholic churches from the laity to the clergy; the Catholic drive to ban the Protestant Bible from public schools; and most important, the Catholic drive to get public tax support for parochial schools. Defeating these Catholic initiatives required control of local and state governments, not Congress or the presidency; hence Know Nothings placed first priority on capturing subnational offices. True, extending the naturalization period for immigrants from five to twenty-one years, just like repealing the Kansas-Nebraska Act, required gaining control of Congress; and the Know Nothings, like the embryonic Republican party, competed with Democrats and Whigs for control of House seats in 1854 and 1855. Even that goal, however, necessitated a focus on state legislative races, because in the 1850s state legislatures, not popular voters statewide, elected United States senators. For all of these reasons, the emerging rivals to the Whigs first aimed their efforts at state and local races, not the presidency.[24]

24. I have discussed these matters more fully in "The Politics of Impatience"; "The Antimasonic and Know Nothing Parties," in *History of U.S. Political Parties*, ed. Arthur M. Schlesinger, Jr. (4 vols.; New York, 1973), I, 575–737; and *Political Crisis of the 1850s*, 155–69.

The point is crucial, for, given the organizational difficulty of se-
lecting candidates and distributing ballots, the smaller the geographical
size of a jurisdiction the better the chances that a new party could successfully challenge an existing organization. It was far more difficult to
launch a new party in a presidential or even gubernatorial election than
in races for mayor, county commissioner, state legislator, or congressman.
The new Republican and Know Nothing parties—and the dozens of other
new parties that contested elections in the chaos of 1854 and 1855—
picked precisely those elections in which it was easiest to wean away Whig
voters. Building a coherent nationwide or even statewide organization
across hundreds of local jurisdictions, of course, required an exceptional
degree of coordination, one that did not exist in 1854 or 1855 and
emerged only fitfully in 1856. Yet those local jurisdictions proved perfect
battlegrounds on which a bewildering variety of insurgent new parties
could both smash the Democracy and annihilate Whiggery.

In addition to the shift within the federal system, there was a second
reason why it was far easier to build successful new parties in the 1850s
than in the 1970s. It can be summarized in two words—ballot access.
Prior to the adoption of state-printed secret ballots in the 1890s, political
parties themselves had the obligation to print and distribute ballots. In a
host of ways, this requirement made political parties far more powerful
than they are today, for candidates were absolutely dependent upon the
party organization to give people a chance to vote for them. But this
practice also meant that anyone who had access to a printing press and
enough manpower to distribute ballots could start a new party. In sum,
challengers to the major parties did not have to clear a series of legal
hurdles to get "on the ballot." They could print their own ballots that
were just as legal as those printed by the major parties.

Since the so-called reforms of the 1890s, in contrast, places on the
state-printed ballots are reserved for officially sanctioned or recognized
political parties. Evidence indicates, indeed, that in many states the major
parties adopted the Australian ballot with the explicit intention of denying
third parties like the Socialists and Populists access to the electorate.[25] The

25. Richard L. McCormick, *From Realignment to Reform: Political Change in New York State, 1893–1910* (Ithaca, 1981), 114–18; John F. Reynolds and Richard L. McCormick, "Out-lawing 'Treachery': Split Tickets and Ballot Laws in New York and New Jersey, 1880–1910,"

two major parties, in sum, monopolized ballot access for themselves specifically to quash third-party challenges. To break that monopoly, minor or third parties face severe hurdles. Either they must prove that they received a certain proportion of the vote in a previous election, literally an impossible task for a new party, or they must secure a specified number of validated signatures on petitions to gain a place on state-printed tickets—arduous tasks that, one can recall, obsessed the Wallace and Anderson campaigns of 1968 and 1980.

A comparison of the respective fates of the Whigs in the 1850s and of the Republicans in the 1970s, therefore, offers an important clue about the death of the Whig party. It disappeared because it was quickly replaced by new parties that outbid it for the anti-Democratic vote; and it was the rules of the political game and the nature of the federal system in the 1850s, and not simply the undeniable power of the issues that the new parties exploited, that explains why successful new parties could emerge in that decade when they have not in the twentieth century.

The British Conservative party of the 1850s provides another example of an organization that survived in the face of conditions amazingly similar to those that confronted the Whigs. Although the Conservative party was formed in 1832, only two years before the creation of the Whig party, to my knowledge no one has ever made a systematic attempt to compare the two organizations. Perhaps that failure is attributable to the confusing fact that the opponents of the Conservatives were themselves called Whigs. But I suspect that the primary reason is that Louis Hartz and others have persuaded historians that Americans never had an authentic conservative tradition and that because the Whigs lacked a genuinely conservative pedigree, any comparison between the two would be spurious.[26] Ideology aside, however, the two parties had remarkably similar

---

Journal of American History, LXXII (1986), 835–58; Peter H. Argersinger, "A Place on the Ballot: Fusion Politics and Antifusion Laws," *American Historical Review*, LXXXV (1980), 287–306.

26. Louis Hartz, *The Liberal Tradition in America* (New York, 1955), 22, 89–113; Hartz, *The Founding of New Societies* (New York, 1964), 34–37, 82–92. Robert Kelley's otherwise admirable comparative analysis of liberal ideology in England and the United States complicates the problem in another way because he insists on identifying the great Conservative leader Robert Peel with the American Democrats. See Robert Kelley, *The Transatlantic Persuasion: The Liberal-Democratic Mind in the Age of Gladstone* (New York, 1969), 184–93. One can hope that the appearance of books

careers as competitive political organizations within the emerging two-party systems of the two nations.[27]

The history of both parties, for example, can be understood in terms of the efforts of leaders to attract new elements into a coalition with an older, narrower, and discredited conservative predecessor. In the case of the Whigs, that predecessor was the candidly elitist National Republicans, who self-destructed in the South and West by opposing Indian removal, espousing ultranationalism, which seemed to threaten slavery, and championing the Bank of the United States. For the Conservatives, it was the "Ultra" Tories, whose intransigent opposition to the Catholic Emancipation Act of 1829 and Reform Bill of 1832 stigmatized them as unpopular, and politically unrealistic, reactionaries. To build broader conservative coalitions in the face of prevailing "liberal" majorities, leaders such as the Whigs Henry Clay and Thurlow Weed and the Conservative Robert Peel attempted to establish new and distinctive identities for the new parties, identities that were symbolized by new names and that would differentiate those organizations both from their defeated conservative predecessors and from their victorious opponents. The Whigs had accomplished this feat by 1841, when they controlled the presidency, both houses of Congress, and two-thirds of the state governments. Under Peel's leadership, which was absolutely critical to building a broader Conservative coalition on the Tory base, the Conservatives captured control of Parliament in the same year.

After 1841 both parties suffered fragmentation and electoral defeat and faced the task of finding new strategies to make a comeback. The Whigs split immediately when John Tyler became president, and their

---

like John Ashworth's *"Agrarians" & "Aristocrats,"* which assert that the Whigs were indeed conservative, will spur comparative analysis of the Whigs and Conservatives.

27. I claim no expertise on nineteenth-century British politics, and the following account of the Conservative party is exclusively based on Norman Gash, "From Origins to Sir Robert Peel," in *The Conservatives: A History from Their Origins to 1965*, ed. Lord Butler (London, 1977); Robert Blake, *The Conservative Party from Peel to Churchill* (London, 1970); Robert Stewart, *The Foundation of the Conservative Party, 1830–1867* (London, 1978); and Angus Macintyre, "Lord George Bentinck and the Protectionists: A Lost Cause?" *Transactions of the Royal Historical Society*, 5th Series, XXXIX (1989), 141–65. I am especially indebted to Professor Macintyre of Oxford University, who, in his role as commentator on my Commonwealth Fund Lecture at University College London, pointed out numerous errors in the portrait of the Conservative party I presented there.

newly won majorities were wiped out within two years. Conservative cohesion lasted slightly longer. As is well known, however, Peel's attempt
to continue to broaden the Conservatives' constituency by wooing Catholics with the Maynooth Grant and urban middle classes with Corn Law
Repeal infuriated the die-hard agrarian Tory base of his party and provoked a bitter rupture in 1846. After that date, there were in effect three
parties rather than two in Parliament—the Conservatives, the Peelites,
and the Whigs—and in the elections of 1847 the Conservatives, or Protectionists as they temporarily called themselves, lost about fifty seats from
their already truncated delegation, just at the time when the American
Whigs were bouncing back.[28]

From 1847 until 1856 and beyond, the Conservatives languished
in the minority, confined effectively to their stubborn agrarian base,
which still denounced the Maynooth Grant and Repeal of the Corn Laws.
True, the Conservatives established a minority ministry in the early
1850s, but the Whig administrations between 1849 and 1853 might also
be considered a minority ministry because Democrats controlled Congress
and most state governments. In any event, Disraeli's provisional budget
of April, 1852, by clearly favoring the party's agrarian constituency at
the expense of other groups, helped tumble it from power, just as the
Whigs were thrashed that year. Through all this time, the Conservatives
and their former Peelite allies, whom one might liken to the Free Soilers,
remained bitter enemies, and that animosity continued when most Peelites
eventually combined with the Whigs in the new Liberal party.

Like the Whigs in the early 1850s, that is, the Conservatives
seemed doomed to permanent minority status. Yet the similarities between
the two parties did not end there. As in the United States, anti-Catholic

28. Stewart, *Foundation of the Conservative Party*, 229. The exact extent of the Conservatives'
losses in 1847 is unclear because of the difficulty of distinguishing Peelite Conservative from Protectionist Conservative candidates, and some historians contend that the Peelites suffered a more severe
defeat than the Protectionist Conservative rump. For example, see Macintyre, "Lord George Bentinck," 150. The authorities also disagree about whether the initial breach between the two wings was
irreparable from the start or was made so by personal animosities. What is certain, however, is that
the leadership split in the Conservative party was more severe than any rupture at the leadership level
the Whig party ever suffered during its entire history, and yet the Conservative party still managed
to survive.

sentiment became a potentially powerful political force in England in the early 1850s when the so-called "Papal Aggression" of 1849 ignited protest meetings in counties throughout the nation. Just as in the United States, where Whigs had traditionally been the anti-Catholic party before 1852, this explosion stood to benefit the Conservatives, the staunchest defenders of the Church of England and foes of any concessions to Catholics. Yet Conservative attempts to exploit anti-Catholic outrage were blunted when Whigs took an equally strong anti-Catholic position. Just as both the Whig and Democratic parties in the United States moved to a pro-Catholic position in 1852, in short, both major parties moved to an anti-Catholic position in England. Unlike the United States, where anti-Catholicism spawned a new party and helped doom the American Whigs, therefore, anti-Catholicism failed to realign British politics in the 1850s or to help Conservatives return to power in 1852.[29]

In another vital respect, however, English politics had assumed a shape by the mid-1850s that was extraordinarily similar to the condition of American politics then. A consensus seemed to prevail between the minority Conservatives and majority Whig-Liberals on virtually every issue. In America, such a perceived lack of partisan difference caused a decomposition of the Whig electorate, but the British Conservatives clung to life throughout the decade. Conservative leaders themselves marveled at the endurance of their party when it had no distinguishing issue to sustain it. Lord Malmesbury, for example, complained to the Earl of Derby in 1856 that "the Conservative body can never be an active one except in office, or in opposition to . . . a Minister who attacks our institutions, and . . . we are without either of these stimulants and therefore dormant." Derby replied that he was less surprised by the apathy of

29. My discussion of the "Papal Aggression" rests on a seminar paper I wrote in 1962, my first year in graduate school, on the county meetings held to protest the Pope's reestablishing Catholic bishropics in Anglican sees. That paper, like the Whig party, alas, disappeared years ago, and my memory is admittedly hazy. But Conservative M.P.s at those county meetings uniformly blamed the pro-Catholic policies of the Whigs for encouraging the Pope's action, whereas Whig M.P.s, mouthing virtually word for word the arguments of John Russell's Durham Letter, denied responsibility and denounced the effrontery of the Catholic Church. Bereft of other issues, many Conservative candidates still ran as defenders of Protestantism in 1852. Stewart, *Foundation of the Conservative Party*, 254–55.

Conservatives than by the fact that the party still survived "in the absence of any cry or leading question, to serve as a broad line of demarcation between the two sides of the House. . . . That a Conservative party should have held together at all in such circumstances is rather to be wondered at, than that there should be apathy and indifference when there is nothing to be fought for by the bulk of the party."[30]

Historians of the Whig party can only share this sense of wonder. In the United States, perceived congruence between the parties produced not just apathy but alienation, fears about the continued existence of self-government, and the immediate formation of new parties that rapidly displaced the Whigs. The potential for similar processes of decomposition, realignment, and party reorganization existed in England, yet none of them occurred. Why, in the face of such similar circumstances, were the fates of the Whig and Conservative parties so dramatically different?

In answer to this question, students of the Conservative party would undoubtedly point to the rocklike support it attracted from an extensive agrarian constituency in England. Its defense of the Church of England and the agricultural interest gave it a lock on rural constituencies in southern England that guaranteed the party an irreducible base in the House of Commons. The malapportionment of that body, which overrepresented England and Wales at the expense of Ireland and Scotland, where Conservatives were far weaker, moreover, gave them greater power in Parliament than even their substantial constituency justified. In short, by assuring Conservatives of at least two-fifths of the Commons, these unshakable bastions seemed to assure the party's perpetuation.[31]

Nonetheless, the contrasting fortunes of the Whigs and Conservatives also reemphasize how crucial the federal structure of American politics was to the demise of the Whigs. Although British parties had developed extensive grass-roots organizations by the 1850s to manage the annual voter registrations and mobilize the electorate, and although there were occasional contests for control of municipal governments, most political activity and attention in Britain focused on Parliament, not counties and localities. At the least, the Conservatives, unlike the Whigs, did not

---

30. Quoted in Blake, *Conservative Party from Peel to Churchill*, 90–91.
31. Macintyre, "Lord George Bentinck," 150, 163–65; Stewart, *Foundation of the Conservative Party*, 84–85, 158–60.

have to worry about the erosion of their support in the constant local and state elections that filled the American political calendar.[32]

But the vulnerability of the Whigs to displacement does not answer another crucial question illuminated by the British example. Why was the reaction of rank-and-file members of the Conservative party to the lack of interparty differences and conflict in the 1850s so different from that of American voters in similar circumstances?[33] Why couldn't American voters tolerate consensus? Why did that perception generate not only apathy, but also fears for the very survival of popular self-government and demands for new parties that would be more responsive to the people, when sheer inertia in the face of apathy seemed to hold the British Conservatives together in their party? To answer that question, we must look at the peculiar ideology shared by American voters in the 1850s, for, I suspect, they placed a much greater ideological burden on the act of voting than did Englishmen in that decade or, it should be stressed, than did Americans in the 1970s.

As historians like Rush Welter and George Forgie have brilliantly reminded us, between 1820 and 1860 Americans of all parties were obsessed with a sense of history and with their historical obligation to protect the republican experiment in self-government that was the product of the Revolution. Liberty, equality, and self-government, Americans were consciously educated to believe, were always threatened by tyranny, privilege, corruption, and subversion; and it was their duty to be ever vigilant that the achievements of the Revolutionary fathers were not squandered by their sons. The way they could perform that duty was to participate in politics, to monitor the men who governed them, and to cast votes for the men who seemed most loyal to republican ideals. Thus voting for Americans became a cathartic act, a way for a new generation to refight the Revolution as their ancestors had to secure freedom. Among other things, I suggest, this conviction that politics remained the chief battleground for

---

32. Stewart, *Foundation of the Conservative Party*, 128–46, 159–62. True, a few by-elections for Parliament were held almost every year in Britain, but elections for local, state, and national offices were far more frequent in the United States, where many localities held two or more elections every year.

33. It is difficult to tell from the quotations in Blake, but it is possible that both Malmesbury and Derby were in fact referring to Conservative members of Parliament rather than rank-and-file supporters.

freedom best explains the pervasive use of military metaphors to describe political life in the antebellum period.[34]

In 1848 an anonymous Whig writer articulated the prevailing value system in a way so apt as to merit extensive quotation.

> When the Constitution confers the power of suffrage upon a citizen, it imposes a duty; he has taken a share in the government. . . . How unworthy, then, of this high privilege are those inert or supercilious citizens, who affect to disregard the elections, or to speak of them as a vain and interested contest of office-seekers. A people who respect their institutions, and who not only know, but *feel* that government emanates from themselves, will not confound the contemptible enthusiasm of place-seekers, with the ardor of *patriots*. . . . Whoever feels within himself the least spark of that generosity of soul which makes men republicans is, so far, a POLITICIAN. Politics, the judging and acting for the honor and the prosperity of the nation, is properly an art to which all of *us* are born. *We*, the citizens, who think we have no masters but the laws, cannot be too careful or too vigilant in the exercise of the power of election, in which we perform the initiative art of government.[35]

For a variety of reasons dating from the 1820s and 1830s, moreover, Americans identified the efficacy of the vote, their weapon for protecting and effecting self-government, with the presence of at least two parties that offered them genuine alternatives on the issues of the day. The legitimacy of the entire political system rested on the belief that men governed themselves. That belief, in turn, required faith that men could determine or change what government did, a faith that depended upon the ability to change the actions of government by voting out an old set of officeholders and replacing them with new men who would pursue a different course. Interparty conflict, a perceived difference between the parties, which assured that government actions would change when one party

---

34. Rush Welter, *The Mind of America, 1820–1860* (New York, 1975), 3–74 and *passim*; George Forgie, *Patricide in the House Divided: A Psychological Interpretation of Lincoln and His Age* (New York, 1979). See also Jean H. Baker, *Affairs of Party: The Political Culture of Northern Democrats in the Mid-Nineteenth Century* (Ithaca, 1983).

35. "Necessity of Party—The Press—The Locofoco Platform," *American Review*, II (July, 1848), 69.

replaced another in power, therefore, seemed indispensable to the perpetuation of republican self-government and of the liberty it protected. As the same Whig writer put it in 1848, "The very life of liberty is maintained only by the strife of contending parties." Nor could that struggle be for office alone. It had to involve the promise of alternative public policies. Thus Preston King, a New York Democrat, wrote to Francis Preston Blair, the former Jacksonian editor, in 1855: "There is no other way to carry out in practice the theory of our Republican Government but openly and clearly to declare principles and measures and for men and parties to divide upon them as they are for them or against them. . . . Our whole theory of Government stands upon the idea that the electors of the whole country can and will understand and choose the right." What King clearly implied but left unsaid is just as important as what he did say. Unless the parties provided the electors with a genuine choice, unless they openly and clearly defined their differences on principles and measures, then republican self-government stood in peril.[36]

This mind-set thus helps explain why the fate of the Whigs in the 1850s was so different from that of the contemporaneous British Conservatives and of the Republicans in the 1970s. Once the Whig and Democratic parties were perceived as no longer offering alternatives to the voters, once they appeared to be merely spoils-oriented machines rather than agents of self-government, citizens feared that their primary objective, the preservation of the republican experiment, stood in jeopardy. Hence they could not simply grouse about an unresponsive political system and abstain as so many did in the 1970s, or wait for new issues to exploit as did the Republicans of that decade, or remain loyal to the old party through sheer inertia as British Conservatives seemed to in the 1850s. To accept the absence of alternatives on public policy, of a genuine choice at the polls, was to strip the vote of its utility as a weapon in the defense of republican self-government. Acquiescing in a struggle between contemptible office seekers who ignored public demands and did not change government policies no matter which party controlled government meant condoning the destruction of the precious Revolutionary legacy of self-government. Given the ideological baggage of Americans in the antebel-

36. *Ibid.*; Preston King to Francis Preston Blair, Sr., November 21, 1855, in Blair-Lee Papers, Princeton University.

lum period, given the supreme importance they placed on active political participation, it was natural, indeed necessary, that they reject the old parties as corrupt, boss-ridden, and useless, and demand new parties that would be more responsive to the people by taking distinctive stands on issues the old parties now agreed upon or refused to address. In sum, federalism and balloting practices allowed the Whigs to follow a different course than did the Conservatives and modern Republicans, but the American value system of the 1850s guaranteed that they would do so.

The Politics of Impatience:
The Origins of Know Nothingism

Although historians still disagree over the ultimate causes of the Civil War, most of them would concur that a major proximate cause was the political realignment of the 1850s. The collapse of the national Whig party snapped a crucial bond of union between North and South. Its replacement in the North, the Republican party, provided a powerful political vehicle for sectional hostility to the South, and Republican victory in 1860 provoked secession.

Viewed with hindsight, the reason for this political reorganization seems clear and compelling. The fragile national coalitions of Whigs and Democrats could not withstand the sectional pressure of the slavery extension issue. When that pressure was reaggravated by the passage of the Kansas-Nebraska Act in 1854, the old parties fragmented, and the northern Republican party emerged as the major opponent of the prosouthern Democratic party. Without the slavery issue, the old parties would not have split along sectional lines, the Democratic party would not have been the target of such great northern anger, and the Republican party would never have been formed.

If, however, one asks why voters deserted the Whig party at the state level, rather than why the national Whig organization was destroyed or why the Republican party emerged, it becomes apparent that the slavery issue alone cannot account for the process of realignment in the 1850s. Although the slavery issue divided northern and southern Whigs, it did not necessarily have to drive Whig voters from the party in the North, especially in the states where the Whigs were competitive with the Democrats. In the 1840s, both Democrats and Whigs had divided in Congress over the Wilmot Proviso along sharp North-South lines, but rank-and-file voters in both sections had remained loyal to their old parties. The major parties in 1848 had run different campaigns in the different sections, opposing slavery extension in the North and favoring it in the South, and they had retained their voting support by this Janus-faced tactic.[1] When the Nebraska bill was first introduced in January, 1854, William Henry Seward shrewdly recognized the possibilities of using the same strategy to resuscitate the Whig party, which had been declining in many areas since its defeat in 1852. The elections of 1854 and 1855 were local and state elections that did not involve the national Whig organization. Northern and southern Whigs could run contradictory campaigns. Seward hoped that southern Whigs could pose as truer defenders of slavery than could southern Democrats because Whig Senator Archibald Dixon of Kentucky had first proposed outright repeal of the Missouri Compromise. Northern Whigs, Seward anticipated, could blame the Democrats for sponsoring the obnoxious bill.[2] Because most northern Whigs had always opposed slavery extension, even when they divided over their response to the Fugitive Slave Act of 1850, Seward's plan made sense. Anti-Nebraska sentiment should have helped northern Whigs, not weakened them, in those crucial state and congressional elections. Whig parties in the northeastern states attempted to follow this scenario, and well into the spring of 1854 both Whig and Democratic politicians expected anti-Nebraska sentiment to unify and strengthen the Whig party.[3]

1. In a study of the election of 1848, Joseph G. Rayback estimates that the Whigs held 98 percent of their 1844 vote nationally and 95 percent in the free states, while the Democrats retained 86 percent nationally and 81 percent in the free states. Joseph G. Rayback, *Free Soil: The Election of 1848* (Lexington, Ky., 1970), 288.

2. Roy F. Nichols, "The Kansas-Nebraska Act: A Century of Historiography," *Mississippi Valley Historical Review*, XLIII (1956), 205; Glyndon G. Van Deusen, *William Henry Seward* (New York, 1967), 150. This view differs from Nichols' interpretation of Seward's strategy by making the point that the state and congressional elections of 1854 and 1855 did not have to involve the national Whig organization.

3. B. Thompson to Daniel Ullmann, May 16, 1854, in Daniel Ullmann Papers, New York Historical Society, New York City. See also J. J. Jones to William L. Marcy, March 21, 1854, in William L. Marcy Papers, Library of Congress; William E. Cramer to Caleb Cushing, January 26, 1854, T. M. Parmalee to Cushing, February 15, 1854, Charles W. March to Cushing, March 10, 1854, all in Caleb Cushing Papers, Library of Congress; Pittsburgh *Daily Gazette*,

Unlike 1848, however, the strategy failed. The Whigs suffered massive defections to new parties in 1854 and 1855, and by 1856 Whig organizations in northern states had virtually disappeared.

A complete analysis of the political reorganization that led to the Civil War, then, must explain why the old parties, and especially the Whigs, could not contain and exploit the slavery issue in the 1850s as they had in the 1840s. Furthermore, such an analysis must account for the actual course voters followed as they left old parties and joined new ones. Had the slavery issue alone motivated northern voters, such an explanation would be relatively clear-cut. But it did not. Therefore, there is a need to illuminate some of the other forces that helped destroy the second American party system and that eventually contributed to the triumph of the Republican party.[4]

Between 1853 and 1856, the fastest growing political force in many parts of the United States was not the antislavery Republican party, but the secret anti-Catholic and antiforeign Know Nothing movement. Just when outrage at the Nebraska Act should have been strongest, many people were apparently more concerned about Catholic immigrants.[5] In an atmosphere of popular hysteria about Catholics and frequent assaults on them by lower-class mobs, hundreds of thousands of men joined Know Nothing lodges. With the backing of men who had never bothered to vote before as well as converts from other parties, the order swept local, congressional, and state elections, North and South.[6] In direct contests with the Republicans in 1855, Know Nothings defeated them in New

---

May 3, 1854. Whigs in Illinois also attempted to run as an anti-Nebraska party. Don E. Fehrenbacher, *Prelude to Greatness: Lincoln in the 1850s* (Stanford, 1962), 25–34.

4. For a multivariate analysis of this problem, see Joel H. Silbey, *The Transformation of American Politics, 1840–1860* (Englewood Cliffs, N.J., 1967), 1–34. See also Paul Kleppner, *The Cross of Culture: A Social Analysis of Midwestern Politics, 1850–1900* (New York, 1970), 77–91, 100–104.

5. A New York observer noted, "The Nebraska Kansas bill is obsolete, or in the language of its famous Author 'is superceded & inoperative' in comparison with these immediate & practical questions." Samuel J. Mills to New York Central Whig Association, August 12, 1854, in Ullmann Papers.

6. Ray A. Billington, *The Protestant Crusade, 1800–1860: A Study of the Origins of American Nativism* (Chicago, 1964), 289–314, 380–89. See also Oscar Handlin, *Boston's Immigrants: A Study of Acculturation* (New York, 1968), 200–201.

York and Massachusetts and overwhelmed them in Pennsylvania. In other northern states, Know Nothings were so dominant that Republican parties could not yet form.[7] The American party's presidential candidate in 1856 garnered 21 percent of the popular vote, even though by then the majority of northern Know Nothings were supporting the Republican John C. Frémont.

An adequate understanding of the realignment of the 1850s, therefore, must account for the extraordinary popularity of the Know Nothings and the strength of anti-Catholicism at that particular time. Historians have demonstrated that ethnocultural and religious antagonisms have been important and persistent determinants of voting behavior through American history, but what accounts for the salience of these sentiments in the mid-1850s and for their ability to draw men into the political arena for the first time?[8] After all, Protestant propagandists had warned of a Catholic conspiracy since at least 1800, and angry crowds had burned convents in the 1830s and 1840s. But never before was belief in a papal plot so widespread or anti-Catholicism so intense.[9] Nativist political parties had won several municipal elections in the 1840s, but, although immigration had been heavy since 1846, it was not until the 1850s that nativism spawned such a powerful third party. Why was it not until then that reaction was so strong? Why, moreover, was this aroused bigotry not channeled through its traditional vehicle, the Whig party? In New York, Pennsylvania, Maryland, and other states where the Know Nothings flourished, the Whigs had been the party of temperance reform and nativism. One must explain why the Whigs did not benefit from the salience of these issues in the 1850s and why a new party was formed.

7. In Massachusetts, the Republicans won approximately 29.6 percent of the vote, while the Know Nothings won 42 percent. The proportions in New York were 31 and 34 percent respectively, and in Pennsylvania they were 2 and 47 percent. In New Hampshire, Connecticut, Rhode Island, New Jersey, California, and Maryland there was no Republican party yet formed.

8. For example, see Lee Benson, *The Concept of Jacksonian Democracy: New York as a Test Case* (Princeton, 1961); Michael F. Holt, *Forging a Majority: The Formation of the Republican Party in Pittsburgh, 1848–1860* (New Haven, 1969); Kleppner, *The Cross of Culture.*

9. For example, see Henry M. Phillips to William Bigler, June 11, 1854, in William Bigler Papers, Historical Society of Pennsylvania, Philadelphia; Marcellus Ells to Hamilton Fish, February 14, 1854, in Hamilton Fish Papers, Library of Congress; L. R. Shepard to William L. Marcy, January 28, 1854, in Marcy Papers.

The traditional answer to these questions stresses the importance of the slavery issue and sees Know Nothingism as a diversion from it. Northern outrage at the Kansas-Nebraska Act supposedly destroyed the Whig party, and the Know Nothing order emerged in the vacuum created by its disappearance. To it flocked opportunistic politicians, homeless voters, and especially conservative Whigs—like New York's Silver Greys—who feared that the radicalism of the new Republican party would destroy the Union but who could not stomach joining their old foes, the Democrats.[10] In short, the Know Nothing movement emerged only after the slavery issue shattered the Whig party, and it gained as much from its availability to political refugees as from its anti-Catholicism.

Although many conservatives did vote for Millard Fillmore in 1856, and Unionism was probably the chief source of his strength in the South, there are several problems with this "political-vacuum" thesis. The northern support Fillmore won differed from the support the Know Nothings attracted in 1854 and 1855, before the Republicans formed a national organization. Conservative fears for the Union cannot account for early Know Nothing voters, many of whom later joined the Republicans. Nor were Know Nothings simply refugees. The northern states in which the order grew fastest in 1854, like New York, Massachusetts, and Pennsylvania, were precisely those states where Whigs ran against the Nebraska bill and where anti-Nebraska sentiment should have aided them. In those years, the Whig party still provided a viable alternative for anti-Democratic voters in state and congressional elections, yet many people preferred new parties to the old Whig organization.

The reasons for the disintegration of the Whig party and its inability to benefit from the aroused anti-Catholic and free-soil sentiments of 1854 are complex and cannot be analyzed here in their entirety. Evidence suggests, however, that the forces leading to the rise of the Know Nothing party—forces that had little to do with the slavery crisis—were not a result of the Whig party's collapse but an important cause of that disintegration. These forces prevented the Whigs from remaining the major anti-Democratic party in the North. Put briefly, in the early 1850s an

10. Billington, *Protestant Crusade*, 390–97; Allan Nevins, *Ordeal of the Union: A House Dividing, 1852–1857* (New York, 1947), 316–32.

intensified anti-Catholicism emerged simultaneously with a hostility to politicians and an impatience with established parties that resulted in huge numbers of voters deserting the Whigs on the grass-roots level. These sentiments in turn were products of a general popular malaise and sense of dislocation caused by rapid social and economic change in those years.

Crucial to the downfall of the Whig party was a widespread revolt against the political system in the 1850s that culminated in the Know Nothing movement. Although the 1840s were years of extraordinary loyalty to party so far as rank-and-file voters were concerned, party discipline was breaking down in the early 1850s among both Whigs and Democrats.[11] The divisions within the New York parties between Hardshells and Softshells and Woolly Heads and Silver Greys were only the more spectacular examples of this party disintegration. A look at the local level—and if any party originated at the grass roots it was the Know Nothings—reveals a plethora of splinter parties in the early 1850s. For example, in Pittsburgh a "People's and Anti-Catholic Candidate" captured the mayoralty in 1850 and ran strongly the next two years. An independent slate of state legislators in 1853 was successful in Philadelphia. In the municipal election that year in Boston, Citizens' Union and Young Men's League parties won more voters than the Whigs and Democrats combined. Four parties, none of which was Whig, ran in Cincinnati's spring elections of 1853, while seven different parties contended there in the fall of that year.[12] Independent tickets opposing regular Democratic and Whig candidates took the field in Maryland's state and congressional elections in 1851 and 1853, where an observer lamented to Caleb Cushing, "I was mortified to find so much disorganization."[13]

11. Charles G. Sellers, *James K. Polk, Continentalist, 1843–1846* (Princeton, 1966), 108–109; Charles G. Sellers, "The Equilibrium Cycle in Two-Party Politics," *Public Opinion Quarterly*, XXIX (1965), 16–38; Benson, *Concept of Jacksonian Democracy*, 125–31; Rayback, *Free Soil*, 288–302.

12. Holt, *Forging a Majority*, 109–14; William Pettit to John M. Niles, December 8, 1853, in Gideon Welles Papers, Library of Congress; Handlin, *Boston's Immigrants*, 355, 85n.; William E. Gienapp, "The Transformation of Cincinnati Politics, 1852–1860" (seminar paper, Yale University, 1969), 24–44.

13. Robert McLane to Caleb Cushing, October 14, 1853, in Cushing Papers. See also Douglas Bowers, "Ideology and Political Parties in Maryland, 1851–1856," *Maryland Historical Magazine*, LXIV (1969), 197–217.

Several elements contributed to this fragmentation. Whig discouragement at their loss in 1852 weakened party loyalty, but it hardly explains Democratic disaffection. Divisions over the Compromise of 1850 exacerbated factionalism in both parties, and intraparty rivalries between politicians engendered a few of the splinter parties. Jealous of foes who received regular party nominations, bitter "outs" started new parties. Much more important, however, is evidence that many people were less concerned with party loyalty than with specific issues produced by massive immigration. Impatient with the refusal of the established parties to address these issues or stifled by intraparty divisions over them that prevented any action, these men formed separate temperance, anti-Catholic, and public school parties in Michigan, Ohio, Pennsylvania, Maryland, and elsewhere.[14] Such parties sprang from the people, not professional politicians.

Many who were violently prejudiced against Catholics and who wanted to take political action against them in 1854 considered Whig leadership too passive or too moderate on this issue. Although the Whigs often made nativist appeals, the party rarely acted against Catholics. Even more so than the Democrats, the Whigs were usually led by the elite of a community, men who did not feel the pressures from poor Catholic immigrants that were so unsettling to the common man.[15] Moreover, important Whig leaders like Seward were friendly toward Catholics. Bigots wanted parties that would more militantly express their biases.

Indeed, after 1852 some considered the Whigs not only too passive but actively pro-Catholic. Winfield Scott's candidacy apparently alienated nativists within and outside the party because of his lenient policy toward Catholic churches in Mexico during the war, his willingness to educate his daughters in convents, and especially the party's efforts to capture

14. See notes 12 and 13. For an excellent analysis of the breakup of parties in Michigan and especially Detroit, where the process was remarkably similar to that in Cincinnati, see Ronald P. Formisano, *The Birth of Mass Political Parties: Michigan, 1827–1861* (Princeton, 1971), 22–38. Formisano's careful study, which appeared after this essay was drafted, confirms many of the conclusions about the importance of anti-Catholicism, temperance, and antiparty sentiment in weakening the Whig party and contributing to the strength of Know Nothingism and Republicanism.

15. Holt, *Forging a Majority*, 42–48; Edward Pessen, *Jacksonian America: Society, Personality, and Politics* (Homewood, Ill., 1969), 251–54.

Catholic votes in that election. Nativist organizations such as the Order of United Americans in New York bitterly opposed Scott, and Lewis C. Levin, chief of Pennsylvania's Native American party, assured William L. Marcy that "the feeling among my friends is intense—intense hostility to the Whigs."[16] Other observers from Pennsylvania wrote Franklin Pierce before the election: "Many honest Protestants among the Whigs (especially Methodists and Presbyterians) are disgusted at the course Scott has taken to secure the Catholic vote and will vote against him."[17] From Westmoreland County in western Pennsylvania a Whig reported after the election, "A Presbyterian doctor, a consistent and old fashioned Whig in politics, who practices in some four or five townships in this county, says that a number of Old Presbyterians refused to vote with the Whigs, because Scott was an Episcopalian and had a daughter in a nunnery."[18]

Closely connected to the feeling that parties did not represent the views of people on issues vital to them, and more important in causing the revolt against parties, was a pervasive loss of faith in and animosity toward politicians and the mechanisms of party politics—especially conventions—or, as Rutherford B. Hayes put it when commenting on Know Nothing triumphs in Cincinnati, a "general disgust with the powers that be."[19] The chief object of many of these independent parties was not the passage of specific laws, but simply the recruitment of new and honest men for public office. An Ohioan expressed to Thomas Corwin what in 1852 must have been a general fear that somehow the people had lost control of political power. "We are Republicans, so-called," he lamented to the secretary of the treasury, "and yet men placed in power are often too far removed from the people—are not easily approached, seldom

16. John McKeen to Franklin Pierce, September 28, 1852, in Franklin Pierce Papers, New Hampshire Historical Society, Concord; Lewis C. Levin to William L. Marcy, October 15, 31, 1852, in Marcy Papers.

17. John H. Brinton to Franklin Pierce, October 6, 1852, John Davis to Pierce, October 25, 1852, in Pierce Papers. See also E. A. Penniman to William Bigler, October 13, 15, 1852, in Bigler Papers.

18. James Johnston to Edward McPherson, December 3, 1852, in Edward McPherson Papers, Library of Congress. This Protestant disgust with Scott appeared in Ohio too. See J. C. Stearns to John McLean, April 19, 1852, in John McLean Papers, Library of Congress.

19. Charles R. Williams, ed., *Diary and Letters of Rutherford Birchard Hayes, Nineteenth President of the United States* (5 vols.; Columbus, Ohio, 1922), I, 470.

comply with the expressed wishes of the people, but on the contrary re-
pulse them." [20]

Complaints about the corruption and tyranny of party bosses and
officeholders who managed conventions, chose unpopular candidates, and
generally frustrated the popular will were universal. From Maryland,
Francis P. Blair wrote that the people were furious at "the prevailing
corruptions in the conduct of public affairs," and a Whig bemoaned the
control of his party by "a Court House clique composed of a set of unprincipled men, selfish, immoral & tyrannical." [21] A St. Louis newspaper
declared that "the convention system must be abolished if we would preserve the supremacy of the popular will." [22] Philadelphia Whigs protested
the "high handed attempt" by Whig officeholders to "frown down an
expression of public opinion," while Connecticut Democrats complained
that "selfish office-seekers," "managers[,] timeservers[,] and place men"
controlled the party and fettered the popular will. [23] Even from San Francisco a Whig wrote to his mother in 1852, "With regard to our State and
city elections a strong effort is being made to dislodge the professional
tacticians and wirepullers who have ruled everything this last three
years. . . . Nominating conventions have fallen into such odium here that
after this I think some new plan will be devised for bringing candidates
forward." [24]

20. Thomas J. McGarry to Thomas Corwin, November 4, 1852, in Thomas Corwin Papers, Library of Congress.

21. Francis P. Blair to Franklin Pierce, November 25, 1852, in Blair Family Papers, Library of Congress; "Truth" to Thomas Corwin, September 1850, in Corwin Papers.

22. St. Louis *Daily Democrat*, September 8, 1853, clipping in the Cushing Papers. Friends
of the Pierce administration said that Thomas Hart Benton wrote this editorial as part of his attempt
to destroy the Democratic party in Missouri and win over the rank and file, but Montgomery Blair
was probably correct when he reported that the attacks on the convention system were popular with
the people. The point is that, even while the attempt of leaders to exploit antiparty sentiment to fight
the "ins" may account for the newspaper expression of that sentiment, the tactic itself shows that the
sentiment was powerful. Thomas C. Reynolds to Cushing, September 17, 1853, in Cushing Papers;
Francis P. Blair to Francis P. Blair, Jr., May 18, 1852, in Blair Family Papers.

23. William Mason to Thomas Corwin, May 27, 1851, in Corwin Papers; C. F. Cleveland
to Gideon Welles, July 22, 1854, and draft of letter by Welles, March, 1855, in Welles Papers,
Library of Congress.

24. Roger Sherman Baldwin, Jr., to Emily Baldwin, October 31, 1852, in Baldwin Family
Papers, Sterling Library, Yale University. See also P. M. Wetmore to William L. Marcy, Novem-

Complaints about the unresponsiveness of government, the unrepresentativeness of party leadership, the self-interestedness of politicians, and the evil of parties themselves have been endemic in American history. Denunciations of the unfairness of party conventions have been especially common among "out" politicians who failed to secure regular nominations. There are hazards, then, in using such a constant phenomenon to explain discrete events at a particular time like the revolt from the established parties in the early 1850s.

But antiparty sentiment is more widespread and more intense at some times than at others. The early 1850s were one of those times. The frequent protests and bolts to splinter parties were not the only manifestations of the unusual impatience with politics as usual. There were more extreme examples. Vigilantes organized by San Francisco's leading merchants in 1856 took control of the city from its government, banished the ward heelers of David Broderick's corrupt Democratic machine, and then formed a People's party to provide honest municipal government. The People's party dominated the city for ten years.[25]

It was this hostility to old parties and politicians that helped destroy the Whig party and prevented its resurrection on the new issues of 1854. Even when the Whigs denounced Catholic "aggressions" and the Kansas-Nebraska Act, they could not hold their former supporters or attract new ones. Many people were too suspicious of old political chieftains, the aura of corruption and expediency around Whig officeholders of all ranks, and especially the lack of popular control of the party to remain in it. Men who rebelled against the Whigs and Democrats wanted new parties that would express their will. Gideon Welles perceptively explained the failure of the Whigs to capitalize on anti-Nebraska sentiment: "It has been one of the mistakes of Seward and his friends—of the Whig leaders in Massachusetts—and in this state [Connecticut] also—that the Whig party would gain what the administration lost. The truth is there is a general

---

ber 2, 1853, in Marcy Papers; G. Godfrey Gunther to Horatio Seymour, September 19, 1853, in Fairchild Collection of Horatio Seymour Papers, New York Historical Society.

25. Samuel J. May to Nathaniel P. Banks, June 4, 1856, in Nathaniel P. Banks Papers, Library of Congress; Richard Maxwell Brown, "Pivot of American Vigilantism: The San Francisco Vigilance Committee of 1856," in *Reflections of Western Historians*, ed. John Alexander Carroll (Tucson, 1969), 105–19.

feeling to throw off both the old organizations and their intrigues and machinery. The country has outgrown them. . . . [T]he state of affairs is much as they were thirty years ago, when the old parties were broken up and again reconstructed."[26]

At the same time that it ruined the Whig party, the impatience with the old political system and the desire for new leadership provided a powerful impetus to the early growth of the Know Nothings. Much of the order's appeal was its purpose, clearly expressed by its members, to destroy the old parties, drive hack politicians from office, and return political power to the rank and file. Henry J. Gardner, Massachusetts' Know Nothing governor, described the strategy of his second victory: "We appealed from the wire pullers to the people & the greatest personal and party triumph was won in our country."[27] A New York Know Nothing vowed in 1854, "*We are* determined to give old party lines and old party hacks a glorious drubbing this fall."[28] Indeed, the correspondence of New York politicians makes it clear that Silver Greys and other Whigs joined the Know Nothings not because they wanted a new conservative party but because they were revolting against the Seward-Weed "dynasty" in their party. They objected to the power and corruption of the Weed machine and to Seward's pro-Catholic proclivities. "Whig young men will not follow the lead of King Weed and Co.," explained a Democrat to Samuel J. Tilden, and a Rochester Know Nothing described the party's chief targets as "Sewardism and Political Catholicism."[29] In Pittsburgh,

26. Draft of letter by Welles, n.d., 1856 folder, in Gideon Welles Papers, Connecticut Historical Society, Hartford. Welles later wrote about developments in 1854: "In the meantime, a new and different organization, hostile to all the old organizations sprang into sudden existence, under the name of Know Nothings. Thousands flocked into the order, not that they approved its principles, but for the purpose of relieving themselves from the obligations and abuses of the old organizations. To rebuke these, to defeat these, to rid the country of what they believed no longer useful appears to have been the mission and purpose of the order." Draft editorial, n.d., *ibid.*

27. Henry J. Gardner to Daniel Ullmann, November 12, 1855, in Ullmann Papers.

28. J. J. Henry to Daniel Ullmann, October 10, 1854, *ibid.*

29. S. B. Jewett to Samuel J. Tilden, October 6, 1855, in Samuel J. Tilden Papers, New York Public Library; James R. Thompson to Daniel Ullmann, March 24, 1855, in Ullmann Papers. The letters in the Ullmann Papers for 1853, 1854, and 1855 indicate how much Silver Greys despised both William Henry Seward and Thurlow Weed. Alex Mann to Ullmann, June 20, 1854, L. L. Pratt to Ullmann, October 17, 1854, L. S. Parsons to Ullmann, November 11, 1854, all in Ullmann Papers. See also Horace Greeley to Schuyler Colfax, August 27, 1854, in Greeley-Colfax Papers, New York Public Library.

a Know Nothing editor reflected in 1855: "One great reason the American orders swelled so rapidly in number was the profound disgust every right-thinking man entertained for the corrupt manner in which the machinery of party had been perverted to suit the base purpose of party wireworkers—an evil they honestly believed the orders would remedy."[30]

One way Know Nothings promised to return power to the people was to provide a kind of direct primary system by choosing the party's nominees by majority vote in the local lodges or councils. Another way was to make sure that candidates represented the people and not the political machine. A Bostonian wrote that one of the Know Nothings' "cardinal principles is to send Representatives 'fresh from the people'—no professional, no politician or any office seeker can have part or lot with them."[31] Pittsburgh's Know Nothings demanded that Pennsylvania's United States senator "should be a statesman, and not a mere politician—that he should be a new man, fresh from the ranks of the people—clad in American raiment, and not the cast off garments of Whiggery or Democracy."[32] A Know Nothing from western New York summarized the party's strategy in December 1854:

> There is a prestige surrounding new measures and particularly new men which it is worth our while to concentrate and secure. Under this we have shook off the yoke of political bondage. Under it more than all else we are indebted for our success. Our acts must tally with our throng. Let it be generally understood during the coming presidential campaign that new men are to be the leaders and all the offices filled from the ranks, and I care little by what name we are known, success is sure—but once by our own acts disipate [sic] this impression and half our prospects are gone.[33]

In its early years, the Know Nothing party did select most of its local leaders from new men, men who were younger and poorer than most

---

30. Pittsburgh *Daily Dispatch*, September 5, 1855. On the connection of antiparty sentiment, hostility to politicians, and independency with the Know Nothings in Michigan, see Formisano, *Birth of Mass Political Parties*, 229–38, 246–50.

31. Moses Kimball to Henry L. Dawes, August 28, 1854, in Henry L. Dawes Papers, Library of Congress.

32. Pittsburgh *Daily Gazette*, February 24, 1855.

33. F. S. Edwards to Daniel Ullmann, December 6, 1854, in Ullmann Papers.

political leaders. Of a sample of Know Nothing leaders in Pittsburgh, more than half were younger than thirty-five, 60 percent owned property worth less than $5,000, a proportion much larger than that of the contemporary Whig and Republican parties, and 48 percent were artisans or clerks.[34] Know Nothings in the Massachusetts legislature had almost identical characteristics. They were predominantly artisans from the building trades and shop industries, clerks, and clergymen, not the farmers and lawyers who had been prominent in former legislatures.[35] A New Haven, Connecticut, resident noted that Know Nothing candidates there were entirely new men, "some of them young men only four years from College and others quite uneducated and as it now appears unfitted for their places."[36] The widespread complaints about the inexperience and incompetence of Know Nothing legislatures suggest that most of the early Know Nothing officeholders were political novices.[37]

The animosity to established officeholders and Know Nothing success at the polls, however, provided an irresistible opportunity to "outs" from the old parties—politicians from the second rank whose ambition was frustrated by the dominance of other factions within their own party or by the dominance of the opposing party in their area. Increasingly, Know Nothing candidates were in fact the "broken-down politicians and persistent office hunters" that their opponents labeled them.[38] The Know Nothing candidate for governor in New York in 1854, Daniel Ullmann, was a classic example. Balked in his pursuit of statewide office for four years by the Seward-Weed wing of the Whig party, he quickly joined the Know Nothings. The ease and rapidity with which old politicians like Simon Cameron, Henry Wilson, and Millard Fillmore achieved control of the party disillusioned the thousands who joined the order to escape the

34. Holt, *Forging a Majority*, 155.

35. George H. Haynes, "A Know Nothing Legislature," *Annual Report of the American Historical Association for the Year 1896* (2 vols.; Washington, D.C., 1897), I, 175–87.

36. Emily Baldwin to Roger Sherman Baldwin, Jr., April 3, 1855, in Baldwin Family Papers. The Know Nothings attracted and appointed young and ambitious politicians in Philadelphia too. The Know Nothing mayor, elected in the spring of 1854, carefully selected new men for the municipal patronage posts, much to the dismay of seasoned Whig politicians. W. S. Hirst to William L. Bigler, June 10, 1854, G. G. Wescott to Bigler, July 14, September 7, 1854, in Bigler Papers.

37. Billington, *Protestant Crusade*, 412–17.

38. Pittsburgh *Daily Gazette*, September 19, 1855.

rule of politicos and return power to the people. A North Carolinian lamented: "This struggling and scrambling for office and promotion was one of the very great evils it was the object of our organization to remedy—and yet our success is likely to be jeoparded by the very same evil. The masses are sound but the old party leaders and political hacks, who have come into the order, from selfish purposes, will ruin us, if we are not strictly on our guard."[39] Such disillusionment was one of the main reasons for the precipitous decline of the Know Nothings after 1855.

Just as the American party was losing its image of newness and representativeness, the Republican party evinced it. Clearly, the most important reason why the Republicans, rather than the Know Nothings, became the major opponent of the Democrats in 1856 was the intensified sectionalism aroused by "Bleeding Kansas" and the caning of Senator Charles Sumner.[40] Almost as important was the bargain Republicans struck with northern Know Nothings. In state and local elections, Republicans openly threw their support to Know Nothings like Gardner in Massachusetts or Union tickets with prominent Know Nothing candidates in return for Know Nothing votes for Frémont, and local Republican newspapers and speakers denounced Catholics to woo Know Nothings.[41] But

39. Kenneth Rayner to Daniel Ullmann, n.d., 1855 folder, in Ullmann Papers.

40. Don E. Fehrenbacher is correct when he says that the Republican party was above all a response to concrete events. Don E. Fehrenbacher, "Comments on Why the Republican Party Came to Power," in *The Crisis of the Union, 1860–61*, ed. George Harmon Knoles (Baton Rouge, 1965), 21–29. See also Eric Foner, *Free Soil, Free Labor, Free Men: The Ideology of the Republican Party Before the Civil War* (New York, 1970), 199–200; T. M. Monroe to Daniel Ullmann, June 13, 1856, in Ullmann Papers; Russell Sage to Nathaniel P. Banks, May 31, 1856, in Banks Papers.

41. Nevins, *Ordeal of the Union: A House Dividing*, 466–71; Holt, *Forging a Majority*, 175–219; Edward L. Pierce to Salmon P. Chase, August 3, 1857, in Salmon P. Chase Papers, Library of Congress; S. J. Welles to Gideon Welles, January 3, 1857, in Welles Papers, Library of Congress. The Republicans tried to capture the anti-Catholic vote not only by defending John C. Frémont from the charges that he was Catholic but also by denouncing the Catholic control of the Democratic party. Cincinnati *Gazette*, October 4, 1856; Cincinnati *Enquirer*, November 6, 1856. Edwin D. Morgan, chairman of the Republican National Committee in 1856, informed a correspondent in Syracuse: "The anti-Catholic tract is to be out soon. So I learn from Mr. Gray. It has been too long delayed." Morgan to Allen Monroe, October 9, 1856, Letterbook Copy, in Edwin D. Morgan Papers, New York State Library, Albany. For the anti-Catholic appeals of the Michigan Republican party, see Formisano, *Birth of Mass Political Parties*, 268, 271–72. Foner recognizes that nativism and temperance were major forces in the breakup of the old parties and that most

an additional reason for the readiness of northern Know Nothings to join the Republican coalition was the skill with which the Republicans presented the appearance of freshness and concern for the people.

From the inception of the Republican party, its leaders had recognized and profited from the popular mood of protest against established parties. Early anti-Nebraska coalitions in Ohio and Indiana were called People's parties, and when Republicans tried to organize independently of Know Nothings in Connecticut in 1856, they adopted that name.[42] The need for an innocuous common denominator that could attract mutually suspicious Whigs, Democrats, and Free Soilers dictated this tactic, but Republicans also hoped to capitalize on the public demand for popularly controlled parties just as San Francisco's vigilantes did. That the Republicans attracted men who hated politicians and the mechanisms of party politics became evident during the initial meeting to organize a national party at Pittsburgh in February, 1856. There a delegate from Cincinnati, Charles Reemelin, opposed holding a national nominating convention because "the people would find their *men*, if it was taken out of the hands of *bargaining politicians*." He protested that he had hoped the Republican meeting "was the inauguration, of a new and purer political party that would avoid the corruptions incident to political conventions, & especially not . . . name, the *time* & place, which was an advertisement to the political jesuits to commence their work."[43]

Although the Republicans held a convention, they took advantage of the old-fashioned machine-controlled aura around the American and

---

northern Know Nothings had joined the Republicans by 1856, but he argues that in many states the Republicans won those accessions without attacking Catholics. Foner, *Free Soil, Free Labor, Free Men*, 226–50.

42. Salmon P. Chase to E. S. Hamlin, January 12, 1855, in Chase Papers; John Law to William L. Marcy, September 3, 1854, in Marcy Papers; Charles L. English to Gideon Welles, January 31, 1856, in Welles Papers, Library of Congress. San Francisco's People's party supported the Republicans. Brown, "Pivot of American Vigilantism," in *Reflections of Western Historians*, ed. Carroll, 105–109. Formisano stresses the importance of antiparty sentiment in the early Republican party in Michigan. Formisano, *Birth of Mass Political Parties*, 264–65, 326–27.

43. Jacob Heaton to Salmon P. Chase, February 25, 1856, in Chase Papers. A Know Nothing wrote Nathaniel Banks that it was important that the Republican nomination come from the people and not just a convention. David K. Hitchcock to Banks, March 28, 1856, in Banks Papers.

Democratic parties. Fillmore's nomination by the Know Nothings, seemingly at the dictation of southerners, fell flat among northern lodge members who demanded, as one informed Nathaniel P. Banks, a candidate "fresh from the loins of the people—a mechanic—able and jealous of the religious hierarchy of Rome."[44] Aware of this sentiment, the Republicans nominated Frémont, a man considerably younger than Fillmore or James Buchanan, the Democratic candidate, and Republican editorialists shrewdly presented the "Pathfinder" as "a new man, fresh from the people and one of themselves . . . [who] has been singled out by the people themselves to retrieve the government from maladministration."[45] As they would in 1860, the Republicans also organized Wide Awake clubs, marching societies whose members paraded the streets in uniform with lanterns burning. These vestiges of the superpatriotic Know Nothing lodges attracted the young and the poor, workingmen and mechanics, precisely the kind of men who had flocked to those lodges in 1854 and 1855.[46] Through their candidate, appeals, and imitative campaign paraphernalia, the Republicans could lure those Know Nothings who resented southern aggressions, found nothing fresh in Fillmore, and yearned for a genuine people's party.

If the significance of the impatience with old parties seems clear, one must still ask why it emerged at this time. Party loyalty had been fervent in the 1840s. What in the early 1850s prompted such widespread feeling among the rank and file that parties no longer served the needs of the people, that the people had lost control of political decision making to secretive manipulators? Know Nothing rhetoric suggests that this feeling

44. Thomas J. Marsh to Nathaniel P. Banks, March 19, 1856, George White to Banks, June 10, 1856, in Banks Papers.

45. In 1856, Millard Fillmore was fifty-six, James Buchanan sixty-five, and Frémont forty-three. Draft editorial, n.d., in Welles Papers, Connecticut Historical Society.

46. Early Know Nothing clubs were called Wide Awakes. Billington, *Protestant Crusade*, 420. For the kind of men who joined the 1860 Wide Awake clubs, see James W. Husted to Edwin D. Morgan, August 1, 1860, Lewis Benedict, Jr., to Morgan, September 11, 1860, James Irving Smith to Morgan, October 8, 1860, all in Morgan Papers. For the early Know Nothing lodges, see H. W. Allen to S. Sammons, October 30, 1854, in Ullmann Papers; John S. Williams to Gideon Welles, November 25, 1854, in Welles Papers, Library of Congress; David Fullwood to Simon Cameron, December 12, 1854, in Simon Cameron Papers, Dauphin County Historical Society, Harrisburg.

was indicative of a much broader uneasiness about the powerlessness of the people to control the meteoric social and economic changes transforming their environment and threatening their most cherished values. Dislocation created the impatience with established parties, the demand that officeholders answer the needs of the people. At the same time, as the phrase "political jesuits" indicates, it intensified a felt need of many people by exacerbating anti-Catholic and nativist prejudices. Because Catholic immigrants could be blamed for perceived evils that were caused by the whole panoply of economic, social, and intellectual forces disordering the lives of many Americans, those Americans began to demand new parties that they would control and that would take action to alleviate their anxieties.

The social forces transforming society in this period are familiar. Immigrants from Ireland and Germany inundated various communities after 1846. The tide of aliens seemed to swell the number of slums, violations of the Sabbath, drunkards, paupers, brawls, and crimes. The cheap competition supposedly offered by immigrant workers could be blamed for forcing wages down. Politically, the immigrants seemed to pervert the democratic process by voting in blocs that were easily manipulated by ward bosses and party wire pullers who appealed to ethnic and religious identity.[47] From these machines sprang the corruption of local government that so appalled the middle class.

The sharp increase in the political participation of foreigners after 1851 was probably the major proximate cause of the formation of the Know Nothing order.[48] Because many states limited suffrage to citizens and because naturalization required five years, immigrants who arrived in the late 1840s were only beginning to vote in the early 1850s. Naturalization laws were frequently broken, however, and they alone cannot account for the increase in immigrant voting. Equally important was the temperance campaign of those years. The passage of the Maine Law in 1851 spurred efforts in many other states to pass similar legislation; those

47. Billington, *Protestant Crusade,* 322–38; George W. Morton to Hamilton Fish, February 27, 1854, in Fish Papers; T. Sherman Bassett to Nathaniel P. Banks, December 9, 1855, in Banks Papers.

48. Billington, *Protestant Crusade,* 325–26; Handlin, *Boston's Immigrants,* 191–92; Pittsburgh *Daily Dispatch,* September 5, 1855.

efforts provided a political issue that seemed relevant to most foreigners, and it drew them into the political arena for the first time—almost always against the liquor law.[49] This increased political participation in seemingly unthinking blocs, the prominence of foreigners and Catholics among Democratic officeholders, and the obsequious efforts of both Whigs and Democrats to capture the foreign vote certainly helped create the disenchantment with old parties and the desire for new ones.

It was the Catholicism of many of the newcomers that seemed most threatening to apprehensive native Protestants. Just when Catholic political influence was increasing, the church's hierarchy provided concrete evidence of the long-warned-of papal plot to control the United States. The Catholic clergy in 1852 began to move for ecclesiastical ownership of church property, and in 1853 the pope sent a special nuncio, Gaetano Bedini, to the United States to arbitrate some disputed claims. Propagandists quickly called Bedini the vanguard of the papal invasion. Most disastrous, in 1852, 1853, and 1854 in states like Ohio, New York, Pennsylvania, and Maryland, the Catholic clergy and Democratic legislators who represented them began to agitate for laws that would stop Bible reading in public schools and divide school funds so that the taxes Catholics paid could be used to support parochial schools rather than the common school system. This apparent papal assault on public schools especially angered the middle and working classes, Protestant immigrants among them, who viewed education as a key to social mobility.[50] By attacking schools and competing for jobs, Catholics seemed to represent just as much of a threat as slavery expansion to the northern vision of the good society, a society that allowed and encouraged upward mobility out of the wage-earner status.[51] To northeastern workers, indeed, they probably seemed a greater threat.[52]

---

49. Silbey, *Transformation of American Politics*, 12–15, 28–32; Holt, *Forging a Majority*, 114–20; Handlin, *Boston's Immigrants*, 195–98.

50. Billington, *Protestant Crusade*, 289–314; Holt, *Forging a Majority*, 132–40; Bowers, "Ideology and Political Parties in Maryland," 197–217. See also Vincent P. Lannie, "Alienation in America: The Immigrant Catholic and Public Education in Pre–Civil War America," *Review of Politics*, XXXII (1970), 503–21.

51. Foner, *Free Soil, Free Labor, Free Men*, 11–39, 40–102.

52. A New Yorker complaining about immigrants wrote to Hamilton Fish: "It is true that much of the evil exists in Cities, but are cities no part of the U.S.? and are American *mechanics* to be

By the mid-1850s, then, what Catholic immigrants represented menaced the dearest values of Americans: social order, political democracy, public education, and social mobility. Many of the splinter parties were formed to meet these threats when the old parties would not address them with sufficient force. In the Know Nothing order, troubled native Protestants hoped to find a weapon to redress these wrongs.

These specific grievances against Catholics after 1852 explain much about the intensity of anti-Catholicism and the impatience with old parties. In many communities, moreover, the menace posed by Irish and German Catholics could be identified precisely at a time when many residents were dislocated and bewildered by the rapidity of economic change. In these cases, it was the coincidence of disruptive economic developments with the increased political activity of despised groups that produced the strength of anti-Catholicism and the emergence of the Know Nothings.

The relationship between economic change and political behavior is the least explored aspect of the politics of the 1850s, but the evidence that exists about economic trends in that period is very suggestive.

There is evidence that the unpredictability of the economy, the fluctuation of prices, and the dependence on uncertain weather conditions increased the instability of the lives of many who simultaneously faced the social disruption caused by pell-mell population growth, urbanization, and immigration. Although it was a period of inflation because of the California gold strikes, indices of business activity show sharp slumps in the latter half of 1851 and 1854 and in early 1855.[53] At those times,

---

borne down, crushed, or driven to western wilds?" In short, northeastern workingmen did not want to go west and were more concerned about what might force them to go there than what they might meet there in competition from slaves. George W. Morton to Fish, February 27, 1854, in Fish Papers.

53. See the graph and tables in *American Business Activity Since 1790*, published by the Cleveland Trust Company in 1966. These are based on an index of ten series that were weighted according to their importance in the overall economy. The ten series are commodity prices, imports, imports retained for consumption, government receipts, ship construction, government expenditures, coal production, exports, iron exports, and tons of registered shipping in service. For tables on wholesale prices for farm products, hides and leather goods, textiles, fuel, and metal products, see George F. Warren and Frank A. Pearson, *Wholesale Prices for 213 Years, 1720–1932* (Ithaca, 1932), 85–98. See also Albert Fishlow, *American Railroads and the Transformation of the Ante-bellum Economy* (Cambridge, Mass., 1965), 54, 112–13.

rising unemployment coexisted with rising prices. A drought produced low water on the Ohio River in 1854, dramatically curtailing trade on that stream.[54] Workers connected with the river trade in Pittsburgh, Cincinnati, Louisville, and St. Louis, where the Know Nothings were strong, may have faced unemployment or lower wages.

Compounding these fluctuations and much more important in creating dislocation was the massive railroad construction between 1849 and 1854. It is not mere chance that the breakup of the second American party system occurred just when the trunk-line railroads connecting the Atlantic Coast with the Midwest were finished. Railroad construction and the completion of the Erie, Baltimore and Ohio, Pennsylvania, and New York Central between 1851 and 1854 produced disruptive changes in patterns of commerce, methods of manufacturing, and, as a New York State official put it, "the social conditions of our people."[55] Relatively isolated and homogeneous communities were now brought into contact with men of different backgrounds as railroads and the telegraph increased communication among towns and as armies of immigrant railroad workers arrived with the tracks in area after area.[56] Although prices rose in general, railroads caused food prices to soar in eastern and especially midwestern cities. As an astute Detroit school teacher noted, "The rise of provisions in consequence of the opening of the Erie railroad, has made living here very much higher the last year, & will probably compel all of us teachers to advance our prices."[57] Because farmers now had easy access to New York and the foreign market by railroad, they could and did raise prices elsewhere.[58]

54. Fishlow, *American Railroads*, 293.

55. Quoted *ibid.*, 11–12. See also Alfred D. Chandler, Jr., *The Railroads: The Nation's First Big Business* (New York, 1965), and Chandler, "The Organization of Manufacturing and Transportation," in *Economic Change in the Civil War Era,* ed. David T. Gilchrist and W. David Lewis (Greenville, Del., 1965), 137–65.

56. Contemporaries were well aware that railroads hired immigrants as construction crews, and they complained about this floating Democratic vote. John Keatkey to Simon Cameron, December 12, 1854, in Cameron Papers; Vesparian Ellis to Daniel Ullmann, May 29, 1855, in Ullmann Papers; J. M. Killinger to Lemuel Todd, July 20, 1857, in McPherson Papers.

57. Mary H. Clark to Mark Howard, June 20, 1852, in Mark Howard Papers, Connecticut Historical Society.

58. Fishlow, *American Railroads*, 43–44; Chandler, *Railroads*, 25–30.

Just when workers faced inflation and increasing competition, many probably lost their jobs as railroads began to take trade away from water routes and to shift commercial courses.[59] Some towns along rivers and canals were bypassed entirely, and communities that suffered from a lack of railroad transportation may have turned to nativism.[60] But railroads disrupted the communities they came to as well. Through railroad lines destroyed the jobs of men in former transfer centers. In numerous towns where rivers connected with canals or railroads or where railroads of different gauges had separate terminals, thousands of dockworkers, draymen, warehousemen, and common laborers had been employed in transferring through freight from one mode of transportation to the next. Once continuous lines were completed through those places, freight no longer had to be unloaded, and jobs disappeared. Merchants and shippers everywhere now became dependent on unpredictable railroad rates, and even in the 1850s discriminatory rates put men in some communities at a serious disadvantage. Midwestern merchants faced increased competition from the East and from the railroads themselves. In Cincinnati and Pittsburgh, for example, forwarding and commission merchants lost business to the railroads who gave that service free of charge, and the teamsters and rivermen employed by those merchants may have been displaced.[61] It seems clear that the dislocation of the river traffic produced by the sum of these causes contributed to Know Nothingism in both Pittsburgh and Cincinnati. In Pittsburgh, Know Nothings came from the poorest Protestants, some of them from the transient population who worked on the docks or were involved in the decreasing transfer functions of the city.[62]

59. For the shift in trade, see Fishlow, *American Railroads*, 18–33, 279–97; Harry N. Scheiber, *The Ohio Canal Era: A Case Study of Government and the Economy, 1820–1861* (Athens, Ohio, 1969), 272, 319–43. Contemporaries worried about the gains of railroads at the canals' expense. A. C. Flagg to George W. Newell, May 26, 1852, J. Center to H. H. Van Dyck, July 9, 1852, clipping of the Albany *Evening Atlas*, October 29, 1855, all in William L. Marcy Papers, New York State Library.

60. Complaints that towns faced economic disaster because of the lack of railroad transportation were numerous. B. F. Cooper to Myron H. Clark, April 2, 1853, in Myron H. Clark Papers, New York State Library.

61. Scheiber, *Ohio Canal Era*, 337–38; Holt, *Forging a Majority*, 228–34.

62. Holt, *Forging a Majority*, 149, 169–70, 83n.

Cincinnati's major Know Nothing strongholds were Wards 3 and 17, along the Ohio River, and 1, 2, 8, 14, and 16, close to the river.[63]

The trunk-line railroads also changed methods of manufacturing in the Midwest as they brought increased competition from the East. One result was that those manufacturers who could centralized their operations in the cities into fairly large-scale enterprises. For example, in Pittsburgh at that time the iron industry began to integrate vertically and concentrate. Before the 1850s, iron making had been decentralized in the Midwest. Pig iron was smelted from ore in thousands of small furnaces in western and central Pennsylvania, Ohio, New York, Kentucky, Tennessee, and Missouri. Located at ore deposits and close to timber, those furnaces used charcoal as fuel. The pig iron was then shipped to centers such as Pittsburgh where it was rolled and molded into retail products such as nails and stoves or iron bars that were shipped to blacksmiths in hundreds of communities. In the 1850s, however, because railroads brought eastern and imported iron products across the Alleghenies more cheaply than before, iron makers in Pittsburgh began to combine the two-phase process, bring in iron ore, and smelt their own pig iron with coke as fuel.[64] Similarly, railroads transformed the entire structure of Cincinnati's econ-

63. Cincinnati *Enquirer*, April 6, October 11, 1855. Walter Glazer notes that by 1840 Ward 3 had a large concentration of rivermen and Irish, as well as many foundries, boiler yards, and stables. In the 1840s and 1850s, moreover, "the poorer and more disreputable elements began to take over the riverfront wards," as well as the western part of the city where Wards 8, 14, 15, and 16 were filled with run-down, cheap houses. Walter Glazer, "Cincinnati in 1840: A Community Profile" (Ph.D. dissertation, University of Michigan, 1968), 137–38, 223–27. The other riverfront wards, 4 and 6, generated large Know Nothing votes, but even larger Democratic totals, probably because of the heavy concentrations of Irish in them. *Ibid.*, 138–40.

64. Holt, *Forging a Majority*, 19–20, 230. Louis C. Hunter argues that concentration occurred because of the shift in the market provided by railroads. Pittsburgh iron makers began to produce structural iron for rails rather than malleable wrought iron bar for western blacksmiths. Louis C. Hunter, "Influence of the Market upon Technique in the Iron Industry in Western Pennsylvania up to 1860," *Journal of Economic and Business History*, I (1929), 240–81. Contemporary editors, however, noted that increased competition from eastern iron manufacturers and discriminatory railroad rates on pig iron also forced concentration. Pittsburgh *Daily Gazette*, April 21, December 3, 1859; Pittsburgh *Morning Post*, April 29, 1859. For the sudden and disastrous impact of the completion of the Pennsylvania Railroad on the iron industry west of the Allegheny Mountains, see Peter Temin, *Iron and Steel in Nineteenth Century America: An Economic Inquiry* (Cambridge, Mass., 1964), 76–95. Eastern pig iron made with anthracite coal as fuel drove out of business western furnaces that used charcoal and forced sharp changes in production techniques.

omy. Shipments on canals and the Ohio River declined, meat-packing became less important as livestock was shipped directly east, and the milling of flour increased. At the same time, the factory production of clothing that employed German and Jewish tailors grew.[65]

If some manufacturers in cities could enlarge and mechanize their production, that option was denied to others in those cities and to small manufacturers and artisans in small towns and rural communities. The very concentration of factory production in urban centers only increased the plight of such men—whether they be tailors, spinners involved in the home manufacture of cloth, or iron furnace operators who lacked the financial resources to achieve economies of scale. The products of midwestern cities only added to the deluge of cheaper goods from the East that eliminated the competitive advantages of small-town businessmen in their own local communities. If the lower transportation costs provided by railroads helped consumers, temporarily at least, the rates could prove ruinous to local producers whose communities were brought into the economic nexus of larger cities by those roads. In both small towns and cities, artisans and the employees of smaller firms that were shut down or had to lower wages because of increased competition could easily blame cheap immigrant labor for their plight, especially if the new factories, like those in Cincinnati, employed skilled immigrants.[66]

The point is not that railroads harmed all communities absolutely; most eventually grew and benefited from them. But during the 1850s, railroads caused wrenching structural changes in the economies of many communities that necessarily involved the displacement of men employed in the old businesses—whether they be river and canal men or artisans not employed in the new factories. By linking communities and increasing the ease of communication among them, moreover, railroads and the telegraph often tended to increase the economic domination of larger communities over smaller ones and thus to undermine the economic and social security of men who lived in the latter.

The impact of railroads on the East, especially New England, is less

65. Scheiber, *Ohio Canal Era*, 319–25, 337–39.

66. George Morton blamed immigrants not only for depriving native workingmen of jobs and forcing down wages but also for forcing up the cost of rent and food. "From this state of things a thousand evils arise to the working classes," he lamented. Morton to Hamilton Fish, February 27, 1854, in Fish Papers.

clear. The agricultural regions suffered from western competition, and, as elsewhere, small towns connected to larger cities by railroads increasingly fell under their economic sway.[67] But economic historians disagree about the effect of railroads on eastern manufacturing. Some argue that railroads allowed increased mechanization of factories and the use of interchangeable parts in the 1850s—developments that would cause technological unemployment among skilled workmen or reduce them to dependent wage-earner status.[68] Other maintain that the development of factory production in New England had little to do with the wider market opened by railroads.[69] There is a good deal more to be learned about the structural impact of railroads in New England. It seems clear, however, that machine-powered factory production and the use of interchangeable parts increased in the 1840s and 1850s, that New England textile manufacturing peaked in the 1840s and grew at a slower rate in the 1850s, and that the Know Nothings, as studies of the membership of various Massachusetts lodges show, came disproportionately from manual workers and artisans—shoe-makers, carpenters, wheelwrights—who may have suffered displacement or lower wages just as they faced higher prices.[70] Even where production in an industry was not yet mechanized, workers were threatened with the possibility of that change because many were aware of the rapid growth of factories in other businesses. Outside of New England in cities such as Philadelphia, moreover, the dislocation caused by industrialization and mechanization of factory production drove some workers to nativist politics.[71]

What quantitative and qualitative evidence exists indicates that Know Nothingism was overwhelmingly a movement of the laboring and middle classes.[72] Workers and many from the huge floating popula-

67. Paul W. Gates, *The Farmer's Age: Agriculture, 1815–1860* (New York, 1960), 416–17.

68. Chandler, *Railroads*, 23; Chandler, "The Organization of Manufacturing and Transportation," in *Economic Change*, ed. Gilchrist and Lewis, 137–65.

69. Fishlow, *American Railroads*, 237–61. Fishlow does admit, however, that railroads contributed to the shift from home to factory manufacture of woolens in New York. *Ibid.*, 256.

70. *Ibid.*, 248–60; Seymour Martin Lipset and Earl Raab, *The Politics of Unreason: Right-Wing Extremism in America, 1790–1970* (New York, 1970), 55–57.

71. For an analysis of the dislocating effects of industrialization and the tendency of unskilled workingmen to express their frustration in political nativism, see Sam Bass Warner, Jr., *The Private City: Philadelphia in Three Periods of Growth* (Philadelphia, 1968), 63–78.

72. Lipset and Raab, *Politics of Unreason*, 55–57; see also note 46.

tion—men who appeared one year in a town's directory and were gone the next, probably because they had left in search of a job—voted for the first time. Because these men suffered most from the traumatic economic changes of the decade, they became most susceptible to the cries of Catholic conspiracy raised at that time. Among members of the old parties, it was precisely those people who were most disturbed by the changes in their environment who were most impatient with the parties because they did nothing to meet their needs and because they seemed beyond popular control. As Welles thought, some people may have been more interested in joining a new party, any new party, than in anti-Catholicism, but both sentiments probably motivated the vast majority. Know Nothingism provided a way for them to seek to control the arcane forces changing their lives. They joined the order simultaneously to regain control of political power and to use that power to attack Catholic immigrants on whom much of the unsettling disorder could be blamed.

In one sense, Know Nothingism was a combination of the responses to disruptive change that David Brion Davis and Rowland Berthoff have suggested. Davis argues that accelerated mobility and institutional change induce belief in conspiracy theories of subversive forces.[73] Berthoff has hypothesized that the popularity of fraternal organizations like the Masons and Odd Fellows at the end of the nineteenth century indicates the desire of people for a stable and ordered community they could not find in the chaotic larger society.[74] Know Nothings joined a secret fraternal organization and believed in a Catholic conspiracy, and perhaps the fact that they did so in larger numbers than at other times in our history indicates that the social disruption of the 1850s was unusually severe.

An even better model by which to understand the origins of Know Nothingism, however, is that offered by Samuel Lubell in *The Hidden Crisis in American Politics,* from which is borrowed the phrase "politics of impatience." To explain the turbulent politics of the late 1960s, Lubell argues that the rapidity of social change had created an intense emotional involvement with issues that caused people to revolt against the party

73. David Brion Davis, *The Slave Power Conspiracy and the Paranoid Style* (Baton Rouge, 1969), 28–29.
74. Rowland Berthoff, "The American Social Order: A Conservative Hypothesis," *American Historical Review,* LXV (1960), 495–514. Sam Bass Warner makes this point explicitly about nativist groups in the 1840s and 1850s and the Know Nothings. Warner, *Private City,* 61–62.

system because it did not represent their views or give them an active enough role in political decision making.[75] Remarkably similar anxieties and frustrations engendered the Know Nothing movement. Sudden economic dislocations and rising prices increased the fears of thousands of native-born Protestants who felt threatened simultaneously by what seemed to be Catholic attacks on local school systems and by the job competition and increasing political power of immigrant groups they regarded as dangerously un-American. When both the Democrats and Whigs courted those groups rather than redressing the Protestants' grievances, voters bolted to the Know Nothing order, which promised that it would jettison the unresponsive political power brokers who ran the major parties and then take action against Catholic immigrants. By embodying so well the popular impatience with the two-party system, by demanding power for the people, and by pandering to intense and widespread prejudices, Know Nothingism became an enormously potent force at a decisive period in American political history.

The forces producing Know Nothingism had immense significance for the incipient Republican party. The revolt against the Whigs aborted their efforts to channel northern antisouthern sentiment and allowed the Republicans, instead, to exploit it. Anti-Catholicism turned massive numbers of middle- and working-class voters against the Democrats, and most of these eventually joined the Republicans who, in addition to their defense of free white labor, conspicuously nominated Know Nothings to state and local offices and consciously presented the appearance of newness and true representativeness that the Know Nothings had lost by 1856. Finally, the same sense of dislocation that engendered antiparty sentiment and anti-Catholicism also intensified northern belief in a slave power plot when the Kansas-Nebraska Act, "Bleeding Kansas," and the Lecompton Constitution provided concrete evidence of such a conspiracy. Apparent Democratic complicity in both the slave power plot and the papal plot almost assured Democratic defeat. In 1860, when the Republicans ran a virtual unknown, a true man of the people, a rail-splitter, the Democrats suffered that loss, and it in turn brought on the Civil War.

75. Samuel Lubell, *The Hidden Crisis in American Politics* (New York, 1970), 17–26, 39–68, and *passim*.

The New Political History
and the Civil War Era

In the 1960s and 1970s, historians who focused on the identity, values, and behavior of voters rather than on political elites challenged the prevailing interpretations of nineteenth-century politics. Drawing on the research of political scientists like Walter Dean Burnham, they organized their investigations around a model of successive two-party systems that consisted of long periods when the alignment of voters on opposite sides was stable and that were separated by shorter periods of massive and enduring change in voter affiliation known as critical realignments.[1] In addition, most insisted that ethnic and religious tensions motivated voters more than class conflict or the sectional, racial, and economic issues that were of such concern to national political leaders. For example, some, including this reviewer, argued that the realignment of the 1850s that culminated in the triumph of the Republican party was caused as much by prohibitionism, nativism, and anti-Catholicism as by antislavery sentiment and that the Republicans, after absorbing the great majority of northern Know Nothings, were as much an anti-Catholic as an antislavery party. Others, the foremost of whom is

---

This essay originally appeared as a long review of Stephen E. Maizlish, *The Triumph of Sectionalism: The Transformation of Ohio Politics, 1844–1856* (Kent, Ohio, 1983) and Dale Baum, *The Civil War Party System: The Case of Massachusetts, 1848–1876* (Chapel Hill, 1984). Page references to these books will appear in the text.

1. Walter Dean Burnham, *Critical Elections and the Mainsprings of American Politics* (New York, 1970); see also Paul Kleppner, ed., *The Evolution of American Electoral Systems* (Westport, Conn., 1981).

Paul Kleppner, asserted that during the life of the third or Civil War party system, between 1853 and 1892, the fundamental source of cleavage between Republican and Democratic voters in the North was an irreconcilable conflict between pietistical and liturgical religious values.[2] For these historians, in sum, voters, their values, and their movements, and not governmental policies or leadership decisions, provide the key to explaining American political development.

Both the quantitative methods and the interpretations of this so-called "new political history" were met with skepticism and increasingly with criticism from quantifiers and nonquantifiers alike. These new books by Stephen Maizlish and Dale Baum join that assault.[3] Although they differ slightly in the chronological periods they cover and profoundly in their methods and approach, they are linked by their common attack on the ethnocultural interpretation that came to the fore in the past two decades.

Maizlish's *The Triumph of Sectionalism* reasserts the value of traditional methods as well as the validity of the traditional interpretation that the slavery issue shattered the second party system and shaped the realignment that brought Republicans to power. Although he includes regression estimates of the movement of Ohio's voters between 1848 and 1856, they were not generated by Maizlish himself and are largely peripheral to his analysis. His preference is for traditional political history written from the perspective of the political elite, and he explicitly asserts that public opinion can be inferred from leaders' speeches, editorials, and correspondence. Thus the chief—and immense—value of this thoroughly researched book is its clear and detailed chronological account of the reaction, strategies, and factional divisions of Whig, Democratic, and Free Soil politicians in Ohio between 1844 and 1856.

During those years, Maizlish asserts, the orientation of partisan conflict in Ohio shifted from the economic issues at the core of the second party system to one dominated by the sectional conflict over slavery expan-

2. Paul Kleppner, *The Third Electoral System, 1853–1892: Parties, Voters, and Political Cultures* (Chapel Hill, 1979).

3. I am obliged to state that I read manuscript versions of all of one and part of the other book under review and am thanked by both authors in their acknowledgments. Lest that fact create concern about a conflict of interest, careful readers will note that my own work is one of the chief targets of both authors. My prior acquaintance with the two authors, therefore, has not assured acquiescence in their views.

sion. This transformation was effectively completed by the winter of 1848–1849 when a coalition of Democrats and Free Soilers elected Salmon P. Chase to the United States Senate. Both Whig and Democratic politicians helped place slavery at the center of Ohio politics, the Whigs by emphasizing the antislavery reasons for opposing Texas' annexation in 1844–1845 and the Democrats by consciously stressing territorial expansion and the Mexican War after 1846 in order to avoid internal divisions over the state banking issue. In sharp contrast to James Roger Sharp and William G. Shade, indeed, Maizlish insists that banking and other economic issues lost salience in Ohio after 1846.[4] From that point on, the slavery issue dictated political development in the state. The bolt of almost two-fifths of the Whigs to the Free Soilers in 1848 and the Whigs' failure to prevent a Democratic–Free Soil alliance in the legislative session of 1848–1849 left that party "powerless" and traditional alignments in "chaos." Contrary to other interpretations, in short, the second party system in Ohio was dead as early as 1849. "The old structures of the Jacksonian political order remained, but they were empty shells, lacking ideological content" (146).

Because slavery had displaced economics as the central concern of Ohio's voters and because both major parties divided over their response to the Free Soilers, the years 1849 to 1853 witnessed a structural and ideological vacuum as parties failed to provide clear alternatives on issues. Antislavery sentiment could not be expressed at the polls, Maizlish contends, because "the political environment of the early 1850s simply did not offer a context within which sectional issues could be aired" (167). Instead, in 1852 and 1853, nativism and prohibition temporarily emerged as issues; but, he insists, in contrast to the ethnocultural interpretation, that they entered the political arena only because the slavery issue had previously destroyed the second party system. They did not reflect the dominant concern of voters, which was still slavery.

The overriding force of the slavery issue was reaffirmed between 1854 and 1856 when anti-Nebraska sentiment precipitated the voter realignment and reorganized the party system along lines explicitly oriented

---

4. James Roger Sharp, *The Jacksonians Versus the Banks: Politics in the States After the Panic of 1837* (New York, 1970); William G. Shade, *Banks or No Banks: The Money Issue in Western Politics, 1832–1865* (Detroit, 1972).

toward sectional issues. He admits that the Know Nothings played a role in these developments, but he argues that the order appeared only because homeless Whig conservatives sought a refuge from a sectionally extreme party like the Republicans. That party's nomination of Chase for governor in 1855, its refusal openly to endorse nativist and anti-Catholic principles, and its victories in 1855 and 1856 demonstrated that antislavery sentiment was the primary determinant of Ohio voting behavior as it had been since the mid-1840s.

Maizlish is surely correct that the slavery issue had a particularly disruptive impact in Ohio compared with, say, Pennsylvania or New Jersey, and it is also true that by 1856 Republicans had managed to confine partisan dialogue almost exclusively to sectional issues. In my opinion, however, he greatly exaggerates the centrality of the slavery issue in the period as a whole, misdates the demise of the second party system and thereby grossly distorts the weakness of both the Whig party and economic issues after 1846, and underestimates the real saliency of ethnocultural concerns.

According to Maizlish, the second party system was "crippled indeed" in 1844 (34), could not depend on economic issues "to give it coherence" after 1846 (40), and collapsed in 1848 because of huge defections to the Free Soil party. After that election, the Whigs were "permanently powerless" (73), and the parties and factions that remained were "empty shells, lacking ideological content" (146). One way to dispute these claims is to examine the share of the popular vote retained by the two major parties. Because the tables he had borrowed contain no elections before 1848, Maizlish badly inflates the extent of Whig defections to the Free Soilers. Moreover, Whigs and Democrats combined captured 97.5 percent of the vote in 1844, 89.1 percent in 1848, and 91.2 percent in 1852. Even when one considers nonvoters, they garnered over four-fifths of the potential vote in all those elections. If the two-party system had collapsed as early as Maizlish says it did, Ohio's voters apparently did not know it.

Election returns also throw light on the date of and the reasons for the death of the Whig party. Like some other historians, Maizlish mistakenly attributes the Whigs' inability to retain their electorate to antiparty sentiment that prevented institutional loyalties from forming among Whig voters and politicians. Throughout the 1840s, he argues, "Whigs found it difficult to function in the modern political world" (80) because of this supposed hostility to party organizations. Yet this was a party that displayed great cohesion in the legislature and won two-thirds of the elections held in the decade. Although the Whigs never won an election after 1848, between 1848 and 1852 the margin separating Democrats from Whigs averaged only 6.1 percentage points, and the Whigs remained a viable alternative for anti-Democratic voters. In 1853, however, the Whig coalition disintegrated when it attracted only 30 percent of the vote, and the margin between the major parties jumped to 22. Yet as Maizlish himself admits, prohibition was the central issue that year. In terms of voting support, the slavery issue may have weakened the Whig party, but an ethnocultural issue destroyed it. Maizlish's rebuttal that the structure of the political system between 1849 and 1853 prevented voters from expressing their dominant concern with slavery is surely wrong. The Free Soil party continued to run separate candidates in those years, and voters outraged at the Compromise of 1850 or worried about slavery had a way to channel those emotions. Yet the Free Soil vote plunged even more than the major party vote in 1850 and 1851, rebounded partially in 1852, and soared in 1853 when the Free Soilers were the only party to endorse prohibition. Either antislavery voters retained confidence in the major parties until 1852 or antislavery sentiment was not their major concern.

Another way to dispute Maizlish's contentions is to look at policy making. One of the chief weaknesses of Maizlish's book—and also of Baum's for that matter—is that although both are ostensibly studies of state politics, both ignore the chief arena of state government, the legislature. Politics, after all, is more than the sum of elections, patronage distribution, and factional quarrels. It also involves governance and the making of policy, and on the state level most policy concerned economic matters. Examination of roll-call votes in Ohio's legislature, for example, indicates that economic issues had vitality long after Maizlish says they did, at least insofar as providing a distinctive identity for Democrats and Whigs. Those parties were not devoid of substantive meaning after 1848. Although the Whigs' ability to win elections may have disappeared after that date, the same was not true of their ability to shape the substantive aspects of state politics. The Free Soilers cooperated with Whigs on economic policy and thereby gave them the power to defeat Democratic assaults on their economic programs. For example, the average index of likeness between Whigs and Democrats on 138 roll-call votes in the state house of representatives involving banking and currency between 1849 and 1852 was only 20, indicating sharp conflict between the major parties, whereas the average index of likeness between Whigs and Free Soilers on those same votes was 79. A similar pattern appeared in roll-calls on stockholder liability and charters of business incorporation.[5] Although the Whigs no longer controlled the offices of state government, they continued to control its economic policies through the aid of the Free Soil party, which Maizlish says ruined them.

Finally, proponents of the ethnocultural interpretation would object that Maizlish's contention that nativism could enter the political arena in either its pre–Know Nothing or Know Nothing forms only because the slavery issue had disrupted old party lines seriously minimizes the force of those issues in their own right and the extent to which they became issues because of grassroots pressure. One of the difficulties in assessing the impact of nativism on Ohio's realignment in the 1850s is that there was no separate Know Nothing vote, except for a splinter faction in 1855 that was as much a protest against Chase personally as a reflection of nativism. Still, Maizlish's analysis of voter motivation in these years involves questionable assumptions about the response of voters to party platforms, assumptions that can better be examined in the discussion of Dale Baum's *The Civil War Party System: The Case of Massachusetts, 1848–1876*.

Like Maizlish's study, Baum's book is an exceedingly valuable contribution to our knowledge of nineteenth-century politics. But it is more ambitious and a very different kind of book. Baum is a quantifier, and he directly employs, even while revising, the realignment/party system model of the new political history. Seventy-seven tables are scattered throughout the text of the book, and virtually every chapter concentrates on interpreting a particular set of voting returns. The extraordinarily useful tables reflect an impressive command of sophisticated statistical techniques. His regression estimates of the movement of voters between elections are the first I have seen that distinguish between eligible voters who abstained in one election and new voters who had not been able to vote in the first election. Indeed, his consistent attention to movement in

5. These figures were taken from Kurt P. Shadle, "Consensus and the Decline of the Second Party System in Ohio, 1848–1854" (seminar paper, University of Virginia, 1978).

and out of the active electorate by different occupational and ethnic groups is one of the chief strengths of the book. Moreover, he runs multiple regression analyses to measure the relative weight of economic versus ethnic and religious variables in determining the parties' respective voting support.

Baum's assault on the prevailing interpretation offered by new political historians proceeds along three interrelated paths. First, he demonstrates that Massachusetts voting patterns did not conform to the chronology Paul Kleppner has ascribed to the Civil War party system in *The Third Electoral System, 1853–1892* (1979). There was no critical election sequence between 1854 and 1860 or a prolonged realigning phase from 1854 to 1874 that was followed by a stable phase from 1874 to 1892 that in turn was reshaped by a realignment in the 1890s. Realignment began in the Bay State in 1848 and lasted until 1863 when voting lines stabilized until the end of the decade. Then the 1870s saw more realigning activity than did the 1890s; in Massachusetts, indeed, there was no realignment ending the third party system in 1894 or 1896. Contrary to Kleppner, Baum also argues that the voting alignments established by 1876 were completely new because the Democrats gained enough accessions from the Republicans and mobilized enough new voters to change their coalition dramatically from what it had been in the 1850s and 1860s. The prevailing model for the third party system, in sum, misdates its beginning, its internal transformations, and its demise, at least for Massachusetts.

Second, Baum explicitly rejects the centrality of ethnocultural factors throughout the entire period covered in his study. Repeating the arguments of his influential article in the *Journal of American History*, he contends that Know Nothingism and therefore anti-Catholicism played an insignificant role in the Massachusetts Republican party in the 1850s.[6] A large share of the original Know Nothing coalition in 1854 were not nativists; most authentic nativists did not vote Republican until 1860, and the party could have won then even without their support; Republican leaders emphatically repudiated nativism; therefore antislavery sentiment primarily accounts for the rise and triumph of the Republican party.

6. Dale Baum, "Know Nothingism and the Republican Majority in Massachusetts: The Political Realignment of the 1850s," *Journal of American History*, LXIV (1978), 959–86.

Furthermore, a cleavage between evangelical or pietistic and liturgical religious orientations did not shape Republican and Democratic voting support in the 1860s and 1870s. Although foreign-born voters and liturgical religious denominations did disproportionately support the Democrats, the Republicans did not represent evangelical Protestantism or anti-Catholicism. His multiple regression analysis indicates that economic, not ethnoreligious, factors best identify who voted Republican and who did not vote at all. "The conclusion is inescapable that voter turnout and political conflict in Massachusetts during the Civil War years were largely determined by the economic milieu in which men lived and worked, and by an antislavery commitment that transcended religious considerations as the primary basis for partisan identification" (100). Even though ethnic variables had greater weight in explaining the Republican vote in the new alignment established in 1876, moreover, the religious divisions so cherished by Kleppner did not. Nor should one exaggerate the importance of ethnic variables, because economic factors remained more important and naturalized voters constituted only 20 percent of the eligible electorate. Contrary to Kleppner, in sum, growth of the immigrant population did not account for the Democratic comeback of the 1870s.

Third, and of most importance, Baum offers an alternative interpretive framework with which to conceptualize the Civil War era that does not rest on the voter alignments that are so central to the party system paradigm of the new political history. Ironically, given his own heavy emphasis on voting analysis, this framework is based on elite strategies, the issues they chose to contest, and the ideological content those issues had. In short, it is quite similar to the approach Maizlish adopts in his study of Ohio. Briefly put, Baum argues that Massachusetts politics between 1848 and 1876 underwent a dual transformation away from nonideological politics in the 1840s to a period in the 1850s and 1860s when the parties were ideologically polarized over sectional and racial issues and back again to a nonideological or pragmatic politics in the 1870s as sectional and racial issues lost their salience. Precisely because party lines were most sharply drawn in the 1860s over issues involving the conduct of the Civil War, black rights, and Reconstruction policy, voting alignments were more stable in that decade than in either the 1850s or the 1870s. Only when Democrats and Republicans ceased to offer clear alternatives on race and reconstruction in the 1870s did the voter shuffling occur that reshaped the system by 1876. In sum, Baum argues compellingly and correctly that the major parties' ability to retain their voter support and prevent defections was a function of the sharpness or clarity of the issue conflict between them.

These transformations, Baum contends, can best be understood by tracing the ascendancy of the Bird Club, or radical faction, of the Republican party in the 1860s and its fall from power in the 1870s. During the war, these extreme antislavery men advocated immediate emancipation and harsh policies against the Confederacy; in the early years of Reconstruction, they committed the state Republican party to unabashedly radical policies like black suffrage and confiscation. The extremism of Republican leadership in turn drove racist Democrats who feared revolutionary social and constitutional changes to the other end of the ideological spectrum. With the parties polarized over war and reconstruction policies, the Republicans consolidated their hold on the majority of Massachusetts voters, with the brief exception of 1867. Democrats made a minor comeback that year, moreover, not because voters repudiated radicalism on racial matters but because the Democrats temporarily exploited the prohibition issue.

Only after the presidential election of 1868 did Republicans lose their overwhelming command of the electorate, and in the most impressive section of the book Baum details the radicals' fall from power that accompanied the shift from ideological to pragmatic politics between 1869 and 1876. Interested only in the South and black rights, the radical leadership refused to take clear stands on new issues emerging at the state level, such as prohibition, labor rights, and corruption. At the same time, the Democrats' adoption of the New Departure obfuscated party differences on Reconstruction. As a result Republicans became vulnerable to incursions into their voting base by Labor Reform and Prohibition parties. Simultaneously, the Republican leadership fragmented as the Bird Club broke with Grant and his Massachusetts lieutenant Ben Butler, and in 1872 Francis Bird himself led a tenth of the Republican electorate into the Liberal Republican column, most of whom never returned to Republican ranks. By 1876, they were joined in the Democratic party by still more former Republicans and new voters who protested against the Republicans as a corrupt, missionless, and spoils-oriented machine that offered them no clear party alternatives to the Democratic stands for solving the depression or meeting any other pressing issue of the day.

One can quibble with certain aspects of this portrait. Baum never explains why sectional and race issues are more ideological than economic or ethnocultural issues. It is unclear to me at least that politics in the 1860s was uniquely ideological compared, say, with the sharp polarization between Whigs and Democrats over economic policy from 1837 to the early 1850s. Baum also minimizes the extent to which Republicans and Democrats did offer sharp partisan alternatives to the voters in 1876 by ignoring the clear national party differences over the Specie Resumption Act, the tariff, and the anti-Catholic Blaine Amendment. The issue agenda of party combat did change from the 1860s to the 1870s, but that transformation was not necessarily one from an ideological to a pragmatic politics. Attention to the partisan dimensions of state economic policy making in the 1860s and 1870s may have helped Baum explain the voting patterns he has identified. Nonetheless, these are relatively minor suggestions for improving an otherwise compelling interpretative framework. Baum's book ranks with James Mohr's study of New York as the finest analysis of northern state politics in the 1860s and 1870s I have read, and it should be a model for the monographs on other northern states in those years that we so badly need.[7]

On the other hand, I find Baum's contention that Know Nothingism and anti-Catholicism played an insignificant role in the rise of the Republican party in the 1850s unpersuasive. First, he never explains why, if antislavery sentiment was the dominant motivation of Republican voters, the Bird Club could not gain control of the state party until 1860. Against its wishes, most Republicans voted for the Know Nothing gubernatorial candidate in 1856, while Nathaniel P. Banks, a former Know Nothing who openly courted nativist voters, led the party from 1857 until 1860. Baum, for example, makes much of the failure of Republicans to vote in 1859 for a constitutional amendment denying foreign-born citizens the vote until two years after their naturalization. Yet he never admits that Republican-dominated legislatures continually passed this amendment

7. James C. Mohr, *The Radical Republicans and Reform in New York During Reconstruction* (Ithaca, 1973).

and that Republican governor Banks endorsed it. If the influence of Know Nothings in the party was so small, how could this be? Clearly, the Republican party consisted of more than its extreme antislavery, anti–Know Nothing wing.

Second, the turning point in the rivalry between Republicans and Know Nothings to replace the Whigs as the major anti-Democratic party was the presidential election of 1856, not 1860. After that election, most voters who wanted to defeat Democrats for whatever reason knew that the Republicans, not the Know Nothings, had the best chance to do it. Yet Baum never supplies tables indicating what proportion of the 1856 Republican vote was supplied by 1854 and 1855 Know Nothings, information that is far more crucial in terms of the success of the party than their share of Lincoln's vote. Other studies indicate that the vast majority of Massachusetts Know Nothings voted Republican in 1856, but alas, they do not calculate the Know Nothing share of the Republican vote.[8]

Third, both Baum and Maizlish make a questionable assumption about the reasons men voted as they did. Baum argues explicitly, and Maizlish implicitly, that nativism did not motivate voters unless they supported Know Nothing candidates. Because Republicans stressed the slavery issue, Republican voters must have been motivated by antislavery or at least antisouthern sentiment, not nativism. Republican voters were hostile to the South and slavery expansion, but that fact does not mean those sentiments were the only, or even the chief, reasons they supported the party. The ethnocultural analysis rests largely on the theory of negative reference group behavior, which is ignored by both authors. By this

8. Regression estimates showing very heavy Know Nothing support for the Republican presidential candidate in 1856 have been calculated by William E. Gienapp, "Nativism and the Creation of a Republican Majority in the North Before the Civil War" (unpublished paper in my possession) and his "Origins of the Republican Party, 1852–1856" (Ph.D. dissertation, University of California at Berkeley, 1980). Gienapp's dissertation is also the source of the regression estimates included in Maizlish's study of Ohio, and it will soon be published in revised form by the Oxford University Press.

Note: In the published versions of Gienapp's book and article, which appeared after this review was written, he *does* calculate the percentage of Frémont's voters in 1856 who had previously voted Know Nothing. Contrary to the thrust of Baum's argument, over one-half of the 1856 Republican voters had supported the Know Nothings in 1854, and over a third had voted Know Nothing in 1855. It is true, however, that Republicans could have carried Massachusetts in 1856 even without these former Know Nothing voters because the Democratic party was so weak there.

theory, men vote for one party as much because they dislike the membership of the other party as because they are responding positively to the platform of their own party. In the 1850s, the Democrats were undeniably the party of the Catholics. Hence, once the Republicans became the major anti-Democratic party, it is likely that anti-Catholics, especially those who refused to join the Know Nothing order, voted for them as much to defeat the pro-Catholic party as to defeat the Slave Power.

In my judgment, then, these two fine studies have not totally demolished the validity of the ethnocultural interpretation of the realignment of the 1850s. But they have raised penetrating questions about the entire focus of the new political history by forcefully reminding us that voters' values do not explain political change over time. Leadership decisions do. I have profited greatly from reading both books, and they fully deserve the close attention of students of the period.

Two Roads to Sumter

Exactly why seven Deep South states seceded in response to the election of Abraham Lincoln while the eight other slave states refused to do so is still unclear. Fears for slavery are normally cited, but historians disagree about how it was menaced and who was most alarmed. The determination of a small, all-powerful planter class to extend slavery to perpetuate its hegemony, fears of economic loss by the more numerous slaveholding element, and the racial anxieties of both slaveholders and nonslaveholders that Republican rule meant abolition, insurrection, and race war have all been suggested to explain secession. Planters and poor whites could, of course, have supported secession with equal fervor for different reasons. Still, all of these theories suffer from two main problems. First, they would seem to apply equally well to the states that refused to secede merely because Lincoln won as to those that did so enthusiastically. Second, by relying on the motives of entire groups, they cannot account for the divisions within Deep South states during the presidential election of 1860 and subsequent contests over secession. We have, in fact, little precise knowledge about who had the political power to effect secession, who supported it, and who balked at it, but clearly, planters, slaveholders, and whites did not act as cohesive groups. We need, in short, to develop a more sophisticated interpretation

This essay originally appeared as a long review of William L. Barney, *The Secessionist Impulse: Alabama and Mississippi in 1860* (Princeton, 1974) and William J. Evitts, *A Matter of Allegiances: Maryland from 1850 to 1861* (Baltimore, 1974). Page references to these books will appear in the text.

of the forces behind secession that explains both the different behavior of groups within the Deep South states and the sharply contrasting reactions to immediate secession in the Upper and Lower South. By focusing respectively on Maryland and on Alabama and Mississippi, the excellent studies under review here provide some possibilities for, as well as illuminate some of the pitfalls in, the generation of such an interpretation.

William Barney's *The Secessionist Impulse* directly addresses the problems of why Alabama and Mississippi were divided in 1860 and why they seceded. Secession, he argues, had its immediate impetus in the presidential election, which was, in effect, a referendum on the future of the South. Alabamians and Mississippians were presented with clear ideological and political alternatives in the election. With few exceptions, the supporters of John C. Breckinridge led the drive for immediate secession, while the conservative followers of John Bell and Stephen A. Douglas tried to delay it. The Breckinridge men insisted that slavery was doomed unless it could expand. Hence they demanded a federal slave code in existing territories, the acquisition of additional territory for slavery, and, should Lincoln win, secession to keep the hope of expansion alive. In sharp contrast, conservatives denied the need for a slave code, more slave territory, or secession. The Union contained no territory suited to slavery, and the South no slave surpluses to send there. Expansion was a bogus issue agitated by disunionists.

The conservative appeal seemed pallid next to the Breckinridge ideology, Barney argues, for southerners in 1860 were convinced, with good reason, that they faced a crisis. Food shortages produced by a drought that summer, widespread rumors of slave revolts, and constant secessionist agitation by Minute Men clubs, vigilance committees, and volunteer militia companies fed that sense of alarm. But the major reasons were economic. Following closely the arguments of Eugene Genovese in *The Political Economy of Slavery*, Fabian Linden, and others, Barney insists that, despite the cotton boom of the 1850s, the South had severe economic woes.[1] Soil erosion and exhaustion diminished the availability of cotton land; scarcity and heavy demand forced the price of the remaining land

---

1. Eugene Genovese, *The Political Economy of Slavery* (New York, 1965); Fabian Linden, "Economic Democracy in the Slave South: An Appraisal of Some Recent Views," *Journal of Negro History*, XXXI (1946), 140–89.

and also of slaves beyond the reach of most; profit margins of small slave-holders fell as costs rose; and in the newer cotton regions yeomen farmers were squeezed off the land when planters expanded their holdings. As opportunities shrank for the landless, the slaveless, and the aspirants to planter status who could not afford more land or slaves, they turned to expansion to satisfy their ambitions. Convinced that slavery would wither and die without expansion, nonslaveholding whites whose sense of worth depended on continued debasement of blacks through slavery and whose sense of security depended on their continued dispersal to new areas also demanded it. The Republican program of confining slavery thus menaced "the profits of the plantation, the hubris of the planter, and the racial phobias of all Southern whites" (23).

The Breckinridge-secessionist ideology, then, reflected the deepest hopes and fears of the vast majority of voters. Because the Breckinridge forces also controlled the regular Democratic machinery in heavily Democratic states, Breckinridge won easily. Utilizing their control of that machinery, the governorships, newspapers, and apolitical pressure groups, and exploiting even more racist fears that Republican rule meant black equality, the secessionists then swept their states out of the Union. The conservatives, frequently intimidated into silence, agreeing that slavery required protection and admitting the right if not the expediency of immediate secession, could offer little resistance.

Given Barney's formulation, the wonder is not that Breckinridge and the secessionists triumphed but that they faced any opposition at all. In the most original and ambitious portions of the book, Barney attempts to explain those divisions. Through quantitative analyses of the leadership and voting support of the two sides, he provides some provocative answers. The battles of 1860 pitted the young, upwardly mobile, and ambitious against older men who had already made it to the top of southern society or who had given up hope of ever getting there. Breckinridge leaders were generally younger, wealthier, and more involved in slaveholding and cotton-planting than their Bell-Douglas counterparts. Slaveholding lawyers were more prominent among Breckinridge leaders, nonslaveholding merchants among Bell-Douglas activists. The sole exception was the Mississippi Delta, an old Whig stronghold. Old wealth there supported Bell; young wealth, Breckinridge. Outside of the Whig Delta and Alabama's hill country, whose nonslaveholding whites supported

Breckinridge because of fervent party loyalty, Breckinridge's support came from the "cotton frontier" where slaveholding and cotton production grew at the fastest rates. Bell voters, in contrast, came from the older cotton areas that had passed their peak, from nonslaveholding subsistence farmers, and from town artisans and businessmen "on the periphery of Southern expectations" (97). These economic divisions became even clearer in the secession convention elections, for the Alabama hill whites, always firm unionists, now switched to the cooperationist camp while the Alabama black belt went solidly secessionist.

Although all southerners feared abolition, then, different groups perceived the Republican threat with different intensity. "The young slaveholding planters, farmers, and lawyers of the Breckinridge Democrats, the most ambitious and dynamic elements in the South's political economy" (313), believed that Republican free-soilism "imperiled [their] newly won and not yet solidified status" and denied them the "opportunity to start anew in virgin land" (93). "With their hopes for advancement not yet abandoned, still in the process of accumulating rather than protecting property, these younger social elements were prepared to believe the worst of those pledged to destroy the basis of their future wealth and position" (187). In contrast, "the older Whig planters and farmers either already enjoyed an acceptable preeminent prestige or were more rooted in their social station" (187). "With the drive and ambition of youth behind them, they had little use for an ideology that stressed growth and a widening of opportunities for slaveholders" (95).

Barney's explanations are usually plausible and often ingenious. But are they persuasive? His portrait of real economic crisis may be badly overdrawn if Robert Fogel and Stanley Engerman's *Time on the Cross* is correct about the prosperity of the plantation system and the resulting optimism of planters in the 1850s.[2] Even if Barney is right about the economy, one might expect the contending groups he identifies to react to slavery expansion in ways precisely the opposite of those he depicts. Why should the youngest, most prosperous planters from the booming cotton areas demand expansion while planters from declining areas whose land was indeed exhausted oppose it (138–39)? The argument that the concern

2. Robert Fogel and Stanley Engerman, *Time on the Cross: The Economics of American Negro Slavery* (2 vols.; Boston, 1974).

was for future growth seems refuted by his own evidence in the suggestive tables on pages 136–37. Those data show that, with the exception of the Delta, Breckinridge ran best in those areas with the greatest amounts of unimproved acreage—land that could be devoted to cotton in the future—whereas he was weakest in the areas that had the least land for additional cotton planting.

These inconsistencies stem from two related sources. One is Barney's insistence that the thirst for expansion was the major impetus behind secession. No doubt demands for slave expansion pervaded the rhetoric of the period. Democrats had made such demands for years. Yet important leaders like William L. Yancey, curiously a minor figure in Barney's book, denied the need of actual expansion. Could it be that the most salient feature of the expansion issue was not the real need for it but instead the denial of southern equality inherent in Republican prohibition of it? The southern refusal to be treated as less than equal, to accept minority status, had laid behind the insistence on the right to expand since the Wilmot Proviso. J. Mills Thornton, indeed, has brilliantly argued that the determination to protect southern equality and liberty, a symbolic issue that could be translated into Jacksonian terms, was more important in Alabama's drive for secession than either the need for expansion or fears of abolition.[3]

Second, Barney may overlook alternative explanations for his behavioral patterns because of his ahistorical analysis. He looks only at 1860, finds divisions, and attempts to explain them by economic and social variables for 1860. Long ago, however, Lee Benson warned against studying elections without some temporal perspective.[4] Habit or party identity shapes voting as much as active responses to ideologies or current issues. The patterns Barney detects could have been less the response to a referendum on secession than the product of long-term interregional and Whig-Democratic conflict in those states. Barney does not ignore tradition or political motives entirely, but he emphasizes competing ideologies to explain behavior. Yet surely the presence of young men among Breck-

3. J. Mills Thornton III, "Politics and Power in a Slave Society: Alabama 1806–1860" (Ph.D. dissertation, Yale University, 1974), 273–99, 509. Thornton's dissertation was later published as *Politics and Power in a Slave Society: Alabama, 1800–1860* (Baton Rouge, 1978).

4. Lee Benson, "Research Problems in American Political Historiography," in *Common Frontiers of the Social Sciences,* ed. Mira Komarovsky (Glencoe, Ill., 1957), 113–83.

inridge leaders and old men among Bell leaders is as readily explained by the bankruptcy of the Whig party in those states after 1852 as by expansionist desires. Men with political, if not territorial, ambitions had no place to go but the Democratic party. Not only the collapse of Whig effectiveness at the state level, but also internal rivalries within the Democratic party are important. Thornton demonstrates, for example, that old jealousies between north and south Alabama Democrats, rivalries in which Yancey and his clique of young lawyers were key figures throughout the 1850s, accounted for the apparent shift of North Alabamians after the election. Hatred of Yancey, not unionism, caused them to oppose him at the secession convention.[5] Had Barney examined previous political developments and voting patterns, he may not have been so dependent on differing responses to expansion to explain the divisions he found.

Precisely because it places Maryland's decision not to secede in a historical context, William J. Evitts' admirable *A Matter of Allegiances* is persuasive. Evitts' major thesis is that although Marylanders always worried in the 1850s about whether to align with the South or the Union in the event of secession, they were not preoccupied with that decision. Internal problems growing out of rapid industrialization, urban growth in Baltimore, immigration, and interregional rivalries vied for their attention. National and local concerns became inextricably entangled in the political arena. The combination, but especially local issues, forced a major realignment of Maryland's voters and a reorganization of her parties. That realignment both reflected intense emotions and shaped strong allegiances to new parties that mattered as much if not more to Marylanders than the sectional conflict itself.

Maryland's politics in the 1850s followed a course remarkably similar to that in many northern states. By 1850, the Whigs had consistently dominated national elections. Strongest in Old Maryland, the southern and Eastern Shore counties where slavery was concentrated, they also carried the western counties by smaller margins because of their commitment to federal internal improvements. Baltimore City, which contained almost a third of the state's voters, was Democratic. These lines held in state elections, but enough voters in western counties switched to give those contests to the Democrats. The Democrats favored revision of the state's

5. Thornton, "Politics and Power," 510–22.

constitution and legislative reapportionment, which were enormously popular issues in the west and Baltimore, whereas the Whigs of Old Maryland opposed these measures. Between 1850 and 1852, the Democrats exploited those state issues, the disappearance of the internal improvements question with the completion of the Baltimore & Ohio Railroad and Chesapeake & Ohio Canal, and Whig divisions at the national level over the Compromise of 1850 to erode Whig support and capture the presidential election in 1852. Increasing political corruption, the lackluster performance of the constitutional convention in 1851, and the issueless nature of the 1852 election also spawned an antiparty, antipolitician sentiment that led to the repudiation of both old parties as meaningless and to a demand for reform. That demand was expressed first through a plethora of independent candidates and an apolitical temperance movement in 1853, and then more successfully through the Know Nothing movement in 1854 and 1855. Frightened by economic and social changes, the rapid growth of the Catholic immigrant population, Democratic efforts to share the public school fund with parochial schools, political corruption, and the unresponsiveness of the old parties, Marylanders saw Know Nothingism as a reform movement that would clean up politics, respond to the people's will, and restore the purer political and moral values of an earlier age. Most important, the emergence of the Know Nothings worked a fundamental realignment in Maryland's voting patterns. Whig bastions in Old Maryland became Democratic, a process that had begun in 1852. Not only the slaveholding but the Catholicism of many of those old counties caused the shift. At the same time, Democratic western Maryland and Baltimore became Know Nothing strongholds.

Once in office, the Know Nothings became the target of reform, not its vehicle. They jettisoned the nativist issues that had brought them to power and relied instead on a program of fervent unionism and on massive violence, intimidation, and fraud in Baltimore to control the state until 1859. The Democrats, in turn, became more prosouthern on national issues, but during the state elections between 1856 and 1860 they demanded reform in Baltimore and an end to Know Nothing rule. Supported by anti-Baltimore voters in the rural counties and an independent reform organization in the city itself, the Democrats finally captured the legislature in 1859 and passed laws to reform Baltimore's elections that broke the grip of the Know Nothing machine there. In sum, state level politics in Maryland from 1850 to 1859 had real substance, a substance provided largely by the issue of reform in one version or another—revision of the constitution, the Know Nothings in mid-decade, and the anti–Know Nothings at its end.

This background shaped the results in 1860. As in Alabama and Mississippi, the race in Maryland was essentially between Bell and Breckinridge. Lincoln and Douglas were both spurned as too northern. Proclaiming that "Maryland Must and Will Be True to the South," Breckinridge men demanded a federal slave code, dismissed Bell as unsafe, and drew solid support from slaveholders. There, too, Bell men stressed unionism, denounced secessionists, and proclaimed slavery extension a phony issue. As in the Deep South, moreover, Breckinridge won, but not, Evitts insists, because of his ideology. Bell reflected the real values of Marylanders. Breckinridge triumphed because he carried Baltimore, where he had the support of the independent reform organization. The stigma of Know Nothingism cost Bell the city and thus the state. Although Evitts implies that outside of Baltimore national issues were most important, his own evidence here as throughout the book indicates that local concerns were far more important. He found stunningly high correlations between Bell's vote in the counties and the Know Nothing votes in the state elections of 1855, 1857, and 1859, elections where local concerns were clearly salient. The realignment of the 1850s, in short, forged such powerful allegiances to competing parties that they alone could have accounted for the results in 1860, no matter what the issue.

Although Minute Men formed clubs, militia companies armed, and fears of slave revolts intensified after John Brown's raid in neighboring Virginia, Maryland, unlike Alabama and Mississippi, refused to secede. Evitts offers cogent reasons why. For one, Know Nothing Governor Thomas Hicks, unlike his counterparts to the south, opposed secession and refused to call a special session of the legislature when Breckinridge men demanded it. Second, unionists simply outnumbered secessionists. The Baltimore businessmen who led the reform movement and backed Breckinridge ardently supported the Union to preserve their economic ties to the North. Finally, slavery was a much less vibrant institution in Maryland than in the Deep South. "By 1861 Maryland had evolved into a pattern of life so different from that of the Southern states that secession was never more than a distant possibility" (190).

Without quarreling with these explanations, a political historian can suggest that the different political experiences of Maryland and the Deep South states, aside from any economic and social distinctions, offer another reason why the Upper and Lower South responded so differently to Lincoln's election. Whatever else it represented, immediate secession was a repudiation of the normal political process, a rejection not only of Republican rule but of the national Democratic party that would have controlled Congress. Even Barney notes that southerners rejected old institutions and "the legitimacy of the status quo" (237), that national Democratic leaders like Jefferson Davis and Benjamin Fitzpatrick were ignored, and that secessionists stressed that ties to corrupt and useless party organizations must be broken. In short, the Deep South states had lost faith in politics as usual, in the safety provided by party competition and the ebb and flow of elections. In its narrowest terms, what distinguished the Upper South states that refused to secede immediately, even those that later joined the Confederacy, was that, at least until Fort Sumter, they continued to have faith in normal political processes to protect the South. If Maryland was at all typical of the Upper South states, they may have had faith precisely because state level politics during the 1850s had revolved around substantive issues, the system had been responsive even if it had required a realignment, and reform had been achieved. It may be possible to apply to the antebellum South, which has always seemed exotic terrain to political historians, the theories recently advanced by such political scientists as Walter Dean Burnham and James L. Sundquist. They have argued that, historically, voter realignments have defused crisis situations growing out of the unresponsiveness of the political system to emergent public demands by forcing the old parties or creating new ones to address the needs of the voters.[6] Though startling, it may not be too far-fetched to suggest that secession was an effort to achieve reform and the overthrow of an unresponsive party system that Marylanders and

6. Walter Dean Burnham, *Critical Elections and the Mainsprings of American Politics* (New York, 1970); James L. Sundquist, *Dynamics of the Party System: Alignment and Realignment of Political Parties in the United States* (Washington, D.C., 1973).

most northerners had achieved through their realignments of the 1850s. Whether this theory has wider applicability will only be determined by intensive investigations of political developments during the 1850s in other southern states. Evitts has provided a fine model for such studies.

The Problem of
Civil War Causation

Long before David Potter died in 1971, historians had impatiently awaited his volume on the coming of the Civil War for the New American Nation Series. Widely admired for the sagacity of his judgments, the clarity of his mind, and his awesome ability to dissect and simplify complex problems, Potter was without peer in the historical profession as a pure logician. He had devoted more than a decade of reading and reflection to the preparation of this study. Now, five years after his death, edited and ably completed by his colleague at Stanford University, Don E. Fehrenbacher, the product of that effort has finally appeared, and we can all be grateful. *The Impending Crisis, 1848–1861*, is the fairest and most intelligent history of the antebellum period yet to appear in print. Because it both synthesizes and comments upon a vast body of scholarship and because it is literally crammed with penetrating insights and perceptive judgments about a host of events and controversies, it should be the first place that one looks henceforth for an assessment of those troubled years.

At the outset, Potter shrewdly evaluates the lengthy historiographical debate over the nature of the sectional conflict and clearly stakes out where he stands. Though that debate has gone in cycles, essentially there have been two sides. Fundamentalists argued that basic and irresolvable

This essay originally appeared as a long review of David M. Potter, *The Impending Crisis, 1848–1861*, completed and edited by Don E. Fehrenbacher (New York, 1976). Page references to this book will appear in the text.

ideological, economic, and cultural differences between North and South produced the conflict that led to war. Though they have disagreed among themselves, most have insisted that slavery was the crucial issue. Opposing revisionist historians insist that neither the slavery issue nor economic and cultural differences were sufficiently serious to cause war. Instead, they blame the mistakes of political leaders and the agitation of sectional extremists for blowing inherently manageable problems out of proportion. Recently, neofundamentalists like Eugene Genovese and Eric Foner have reasserted the importance of slavery in generating antithetical cultures, economies, and ideologies in the North and South. Unlike earlier fundamentalists like James Ford Rhodes and Dwight L. Dumond, however, they have not attributed the war to disagreement over slavery's morality or immediate pressures for its abolition.[1] Rather, they have argued that because each section viewed the extension of the other's civilization to the West as a threat to its own, the sections went to war over the question of slavery extension.

Since the publication of his *Lincoln and His Party in the Secession Crisis* in 1942, David Potter has normally been consigned to the revisionist side of this debate, but here he emphatically embraces fundamentalism, and the older version at that. He flatly rejects the notion that slavery was not basic to all other sectional differences. Echoing Rhodes and Dumond, moreover, he insists that a profound disagreement over the morality of slavery was the core of the sectional conflict. "A conflict of values, rather than a conflict of interests or a conflict of cultures, lay at the root of the sectional schism" (46). Potter admits that the main political goal of the North was prevention of slavery expansion, not abolition, and that many northerners were racists. Still, he explicitly rejects the arguments recently advanced by historians like Eugene Berwanger, James A. Rawley, Chaplain Morrison, and others that these facts indicated that overt dedication to white supremacy in the West and antipathy toward white slaveholders, not sympathy for black slaves, impelled northerners. Instead, he endorses the old argument of Arthur M. Schlesinger, Jr., that

1. Eugene Genovese, *The Political Economy of Slavery* (New York, 1965); Eric Foner, *Free Soil, Free Labor, Free Men: The Ideology of the Republican Party Before the Civil War* (New York, 1970); James Ford Rhodes, *History of the United States from the Compromise of 1850* (7 vols.; New York, 1892–1906); Dwight L. Dumond, *The Antislavery Origins of the Civil War* (Ann Arbor, 1938).

because northerners venerated the Constitution, they felt powerless to attack slavery within southern states no matter how much they despised it.[2] The emergence of the territorial issue in 1846, however, unleashed their genuine "moral indignation" from its constitutional restraints.

Although Potter resurrects the earliest fundamentalist belief about the crux of the sectional conflict, he wisely rejects the corollary assumption of historians like Rhodes that such a value conflict made war inevitable. Moral differences over slavery had long existed, he correctly recognizes, and their presence alone did not produce war. The central question concerning the coming of the Civil War is not what caused sectional conflict but why that conflict became so disruptive in the 1850s when it had not been earlier. The key to the war's coming, he insists, was the process by which sectional conflict became politicized. Only when it did so could it rend the nation. Thus *The Impending Crisis* is primarily an analysis of political developments from the outbreak of the Mexican War to the firing on Fort Sumter, and his most important contributions come as insights into particular events along the way.

For one thing, Potter provides perhaps the best account of the last years of the Polk administration we will have until the third volume of Charles Sellers' biography of Polk is published. His handling of the stalemate over the disposition of slavery in western territories during the late 1840s is especially adept. Here he makes the brilliant point that extension of the Missouri Compromise line to the coast was potentially a better compromise solution than popular sovereignty until the separate organization of Oregon in 1848 destroyed its utility. By reducing the area north of 36°30′, the Oregon bill rendered extension of the line too advantageous to the South to be acceptable any longer in the North. Thus the Democrats resorted to the dangerously ambiguous popular sovereignty formula as a middle ground between the Wilmot Proviso and the Calhounite position of unlimited expansion.

2. David M. Potter, *Lincoln and His Party in the Secession Crisis* (New Haven, 1942); Eugene H. Berwanger, *The Frontier Against Slavery: Western Anti-Negro Prejudice and the Slavery Expansion Controversy* (Urbana, Ill., 1967); Chaplain W. Morrison, *Democratic Politics and Sectionalism: The Wilmot Proviso Controversy* (Chapel Hill, 1967); James A. Rawley, *Race & Politics: "Bleeding Kansas" and the Coming of the Civil War* (Philadelphia, 1969); Arthur M. Schlesinger, Jr., "The Causes of the Civil War: A Note on Historical Sentimentalism," *Partisan Review*, XVI (1949), 969–81.

Potter follows Holman Hamilton in arguing that Democratic votes and leadership were more important than Whig oratory in securing the passage of the Compromise of 1850. Yet, anticipating the arguments of recent historians like Robert F. Dalzell, Jr., he insists that there really was no compromise between the opposing sections; the measures of that year constituted an armistice at best. Potter breaks sharply with the revisionist orthodoxy as to what the compromise actually said concerning slavery in Utah and New Mexico Territories, however. Disagreeing with Robert Russell and Hamilton, he argues that the laws did not explicitly give territorial legislatures the authority to rule on slavery during the territorial stage. Here I think Potter would have benefited from Robert Johannsen's biography of Stephen A. Douglas, which appeared after his death. Douglas was the chief manager of the legislation in the final stages, and Johannsen presents impressive evidence that explicit popular sovereignty was indeed incorporated in the territorial laws.[3]

Johannsen's biography also probably would have forced a reworking of Potter's chapter on the Kansas-Nebraska Act, surely the most curious in the book. Ignoring the political pressures that contributed to the framing of the law and that are stressed by both Johannsen and Roy F. Nichols, Potter once again returns to a much older interpretation.[4] Douglas' chief goal, he asserts, was building a Pacific railroad on a central route, and he agreed to the overthrow of the Missouri Compromise ban on slavery in Nebraska as part of a logrolling operation to win southern votes for the railroad scheme he favored. Where Potter does accept Nichols is in his insistence that once Douglas introduced the bill, he lost control of events and was forced beyond his initial concessions by southern pressure. Johannsen argues compellingly, however, that Douglas from the first intended to apply popular sovereignty in the territorial stage to the Nebraska bill; he wasn't forced to. He makes clear as well that while Douglas was genuinely interested in western development, he was equally interested in using that program, not to forward his presidential candidacy in 1856, as

3. Holman Hamilton, *Prologue to Conflict: The Crisis and Compromise of 1850* (Lexington, Ky., 1964); Robert F. Dalzell, Jr., *Daniel Webster and the Trial of American Nationalism, 1843–1852* (Boston, 1973); Robert Russell, "What Was the Compromise of 1850?" *Journal of Southern History*, XXII (1956), 292–309; Robert W. Johannsen, *Stephen A. Douglas* (New York, 1973).
4. Roy F. Nichols, "The Kansas-Nebraska Act: A Century of Historiography," *Mississippi Valley Historical Review*, XLIII (1956), 187–212.

some historians charge, but as a way to reunite the disintegrating Democratic party in 1854. The political purposes of the bill were just as important to Douglas as the program itself.

If Potter's account of the framing of the Kansas-Nebraska Act is questionable, his succinct analysis of events in "Bleeding Kansas" is the finest brief treatment I have ever read. Agreeing with revisionists that conflicting attitudes toward slavery did not produce the strife among settlers in the territory, he brilliantly shows how the politicization of the slavery issue was crucial "in structuring and intensifying the friction." Sectional conflict outside of Kansas worked "to polarize and organize all the diffused and random antagonisms, which might otherwise have remained merely individual and local" (203–204).

Similarly, Potter's chapter on the political realignment of the 1850s is generally first-rate. Here again he focuses on exactly the right question—why the northern Whig party disappeared after 1854 rather than benefiting from the renewed antislavery sentiment sparked by the Nebraska Act. As Potter notes, other historians have insufficiently appreciated the critical difference between the sectional rupture in the national Whig party caused by slavery and the disintegration of state Whig parties in the North after 1852 even when they tried to exploit the slavery issue against the Democrats. Logically, antislavery sentiment alone cannot account for the death of the Whigs. Utilizing recent scholarship, Potter argues that the surge of anti-Catholic, nativist, and prohibitionist sentiment reflected in the phenomenal rise of the Know Nothing movement in the mid-1850s is what really gutted the Whig party in the North and later contributed significantly to the triumph of the Republicans. Potter calls the Republicans' merger with the nativists in 1856 the most critical event in the history of the party. More than the sudden salience of ethnocultural issues produced the Whig collapse, but Potter's sophisticated account marks a great advance over simplistic theories that the slavery issue alone destroyed the Whig party and shaped the realignment from which the Republican party emerged.

Potter's chapters on the Dred Scott decision, the Lincoln-Douglas debates, and John Brown's raid are also gems, but because Potter was one of the foremost students of the elusive problem of southern identity, his judgments about the impulse behind secession especially merit attention. He argues cogently that secession did not result from a preexisting southern nationalism based on cultural affinities and common values—in short, on a distinct southern identity. "The Civil War did far more to produce a southern nationalism which flourished in the cult of the Lost Cause than southern nationalism did to produce the war" (469). Fear of the North, not some positive affirmation of culture, produced secession. Potter, however, rejects the notion advanced by Genovese and iterated since Potter's death by William L. Barney that what the South feared was that the Republicans would successfully prevent slavery's extension, which southerners by 1860 regarded as a social, economic, political, and racial necessity. Instead, Potter argues in the vein of Stephen Channing that the South seceded because it was terrified that Republican propaganda and Republican toleration of the circulation of abolitionist literature in the South would provoke slave insurrection.[5] By 1860, southerners were not united culturally, but they "*were* united by a sense of terrible danger. They were united, also, in a determination to defend slavery, to resist abolitionism, and to force the Yankees to recognize not only their rights but also their status as perfectly decent, respectable human beings" (478).

It would be an injustice to end this summary without including the final two chapters on the secession crisis written by Professor Fehrenbacher. They sustain the same high literary and interpretative quality that graces the rest of the book. Particularly noteworthy is Fehrenbacher's stunning insight that secession, the Deep South's refusal to tolerate Lincoln's election, abruptly transformed the entire sectional issue and ensured that the North would be much more united in resisting the South than it ever had been before. "Here is the key to understanding why many Republicans seemed to become more intractable as the danger of disunion became more palpable. . . . . The main problem at hand was no longer the expansion of slavery, but the survival of the United States, and the most pressing moral issue was not now slavery, but majority rule" (527). What motivated northerners during the ultimate crisis, in short, was not moral antipathy to slavery but determination to preserve the principles and existence of republican government itself.

These and many other thoughtful insights evoke profound admiration from a reader, yet upon concluding the book one still has a vague

5. William L. Barney, *The Secessionist Impulse: Alabama and Mississippi in 1860* (Princeton, 1974); Stephen Channing, *A Crisis of Fear: Secession in South Carolina* (New York, 1970).

sense of disappointment and incompleteness. The sum of its parts seems stronger than the whole. In part, this uneasiness stems from Potter's failure to answer conclusively the questions he does ask. With all its extraordinary wisdom and learning, the book tells more about *how* the Civil War came than about *why* it came. It raises disturbing doubts whether any such broad-scale synthesis can ever satisfactorily unravel the greatest puzzle in American history—exactly what caused the Civil War? In part, however, disappointment arises because the book is almost defiantly old-fashioned. It is largely shaped and restricted by questions historians have been debating for almost a hundred years. One wishes Potter had gone beyond the traditional issues, broken new ground, and charted new approaches to the antebellum period. Only with fresh perspectives can we gain new insight into what caused the war in April, 1861.

Potter's traditionalism is perhaps best exemplified in his treatment of antebellum politics. In recent years, several political historians have argued that grass-roots voters were normally unconcerned with the great national issues that have dominated previous interpretations of politics. These studies of the 1850s and other periods vary in quality, but their central message is that one cannot possibly get an accurate picture of political development by focusing only on national politics—congressional debates, presidential elections, and so forth. Potter exploited these studies in his account of the realignment of the 1850s, but he is distressingly ambiguous on the crucial question of how much people really cared about national, slavery-related events. The series editors properly say that Potter recognized that slavery did not monopolize the politics of the period (xiv), and Potter himself argues that most people did not "have any fixation on the issue of slavery" (145). Yet elsewhere he seems to take precisely the opposite position. After 1846, he argues, "the slavery question would grow to dominate national politics, and Congress would become for fifteen years the arena of a continuous battle watched by millions of aroused sectional partisans. No other issue in American history has so monopolized the political scene" (49). Throughout the book, he stresses that "public attention was focused intently on events in Congress" (73, 320). Neither Potter nor any other historian has proved that millions of Americans were "aroused sectional partisans," but in that belief he devotes the book almost exclusively to national-level politics. Although he correctly notes that "state government rather than federal government symbolized public authority for most citizens" in the nineteenth century (52), he ignores the state level of politics except to deal with local responses to the national slavery issue. But the slavery issue was not the major concern of state governments, and state-level political developments exclusive of slavery did as much to shape the political transformation that led to war as did the national events on which Potter focuses. Finally, Potter reflects the rather dismal state of political historiography when he does examine the voting realignment and political reorganization of the decade. Like most other historians, he deals almost exclusively with the North; we learn very little about what happened in southern politics between 1852 and 1860. One can argue, however, that the differing political experiences of southern states in those years helped determine which slave states seceded and which did not in response to Lincoln's election. It is difficult to fault Potter for this lapse, for with the exception of an excellent study of Maryland, which appeared after his death, we simply have no modern studies of southern politics in the 1850s. One might say, indeed, that it is unfair to fault Potter at all for his treatment of politics, for the real focus of the book is the escalation of sectional conflict between 1848 and 1861.

Yet it is fair to examine how cogently he answers the crucial question he raises at the beginning of the book—why the long-standing sectional conflict over slavery became so disruptive in the 1850s. Potter never provides an explicit answer to this question. One must infer what he thinks from the book as a whole. He does make clear from the beginning that the North and South were profoundly divided over slavery. Northerners condemned it as immoral, and southerners feared any antislavery agitation that might produce abolition or provoke slave revolt. What Potter seems to argue is that events between 1846 and 1861 intensified those basic emotions in both sections until they engendered the triumph of the antislavery Republican party in 1860 and southern secession in response to it. The problem is that he is again ambiguous or inconsistent about exactly what emotions were intensified. Put another way, it is unclear how the slavery issue was politicized, why it had the resonance with the northern electorate he claims it had. At places, he reasserts that moral antagonism was heightened by events, yet elsewhere he admits that northern propaganda about the Nebraska Act, Bleeding Kansas, and the Dred Scott decision focused on the iniquity of slaveholders, not slavery, and shrilly warned of the Slave Power's plot to subvert republican values of liberty, equality, and self-rule. Even Lincoln depended upon such rhetoric in his debates with Douglas. Such accusations, he correctly states, had much more impact in the North than denunciations of slavery itself would have had (163–64). The distinction is absolutely critical, for Republican propaganda did not appeal to the moral concern for the Negro slave Potter says was the fundamental emotion. I think, in fact, that Potter is more accurate about the nature of Republican rhetoric than about the northern mind, but even then it is unclear exactly what the North was bothered about.

There are two alternative interpretations of northern sentiment, as inferred from Republican rhetoric, that seem more persuasive than Potter's contention that northerners "accepted [the] doctrine that slavery was morally intolerable" and sincerely "opposed the oppression of a racial minority" (143, 251). Most simply, one can argue that the evidence supports the hypothesis Potter rejects. The basic northern sentiment may have been anti-southernism, opposition to white slaveholders, not sympathy for black slaves. Sheer hatred of the arrogance and aggressiveness of the Slave Power mobilized northerners.

It is possible, however, to extend Professor Fehrenbacher's brilliant observation about the secession crisis to the entire period covered in the book to arrive at a more complete understanding of the northern mind that incorporates its undoubted hostility to the Slave Power. From the northern point of view, what may have been at stake in the entire sectional conflict was not the moral wrong of Negro slavery but the continued viability of republican government itself, a much more basic issue. Since the Revolution, Americans in both sections had been obsessed with the fragility of republics, with the danger power in any form posed to liberty, and with the susceptibility of republican self-government to usurping conspiracies and plots. Thus the numerous accusations about tyranny-threatening plots and conspiracies that pervaded northern and southern rhetoric in the 1850s may have represented, not as Potter asserts, "the psychological tendency to interpret the behavior of the opposition in conspiratorial terms" (287), but the real and basic fears of Americans in both sections that powerful groups in the other section meant to subvert true republican government, to strip them of liberty and equality, and to make them figuratively slaves to the other's domination. As Bernard Bailyn has pointed out, the word *slavery* had a definite political meaning in the eighteenth century that had little to do with the institution of Negro slavery.[6] It implied subjugation to another's power; it meant the absence of liberty; it was the antithesis of republicanism. The rhetoric of the 1850s suggests the possibility that the politicization of the slavery issue in this abstract sense best explains why the sectional conflict became more disruptive in the 1850s than it ever had been before. The basic issue, in sum, may have been the fear of white slavery, not the reality of Negro slavery.

If so, the task for historians is to look beyond the escalating sectional conflict itself to discover why fears for the security of the republic were more widespread and intense in the 1850s than at any time since the 1790s. To do that is precisely why one must look below the national level of politics when examining the antebellum period. What may have brought the sectional conflict to a point of crisis in 1861, in other words, was not simply the series of events that aggravated it but the development of a popular mood that made northerners and southerners much more responsive to sectional propaganda about threats to republicanism than they had previously been.

6. Bernard Bailyn, *The Ideological Origins of the American Revolution* (Cambridge, Mass., 1967).

Abraham Lincoln and the Politics of Union

One of the most stimulating analyses of Civil War politics ever written is a brilliant essay by Eric McKitrick called "Party Politics and the Union and Confederate War Efforts."[1] In it, McKitrick argues that the North had a decisive advantage over the South because it continued to have two-party rivalry during the war whereas the Confederacy did not. The presence of the Democratic party forced Republicans of all kinds to rally behind the policies of the Republican government to win elections. As a result, the North remained more united during the long ordeal than the division-plagued Confederacy.

According to McKitrick, party politics also made Abraham Lincoln a more effective presidential leader than his Confederate counterpart, Jefferson Davis. The organization and partisan needs of the Republican party provided Lincoln with guidelines, first to select and then to reshuffle his cabinet, with ways to ensure the loyalty of his vice presidents, with incentives to gain the cooperation of state governors, and with sanctions to punish political opponents both inside and outside his own party. In contrast, the hapless Davis lacked party lines to separate friends from foes and to generate institutional loyalty to his administration. Hence he could not control his cabinet, Vice President Alexander Stephens, obstreperous governors like Joe Brown of Georgia and Zeb Vance of North Carolina,

---

1. Eric McKitrick, "Party Politics and the Union and Confederate War Efforts," in *The American Party Systems: Stages of Political Development*, ed. William N. Chambers and Walter Dean Burnham (New York, 1967), 117–51.

or political opponents in Congress and the electorate. McKitrick concludes that it was because of the presence of a two-party system that Lincoln was able to hold the North together long enough to win the war. Without the glue that parties provided, Davis could not prevent centrifugal forces from tearing the Confederacy apart.

Despite the stunning originality of McKitrick's argument, it leaves several crucial questions unanswered. Most important, it slights the critical matter of Lincoln's relationship with the Republican majority in Congress. If the presence of the Democratic opposition pressured Republicans to pull together, how can one explain the well-known hostility of many Republicans to Lincoln, the effort of Republican senators to purge his favorite William Henry Seward from the cabinet, or the palpable conflict between Lincoln and the congressional wing of his party over emancipation, the arming of blacks, reconstruction, and other wartime policies?

At one time it was fashionable to blame these clashes on a cabal of vindictive radicals who frustrated the benevolent plans of the magnanimous president. Now we know that such a melodramatic interpretation is misleading. Although there were indeed radical and moderate factions in the Republican party during the war, virtually all congressional Republicans, not just the radicals, blamed Lincoln for failing to prosecute the war vigorously enough and to move against slavery rapidly enough, and virtually all voted for the measures that set Congress's policy apart from Lincoln's. Nor is it satisfactory to contend, as some historians have, that Lincoln and congressional Republicans had the same fundamental goals, that they were traveling the same road at different rates, and that Lincoln was really happy to have the more radical congressmen blaze the trail. Timing is almost everything in politics, and that line of argument fails to explain why Lincoln and Congress wanted to move at different speeds while it simultaneously minimizes the seriousness of the disputes between them. Finally, it is not terribly convincing to assert that the pragmatic and sagacious Lincoln, alone among the Republican politicians in Washington, recognized the need to keep the border slave states and northern Democrats behind the war effort and therefore resisted congressional demands concerning emancipation and the use of black troops that might alienate them. Lincoln had no monopoly on political wisdom or common sense. Congressional Republicans must have recognized the potential political impact of the policies they advocated. Nonetheless, they vigorously demanded them, often against Lincoln's wishes. Why?[2]

This essay suggests that the continuation of the two-party system, which McKitrick sees as the cause of Republican unity during the war, was in fact the source of the division between Lincoln and Congress over wartime policy. Because Lincoln and congressional Republicans adopted different political strategies in response to the challenge posed by the Democratic party, they also pursued different paths to fight the war they both wanted to win. The result of Congress going one way and Lincoln another, however, was a more successful war effort than the North would have achieved had it followed either course alone. McKitrick may not be correct about the precise way in which a two-party system helped the northern war effort, but he is correct about the result. It significantly contributed to northern victory.[3]

To understand Civil War politics it is necessary to remember three facts of political life. First, the Democratic party remained a potent challenger to Republicans in the North. Though divided between two candidates and forced to defend one of the most unpopular and corrupt administrations in American history, the Democrats still won almost 44 percent of the popular vote in the free states in 1860. As the war progressed,

2. The historiographical debate on this topic has been extensive. Among the more important titles are T. Harry Williams, *Lincoln and the Radicals* (Madison, 1941); David Donald, "The Radicals and Lincoln," in *Lincoln Reconsidered: Essays on the Civil War Era* (New York, 1961), 103–27; David Donald, "Devils Facing Zionwards" and T. Harry Williams, "Lincoln and the Radicals: An Essay in Civil War History and Historiography," in *Grant, Lee, Lincoln and the Radicals,* ed. Grady McWhiney (New York, 1966), 72–177; Hans L. Trefousse, *The Radical Republicans: Lincoln's Vanguard for Racial Justice* (New York, 1969); Herman Belz, *Reconstructing the Union: Theory and Policy During the Civil War* (Ithaca, 1969); Michael Les Benedict, *A Compromise of Principle: Congressional Republicans and Reconstruction, 1863–1869* (New York, 1974); James A. Rawley, *The Politics of Union: Northern Politics During the Civil War* (Hinsdale, Ill., 1974); and LaWanda Cox, *Lincoln and Black Freedom: A Study in Presidential Leadership* (Columbia, S.C., 1981).

3. My argument here in no way denies the importance of other factors that contributed to tensions between Lincoln and Congress, such as jurisdictional conflicts between the executive and legislative branches or Congress's ideological opposition to Lincoln's reconstruction policies because they inadequately protected blacks or secured republican self-government. Rather, my point is that the different political strategies pursued by Lincoln and congressional Republicans was the chief source of the conflicts over policy between them. David Donald has briefly suggested a somewhat similar interpretation in *The Politics of Reconstruction, 1863–1867* (Baton Rouge, 1965), 11–17.

moreover, controversial Republican policies like emancipation, conscription, and the suspension of habeas corpus gave them golden issues to campaign on. The menace of a Democratic comeback, in sum, was no chimera.

Second, the Republican party had no base of any consequence in any slave state. In 1860 Lincoln's support in the border states that remained in the Union ranged from 24 percent in tiny Delaware to a pitiful 1 percent in his native Kentucky. In the slave states that seceded, Lincoln received a handful of votes only in Virginia; no Republican tickets had even been distributed in the other ten states that joined the Confederacy. It may strike some as odd to include Confederate states in a discussion of the political situation that shaped the clash between Lincoln and congressional Republicans, but one must remember that the fundamental northern purpose in the war was to restore those states to the Union. Certainly, Lincoln hoped they would be voting again in the congressional and presidential elections of 1864, if not earlier, and they seemed likely to vote against Lincoln and other Republican candidates unless support were developed within them.

Third, and most important, Lincoln and congressional Republicans had different constituencies. Lincoln faced a national electorate, not a local one, and he had won less than 40 percent of the popular vote in 1860. To achieve reelection he had to worry about winning statewide pluralities both in the free states, where the race had often been close even in 1860 when the opposition divided among three candidates, and in the border and Confederate slave states, where he had virtually no organizational or popular support. There is no need to question Lincoln's desire for reelection. Virtually everyone who knew him commented on his insatiable political ambition. Like most politicians, moreover, Lincoln convinced himself that his reelection was in the best interest of the nation and that the political strategy he pursued to achieve it was the best way to restore the Union.

Unlike Lincoln, congressional Republicans did not have to consider areas of existing or potential Democratic strength in their own political calculations. By definition, the vast majority of them came from districts where the Republican party was strongest and most secure from the Democratic challenge. Most of them, that is, received a larger proportion of the vote in their local congressional districts than Lincoln did of the statewide vote in their states, especially in the hotly contested battle-grounds of Illinois, Indiana, Ohio, and New York (see Table 1). To such men, the campaign formula that had brought Republicans to power in the late 1850s seemed perfectly capable of keeping them in power in the 1860s. That strategy was to denounce southern political power as unfair and dangerous, to expose a supposed Slave Power conspiracy against northern liberties, to arraign northern Democrats for complicity in that southern plot, and to promise to eradicate that southern threat once Re-

Table 1   Lincoln's Percentage of the Popular Vote in 1860 Compared with the Percentage of the Popular Vote Won by Victorious Republican Congressional Candidates in Northern States in 1860 and 1861

	Lincoln	Congress	
		Median	Average
Maine	64%	55.3%	56.7%
New Hampshire	57	52.8	53.1 (1861)
Vermont	75	75.2	75.7
Massachusetts	62.5	64	63.7
Connecticut	54	53.7	53.7 (1861)
New York	53.7	58.8	57.5
New Jersey	48	52.7	52.7
Pennsylvania	56	54.2	57.2
Ohio	52.3	57.2	58.2
Indiana	51.1	54.5	55.4
Illinois	50.7	62.2	62.5
Michigan	57.1	57.5	57
Iowa	55.1	55.2	55.2
Wisconsin	56.5	54.5	56.5
California	32.2		
Oregon	37.9		

NOTE: This table includes congressional percentages only for victorious Republican candidates, not for all Republican candidates. Returns were taken from the *Tribune Almanac*, which listed no popular results for congressional races in California and Oregon.

publicans achieved power.[4] In short, Republican congressmen believed that they had won office in the past and could win again in the future by running as an antisouthern party.

Because they had different constituencies, Lincoln and Republican congressmen reacted differently to the problems posed by the Democratic opposition and the conduct of the war. Usually familiar with public opinion only in the staunchest Republican strongholds, congressional Republicans believed their constituents demanded a ruthless, no-holds-barred crusade to crush the South and humble the Slave Power. Aghast at reports that northern generals protected civilian property in the South, an Ohio Republican senator ranted in 1862, for example, that "this was not the way in which the people desired the war to be conducted, and . . . [that] generals were trying the patience of the country too far." Before the people of the North would accept a Confederate victory, a New Jersey Republican congressman vowed, "they will arm every slave against his rebel master; will drive the whole white population beyond the borders; and hold the once proud states . . . as Territories for the home of the enfranchised negro."[5] Republican congressmen were therefore convinced that what was best for their own prospects of reelection, for the Republican party as a whole, and for the nation was the most vigorous prosecution possible of the war against the Confederacy. Hence Congress constantly thrust powers on Lincoln he was reluctant to use and insisted on the retention of fugitive slaves who fled to Union armies, the confiscation of rebel property, emancipation, the enlistment of black troops, conscription, test oaths, and a host of other measures it believed necessary to win the war and punish the planter aristocracy.

That Democrats protested many of their measures worried most congressional Republicans not a whit. Except for a few Republicans who had slipped into office in 1860 and 1861 with a minority of the vote in multicandidate races,[6] they were relatively immune to Democratic efforts to exploit resentment at their actions because of the strength of the party

---

4. For an elaboration of my understanding of Republican appeals in the 1850s, see Michael F. Holt, *The Political Crisis of the 1850s* (New York, 1978), 183–217.

5. New York *Tribune*, June 18, 1862, quoting Benjamin Wade and Congressman John T. Nixon, both quoted in Williams, *Lincoln and the Radicals*, 139, 159.

6. These were primarily the Republican congressmen from New York City, Philadelphia, and California.

in their own districts. Besides, Democratic opposition allowed Republicans to continue to portray northern Democrats as allies of the Slave Power. In their eyes, in short, harsh antisouthern measures would not only help win the war; they would also provide a platform to help Republicans win elections.

Nor, so long as Republicans maintained majorities in Congress and northern state legislatures, were congressional Republicans concerned that their policies might strengthen Democrats outside their own strongholds. After all, they personally did not have to run in such areas. On the other hand, they would brook no serious threat to their own hold on state and national governments. They bitterly protested the appointment of Democrats as civilian or military leaders of the war effort. They also tried to deny power to or strip effective power from offices and jurisdictions that Democrats controlled. In January, 1862, for example, Republicans expelled the Indiana Democrat Jesse Bright from the Senate on the flimsiest of pretexts. Similarly, when Democrats captured a number of northern legislatures and the governorship of New York and New Jersey in the fall of 1862, Republicans rushed the most nationalistic legislation of the war through Congress between December, 1862, and March, 1863. The explicit purpose of the National Banking Act, the draft, and the Habeas Corpus–Indemnity Removal Act was to shift control of banking, manpower, and legal suits against federal officials from state governments, which Democrats now controlled, to the national government, which Republicans still dominated.

This same unwillingness to see Democrats exercise power, finally, explains the Republicans' hostility to a rapid readmission of Confederate states to political rights. Those states seemed sure to aid the Democrats whatever the nominal partisan affiliation of the men they sent to Congress. "What!" an Illinois Republican protested in February, 1862, "Bring back the rebel States into full fellowship as members of the union, with their full delegations in both Houses of Congress. They, with the proslavery conservatives of the Border States and the Democrats of the Northern states, will control Congress. Republicans and Republican principles will be in the minority." As early as January, 1863, therefore, the Republican caucus in the House determined not to seat men elected from occupied Confederate states. So too they fought Lincoln's 10 percent plan, attempted to substitute the more rigorous Wade-Davis bill that would delay restoration, and resisted the readmission of Louisiana until after Lincoln died.[7]

Congressional Republicans, in sum, approached the military conflict with the Confederacy and the political conflict with the Democracy in exactly the same way. In neither would they make concessions to induce cooperation; in neither did they seek compromise or accommodation. In both they demanded war to the hilt.

Lincoln's responses to the Democratic and Confederate challenges were dramatically different. Consolidating the Republican party in its existing strongholds by baiting Democrats and humiliating the South did little to improve his personal prospects for reelection. He could not afford to alienate non-Republicans in the northern, border-state, and Confederate areas outside of those established bastions. His solution was not to confront Democrats with distinctively Republican policies or to deny Democratic areas the power they deserved. Instead, he attempted to build a new coalition under his leadership that included proslavery conservatives from the border states, northern Democrats, and former rebels from the Confederacy, just the groups congressional Republicans feared would put Republican principles in the minority. This was *not* simply a matter of broadening the base of the Republican party, as some historians have maintained. Rather, it was an attempt to replace the Republican party with a new bisectional organization to be called the Union party.

To state the argument most boldly, Lincoln almost from the moment he was elected set out to destroy the Republican party as it existed in 1860, that is, as an exclusively northern party whose sole basis of cohesion was hostility toward the South and the Democratic party. Instead, Lincoln wanted to create a new national coalition with support in both sections, a party built around the issue of restoring the Union rather than the issue of crushing the Slave Power or abolishing slavery, as congressional Republicans wanted. To achieve his own political goal, in short, Lincoln had to jettison the antisouthern platform that congressional Republicans insisted on retaining.

Some years ago, David Donald suggested that Lincoln's actions as

7. J. H. Jordan to Lyman Trumbull, February 20, 1862, quoted in Williams, *Lincoln and the Radicals,* 11. Belz, *Reconstructing the Union,* provides extensive evidence that, except for a brief period in 1863, Lincoln and congressional Republicans disagreed about the manner of and conditions for restoring Confederate states to the Union from the summer of 1861 until the end of the war.

president reflected his political upbringing, that he was an exemplary Whig in the White House because he deferred to Congress on virtually all nonmilitary legislation.[8] In attempting to change the name, the program, and the constituency of the party that elected him, Lincoln also acted like a good Whig. All of his Whig predecessors in the office—John Tyler, Zachary Taylor, and Millard Fillmore—had tried to create a new party to replace the Whig party that had put them in office. As Lincoln would during the Civil War, moreover, they too had met fierce hostility from the congressional wing of their party because congressmen wanted to perpetuate rather than abandon the existing organization.

Lincoln clearly hoped to enhance his chances for reelection by forging a new party that would broaden support for him in the North and marshal it in the South. But personal political expediency alone did not dictate his course. Lincoln's lifelong beliefs about the nature of the American republic also impelled him toward the same solution. Perhaps no politician has ever articulated so elegantly and succinctly as Lincoln the fundamental premise of American republicanism, that ours is a government of the people, by the people, and for the people. And the people exercised self-government, he believed, through the votes they cast at elections. As he argued in his message to Congress in July, 1861, for example, the purpose of the war was to demonstrate "that ballots are the rightful, and peaceful, successors of bullets; and that when ballots have fairly, and constitutionally, decided, there can be no successful appeal back to bullets; that there can be no successful appeal, except to ballots themselves, at succeeding elections."[9]

For Lincoln, then, the restoration of the Confederate states to the Union was preeminently a political process, a matter of the people of those states going to the polls and voting to return to the Union. Almost as soon as Yankee armies secured various parts of the South, therefore, Lincoln pressed his military governors to hold elections. "If we could somehow, get a vote of the people of Tennessee and have it result properly," he wrote Andrew Johnson on July 3, 1862, "it would be worth more to us than a battle gained." Throughout the war, indeed, Lincoln wheedled, cajoled,

8. David Donald, "Abraham Lincoln: Whig in the White House," in *Lincoln Reconsidered*, 187–208.

9. Roy P. Basler, ed., *The Collected Works of Abraham Lincoln* (9 vols.; New Brunswick, N.J., 1953–55), IV, 439.

and threatened southerners in attempts to induce them to vote themselves back into the Union. The major purpose of Lincoln's preliminary emancipation proclamation in September, 1862, for example, was not to appease congressional Republicans or European governments or even to prepare the way for actual abolition. Rather, it was to pressure Confederates to hold elections before January 1, 1863, in order to avoid emancipation. Lincoln made his purpose clear when he ordered his military governors in Louisiana, Tennessee, Arkansas, and North Carolina to arrange elections before that date to demonstrate the fidelity to the Union of those occupied areas. When the army commander in eastern Virginia specifically asked Lincoln if occupied areas that held congressional elections would be exempted from emancipation, Lincoln, referring to the proclamation, replied, "It is obvious to all that I therein intended to give time and opportunity. Also it is seen I left myself at liberty to exempt *parts* of states. Without saying more, I shall be very glad if any Congressional District will, in good faith, do as your dispatch contemplates." Similarly, Lincoln's famous amnesty proclamation and 10 percent plan of December, 1863, were meant to hasten the holding of elections to restore southern states by creating an electorate to vote in them, a policy at odds with the wishes of congressional Republicans. In short, whereas congressional Republicans wanted to subdue the Confederacy with bullets, Lincoln wanted to redeem it with ballots cast by southerners themselves.[10]

Lincoln realized, moreover, that for elections in occupied areas to "result properly," southerners needed something more tangible to vote for than the mere idea of reunion. They had to elect politicians who would establish loyal state governments. For those politicians to be able to retain political control of their states against pro-Confederate elements within them, in turn, voter support had to be institutionalized. Because those pro-Confederate elements were overwhelmingly Democratic, finally, Lincoln had to establish a new anti-Democratic political party in the South in order to achieve reconstruction through the political process as he desired.

Such a party, however, could not be called or even allied with the Republican party as long as the congressional Republicans pursued

10. Abraham Lincoln to Andrew Johnson, July 3, 1862, and Lincoln to John A. Dix, October 26, 1862, *ibid.*, V, 302–303, 476. See also Belz, *Reconstructing the Union*, 105–10 and *passim*.

the harsh antisouthern policies they favored. Events in the South after the collapse of the Whig party in the mid-1850s had demonstrated that no matter how much southern voters and politicians disliked Democrats, they would not and could not support a palpably antisouthern party like the Republicans. Instead, they had been compelled to join southern Democrats in denouncing the Republicans while simultaneously attempting to rally opposition to the Democrats through a series of ephemeral non-Republican, anti-Democratic organizations, the most recent of which had been the Constitutional Union party, which supported John Bell for president in 1860.[11]

Yet as long as anti-Democratic voters in the South were organized in a party different from Lincoln's own, they would not enhance his chances for reelection against the Democrats once Confederate states returned to the Union. Nor could such a party secure the permanent restoration of the South that Lincoln sought. The course of political history in the antebellum South had demonstrated that no party could survive in the region unless it was an authentic national party with a northern wing, a party with a genuine chance to win the presidency and control Congress.[12] To build a successful anti-Confederate, pro-reunion party in the Confederate states, in short, Lincoln also had to replace the Republicans with a more palatable anti-Democratic party in the North, one that could serve as the northern wing of the party he needed in the South—at least as long as the southern electorate was confined to whites. Both to further his own chances for reelection in 1864 and to effect reunion, therefore, Lincoln attempted to jettison the name and the antisouthern program of the Republicans and to build a new Union party attractive to non-Republicans in both sections.

To understand why Lincoln believed he could accomplish this feat, one must appreciate that few people in the 1850s and 1860s anticipated that the Republicans would remain the permanent successors to the Whigs as the major anti-Democratic party in American politics. Accustomed to twenty years of bisectional interparty competition between Democrats and Whigs, many regarded the exclusively northern Republican party as a

11. Holt, *Political Crisis of the 1850s*, 219–59; William J. Cooper, Jr., *The South and the Politics of Slavery, 1828–1856* (Baton Rouge, 1978), 341–74; and William J. Cooper, Jr., *Liberty and Slavery: Southern Politics to 1860* (New York, 1983), 243–81.

12. This point is forcefully argued in the two books by Cooper cited above.

temporary aberration. As a result, proposals for displacing the Republicans with other anti-Democratic parties that eschewed sectionally oriented attacks on the South had abounded in the late 1850s. For example, it had required a terrific struggle for Republicans to overcome the Know Nothing challenge to their credentials as the new anti-Democratic party in 1855–1856, and they had been forced to beat back another attempt to launch a conservative, bisectional anti-Democratic party in 1858–1859. Although John Bell's Constitutional Union candidacy had fared poorly against Lincoln in the free states in 1860, his virtual monopoly of the anti-Democratic vote in the slave states reaffirmed the potential that a different, non-Republican opposition party might have if it could secure that southern support.

The precarious position of the Republican party in certain northern states at the end of 1860 also encouraged Lincoln to hope that most Republicans might go along with his attempts to refashion the party. The Republicans carried California and Oregon in 1860 and again in 1861, for example, with less than 40 percent of the vote because the majority Democrats were divided into pronorthern and prosouthern wings. Republicans from such states might well see the wisdom of combining with the pro-Union wing of the Democracy. Republicans from Ohio, Illinois, Indiana, and New York, where the 1860 race had been exceedingly close, might also acquiesce in a change of name and platform that could add Bell men and some Democrats to their column. Such a change might be especially appealing to his supporters in New Jersey and Pennsylvania who did not even dare call themselves Republicans because of the antislavery, antisouthern connotations of the name. Instead, they assumed the label "People's Party," which, as its adherents in Pennsylvania repeatedly told Lincoln, was decidedly different from the Republican party. "The Party in Pennsylvania are thoroughly *Anti* Abolitionist," wrote a Philadelphian, "and it is [only] with difficulty [that] we can keep them solid with the *Republican* party." Lincoln must not "give the *negro* question too much prominency," he added, "or I fear a reaction which will again throw our State into the ranks of the Democrats." When congressmen from Pennsylvania and other northern states urged Lincoln in the weeks following his election to appoint John Bell and other southern Constitutional Union men to the cabinet in order to effect a merger between the Republicans and "the Union element of the South" in the next Congress where Republicans expected to be in the minority, Lincoln's belief that he could fundamentally transform the party must have been strengthened.[13]

Political developments in the North and the South during the secession winter of 1860–1861 both cemented that conviction and inspired the name and platform of the party Lincoln attempted to build during the war. Throughout the South in the elections to choose delegates to secession conventions, a voter realignment seemed to begin as Douglas Democrats and some nonslaveholding Breckinridge Democrats joined Constitutional Unionists in opposing immediate secession. In the Upper South where these antisecession coalitions prevailed, they quickly moved to form Union parties to contest the congressional, gubernatorial, and state legislative elections scheduled for the spring, summer, and fall of 1861 against the remaining Democrats who favored secession.[14]

Almost immediately, these southern Unionists contacted high-ranking Republicans like William Henry Seward, Thurlow Weed, Thomas Corwin, and Lincoln himself, begging them to drop their antisouthern stance and to join the southerners in a new national Union party. Such a new party was necessary, they insisted, because the issue was no longer slavery's expansion versus free soil or North versus South, the dichotomies that had defined the Republican/Democratic rivalry of the late 1850s. Now the only issue was union or disunion.

Hence John Gilmer of North Carolina, whom Lincoln fervently wanted in his cabinet, advised the president-elect in December, 1860, to disregard extremist Republicans when he formulated policies and "to come as far South as you can. You may divide from your many party friends, but by the preservation of the peace of the country, you will nationalize yourself and your party." Similarly, in January, 1861, Gilmer urged the New York Republican boss Weed to help build "a great national

13. Francis Blackburn to Abraham Lincoln, Philadelphia, November 24, 1860, James K. Moorhead to Lincoln, Pittsburgh, November 23, 1860, in Abraham Lincoln Papers, Library of Congress. On the difference between the Republican party and the People's party in Pennsylvania and New Jersey, see also Michael F. Holt, *Forging a Majority: The Formation of the Republican Party in Pittsburgh, 1848–1860* (New Haven, 1969), 264–69.

14. The best study of the Union party movement in the Upper South is Daniel W. Crofts, "The Union Party of 1861 and the Secession Crisis," *Perspectives in American History*, XI (1977–78), 327–76. For the embryonic realignment in the Lower South, see Peyton McCrary, Clark Miller, and Dale Baum, "Class and Party in the Secession Crisis: Voting Behavior in the Deep South, 1856–1861," *Journal of Interdisciplinary History*, VIII (1978), 429–57.

party." In February the Richmond *Whig* concluded in a widely reprinted editorial that "the conservative Whigs and Democrats of the South and the conservative Republicans of the North must unite to form a new Union party."

> We predict that before the 4th of July this will be the arrangement of parties. The Republican party cannot exist in its present basis. Lincoln and Seward will have the sagacity to see this, and they will promptly give the cold shoulder to the extreme men of their party and try to establish a national party, which will repudiate the wild absurdities of the Abolition school. A political necessity will constrain them to abandon not only the extreme dogmas of their party, but also to adopt a new name significant of the policy of the new party, and this name must be the UNION PARTY.[15]

Before Lincoln's inauguration, a number of northern Republicans appeared receptive to the idea. The Washington correspondent of the New York *Times* wrote in February, 1861: "The question pending is one as to whether Mr. Lincoln shall become the head of the great 'Union Party' of the country, or whether a party upon that issue shall be permitted to grow up in hostility to his Administration." The incoming administration, he added, must choose between "the party issues of the *past*" and "the necessities of the future." Earlier that paper's editor, Henry J. Raymond, had privately advised Lincoln that "the Union men of the South must belong to our party—and it seems to me important that we should open the door to them as wide as the hinges will let it swing." In the present crisis, a founder of Ohio's Republican party warned, Lincoln must rally men of all parties who were loyal to the Union and not just Republicans. To do that, he must exclude from his administration "men, however worthy and prominent, who would be objectionable to the friends of the Union in other parties." Similarly, John Defrees, editor of the principal Republican newspaper in Indiana, wrote Lincoln that "'Union' or 'dis-union' will soon be the division of the parties North and South, and your administration must be sustained by the Union men North and South." Appointing

15. John A. Gilmer to Abraham Lincoln, December 29, 1860, in Lincoln Papers; John A. Gilmer to Thurlow Weed, January 12, 1861, and Richmond *Whig*, February 11, 1861, quoted in Crofts, "The Union Party of 1861," 357.

southerners like John Bell to the cabinet would not only "build up a party" that would sustain Lincoln in the South, but it would "give us even additional strength in the North by bringing to us moderate Douglas men." "Some of our radicals might object," he confessed, "but most of them would soon be convinced of the wisdom of the movement." [16]

This last prediction proved erroneous. Even before the culmination of secession, many Republicans protested against any abandonment of Republican principles, "the party issues of the *past*" as the *Times* reporter had called them, to appease the South or any attempt to attract southerners and northern Democrats to the party through patronage appointments. Thus a dismayed Indiana Republican asked his congressman in January, 1861, "Is there not a movement . . . to build a 'union party' in the north which shall absorb Americans and Douglas men and Conservative Republicans; done for the purpose of killing what they term the Abolition element in the Republican party, aimed at men of our Stamp? The movement cannot amount to anything unless it should be the disruption of the Republican party." [17]

The completion of secession and outbreak of warfare widened Republican opposition to changing the party. Secession manifestly meant that attempts to deter it by wooing southerners had failed. More important, the withdrawal of southerners meant that Republicans could dominate Congress without southern support. War against the Confederacy, finally, offered an opportunity to build a platform of concrete antisouthern actions, actions they could not have taken against the Slave Power without the excuse the war provided. However amenable some Republicans had been to changing the image and broadening the constituency of the party in the winter of 1860–1861, therefore, few remained so six months later. Instead of worrying about extending the party to the South, they focused

16. New York *Times*, February 26, 1861, quoted in Crofts, "The Union Party of 1861," 358; Henry J. Raymond to Abraham Lincoln, December 14, 1860, Thomas C. Jones to Lincoln, December 24, 1860, and John D. Defrees to Lincoln, December 15, 1860, all in Lincoln Papers.

17. B. F. Diggs to George W. Julian, January 16, 1861, quoted in Williams, *Lincoln and the Radicals*, 15. For examples of letters warning Lincoln not to compromise, see C. F. Jack to Abraham Lincoln, December 5, 1860, and Carl Schurz to Lincoln, December 18, 1860, in Lincoln Papers. Lincoln's correspondence prior to his inauguration was filled with such letters, but it also contained many urging him to make concessions to the South. The basic study of the hardening of Republican opinion against compromise with the South during the secession crisis is Kenneth M. Stampp, *And the War Came: The North and the Secession Crisis, 1860–61* (Baton Rouge, 1950).

throughout the war on consolidating its power in the North, a project that seemed to require no change in the party's image or constituency whatsoever.

Nonetheless, as is well known, during the war Lincoln's party did exchange the Republican name for the Union label, first at the state level in 1861, 1862, and 1863 and then at the party's national convention in 1864. Most historians, echoing contemporary Democrats, have regarded this action as a transparently cosmetic attempt by cynical Republicans to lure gullible Democrats and Unionists into supporting Republican candidates and Republican policies, not a genuine transformation of the party's constituency and principles. We in fact know very little about where the impetus for this change came from or what the reaction of regular Republicans to it was. Evidence from several northern states like Illinois, Ohio, Massachusetts, and California, however, suggests that some Republicans resented even changing the party's name. Many more vehemently opposed the steps Lincoln took to give that change real substance—sharing offices with Democrats and Unionists and trying to scuttle the antisouthern policies congressional Republicans demanded.[18]

There is, alas, no "smoking gun" in the form of a letter in which Lincoln explains his purpose or urges state Republican politicians to start

18. For examples of historians who consider the adoption of the Union name a facade, see James G. Randall, *Lincoln the President* (4 vols.; New York, 1945–55), II, 214–16; and Joel H. Silbey, *A Respectable Minority: The Democratic Party in the Civil War Era, 1860–1868* (New York, 1977), 40–61. We need much more systematic study of the reactions by congressional Republicans and state-level Republican politicians to the formation of Union coalitions in the North. I have not done that research myself and have gleaned information about the states mentioned from the following sources. For Illinois, there is an excellent discussion of the origins of and reaction to the Union party movement in Gary Lee Cardwell, "The Rise of the Stalwarts and the Transformation of Illinois Republican Politics, 1860–1880" (Ph.D. dissertation, University of Virginia, 1976), 37–89, esp. 52–76. On Ohio, I have had an opportunity to read Frederick J. Blue's manuscript biography, "Salmon P. Chase: A Life in Politics," which suggests a negative reaction on p. 584 n. 57. For California, I have relied on conversations with my colleague Professor Charles W. McCurdy, who is writing a biography of Stephen J. Field, one of the leaders in forming California's Union party. Finally, for Massachusetts, where the Union or People's party formed explicitly as a conservative foe of the Republicans and of the reelection of Charles Sumner to the Senate, I used David Donald, *Charles Sumner and the Rights of Man* (New York, 1970), 67–86. In addition to the specific examples included below in the text, Williams, *Lincoln and the Radicals*, is a compendium of Republican complaints about Lincoln's appointments and policies.

Union organizations. Therefore, one cannot prove that Lincoln initiated the creation of Union parties that began to appear in the North in the fall of 1861. Nevertheless, one can infer Lincoln's intentions from his behavior, especially when that behavior is correlated chronologically with efforts to start Union parties and help them win elections in various states. Specifically, his attempt to build a new bisectional Union party can be seen in his dispensation of federal patronage, his use of the presidential pulpit to define the purpose of the war as restoration of the Union rather than abolition or social revolution in the South, and his attempts to shape wartime politics toward the South, toward slavery, and toward blacks.

Contrary to the McKitrick thesis, for example, building the Union party rather than balancing factions within the existing Republican party determined Lincoln's cabinet selections throughout his presidency. For the most important post, secretary of state, he chose Seward who, he had been warned, favored the "abandonment" of the Republican party and "the early formation of new combinations, under the name of a 'Union party,' or something of that kind." No Republican, indeed, had been more sympathetic than Seward to the Union party movement in the Upper South during the secession crisis, and no Republican knew so well what was needed to gain the Union party's support for the Lincoln administration. Thus the purpose of Seward's notorious memorandum to Lincoln (April 1, 1861) was contained in its emphatic insistence that "we must *Change the question before the Public from one upon Slavery, or about Slavery* for a question upon *Union* or *Disunion*." Although Lincoln disregarded the accompanying advice in this note to start a foreign war and to abandon Fort Sumter to prevent a collision with the Confederacy, he was in perfect agreement with Seward about changing the issue from slavery to union. Indeed, Seward remained Lincoln's primary coadjutor in the Union party scheme throughout the war. Hence it is no coincidence that at precisely the time in September, 1862, that Gideon Welles was complaining in his diary that Seward was always closeted with Lincoln, "inculcating his political party notions," Salmon P. Chase was protesting in *his* diary that Lincoln "has already separated himself from the great body of the party which elected him." Nor is it a coincidence that Seward was the chief target in the cabinet of angry congressional Republicans. They knew that Seward's and Lincoln's hopes of a bisectional Union party directly conflicted with their own hope of preserving the Republicans as an exclusively northern and vigorously antisouthern, anti-Democratic organization.[19]

Lincoln also expected that his appointees as secretary of war would further the development of the new party, if only by attracting northern Democrats to it. One of the things that finally persuaded Lincoln to appoint the unsavory Simon Cameron was that he had been assured that "there are thousand of influential democrats in Pennsylvania, who would feel disposed to sustain an administration, of which he should be a member." Cameron lost his value as a lure to Democratic defectors, however, when he endorsed the recruitment of black troops in December, 1861. So Lincoln exiled Cameron about as far away from negrophobic northern Democrats as he could—to Russia—and replaced him with another Pennsylvania Democrat, Edwin Stanton. Unlike Cameron, indeed, Stanton had never joined the Republican party, and he had even served briefly in Buchanan's cabinet. Thus an Ohioan gushed to the new secretary, "The great democracy of the West feel especially grateful that the administration has at last called into its councils so thorough and pure a Democrat as Edwin M. Stanton." That gratitude, Lincoln hoped, would be translated into Union votes in upcoming northern elections.[20]

Lincoln's selections from the border states even more clearly illustrate his intentions to replace the Republican party. The tiny Republican organizations there denounced Bell supporters and former Know Nothings as "our enemies" and demanded posts in the cabinet for pure antislavery Republicans such as the Kentucky abolitionist Cassius M. Clay or Judge William Marshall of Maryland. Maryland Republicans specifi-

19. George Fogg to Abraham Lincoln, February 5, 1861, quoted in Crofts, "The Union Party of 1861," 368 n.48; Leonard Swett to Abraham Lincoln, December 31, 1860, and Seward to Lincoln, December 25, 1860, in Lincoln Papers. Seward's April 1 memorandum is printed in Basler, ed., *Collected Works*, IV, 317. The Crofts article is the best account of Seward's attempt to build a Union party in 1860–1861, but for his continuing efforts during the war, see also LaWanda Cox and John H. Cox, *Politics, Principle, and Prejudice, 1865–1866: Dilemma of Reconstruction America* (New York, 1963), 31–49. The quotations from the cabinet diaries come from Welles's entry for September 16, 1862, and from Chase's entry for September 12, 1862. See Howard K. Beale, ed. *Diary of Gideon Welles* (3 vols.; New York, 1960), I, 136; and David Donald, ed., *Inside Lincoln's Cabinet: The Civil War Diaries of Salmon P. Chase* (New York, 1954), 136.

20. David Taggart to Abraham Lincoln, December 17, 1860, in Lincoln Papers; A. G. W. Carter to Edwin M. Stanton, January 17, 1862, quoted in Williams, *Lincoln and the Radicals*, 91.

cally warned Lincoln that the appointment of Montgomery Blair would destroy the Republican organization in that state because Blair favored "a *de*-republicanizing of the party, and a coalition administration," "a sort of 'Union' party to take the place of the Republicans." Precisely because Lincoln sought the same kind of party reorganization, he ignored the pleas of Republicans and selected Blair as well as Edward Bates, another favorite of the proslavery conservatives who were the political enemies of border-state Republicans. For the same reason, despite the anguished protests of Republicans, he divided the lesser federal posts in the border states among Republicans, Bell men, and Democrats who supported the new Union parties.[21]

As the war dragged on, both Bates and Blair, like Seward, drew fire from angry congressional Republicans for delaying the harsh antisouthern, antislavery measures they demanded. Thus Lincoln's decision to replace both men in 1864 is usually interpreted as a concession to radical elements in the Republican party, an attempt to balance the dismissal of the radical Chase from the cabinet, or a quid pro quo for John C. Frémont's withdrawal as an independent radical Republican candidate from the presidential campaign that year. Yet equally important in shaping Lincoln's decision was his awareness that the Union parties in both Missouri and Maryland had undergone fundamental transformations. By 1864 radical elements committed to immediate, uncompensated emancipation and the use of black troops had taken them over. Hence conservatives like Bates and Blair no longer served as adequate bridges to the Union parties whose support Lincoln sought. For him to retain their backing, Blair and Bates had to go.[22]

Lincoln also manipulated other federal appointments to build the Union party, especially in 1861 and 1862 when his attention was focused

21. Curtis Knight to George D. Blakey, Kingston, Ky., December 15, 1860, Joseph Calvert to Abraham Lincoln, Bowling Green, Ky., December 28, 1860, and W. G. Snethen to Lincoln, Baltimore, November 26, December 8, 13, 1860, all in Lincoln Papers. For Lincoln's other patronage appointments in the border states, see Harry J. Carman and Reinhard B. Luthin, *Lincoln and the Patronage* (Gloucester, Mass., 1964), 186–227; and William B. Hesseltine, *Lincoln's Plan of Reconstruction* (Chicago, 1967), 19–30.

22. For these developments in the border states, see Jean H. Baker, *The Politics of Continuity: Maryland Political Parties from 1858 to 1870* (Baltimore, 1973), 77–110; and William E. Parrish, *A History of Missouri: Volume III, 1860–1875* (Columbia, Mo., 1973), 87–115.

primarily on the North and the border states. It is true that outside of the border states the vast majority of civilian positions went to regular Republicans recommended by Republican congressmen. Nonetheless, Lincoln carefully placed Democrats in highly visible posts in order to woo Democratic backing for new Union organizations in the North. Not only the fact but the timing of these appointments reveals his purpose. The most conspicuous examples were the military commands he showered on Democratic favorites like John McClernand, Don Carlos Buell, and George B. McClellan, appointments that Seward heartily favored and that congressional Republicans increasingly denounced by 1862. Despite this growing protest, Lincoln retained them in command as long as they might lure Democratic votes to the Union parties in northern states—and only that long. Buell was dismissed on October 24, 1862, after the October congressional elections in Illinois, Indiana, Ohio, and Pennsylvania. McClellan received the axe on November 5, 1862, the day after elections in New York and New Jersey.[23]

Lincoln also attempted to attract Democrats to influential civilian or quasi-civilian positions at times when he hoped to advance the building of Union parties in particular states. The Union party held its organizing conventions in Indiana in June, 1862, and in Illinois in September, 1862, for example. On July 31, 1862, Lincoln asked the widely popular former Democratic governor of Indiana, Joseph Wright, to run as a Union candidate for Congress to help bring Democrats to the new organization. Failing in that endeavor, he appointed the Kentucky Democrat Joseph Holt to the new post of judge advocate general of the army on September 3. Holt was a great favorite among Indiana and Illinois Democrats, who had boomed him as a Democratic presidential possibility in January, 1862. Holt, of course, was also a prominent leader of Kentucky's Union party, which, in a special session of the Kentucky legislature in August, 1862, had spurned Lincoln's offer of compensation and denounced as intolerable the antislavery actions of Republicans in Congress. Thus Lincoln with a single stroke tried to pacify the Union party in Kentucky and to persuade Democrats to join it in Indiana and Illinois.[24]

23. Williams, *Lincoln and the Radicals*, 190–95; Carman and Luthin, *Lincoln and the Patronage*.

24. Basler, ed., *Collected Works*, V, 351–52, 358 n.; Randall, *Lincoln the President*, II, 213; *Appleton's Annual Cyclopaedia for 1862*, 519, 527–28, 541.

One final example must suffice. Since 1860 California's Republican party had clung to power only because the Democrats were divided into pro-Union and prosouthern wings. In 1862 the leader of the Union Democrats, John Conness, approached the Republicans about merging the two organizations into a Union party, a merger that reached fruition in the state legislative session that began in January, 1863, when Conness, to the dismay of many original Republicans, was elected to the United States Senate. Conness' chief ally as leader of the Union Democrats was Stephen J. Field. Hence, when Lincoln nominated Field as a Supreme Court Justice and circuit judge for California in late February, 1863, he not only nurtured the new Union coalition emerging in California, but he dramatically gave his blessing to the prominent role of Democrats in it, a prominence resented by most California Republicans.[25]

A closer look at the chronology of conventions and elections involving the Union party in the North and border states also helps explain Lincoln's attempts to delay or frustrate congressional and military initiatives toward abolition and the arming of blacks. One reason for Lincoln's cautious movement on these matters surely was his concern about keeping proslavery southerners and negrophobic northern Democrats behind the war effort. Arming blacks, he declared in August, 1862, could "turn 50,000 bayonets from the loyal Border States against us that were for us."[26] Yet Lincoln was equally worried about turning ballots against his cherished Union party.

Take, for example, his rapid reaction to Frémont's emancipation decree of August 30, 1861. That edict not only menaced Kentucky's future loyalty to the Union, but it also could, in the words of Kentucky's James Speed, "crush out every vistage [sic] of a union party in the state." Although the Kentucky Union party had already won congressional elections in June and the state's legislative elections in August, before Frémont's actions, the legislature itself was due to meet on September 2. More important, state conventions to organize Union parties that would combine Democrats and Republicans were scheduled to meet in September in both Ohio and New York, conventions that could easily fizzle un-

25. Basler, ed., *Collected Works*, VI, 113. Again, I have relied primarily on my colleague Professor Charles W. McCurdy for information on the political situation in California.

26. "Remarks to Deputation of Western Gentlemen," August 4, 1862, in Basler, ed., *Collected Works*, V, 356–57.

less Frémont were rebuked. Thus Lincoln requested Frémont to revoke his order on September 2 and commanded him to on September 11, much to the displeasure of congressional Republicans. Nor was it coincidental that Lincoln first sent the orders to remove Frémont from command on October 24, orders that were finally implemented on November 2. Though firing Frémont angered Republicans, it helped the broad-based Union parties score decisive triumphs in New York and Maryland on November 6.[27]

Lincoln's public revocation of General David Hunter's emancipation decree on May 19, 1862, must also be understood in terms of the political calendar. State conventions to launch the Union party were scheduled in Indiana on June 24, Pennsylvania and New Jersey on July 17, and Illinois on September 24. In addition, Ohio's Union party, which had elected Democrat David Tod governor in 1861, was due to hold another state convention on August 21, 1862. Lincoln had to revoke Hunter's order, lest potential Democratic supporters for these parties be frightened away. For the same reason, he made a point of publicizing his rejection of an offer of two Negro regiments from Indiana on August 4, his advice to a delegation of free blacks on August 14 that colonization was the best solution to the country's racial problem, and his famous reply to Horace Greeley on August 22 that restoration of the Union, not abolition, remained his primary goal. For Lincoln, of course, building a successful bisectional Union party was integral to restoring the Union. And his disavowal of any intention to emancipate the slaves or arm blacks was clearly meant to help build that party.[28]

It is true that Lincoln seemed to contradict these efforts to reassure negrophobic northern Democrats and proslavery border-state Union men when he issued his preliminary Emancipation Proclamation on September 22. But he tried to make even that palatable to the groups he was wooing. For one thing, the emancipation provision of Congress's confis-

27. James Speed to Abraham Lincoln, September 3, 1861, *ibid.*, IV, 506–507 n; Lincoln's actions can be followed *ibid.*, 506–507, 517–18, 562–63. Dates for convention meetings and elections were taken from *Appleton's Annual Cyclopaedia for 1861* and the *Tribune Almanac*. See also Silbey, *A Respectable Minority*, 39–42.

28. Dates for convention meetings are given under the entries for the respective states in *Appleton's Annual Cyclopaedia for 1862*. Lincoln's statements and orders can be found in Basler, ed., *Collected Works*, V, for the dates indicated.

cation act of July 17 theoretically went into effect in September, so Lincoln's postponement of emancipation until January 1, 1863, seemed to delay actual implementation of abolition by government forces until after the fall elections of 1862.[29] Moreover, by exempting loyal slave states and indicating that Confederate states that returned to the Union before that date would escape abolition, he made it clear that he viewed emancipation as an effort to hasten the restoration of the Union, not to punish southerners. Thus the measure was compatible with his insistence the previous December that "the integrity of the Union" was "the primary object of the contest" and that he wanted to prevent the war from degenerating "into a violent and remorseless revolutionary struggle."[30]

Equally important, Lincoln took steps to balance whatever losses the proclamation might cost the Union parties in the North and border states by reducing the Democratic vote. On September 24, 1862, he suspended habeas corpus throughout the nation for the duration of the war and ordered the military arrest of "all persons . . . guilty of any disloyal practice." Almost by definition, such persons would not be supporters of the Union party; instead, they would be potential voters against it. Thus the thousand of arrests made in 1862, 1863, and 1864, often immediately before elections took place, kept foes of the Union parties away from the polls.[31]

None of Lincoln's efforts, however, prevented a stunning Democratic comeback in the elections of 1862 in New York, New Jersey, Pennsylvania, Ohio, Indiana, and Illinois. The divergent responses of Lincoln and congressional Republicans to this Democratic resurgence illustrate well how their contrasting political strategies led to conflict between the two branches. Both correctly recognized that the Republicans or Union party had lost primarily because they had suffered significantly more

29. David Donald makes this point in *Charles Sumner and the Rights of Man*, 81.

30. Basler, ed., *Collected Works*, V, 49.

31. *Ibid.*, V, 436–37. A number of historians have commented on the calculated reduction of the Democratic vote in the North and border states through the use of arbitrary arrests and military intervention. See, for example, Hesseltine, *Lincoln's Plan of Reconstruction*, 31–47 and *passim*. Forceful suppression of the Democratic vote also forms a central theme of William B. Hesseltine, *Lincoln and the War Governors* (New York, 1948). In a recent book published seven years after my essay was written, however, Mark Neely vigorously and compellingly denies that most arrests of civilians in the North and border states had a political motivation. Mark E. Neely, Jr., *The Fate of Liberty: Abraham Lincoln and Civil Liberties* (New York, 1991).

drop-off in their vote since 1860 than the Democrats, but they differed in their explanation of that erosion. Lincoln attributed it to the absence of potential Union voters in the army. Most Republicans instead blamed it on abstention by disgusted northerners who wanted much harsher policies toward the South and slavery, the kinds of policies Republicans thought Lincoln had thwarted. Congressional Republicans, in other words, believed that former Republican voters had abandoned the party when it in turn seemed to abandon its antisouthern platform.[32]

Equally revealing, angry Republicans bluntly pointed to Lincoln's attempt to include Democrats and southerners in a new Union party as the chief cause of the debacle. "The Republican organization was voluntarily abandoned by the president and his leading followers, and a no-party Union was formed," fumed Ohio Senator John Sherman. If the Republicans "have the wisdom to throw overboard the old debris that joined them in the Union movement, they will succeed. If not, they are doomed." "Fear of offending the Democracy has been at the bottom of all our disasters," echoed Maine's William Pitt Fessenden. Chicago's Republican editor Joseph Medill also castigated Lincoln's courtship of Democrats: "It is enough to make the strongest men weep tears of blood. The President has allowed the Democratic party to shape the policy of the war and furnish the Generals to conduct it, while the Republicans have furnished the men and the money." What galled these Republicans, it bears repeating, was not simply sharing leadership positions with Democrats and border state Unionists. It was that courting such men precluded or at least obfuscated the punitive actions against the Slave Power like confiscation, abolition, and the arming of former slaves that Republicans thought their constituents wanted. By watering down the Republicans' antisouthern principles in favor of the diluted Union platform, Ohio's Joshua Giddings complained, Lincoln had condemned Republican candidates to enter the elections "without doctrines, principles, or character." The Democratic comeback of 1862, in sum, reinforced the conviction

32. See, for example, the revealing exchange between Lincoln and Carl Schurz about the reasons for the Republican and Union defeats in Basler, ed., *Collected Works*, V, 493–95, 509–11. On the dramatic difference between the size of Democratic and Republican drop-off in 1862, see Table 3.4 in Paul Kleppner, *The Third Electoral System, 1853–1892: Parties, Voters, and Political Cultures* (Chapel Hill, 1979), 77.

among congressional Republicans that they could defeat Democrats in the North only be retaining the Republican party's exclusively northern, antisouthern, anti-Democratic identity.[33]

That hardening of Republican opposition to the Union party strategy made further clashes with Lincoln inevitable, for the president viewed the Democratic comeback in the North as an even greater reason to press ahead with his plans before the 1864 presidential contest. The palpable failure of substantial numbers of northern Democrats to join the Union coalition probably made them less important in his calculations after 1862. We know he sacked Buell and McClellan immediately after the elections ended, and in January, 1863, he went ahead with emancipation and the concomitant enrollment of black troops, policies he had tried to delay earlier. It is also clear that in 1863 and 1864 he relied less on inducements to Democrats than on the soldier vote he thought had been absent in 1862 to carry northern elections. On the other hand, after the 1862 debacle, he sought frantically to shore up Union organizations in the border states and to build them in the Confederate states in order to offset the renewed strength of the Democracy in the North with new support for himself in the South.[34]

By 1863 and 1864, Union parties had been successfully established in the border states. Moreover, they were increasingly falling under the lead of more radical men, at least in Missouri and Maryland, men who wanted to abolish slavery and ruthlessly proscribe their political enemies from voting. In the border states as in the North, therefore, Lincoln shifted course from seeking support for the Union parties to trying to weaken the Democratic challenge to them. He increased arrests of supposed Confederate sympathizers at election times and dispatched troops to

33. John Sherman to William T. Sherman, November 16, 1862, William Pitt Fessenden to John Murray Forbes, November 13, 1862, Joseph Medill to Lyman Trumbull, November 14, 1862, and Joshua Giddings to George W. Julian, March 22, 1863, all quoted in Williams, *Lincoln and the Radicals*, 15, 188–90. Note that it was immediately after these defeats in the fall of 1862 that Senate Republicans tried to purge Seward and that Congress passed nationalistic legislation aimed at stripping state governments of their jurisdiction over banking, manpower, and legal proceedings against federal military and civilian officials.

34. Belz, *Reconstructing the Union*, 109–10, also recognizes that Lincoln pressed ahead with his party-building efforts in the South in order to offset Democratic gains in the North.

guard the polls, troops that, not incidentally, intimidated potential Democratic voters. As a result, Democratic turnout in the border states in 1863 and 1864 dropped substantially from its 1860 levels. In this regard, it is quite significant that Lincoln's amnesty proclamation of December, 1863, however magnanimous it was toward Confederate states, specifically excluded the border states and the North from its provisions. Lincoln had no intention of restoring the vote to the most determined foes of the Union party in those states, especially because presidential amnesty would have overturned the draconian laws disfranchising Confederate sympathizers that state Union parties themselves had passed.[35]

Congressional Republicans readily approved Lincoln's new policies in the border states because they embodied the hard-nosed course they had long advocated. Furthermore, by 1863 and 1864 those Union parties and even the incipient Union organizations in Louisiana, Tennessee, and Arkansas were moving toward emancipation on their own. By 1864, in sum, the goal, if not the precise method, of abolition had ceased to be a bone of contention between Lincoln and Republican congressmen, and Lincoln happily endorsed the Thirteenth Amendment in the 1864 Union platform now that southern Union organizations accepted the inevitable end of slavery. The restoration of political rights and congressional representation to Confederate states and the inclusion of former Confederates in the Union party, however, were another matter. Here Lincoln and the congressional wing of his party remained at odds.

Almost as soon as the 1862 returns came in from the North, Lincoln bombarded his military governors in the occupied South with instructions to hold congressional elections, but Republicans in Congress refused to seat the few men who were chosen.[36] These Republicans were even more

35. In addition to the books on Maryland and Missouri by Baker and Parrish cited earlier, see the discussion of the wartime political experience of the different border states in the essays in Richard O. Curry, ed., *Radicalism, Racism, and Party Realignment: The Border States During Reconstruction* (Baltimore, 1969).

36. Five congressmen elected from occupied areas of the Confederacy sought to be seated when Congress met in December, 1862. The House refused to seat three from Virginia, North Carolina, and Tennessee. On the other hand, it did admit the two men elected from Louisiana, but only in late February, 1863, a few days before the Thirty-seventh Congress permanently adjourned in early March. See Belz, *Reconstructing the Union*, 110–15.

upset by the lenient terms of Lincoln's amnesty proclamation and 10 percent plan, which, with the exception of a small group of Confederate civilian and military officials, restored political and property rights to those who took an oath of future allegiance and encouraged such men to establish and control civil governments that would replace the military regimes in their states. In contrast, congressional Republicans regarded former Confederates as traitors who did not deserve to vote, hold office, or be represented in Congress.

Lincoln's reconstruction policy of December, 1863, was in fact a classic example of his attempt to find a middle road for his new Union party between the positions staked out by Democrats and congressional Republicans. Because Lincoln required Confederates who sought amnesty to swear that they and their new state governments would abide by his Emancipation Proclamation, Democrats who objected to any conditions being imposed on southern states as a price of restoration denounced the plan as too harsh. Besides, Democrats regarded the 10 percent provision as evidence that Lincoln was creating rotten boroughs to support him in 1864. Republicans, on the other hand, regarded the plan as far too lenient toward the Slave Power and therefore inimical to their attempt to run on an antisouthern platform in the North. For one thing, they wanted to require Confederate states to revise their constitutions to abolish slavery *before* they elected new state governments and sought readmission. Lincoln said nothing about this requirement in his proclamation, and he seemed prepared to ignore it when he allowed the Union party in Louisiana to elect new state officials in early 1864 before holding a constitutional convention. The difference was one of substance and not just procedure, for the area of Louisiana and Tennessee where Lincoln first tried to apply his policy had been exempted from emancipation by his proclamation. Lincoln's policy, in short, seemed far less certain than their own plan to eradicate slavery permanently, at least until the Thirteenth Amendment passed Congress and was ratified by the states. In addition, congressional Republicans wanted to force southern states to repudiate the Confederate debt as a price of readmission, a matter on which Lincoln's plan was silent. Finally, they wanted to limit the period during which Confederates could apply for pardon and to exclude many more former Confederates from the political process than Lincoln's plan seemed to. For all these reasons, Republicans in July, 1864, passed the more stringent Wade-Davis bill as a congressional alternative to Lincoln's plan of reconstruction.

Although genuine differences of opinion over the proper policy as well as a jurisdiction conflict over control of reconstruction separated Lincoln from congressional Republicans, their contrasting political strategies also divided them. Lincoln clearly hoped to restore Confederate states to the Union as rapidly as possible, not only because he wanted their votes in 1864 but also because he wanted to prevent Congress from imposing radical changes on the South that might alienate white southerners from the Union party. Congressional Republicans, in contrast, believed that Lincoln's efforts to lure such men to the Union party through generous policies repeated the mistake of 1862 that had produced Democratic victories in the North. As Herman Belz has ably demonstrated, congressional Republicans wanted to go before the northern electorate in 1864 with a concrete antislavery, antisouthern record. Thus, when the Thirteenth Amendment failed to pass Congress that year, they frantically framed the Wade-Davis bill and begged Lincoln to sign it so they could trumpet their anti–Slave Power credentials to their constituents. Yet precisely because the bill would postpone indefinitely the return of Confederate states to political participation and drive southerners from the Union party Lincoln had worked so hard to build, he vetoed it. That veto, in turn, provoked a storm of protest from Republican leaders in Congress who refused to count the electoral votes cast by those Union parties in 1864 or to admit their chosen representatives to Congress after the election.

Perhaps no document reveals so plainly the differences between Lincoln and congressional Republicans, indeed, as does the extraordinary Wade-Davis Manifesto of August, 1864, in which the Republican leadership spelled out for the northern public why the congressional plan was superior to the president's. Their own bill "exacted" as the price of readmission the "exclusion of dangerous enemies from power and the relief of the nation from the rebel debt, and the prohibition of slavery forever." In contrast, "the President is resolved that people shall not *by law* take *any* securities from the rebel States against a renewal of the rebellion, before restoring their power to govern us." Furious that Lincoln's veto and his own policy would undercut their preferred campaign strategy, congressional Republicans thus publicly repudiated the plan of their presidential candidate in order to reaffirm their own antisouthern credentials with the northern electorate.[37]

At the time of his death, therefore, Lincoln and congressional Republicans remained stalemated over reconstruction and the desirability of including former Confederates in a bisectional Union party. Still, one might argue that Lincoln achieved considerable success with his efforts at partisan reorganization. Despite considerable antagonism from congressional Republicans to his renomination in 1864, the state Union organizations he had worked so hard to nurture in the North, the border states, and the occupied South supported him, and he easily won renomination. Moreover, he engineered the dumping of Hannibal Hamlin and the selection of the Tennessee Democrat Andrew Johnson as his running mate on a ticket that carried the label of the National Union, not the Republican, party. Clearly, Lincoln intended the substitution of Johnson for Hamlin as a signal that the Union party was both bipartisan and bisectional.[38] Finally, and most important, Lincoln received about 340,000 more votes in 1864 than in 1860, and about 146,000 of these new votes came from border states, where he actually carried Maryland, Missouri, and West Virginia. Here indeed was evidence that the party had extended its base to the South.

Yet it would be a profound mistake to conclude that Lincoln succeeded in transforming the Republican party into a genuine bisectional Union party dedicated to reunion rather than the humbling of white southerners. For one thing, there is little evidence outside California of a substantial swing of northern Democrats to the Union party. Those northern Democrats who permanently joined the party, moreover, were men like John A. Logan of Illinois, later a famous waver of the Bloody Shirt and Stalwart supporter of Ulysses Grant. Most Democrats who joined the Union party during the war, just like most young soldiers who cast their

---

37. The Wade-Davis Manifesto is quoted *ibid.*, 229, 242–43. I have relied primarily on Belz, *Reconstructing the Union*, 168–243, for the analysis of the split between Lincoln and Congress over reconstruction in 1864. Other recent accounts that explore the Wade-Davis bill in detail and that also stress the crucial role of developments in Louisiana are: Benedict, *A Compromise of Principle*, 70–99; Cox, *Lincoln and Black Freedom*, 46–139; and Peyton McCrary, *Abraham Lincoln and Reconstruction: The Louisiana Experiment* (Princeton, 1978).

38. The best discussion of the maneuvering behind Johnson's nomination is James G. Randall and Richard Current, *Lincoln the President: Last Full Measure* (New York, 1955), 130–34.

first presidential ballot for Lincoln in 1864, were motivated primarily by hatred of the South engendered by the war itself, not by the spirit of sectional reconciliation Lincoln hoped to foster through the new party. Instead of changing or mitigating the antisouthern thrust of the Republican party, indeed, the Civil War only increased it by reinforcing the bitterness of northerners toward their southern enemies. Thus, in the years immediately following the war, congressional Republicans would strive to make their reconstruction policies and their rhetoric the political equivalent of war against the South.[39]

Given this intensification of antisouthern sentiment in the North, Lincoln's hope of creating a permanent new anti-Democratic Union party that could incorporate white southerners in its ranks was doomed. Whatever the reasons for men from the border and Confederate states joining the Union party, they were not antisouthern. Hence the interests of northern and southern opponents of the Democrats were as much at odds as they had been in 1860. The inevitable failure of the Union party became evident when Lincoln's successor, Johnson, who continued Lincoln's efforts to include northern Democrats and anti-Democratic white southerners in a national Union party, broke with congressional Republicans in 1866. By the fall of that year, those congressmen were campaigning once again as Republicans in open hostility to Johnson's—and Lincoln's—Union party. By the end of 1866, therefore, all hope of substituting a bisectional Union party for the Republicans as the major anti-Democratic party in American political life was gone.

The purpose of this essay, however, has not been to focus on the success or failure of the Union party. Rather, it has been to suggest that Lincoln's attempt to build a Union party in response to the Democratic challenge and the determination of congressional Republicans to take a different tack to defeat Democrats was the chief source of the disagreements between Lincoln and Congress during the war. Furthermore, one can argue that their very divisions helped the North win the war. For

39. The constancy of Democratic voting support during the war is a central theme of Silbey, *A Respectable Minority*. The extent to which hatred of the South motivated Democrats who joined the Illinois Union party during the war and remained in the Republican party after the war is a central theme of Cardwell, "The Rise of the Stalwarts and the Transformation of Illinois Republican Politics." Studies of the motivations of Democrats who joined the Union party in other northern states would be most welcome.

where Lincoln took the lead, as in the use of arbitrary arrests and military intervention to bulwark Union parties in the border states or of amnesty and the ten percent plan to extend them to the Confederate South, or where Congress took the lead, as in the push for emancipation and the arming of black troops or with the nationalistic legislation passed to remove power from Democratic jurisdictions, the central tendency was toward a stronger war effort or greater weakening of the South. Put differently, Lincoln in effect used a carrot to induce southerners to renounce the Confederacy and join a Union party that was not based on unremitting hostility to them, as the prewar Republican party had been. Congressional Republicans, in contrast, wanted to use a stick to beat southerners into submission and thus please their northern constituents. The combination of the carrot and the stick, I suggest, was more successful than either would have been alone.

Index

Whig party, 115, 195–98, 230, 232, 234, 236, 244, 265–67, 269, 293; and Know Nothing party, 133–41; impact on second party system, 292–96; and Republican party, 301, 302; and secession, 303, 304–306

Slidell, John, 84

Smith, Mary Louise, 250

Smith, Truman, 197, 215

Soulé, Pierre, 73

Southern Rights parties, 68, 71, 72, 73, 196

Southwick, Solomon, 93

Specie Circular, 50, 51

Specie Resumption Act, 300

Stafford, Edward, 239–41

Stanton, Edwin, 340

State Rights parties, 48

Stephens, Alexander, 135, 323

Stevens, Thaddeus, 17, 97, 111

Stewart, Andrew, 234

Stockton, Robert F., 143

Stokes, Donald, 188*n*

Sumner, Charles, 12, 71, 125, 144

Sunday blue laws, 78, 109

Sunday mail service, 105–106, 109

Sundquist, James L., 311

Tallmadge, Nathaniel P., 51, 52

Tariffs, 16, 39, 40, 45–47, 60, 63, 65, 80–81, 194, 207, 215, 216, 219–20, 224–26, 229, 234, 236, 300

Taylor, Zachary: political views of, 17; support for, 69, 70, 197–98, 202–203, 228; election of, 192, 193–94, 230, 232–36, 242, 248; rationale for Whig candidacy, 196; 198–99; Polk's mistreatment of, 221, 223; popularity of, 223; opponents of, 231; death of, 248

Temin, Peter, 170*n*

Temperance movement, 56, 72, 77, 78, 111, 115, 117, 122–23, 134, 268. *See also* Prohibition

Texas: annexation of, 17, 22, 57, 58, 59–65, 206–207, 208–10; admission to statehood, 200

Third parties: formation in nineteenth century, 27; reasons for formation of, 88; strong third parties, 88–89. *See also* names of specific parties

Thirteenth Amendment, 348, 349, 350

Thompson, Richard W., 221, 230

Thornton, J. Mills, 307, 308

Tilden, Samuel J., 275

Timberlake, Peggy O'Neal, 45–46

Tocqueville, Alexis de, 96, 99

Toombs, Robert, 135

Transportation. *See* Canals; Railroads

Trist, Nicholas, 17

Tyler, John, 17, 58–62, 65, 189, 190, 257–58

Ullmann, Daniel, 129, 139, 144, 277

Union Democrats, 73

Union party, 335–39, 341–48, 350, 351–53

Unitarianism, 105

Upshur, Abel P., 59, 61

Van Buren, Martin: leadership of Old Republicans, 37, 38; as Jackson supporter, 39–40, 41, 42; presidency of, 43, 52–54, 153, 166, 225; as secretary of state, 45; and 1832 presidential election, 46; as minister to England, 46; opponents of, 47, 48, 62, 63, 157, 167; preservation of alliance between North and South, 57, 65; and Texas annexation, 58, 61, 62; supporters of, 60, 111; estranged from Democratic party, 63–64, 87; as presidential candidate of Free Soil Party, 69; and Kansas-Nebraska Act, 74; as leader in Democratic party, 92